# Neither Washington
# nor Moscow

## Essays on
## revolutionary socialism■

## Tony Cliff

**Bookmarks**

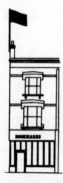

This book is published through the **Bookmarks Publishing Co-operative,** a group of socialists who have loaned money and contributed their skills.

Many socialists have a few savings put aside, probably in a bank or savings bank. While it's there, it's being loaned by the bank to some businessman or other to further the aims of capitalism. We believe it would be better loaned to a socialist venture to further the aims of socialism.

That's how the Bookmarks Publishing Co-operative works. In return for a loan, repayable at a month's notice, members receive free copies of all books published, and other advantages which there isn't room here to mention.

*Like to know more?* Write to Bookmarks Publishing Co-operative, 265 Seven Sisters Road, London N4 2DE.

First published April 1982 by
Bookmarks, 265 Seven Sisters Road, London N4 2DE.

ISBN 0 906224 06 3

Printed by *A Wheaton and Company,* Exeter.
Typeset by *Wayside Graphics,* Clevedon, Avon.
Set in 10/11 point Baskerville.
Production by *Artworkers* and *Niki.*
Design by *Roger Huddle.*
Cover photograph by *John Sturrock (Network).*

# Contents

■ Tony Cliff is a leading member of the Socialist Workers Party.

# Introduction

THIS COLLECTION of articles by Tony Cliff brings together work from 1945 to the 1970s. The common theme is the attempt to turn theory into practice, to act upon Marx's injunction:

'The question of whether objective truth can be attributed to human thinking is not a question of theory but a practical question. In practice man must prove the truth, that is, the reality and power, this-sidedness of his thinking. The dispute over the reality or non-reality of thinking which is isolated from practice is a purely scholastic question.' (**Theses on Feuerbach: 2**)

The unity of theory and practice is not a phrase to be paid lip service but a crucial point of reference. The link between theory and practice in these articles is Marx's own conception of socialism as the emancipation of the working class.

Born in Palestine (a British colony from 1918 to 1948) in 1917, a child of Jewish parents of Zionist persuasion, Cliff came to political consciousness in 1933 and participated, as an internationalist, in the socialist movement in that country. By the middle of the thirties

Cliff had become a Trotskyist in his sympathies. It was, above all, Trotsky's internationalism that appealed to him. Cliff came to Europe in 1946, and since 1952 has lived and worked in Britain.

There were two sorts of difficulties in making this compilation. First, what to include; and second, what to say of the backgrounds against which the various pieces were written.

As far as the first problem is concerned, a large amount of published material already exists. A number of books by Cliff have been published over the years. These include **Russia: A Marxist Analysis**, **Stalin's Satellites in Europe**, **Mao's China**, **The Employers Offensive**, **Rosa Luxemburg** and the four volume political biography of **Lenin**. No extracts from any of these have been included. It has been thought better to reproduce only complete articles written for periodicals, many of which have been, practically speaking, unavailable to the present day reader. Even so, given the limitations of space, it has been necessary to exclude some valuable items, (a list of Cliff's books appears at the end of this book).

The actual selection has been guided by the wish to show something of the development of Cliff's ideas in relation to the changing problems confronting revolutionaries since the Second World War. Inevitably, since the various articles were written for different, sometimes very different, readerships, this makes for a certain unevenness of style. It also calls for some background information.

**Middle East at the Crossroads** was written when Cliff was still an orthodox Trotskyist, as that term was then understood, and was published in *Fourth International*, theoretical journal of the Socialist Workers Party (USA) in 1945, (the promised continuation did not appear).

The organisation, Fourth International, was still numerically insignificant at that time. But, as a 1945 conference resolution of the small but still united organisation of British Trotskyists, the Revolutionary Communist Party, put it:

'The strength of Trotskyism resides in the power of our ideas which alone have shown to be capable of standing up to the test of events.'

There is no doubt that Cliff agreed wholeheartedly with this. He became closely involved with the RCP and prior to 1949 when the organisation collapsed, was one of its leading theoreticians. It became clear however that the 'power of our ideas' was by no means limitless. The Trotskyists were forced to grapple with a series of events unforseen by Trotsky and in direct conflict with his predictions of 1938–40. Also their own confident expectations of rapid growth failed to materialise. In consequence the Trotskyists were thrown into confusion; sharp internal conflicts developed amongst them. Two fundamental issues above all required urgent clarification: First, the prospects for capitalism in the West, and second the nature of the regime of Russia and now the regimes of Eastern Europe and of China.

Trotsky, in his last years, had given Western capitalism very little chance of survival, even in the relatively short run. No peacetime recovery from the slump of the thirties was possible. In the well-known words of his 1938 **Transitional Programme**:

'Mankind's productive forces stagnate. Already, new inventions and improvements fail to raise the level of material wealth. Conjunctional crises under the weight of the social crisis affecting the whole capitalist system weigh ever heavier deprivations and sufferings upon the masses. Growing unemployment, in its turn, deepens the financial crisis of the State and undermines the unstable monetary system. Democratic regimes, as well as fascist, stagger on from one crisis to another.'

The immediate post-war years, however, saw a boom in a number of developed capitalist countries, including the USA, France, Britain, and a little later West Germany, Italy and Japan. Moreover this boom, after a hiccup in 1949, gave way not to a new slump, but to an enormous and prolonged economic upturn on a world scale. For some years, however, it was possible to deny that Trotsky had been mistaken by claiming that the boom was an illusion. This was the position of the leading trend amongst the Trotskyists, led by Germain (Ernest Mandel). There was, argued Mandel, no real economic revival, nor any possibility of one.

**All That Glitters Is Not Gold** is Cliff's reply, written in 1947 on behalf of the RCP leadership, to Mandel's influential article **From ABC To Current Reading**. In this work Mandel 'proved' that capitalist revival was impossible.

It followed that bourgeois democracy would shortly become incapable of managing its increasingly unstable economic base without unleashing violent social and political crisis. And hence, European revolutionaries could expect 'police and military dictatorships' or the proletarian revolution, as an imminent prospect. Against this catastrophic perspective Cliff argued that a certain degree of economic revival was already taking place, that scope for further limited expansion existed and that it was on this basis that the Social Democratic and Stalinist Parties could retain mass support.

Events proved Mandel and the Fourth International majority

wrong. But it should be emphasised that the scale and duration of what we now look back upon as the long boom was not then anticipated by any of the controversialists, Cliff included. The *real* significance of the debate was the differentiation between those who were prepared to look reality in the face, however unwelcome it might be, and those who sought to rationalise, to explain away an unwelcome reality.

Ten years later, the long boom was an established and undeniable fact in the advanced capitalist societies. **The Permanent War Economy** attempted to explain its origins and emphasise its limits to a new political readership, and the **Economic Roots of Reformism** drew the political conclusions.

The future of Western Capitalism caused a sharp dispute within the Fourth International. But this was nothing compared with the controversy over Russia and Eastern Europe. For years, Trotskyists had grappled with the problems of what exactly remained of the conquests of the October Revolution, what *was* the class nature of Stalin's Russia. The orthodox position was set out in the Transitional Programme, in which the Russian state is characterised as:

'a weapon of bureaucratic violence against the working class . . . but it still remains a degenerated workers state'.

This was something of a revision of the nature of the state as Marx and Lenin understood it, and indeed a fair amount of verbal agility was required to make of it any consistent sense. But at least a clear political perspective was drawn from it. First:

'. . . either the bureaucracy, becoming evermore the organ of the world bourgeoisie in the workers state, will overthrow the new form of property . . . or the working class will crush the bureaucracy . . .'

And second:

'The bureaucracy, which became a reactionary force in the USSR cannot play a revolutionary role on the world arena.'

But both aspects of this perspective were subjected to unbearable strain by the events of 1944–9. First, the state ownership of property in Russia emerged intact from the war with its ruling bureaucracy considerably strengthened. And second, in Czechoslovakia, Yugoslavia, East Germany, Hungary, Poland, Albania, Rumania and Bulgaria regimes emerged which closely resembled that of Russia. Were these new regimes also workers states? If so, then this could only come about either through reform, which was unthinkable or through revolution, which was to admit that the Stalinist bureaucracy *could* actually 'play a revolutionary role on the world arena'. If, on the other hand, the new regimes were not workers states, then they had to be some form of class society in which the workers were exploited. But if this were the case, then Russia itself, with a method of social organisation identical to that of the new stratified regimes, was also a class society. That was Cliff's conclusion, first developed in **The Nature of Stalinist Russia** (RCP internal document 1947), in which he argued that Russia was specifically a system of bureaucratic state capitalism. The controversy over this theory led to Cliff's break with the Fourth International in 1950, shortly after the publication of **The Class Nature of the Peoples Democracies** in which the whole issue is rigorously examined.

The other pieces written primarily for readers with Trotskyist assumptions are self explanatory with two exceptions; **The end of the road: Deutscher's capitulation to Stalinism** (1963) and **A Critique of Bureaucratic Collectivism** (1948, revised 1968).

The late Isaac Deutscher was immensely influential amongst the new generation of left-wing socialists which grew up in the decade after Khruschev's 'official' denunciation of Stalinism and the crushing of the Hungarian Revolution in 1956. His writings, especially **Stalin** (1949) and the three volume biography of **Trotsky** (1954 to 1963) were the first widely circulated post-war books on the Russian Revolution and its outcome written from a socialist standpoint which rejected both the Stalinist myths and the virulent anti-socialism of the cold war 'liberals'. They are moreover serious and substantial works – unlike a good deal of Deutscher's prolific journalism, and they are brilliantly written. In consequence, Deutscher became for many thousands, if not tens of thousands on the left internationally *the* authority on Stalinism. Unfortunately, his attitude to it was deeply equivocal. He believed in the possibility, even the inevitability of the self-reform of the bureaucracy from above and, in the last resort, tended to identify with the bureaucracy even against the working classes in the Stalinist states. Cliff's harsh polemic, which gave considerable offence in 'New Left' circles at the time, has obviously been vindicated by later events.

**A Critique of Bureaucratic Collectivism**, written against the now largely forgotten Max Shachtman, is included because the idea (under various fresh labels) that Stalinism represents an entirely new mode of production is again enjoying a certain popularity in the writings of Bahro, Rakovski, Ticktin and others.

In the sixties and early seventies disillusionment with the USSR became widespread on the left, but also widespread became the belief in the new star risen in the East – Mao's China. It was part of the strong tide of 'Third Worldism' that flowed in these years. The three pieces on China included in this volume span ten years (1957–67), and although only a fraction of Cliff's writings on the subject, are more than sufficient to demonstrate a consistent Marxian analysis, unswayed by the shifting fashions of left-wing opinion.

By the time **Crisis in China** appeared the **Socialist Review/International Socialism** group that Cliff had largely inspired was on the eve of a transformation. After many years as a modest propaganda group, growing slowly but unsensationally, it experienced a sudden leap to a four figure membership during the upheavals of 1968. It became possible and necessary to shift the emphasis from propaganda to agitation. **On Perspectives** signals this shift:

'International Socialism, up to now at best an ideological trend, now faces the challenge and opportunity to become linked with the mass working class movement'.

The years spent in creating this 'ideological trend', in defending and developing the marxist tradition provided a solid base for the later progress of International Socialism, now the *Socialist Workers Party*. Without a cadre trained in such a tradition the rapid growth of the late sixties and early seventies would have been quickly dissipated in the downturn that followed, as many of the European revolutionary organisations were to discover.

The new situation called for a new emphasis in Cliff's writing. His first major contribution was **The Employers Offensive**, a tool for intervention in what was then a rising level of class struggle. The four volumes of **Lenin**, which followed between 1975 and 1979, was both a product of and a contribution to the problems of party building which the organisation now faced.

The emphasis on agitation, of course, required an agitational newspaper and for this a very different style of presentation to that of a theoretical journal or magazine of comment. Eight of Cliff's contributions to **Socialist Worker**, covering a ten-year span, are reproduced here.

Finally, **Portugal: Lessons of the 25th November** (1975) speaks for itself. Unfortunately, considerations of space make it impossible to reproduce the much longer and more comprehensive **Portugal at the Crossroads** (1975).

The publishers hope and believe that this collection of writings will be of service to revolutionaries in the nineteen eighties.

**Duncan Hallas**

# The Middle East at the crossroads

THE EVENTS of the last few weeks in the Middle East have drawn the attention of the whole world to what is happening in this region. The terroristic acts of Zionist military organizations, the strikes and demonstrations of the Arab masses in Cairo, Alexandria, Damascus, Beirut and Baghdad against Zionism, and the concentration of British troops in Palestine has aroused numerous questions whose answer will demand an uncovering of the socio-economic roots of the tangle in which this part of the world is involved.

Let us begin, then, with a discussion of the factor which until now has had the last word in the Middle East – imperialism.

## The Imperialist Stake in the Arab East

The Arab East is important to the imperialist powers for four main reasons: first, as a route to other regions – India, Australia, China, etc.; second, as a source of raw materials; third, as an important market for manufactured goods; and fourth, as a field for capital investment. It is self-evident that there is a close connection between these four aspects.

The importance of this region as a route is well-known. The Suez Canal shortens the way from Europe to the East tremendously and through it vital products pass (90–100 per cent of the total British import of jute, tea and rubber, 70–90 per cent of hemp and manganese ore, 40–65 per cent of rice, wool, coffee, zinc ore, lead, etc.).

The Arab East also constitutes a region through which land

routes pass. Germany under the Kaiser planned to construct a railway which would connect her with the Persian Gulf, the Berlin-Baghdad railway. This plan was one of the main immediate causes of the First World War. Germany's defeat put an end to it. Instead Britain constructed a long railway route connecting nearly all the British colonies in Africa (the Cape-Cairo line) which links up with a network of railways connecting the countries of the Arab East: the Cairo-Haifa line, the Haifa-Beirut-Tripoli line (this line connects up with Anatolia and Istanbul), the Haifa-Hedjaz and Haifa-Baghdad lines. These railways constitute an iron hoop which consolidates and binds together the British Empire.

With the rise of the airplane, the ownership of bases in the Middle East becomes an important weapon in the struggle for air supremacy. The air route from London to Bombay, Singapore, Hong Kong and Australia passes through Haifa. The beginning of the air route which passes through the length of British East Africa to Cape Town starts in Cairo. The French air route to Saigon before the war also passed through this region: Marseilles-Beirut-Baghdad-Bombay-Saigon.

The great importance of the Arab East as a route was one of the main reasons for the struggles between the European Powers during the last century – Napoleon's expedition, the war against Turkey in 1832, the Crimean War, and the conquest of Egypt were all connected with this – and also one of the main immediate causes of the First and Second World Wars. Transport routes connecting countries and peoples are not, under capitalism, means for international cooperation, for peace, but for imperialist rivalry, for war.

Renan was most decidedly correct when he mentioned the classic saying, 'I come not to bring peace, but a sword,' when welcoming Ferdinand de Lesseps, builder of the Suez, to the French Academy in April 1885: 'This saying must frequently have crossed your mind. Now that you have cut through it, the isthmus has become a defile, that is to say a battlefield. The Bosphorus by itself has been enough to keep the whole civilized world embarrassed up to the present, but now you have created a second and much more serious embarrassment. Not merely does the Canal connect two inland seas, but it serves as a communicating passage to all the oceans of the globe. In case of a maritime war, it will be of supreme importance, and everyone will be striving at top speed to occupy it. You have thus marked out a great battlefield for the future.'

The digging of the Canal turned the Arab East into a large battlefield, but the growth of air transport has thrown and will throw fuel on the fire of the struggle between the powers.

The most important raw material in the Arab East is petroleum. Until now only a tiny portion of the oilfields has been investigated, and it seems as if all estimates regarding oil reserves in the Middle East tend towards underestimation. In a report prepared for the United States Petroleum Resources Corporation the oil operator, E.

DeGolyer, says: 'The centre of gravity of world oil production is shifting from the Mexican Gulf and Caribbean area to the Middle East-Persian Gulf area and is likely to continue to shift until it is firmly established in that area.'

The truth of this statement is borne out by estimates of Middle East oil resources, one of which says that Saudi Arabia alone can satisfy the total world demand for fifteen years. It is assumed that the quantity in Iran and Iraq is not smaller than that in Saudi Arabia.

At present England has a decisive position in oil production in the Middle East as may be seen from the following figures of its distribution among the different interests. (Figures given are in 1,000 barrels.)

|         | Iraq   | Bahrein | Saudia | Egypt | Iran   | Total   | Percent |
|---------|--------|---------|--------|-------|--------|---------|---------|
| Britain | 13,067 | —       | —      | 9,125 | 75,000 | 97,192  | 79      |
| USA     | 6,533  | 7,300   | 5,475  | —     | —      | 19,308  | 16      |
| France  | 6,533  | —       | —      | —     | —      | 6,533   | 5       |
| Total   | 26,133 | 7,300   | 5,475  | 9,125 | 75,000 | 123,033 | 100     |

There is no doubt that with the increase in the exploitation of the oilfields in Saudi Arabia and Bahrein, the weight of the American companies in the production of oil in the Middle East will grow tremendously. Harold Guise, writing in **The Wall Street Magazine** for 3 March, 1945, is not blind to reality when he says: 'The whole Middle East area today resembles a huge chess-board for economic and political manoeuver seldom matched anywhere else . . . The complex struggle for postwar economic and political power is nowhere potentially so disrupting as in that part of the world.'

Another important raw material which this region supplies is cotton. In face of the USA's nearly complete monopoly of the world cotton supply (producing about two-thirds of the world's cotton and manufacturing only half of her production) and in face of the ousting of Lancashire by the industries in India, Japan, Canada, Brazil, etc., especially in the field of cheaper cotton goods, it became vitally necessary for the English capitalists to keep a monopolistic hold over Egyptian cotton which is of high quality and as such vitally necessary to Lancashire which produces better class goods.

Other raw materials such as potash, bromine, magnesium ore, etc., are produced in large quantities in this region. The potential value of these chemicals is much greater even than their actual value has been, as according to monopolistic international agreements a policy of 'organizing scarcity' has been ruthlessly followed in the East.

The importance of the Arab East as a market is also not to be overlooked as, despite the advance in industrialization, its imports before the war amounted to 78–80 million pounds – quite a substantial sum.

But the greatest importance of this region is its wide field for investment of capital.

### Imperialist Capital Dominates the Arab East

Egypt, which contains the majority of the Arab inhabitants of this region, has been up until now the richest country in the region. For this reason imperialist capital's attention is drawn especially to it. For dozens of years the main investments have been the loans to the Egyptian state, which kept its formal independence. This was a very tidy source of plunder. Thus during the years 1883–1910 the interest alone on a debt of 95 million pounds amounted to 105.6 million pounds. It is interesting to note that Egypt received only 60 million pounds of this debt, the rest being taken by different financial manipulations, so that for 60 million pounds Egypt paid interest of 105.6 million pounds and after this had a debt of 95 million pounds. During the same 28 years the Egyptian fellah paid a sum of 30 million pounds in order to maintain the occupation army in Sudan for the sake of the English plantation companies.

At the same time English, French, Italian, Belgian, German and other contractors were wringing millions of pounds out of the Egyptian people by the construction of works at very exaggerated prices. Thus for instance, the Aswan dam, which, according to the estimate of Sir William Willcocks, the British irrigation expert, should have cost 2.5 million pounds, actually cost 7 million pounds, excluding the 1.2 million pounds for repairs. During these same 28 years when foreign capitalism sucked out of Egypt a sum of about 200 million pounds, the Egyptian Education Department received the almost infinitesimal sum of 3.6 million pounds (less than 130 thousand pounds a year) and the Ministry of Health 3.4 million pounds. Could there be any better proof of the civilizing role of imperialism?

In the last few decades there has been a change in the direction of imperialist capital investment. The place of state loans has been taken by investment in railways, trams, light and power, water, banks and industry, etc. Today all key positions of the economy of the Arab East are in the hands of foreign capitalists.

In Egypt, according to an estimate made by French circles ('L'Egypte Independante par le Groupe D'Etudes de L'Islam', Paris, 1938, pp. 144–5), foreign capital in 1937 amounted to 450 million pounds, the entire wealth of the country being estimated at 963 million pounds, which means that foreigners owned 47 per cent of it.

According to another estimate, capital investment, besides land, in the same year amounted to 550 million pounds (A. Bonne, 'The Economic Development of the Middle East', Jerusalem, 1943, p. 73). Seeing that the price of land is estimated at 500–600 million pounds (and according to another estimate 670 million pounds) the total property of Egypt amounts to 1,000–1,100 million pounds. According to another estimate of 1937 based on English calculations, foreign capital invested in Egypt amounted to 500 million pounds. Thus the property of foreigners constitutes 40–50 per cent of Egypt's total property, which sum does not differ from that arrived at by the French experts.

As far as land is concerned, foreign capitalists have direct proprietorship over 8 per cent of the cultivated land of Egypt, i.e. land worth 50 million pounds. If we deduct this sum from the total of foreign capital invested in Egypt, we get, according to one estimate, 400 million pounds, and according to the other, 450 million pounds.

Taking Bonne's estimate of capital investment, besides land we see that foreign capital accounts for 73–81 per cent.

Thus *foreign capitalists own nearly half the total property of Egypt and about three-quarters of all property besides land.*

The situation in Palestine is not different. Here, too, imperialist capital has overwhelming weight. This is revealed clearly by the census of industry of 1939. This showed that the concessions had 53.2 per cent of all the capital invested in industry and 74.9 per cent of the motor power, despite the fact that some of the biggest enterprises belonging to foreign capital (such as Haifa Refineries, Steel Bros., etc.) were not included. If all enterprises belonging to foreign capital were included it would be clear that at least three-quarters of the industrial capital of the country is imperialist capital, and at least nine-tenths of the motor power is concentrated in its enterprises.

In Syria foreign capital owns a slightly smaller proportion of the wealth of the country. In Iraq practically 100 per cent of industry is in its hands.

With the realization of the giant American petroleum plans in the Middle East – to build pipelines, refineries, etc. – which, according to the most conservative estimates, will demand the investment of at least 300 million pounds, the subjugation of this region will be very substantially increased.

Imperialist capital desires to monopolize the markets of the Arab East for its industrial development there and especially to prevent the rise of a machine industry which would make for economic independence. Seeing that the profits of imperialist capital are dependent on the low wages paid to the Arab workers and the low prices paid for the products bought from the peasants, imperialism is interested in keeping the countryside in the most backward condition, so that it will be an inexhaustible reserve of labour power and cheap raw materials. Imperialism is further interested in this for socio-political reasons: first because only backward, illiterate, sick masses dispersed in tiny villages far away from one another can be ruled easily, and second because its most faithful agents in the colonial countries are the feudal landlords. Thus imperialism is inextricably involved in the agrarian question.

## The Agrarian Question

Three-quarters of the Arab population lives in the country,

subjugated to a tiny handful of big landowners. In Egypt 0.5 per cent of the landowners have 37.1 per cent of all the land while 70.7 per cent have only 12.4 per cent of all the land. 331 men have three times more land than $1\frac{1}{2}$ million poor peasants and there are more than a million land cultivators who have no land of their own whatsoever. One plantation company alone owns such a large area of land as to employ 35,000 workers. The king's estate covers a similar area and maintains about 30,000 small peasants. A calculation of Emile Minost, director general of Credit Foncier Egyptien, a bank connected by every fibre with the existing economic and social order and therefore not likely to exaggerate the extent of exploitation of the masses, gives the division of the net income from agriculture as follows:

|  | Percent |
| --- | --- |
| To taxes | 6.3 |
| To large landowners | 56.6 |
| To merchants | 12.1 |
| To fellaheen | 25.0 |
|  | 100.0 |

Thus a few thousand landowners receive twice the sum that three million fellaheen receive. On an average a poor peasant before the war did not earn more than 7–8 pounds a year. During the war his nominal income rose, but the cost of living rose even more, and his real income therefore decreased. The agricultural worker received even less. The daily wage of a male agricultural worker before the war was 3 piasters (7.2d), of a female, 3 piasters and of a child, 1–1$\frac{1}{2}$ piasters. Furthermore, they were subject to extended periods of unemployment every year as the season of work lasts 6–8 months. Even a foreman did not receive more than 2 pounds a month, a clerk 3 pounds, and a cart driver 1–1.2 pounds. Although during the war wages about doubled themselves, the cost of living rose much more; and there are places where even today the wage of a male agricultural worker does not reach one shilling.

With such low incomes, the food position is obviously terrible. As a matter of fact it is comparable only with that of the Indians. It has been calculated that the consumption of the average Egyptian, which is of course much higher than that of the poor peasant and worker, is only 46 per cent of the optimum in wheat, 25 per cent in sugar, 23 per cent in meat and fish, and 8 per cent in milk products. Furthermore the nutritional value is not improving but steadily deteriorating.

Because of the terrible poverty of the masses, their health conditions are very bad, and the mortality rate is tremendously high, as indicated by the following table, compiled in 1938:

|  | Mortality per 1,000 | Mortality of infants under 1 year of age (for every 1,000 born alive) |
| --- | --- | --- |
| England | 11.6 | 52 |
| Belgium | 13.0 | 73 |
| Poland | 13.8 | 140 |

| India | 24.3 | 167 |
|---|---|---|
| Egypt | 26.4 | 163 |

Only India approximates the death rate of Egypt!

Besides 'normal' deaths, famine and epidemics take their toll of life. Thus during 1944 malaria managed to wipe out tens of thousands of fellaheen in Upper Egypt, whose bodies, weakened by continued hunger, were susceptible to the disease in its severest form. According to one estimate which we may be sure is not exaggerated, 140,000 died of malaria (**Al-Ahram**, 14 April, 1944). 500 workers of the land company Kom Ombo alone died (**Al-Ahram**, 1 March, 1944).

Because of the poor conditions of health, the life expectancy is very low: for males, 31 years and females, 36 years. In the United Kingdom the life expectancy is 60 years for a male and 64 for a female. Those who live to be adults are very weak. Among those conscripted from the villages in 1941, only 11 per cent were medically fit for army service. 90 per cent of Egypt's population suffers from trachoma, 50 per cent from worm disease, 75 per cent from bilharzia, 50 per cent from ankylostoma. The number of people who are afflicted with tuberculosis exceeds 300,000.

Poverty is inevitably accompanied by ignorance, which in Egypt reaches fearful dimensions. Some idea of its extent may be gained from the very succinct remark of el-Mussawar when discussing the results of the 1937 census (28 August, 1942): 'We have 30,000 holders of diplomas as against 14 million who know neither how to read nor write.'

Ignorance is the product of the existing social system, and also one of its pillars. The ruling class knows very well that the illiteracy of the masses is one of the greatest assets of the regime. Thus a certain Egyptian senator thanked God that his country took first place in ignorance (**Al-Ahram**, 7 July, 1944).

Riches, pleasures and hilarity of some tens of thousands of Egyptians and foreigners on the one hand and hunger, disease and ignorance of the *millions* on the other – this is the picture of agricultural Egypt!

The agrarian problem in the other Arab countries is not substantially different to that in Egypt. Thus in Palestine about half the lands are in the hands of 250 feudal families. The feudal lords, being at the same time the usurers, have tremendous power, as has been shown by a British official in these words: 'In one Area Officer's charge extending over three sub-districts there are fourteen government tax collectors; one moneylender alone in one of those sub-districts was said to employ 26 mounted debt collectors.' (L. French, 'Reports of Agricultural Development and Land Settlement in Palestine, Jerusalem, 1931–32', London, p. 77.)

According to the 'Report of a Committee on the Economic Conditions of Agriculturists in Palestine' commonly called the Johnson-Crosbie Report, only 23.9 per cent of all produce of the fellah remains in his hands, while 48.8 goes in taxes to the government, rent to the landowner, and interest to the usurer. In order to understand how low the standard of living of the Arab cultivator is as a result of the backwardness of his economy, his exploitation by different parasites (who constitute the main hindrances to the development of the economy) I have made the comparison between the diet of a fellah and that which the government is supposed to give to convicts (though naturally a large part of this goes into the pockets of the prison officials). I assume that a fellah and his wife are in prison, and that four of his children are in a 'Boys Reformatory School':

|  | Family in Prison (pounds) | Fellaheen (pounds) |
| --- | --- | --- |
| Wheat and millet | 15.1 | 10 |
| Olives and olive oil | 3.8 | 3 |
| Vegetables, lentils and dairy produce | 12.9 | 4 |
| Rice, sugar and other products bought by the fellah outside his plot | 4.7 | 1 |
| Meat | 6.7 | Almost nothing |
| Total | 43.2 | 18 |

(As prices in Egypt are much lower than in Palestine, the figures cannot be used as a basis for comparison between Egypt and Palestine.)

Although this calculation is by no means precise, it nevertheless gives some indication of the terrible conditions endured by the masses of the fellaheens in Palestine.

Conditions in Syria and Iraq are not different. In the latter country there are feudal lords whose estates cover areas of tens of thousands of hectares. Thus the major part of Muntafiq district which covers an area of 6,260 sq. kms. is owned by one family. The income of the fellah in this area is 7–8 pounds a year.

The conditions of the urban masses are not less difficult than those of the agricultural population.

### The Conditions of the Masses in the Towns

Under the double pressure of concentrated imperialist capital and feudalism, because of the small development of industry and the low standard of living of the agricultural toilers in the villages, open and hidden unemployment is very widespread and the conditions of the town workers are very bad. This can well be exemplified by describing the conditions of work in one big industry. Let us take the spinning and weaving works of Mahalla el Kubra, which employs 26,000 workers and 3,000 clerks, inspectors and managers. Beginners receive 1/6 a day, experienced workers 2/7, skilled workers 10 pounds a month. The workers have one day of rest a fortnight and work a ten-hour day. There is no social service and the doctor is there only to give permission for sick leave.

Discipline is kept according to a military system. There are also constant fines which cut into the workers' incomes. As far as the housing conditions of this enterprise are concerned, fifteen workers live in one room sleeping in three shifts on five mattresses (**Al-Ahram**, 21 December, 1944). In other industrial enterprises the conditions are the same.

Obviously the low wages and high prices seriously impair the health of the workers. Thus it is revealed that of 6,000 printing workers in Egypt, 62 per cent suffered from diseases of the digestive system, 85 per cent from anemia, 45 per cent from lead poisoning (**Al-Ahram**, 23 February, 1944). Two incidents bear witness to the extent of the poverty in Egyptian towns: in September 1943, four people were trampled to death when alms were being distributed and in March 1944, an Egyptian woman sold her daughter to a merchant immediately after birth – for 20 pounds.

The condition of the masses in Jaffa and Haifa, Damascus and Beirut, Baghdad and Basra, is a little, but not much, better than in Cairo and Alexandria.

### The Relation of the Ruling Classes to Imperialism

Imperialism could not fortify its domination over the colonial millions if it did not find support in the upper classes of these nations. From what has been said above, it is clear what causes the feudal class to be the agency of imperialism. What is the relation of the Arab bourgeoisie to imperialism?

In order to answer this question it must first be stated that the Arab bourgeoisie is not a homogenous class. Commercial and banking capital intertwines with different modes of production. In the colonies the major part of this capital is connected with the feudal mode of production, enterprises of foreign capital or the import of commodities from abroad. All these sections of the bourgeoisie identify themselves with feudalism and imperialism. The minor part of the Arab bourgeoisie is the industrial bourgeoisie. It rises at a time when the world economy ruled by concentrated finance capital is in decline. It cannot build up its industry, stand in competition with the industries of the 'mother' country, accumulate sufficient quantities of capital and so on except by the harsh exploitation of the workers and peasants and the purchase of cheap labour and raw material, which is made possible for them as the result of the existence of feudalism and imperialism.

This framework of the rule of finance capital on the background of declining world capitalism together with the existence of feudal property relations also determines the weakness of the colonial industrial bourgeoisie and its dependence to a major extent on foreign capital. This is shown in partnerships of foreign and local capital and the dependence of local enterprises on being financed by foreign banks. The existence of the colonial bourgeoisie, the industrial bourgeoisie included, is therefore conditioned by the *super-exploitation* of the workers and peasants – which is the result and the *sine qua non* of imperialism – and by direct economic dependence on foreign capital and imperialism. The colonial bourgeoisie is not the antipodes of imperialism and feudalism, but the antipodes of the workers and peasants. The connection of the colonial bourgeoisie with foreign capital and feudalism on the one hand and the class struggle of the proletariat and peasantry on the other (which two factors are mutually dependent) determine the limits of the struggle of the colonial bourgeoisie for concessions from imperialism.

The Arab bourgeoisie in Palestine is in a special, peculiar position. Here the junior partners of imperialist capital are not the Arab bourgeoisie but the Zionist bourgeoisie. The secondary positions of the economy – such as light industries – are not in the hands of Arab capital as in Egypt or Syria, but in the hands of Zionist capital. Thus according to the 1939 census of industry, the industries of Palestine were distributed thus:

|  | Value of capital investment Percent | Horsepower of engines |
|---|---|---|
| Arab and other non-Jewish | 6.5 | 2.2 |
| Jewish | 40.3 | 22.9 |
| Concessions | 53.2 | 74.9 |

As has been stated the concessions exclude some of the important enterprises of foreign capital. On the other hand some enterprises belonging to non-Arabs are included in the first item. If we correct the table, therefore, we find that foreign capital has at least three-quarters of the capital invested in industry, Jewish capital a fifth and Arab capital only 2–3 per cent.

But this position of the Arab bourgeoisie in Palestine does not make it anti-imperialist, but on the contrary urges it to make efforts to oust the Zionist bourgeoisie in order that it may become the agent of imperialism.

The Arab bourgeoisie cannot and will not wage the anti-imperialist struggle. Despite its wrestling with imperialism for some concessions for itself it is clear that the fate of the bourgeoisie is bound up with that of imperialism.

## Problems Facing Arab Ruling Classes
## With the End of the War

With the end of the Second World War British imperialism is confronted with very serious difficulties in the East and needs to adopt extreme measures to protect its interests. The Arab exploiting classes stand before similar difficulties connected with those of imperialism. An understanding of this calls for a description of the socio-economic situation during the war.

During the war the capitalists and especially the big foreign companies active in the East made tremendous profits. Whereas in the last war the British army spent 45 million pounds in Egypt, in this war the amount is much greater. The war income of Egypt in 1940 was estimated at 34 million pounds, in 1941 at 100 million pounds, and in 1942, '43 and '44 it was at least as much as in 1941. The **Times** of 20 September, 1943 estimated that the army expended 200 million pounds a year in the Middle East. The bourgeoisie has enjoyed extraordinary profits. Thus the big Egyptian sugar company (a French company) ended the year 1941 with 266,000 pounds; 1942 with 1,350,000 pounds. The National Weaving Factories paid 11 per cent dividends in 1938 and 22 per cent in 1942. Misr Weaving Factories in Mahallah paid 7 per cent dividends in 1938 and 28 per cent in 1943. Misr Weaving Factory in the village Dawar paid 12 per cent in 1941 and 20 per cent in 1943. The Marconi Broadcasting Company paid 7 per cent in 1935 and 25 per cent in 1940. Egyptian Hotel Companies paid 10 per cent in 1938 and 25 per cent in 1941. The number of millionaires in Egypt before the war was fifty, and in 1943, four hundred.

The bourgeoisie made tremendous profits in commerce too. Thus in the three years 1941, 1942, 1943, the merchants in Beirut made profits of 16 million pounds. 10 million pounds of this went into the pockets of ten merchants, 2 million pounds went into the pockets of another 20 merchants, and the other 4 million into the pockets of hundreds of smaller merchants.

The banks also enjoyed great prosperity. In all commercial banks in Egypt deposits increased from 44.8 million pounds in 1939 to 116.6 million pounds in 1942. In the Lebanon during the same period it increased from 26.5 million pounds to 84.5 million pounds and in Syria from 6.1 million pounds to 36.4 million pounds. The Arab banks in Palestine paid a dividend of 20 per cent in 1943.

At the same time the suffering of the toiling masses increased very much. The result was a tremendous sharpening of the social tension, which reached its climax in Egypt. Already in January 1942, a bourgeois member of the Egyptian Chamber of Deputies said: 'We have already stood on this platform before and warned the government of the danger of hunger, and we then remarked that he was right who said that hunger is a heretic which knows no compromise or manners. He who looks into history will know that hunger was the cause of many revolutions. And if history tells us that the revolutionary people in one of the biggest states in Europe cried from the depths of their hearts, "We want bread", then we heard a similar rebellious cry of the same tone before the last "Feast of Sacrifice" in the streets of Cairo, a cry that was heard from the mouths of the hungry people attacking the bread vans, in order to snatch bread.' The speaker later described the situation in the country as a 'revolutionary situation' (**Al-Misri**, 6 January, 1942).

Another senator in March 1943 described the situation in these words: 'The war has brought about a concentration of capital in the hands of a few hundreds. The wealth of the rich has increased while the poor have been forced down into more terrible poverty; the gulf between the classes has deepened. The social system is shaky and grave dangers threaten it. A good future cannot be prophesied for the country.'

The peace means a great increase in the sufferings of the masses. The authorities' purchase of products to the extent of tens of millions of pounds will cease, which will lead to the dismissal of about a quarter of a million workers employed in industries supplying the army. The great majority of the 800 thousand workers employed directly by the army will also be discharged. Even industries producing for the civil population will be confronted with grave difficulties in the form of foreign competition which during the war was nearly non-existent, difficulties in the renewal of machinery, etc. The ruling classes are preparing to roll the burden of the crisis onto the backs of the workers and peasants, and make no secret of their intentions. Thus, Fouad Saraj ed-Din, a large landowner who was Minister of Agriculture, Internal Affairs and Social Welfare, said that in order that Egyptian cotton be able to compete with Indian, Chinese and Brazilian cotton, with artificial silk and nylon, the rise of wages in agriculture must be stopped. Hafez Afifi, director of the big bank, 'Misr', also stated that the rise of wages deprived the Egyptian industry of the possibility to compete with foreign products. The paper **Al-Ahram** of 19 July, 1943 stated that the workers were getting a high wage which accustomed them to luxuries *(sic!)*.

### Increasing Antagonism
### Between Bourgeoisie and Imperialists

At the same time the antagonism between the Arab industrial bourgeoisie and imperialism is increasing. There are two main bones of contention: first the problem of the defence of the existing industries from the competition of foreign goods, and second the problem of Britain's tremendous debt to the Eastern countries (to Egypt 350 million pounds, to Palestine – here mainly to Jewish capitalists – 100 million pounds, to Iraq 60 million pounds). The position of the sections of the Arab bourgeoisie regarding these questions is different. The compradore bourgeoisie is much more interested in trade with overseas than in the development of the local industry.

On the other hand the industrialists insist on raising the customs tariffs and are also more assertive as regards the British debt, for they badly need its repayment in order to renew their worn machinery. Thus at the session of the senate on 20 January, 1945, Senator Ahmed Ramzi Bey said that the currency restrictions meant that Egypt could not get dollars and buy in the USA, but only in England, and this was a serious handicap. He proposed that

England supply dollars or even hand over to Egypt some of her shares in companies in Egypt, such as those of the Suez Company, Anglo-Egyptian Co., etc. He also mentioned the decline in practice, if not in theory, of the value of the Egyptian pound compared with the pound sterling. **Al-Ahram** of 19 April, 1944, states that the United Kingdom's debt to Egypt is the debt of the strong to the weak, and of course it was dependent on the will of the strong whether and how to pay. A week later the same paper quotes Senator Mohamed Barakat Pasha as stating that the United Kingdom would not be able to pay her debts and advising Egypt to leave the sterling bloc. The same theme of leaving the sterling bloc and transferring Suez and other shares to Egyptian hands repeats itself over and over again in the Egyptian press.

The Arab bourgeoisie in the neighbouring countries is weaker and therefore less insistent. The position of the Arab exploiting classes may be summarized thus: *all* of them turn their faces towards the cutting of the standard of living of the masses. Some of them, the industrialists, want to use pressure on Britain in order to wring some concessions. But nevertheless one thing must be absolutely clear. Even for the Arab industrialists the first factor takes overwhelming precedence over the second.

In the face of the deep abyss between the masses of workers and peasants and imperialism, the latter is interested, and will be more so in the future, to divert the ire of the masses into a misleading side-track. The majority of the Arab exploiters – the feudal lords, the compradore bourgeoisie, the merchants and usurers – identify themselves in this matter completely with imperialism. (It must not be understood that this means necessarily British imperialism. It may just as well be another, i.e. American.) The industrial bourgeoisie will perhaps try to make use of the masses' ire in order to wring some concessions from imperialism, but before long it is sure to join hands with it in an effort to direct the movement of the hungry masses away from the national and social liberation struggle into a side channel – one of chauvinistic-communal riots.

Jerusalem, 12 November, 1945

# All that glitters is not gold

A Reply to Germain's 'From the ABC to Current Reading: Boom, Revival or Crisis?'

COMRADE E. GERMAIN's article *'From the ABC to Current Reading: Boom, Revival or Crisis?'* has as its objective, according to the writer, to break 'through the curtain of fractional smoke that has been lowered over the debate' in the discussion on Britain. The article, according to its author, is written for educational purposes. But all that glitters is not gold. It abounds with the most elementary mistakes which are put forward as great truths; it reveals a gross lack of knowledge of the Marxist theory of crises and a mechanistic, superficial conception of capitalist decline. To prove this, let us follow Comrade Germain's arguments.

### Germain Misquotes Marx

Germain quotes these sentences from Marx: 'The enormous power, inherent in the factory system, of expanding by jumps, and the dependence of that system on the markets of the world, necessarily beget feverish production, followed by over-filling of the markets, whereupon contraction of the markets brings on crippling of production. *The life of modern industry becomes a series of periods of moderate activity, prosperity, upswing ('essor'), over-production, crisis and stagnation.*'[1] (Germain's emphasis.)

The most important part of this quotation for Germain's analysis is the sentence he emphasises. He concludes from it that Marx's synonym for the word 'boom', which is not to be found in

**Capital**, is 'upswing' (essor). Seeing that this is the key point of his analysis, one would naturally expect Germain at least to quote with meticulous care. In the sentence from Marx's **Capital** under discussion, not six, but only five stages are mentioned: '. . . moderate activity, prosperity, over-production, crisis and stagnation'. *The word upswing (essor) is added to Marx's sentence by Germain.*

I do not wish to imply that this is a conscious falsification. It is probably the result of carelessness and a lack of seriousness in dealing with theoretical problems. He copied too hastily from Kautsky's edition of **Das Kapital**, in which to popularise the work, Kautsky added popular German words to the anglicisms or difficult words used by Marx. These he put in square brackets after the original word. In the sentence quoted by Germain, after the word 'Prosperität' two words are added by Kautsky in a square bracket: 'Gedeihen' and 'Aufschwung'. Germain overlooked the square bracket, arbitrarily deleted one of the two words, and out of the second made a special phase of the economic cycle.

This, to say the least, does not speak well for his scientific conscientiousness.[2]

Germain states that one must identify the boom with only one phase in the ascendance of the cycle: otherwise it 'would lead to this schematism: reduce the whole cycle of capitalist production to two stages: the crisis and the boom'. This argument, which sets out to attack the RCP document, in truth attacks the whole concept of Marx, Engels, Lenin and Trotsky. Sufficient to remind Comrade Germain of the following quotation from Trotsky: '. . . *capitalism does live by crises and booms, just as a human being lives by inhaling and exhaling. First there is a boom in industry, then a stoppage, next a crisis, followed by a stoppage in the crisis, then an improvement, another boom, another stoppage and so on.'* (**The First Five Years of the Communist International,** p. 200, our emphasis).

Of course, these two basic aspects of the cycle, the ascendance and the decline, can be divided into two or three sub-sections: the resumption, moderate activity, the peak of the activity, the beginning of the decline, moderate decline, the end of the decline, etc. For this purpose, we could divide inhalation and exhalation into different sub-sections also. We know that Marx divided the cycle sometimes into two, sometimes into four and sometimes into five parts. But if only one sub-section of the ascending curve is to be termed 'boom' as Germain seeks to do, then Trotsky too must be accused of 'distorting even the ABC' and vulgarising Marxism.

But there are none so confusing as those who forget what they say from day to day. Comrade Germain comes into conflict with what he had to say on another occasion. Thus, according to Comrade O'Daniel, in his document **A Note on Discussion Methods**, Comrade Germain, at the IEC, said: 'The RCP majority leadership make a fifth distortion . . . The PB . . . certainly could not have helped observing that it (the report of Jerome to the October

Plenum of the IEC) described the revival of British economy as an "essor" – a soaring one.'

To make the position perfectly clear, it must be mentioned that the third member of the IS who wrote about British economic perspectives, Pablo, mentions with approval in one and the same document, the analysis of both Germain and O'Daniel. Yet he himself, on another occasion, described the word 'essor' as 'boom'. (**Quatrième Internationale**, Dec. 1946). It is time the Majority IS members found agreement among themselves on this question, which, according to Germain, is the ABC!

Now let us read further and analyse the main traits which Germain considers characteristic of a boom. The first one is that production expands *'in relation to the preceding boom'* (Germain's emphasis).

### Does a Boom Require that Production Expand Beyond the Peak of the Former Boom?

Germain's answer is in the affirmative. While he admits there is lively economic activity in Britain today (which affirms the perspectives of the British majority and contradicts those of the IS of a year and a half ago) he seeks to find a bridge whereby he can attack the RCP and defend the IS. All this amounts to nothing less than a mere sleight of hand trick. *Production in Britain today, he asserts, is lower than the peak of the last boom. Ergo, there is no boom.*

But if his assertion is correct, and a boom requires that production expand beyond the peak of the former boom, then the years 1924–29 in Britain were not years of boom at all, since production was below the level of 1913. In which case, Trotsky made a gross blunder in defining these years as a period of boom. Is this so, Comrade Germain?

More than this. By basing himself on this formulation he does not prove that there is not a boom in England. Unwittingly he proves quite the contrary. British industrial production in 1937 was higher by 23.6 per cent than in 1929. Thus 1937, according to Germain's theory, was a year of boom! Now, is British production today higher or lower than 1937? According to Germain it is lower, proof of which, apparently, is merely the fact that Germain asserts it. Factual evidence he does not find it necessary to adduce. Possibly he relies on the same sources as Pablo did when he wrote: *'The year 1946 ended with a total production which has been estimated at about 80% of 1938.'*

By whom was it estimated? And on what basis? Comrade Pablo lets the cat out of the bag by writing in reference (4) at the conclusion of his article: *'The New York Herald Tribune of 30.3.47, basing its calculation on the indices of imports of raw materials in 1946, on which all industrial activity in Britain depends, evaluated total production at only 72%.'*

Pablo forgot a few not unimportant factors – the shift from

textiles to engineering, which relatively decreases the dependence on foreign sources of raw material; the change in exports from steel to engineering; the big expansion of the chemical industry – all factors which make it fallacious to estimate Britain's production on the basis of her imports of raw materials. But for Comrade Pablo, as it appears for Comrade Germain, it is enough that the imports of raw materials to Britain is about 75 per cent of pre-war for them to conclude that British production today relative to pre-war, must also be about this figure!

A document of the RCP Minority states this even more bluntly. It says: '*A revival of economic activity is taking place in Britain today. It has now reached 72% of the 1938 level of production (Herald Tribune, 30.3.47).*' (Some Comments on the PE Reply to the IS Letter', by the CC Minority.)

Pablo and the British Minority at least explain how they arrived at the idea that production in Britain is lower than pre-war. Germain does not find this necessary. His pontifical declarations, it would appear, are infallible.

What are the facts? According to **The Economist**, the **Financial Times** and other reliable economic journals, employment is higher in Britain than ever before, and furthermore, productivity of labour on the average has risen by at least 10 per cent. It is therefore impossible that production is lower than pre-war. **The Economist** of 2 August, 1947, says: 'There is really very little room for doubt that the aggregate output of the British community today is from 10 to 20 per cent higher in volume than it was in 1938.' An earlier issue of **The Economist** comes to the conclusion that the gross national income is up by 17 per cent in real terms, in comparison with pre-war, or net national income up by 13–14 per cent. (19 April, 1947.) **Labour Research** of May 1947 comes to the same conclusions. We could cite similar conclusions from all the serious economic journals.

If we accept Germain's definition of a boom we will arrive, to say the least, at some very odd conclusions: in 1913 there was a boom; in 1929 there was not a boom; in 1937 there was a boom; yet in 1947, when production is higher than the IS's 'boom' of 1937, Germain says there is not a boom! Also, between two periods of boom, there are sometimes two cycles, and sometimes one cycle! But no matter how he contradicts himself, even if we accept his definition and base ourselves not on his and Pablo's 'facts' but on real facts, the British Majority are right. There is a boom in Britain.

### Is Abundance of Raw Materials and their Cheapness a Condition for Boom?

Germain writes:

'Throughout the period of stagnation and resumption, sufficient stocks of raw material have been built up to create abundance in this field. *The prices of the raw materials* – the principal constituent of the total price of the production of a capitalist commodity – *stand at a level relatively lower than the prices of finished commodities*, allowing in this way a very accentuated rise in the average rate of profit, which constitutes the basis of this extraordinary impetus received by industry during the period of boom.' (Germain's emphasis.)

There are at least four errors in this one paragraph.

**Error No. 1.** It is false to say that 'The prices of the raw materials' are 'the principal constituent of the total price of the production of a capitalist commodity'. In order not to waste too much space, I shall quote only one figure which answers Germain with the facts. In the United States in 1929, raw materials constituted 32.8 per cent of the price of production of total industry. (L. Corey, **The Decline of American Capitalism**, p. 114.)

**Error No. 2.** It is false to say that it is a condition for a boom that at the beginning of the revival the prices of raw materials should 'stand at a level relatively lower than the prices of finished commodities', or that at the end they are relatively dearer. Sometimes it is the case; as often it is not. Sufficient to state that in the years 1866, 1873, 1890 and 1900, which were all years of maximum employment, were peak years of boom, the prices of raw materials were the *lowest* in the whole cycle as against the prices of finished goods. On the other hand, in the years 1825, 1839, 1847, 1857, 1882, 1929 and 1937, also years of the highest peak of production, the prices of raw materials were the *highest* in the whole cycle as against the prices of finished goods. (See **The Conditions of Economic Progress**, Colin Clark, 1940, p. 454.)

To make it absolutely clear that this second allegedly necessary condition for boom, which for Germain is a condition *sine qua non*, is absurd, we add a diagram which makes the position perfectly clear. (See graph 1.)

A little knowledge of the history of capitalism, a little seriousness in relation to it, and more care than to make statements that have no foundation, would have restrained Germain from making the question of price one of prime importance. Fluctuations in price can deepen the fundamental disproportionalities that arise in capitalism, but they are always a secondary factor. We can thus find the interesting fact that there were upswings connected with constant prices (1873, 1893), by rising prices (1907, 1920), and again by constant prices (1929). (Lewis Corey, *op cit.* p. 186.)

**Error No. 3.** It is false to say that necessarily at the beginning of the economic ascendancy of a cycle there are abundant stocks of raw materials. Again, a little knowledge of the history of capitalism will demonstrate the incorrectness of this assertion. Marx dealt with the situation of the weaving industry in England which, despite its acute shortage of cotton yarn due to the backwardness of the spinning industry, experienced a tremendous boom. The American Civil War, which caused a 'cotton crisis' – an acute shortage of cotton –

did not prevent Britian experiencing at the same time, a tremendous boom even in the spinning industry. (**Capital**, I, Modern Library Edition, p. 457.)

**Error No. 4.** It is not true that the relative cheapness of raw materials as against the price of finished goods is a necessary condition for a high rate of profit. The increasing rate of exploitation, the full use of the productive capacity, the low rate of interest, the quick circulation of capital, the cutting of capital values – by these and many other means, does the crisis prepare the ground for the rise of the rate of profit and the boom. The relative cheapness of raw materials as against finished goods was an important factor in many cycles. But it is not the only factor, nor the main one, and

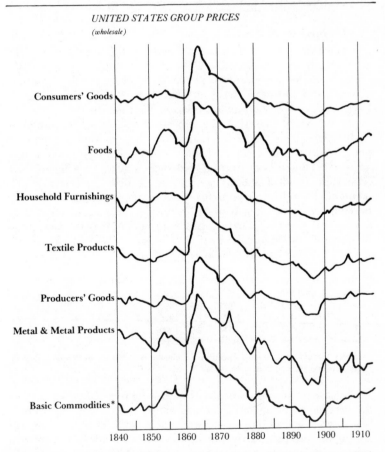

UNITED STATES GROUP PRICES
(wholesale)

Consumers' Goods

Foods

Household Furnishings

Textile Products

Producers' Goods

Metal & Metal Products

Basic Commodities*

1840   1850   1860   1870   1880   1890   1900   1910

(Joseph A. Schumpeter, **Business Cycles**, Vol. II, New York, 1939, p. 478.)

*Includes the prices of 30 basic commodities, farm products, minerals, textiles, and the like.

certainly not the *sine qua non* of a high rate of profit. If it were, many economic cycles of the nineteenth century would have passed by without experiencing any boom, and such a conclusion is too fantastic, even for Germain.

Germain writes:

'Far from being a result of the boom the coal shortage is a factor limiting the revival and making its development towards a boom impossible.'

This conclusion could have some foundation if not for the fact that already today, the consumption of coal in British industry is higher than ever it has been. So that the coal crisis of under production is another proof of the correctness of the characterisation of the existing period in Britain as one of boom.[3]

### The Boom and the Reserves of Labour Power

The third characteristic of a boom that Germain lays down arises also from a misunderstanding of Marx: 'Sufficient reserves of man power,' he writes, 'must be present in order to allow a serious expansion of industry. According to Marx, *the essential basis of the boom is proletarian over-population.*' (Germain's emphasis.)

True, Marx says that the process of capitalist accumulation finds 'a check in the natural limits of the exploitable labouring population'. (**Capital**, I, p. 694.) But this does not mean that if there are not big reserves of unemployed there cannot be a boom. Nor, conversely, (even if one accepts Germain's first characteristic of a boom that production is higher than in the previous boom) that development towards a boom is impossible because of the lack of labour power. It is very easy to prove this. Let us take the percentage of unemployed among industrial workers in Germany[4] for the years 1887–1913. It was as follows:

| Year | % | Year | % | Year | % | Year | % | Year | % | Year | % |
|---|---|---|---|---|---|---|---|---|---|---|---|
| 1887 | 0.2 | 1892 | 6.3 | 1897 | 1.2 | 1902 | 2.9 | 1907 | 1.6 | 1912 | 2.0 |
| 1888 | 3.8 | 1893 | 2.8 | 1898 | 0.4 | 1903 | 2.7 | 1908 | 2.9 | 1913 | 2.9 |
| 1889 | 0.2 | 1894 | 3.1 | 1899 | 1.2 | 1904 | 2.1 | 1909 | 2.8 | | |
| 1890 | 2.3 | 1895 | 2.8 | 1900 | 2.0 | 1905 | 1.6 | 1910 | 1.9 | | |
| 1891 | 3.9 | 1896 | 0.6 | 1901 | 6.7 | 1906 | 1.2 | 1911 | 1.9 | | |

(**A Short History of Labour Conditions in Germany, 1800 to the Present Day**, by Jurgon Kuczynski, London, 1945, p. 163.)

Even Germain could not say that during these 27 years, because the percentage of unemployed was higher than 3 per cent in only four cases, the economy could not reach the level of a boom. His argument becomes clearly ridiculous when we notice that the year 1887 which was the beginning of the ascendancy of the economic cycle, showed an unemployment of only 0.2 per cent, and that other years similarly placed in the cycle showed: 1893, 2.8 per cent unemployment, 1902, 2.9 per cent, 1908, 2.9 per cent. How on earth did the cycle of production reach a boom if, from the beginning, there was almost full employment?

Has Germain heard of the process of rationalisation, the raising of the productivity of labour, etc.? There is in Britain today, about 2 per cent unemployment. *This has not prevented a rise of production.*

Germain writes that '. . . the number of active *men* has *declined* by 211,000 in relation to 1939.' And he adds: 'Really this is a funny kind of boom in man power . . .' (Germain's emphasis.)

What is funny is that Germain does not mention at the same time that the number of active *women* rose by 671,000. More than this, it can happen that during a boom the number of employed men and women not only does not rise, but even declines. This takes place if the volume of production rises less rapidly than the productivity of labour. Thus, for instance, in the years 1920–29 the number of workers in American manufactures, railroads and coal mining decreased by 1,003,000. (L. Corey, *op cit,* p. 227.)

To say that the lack of labour power proves either that there is not a boom in Britain, or that there cannot be a big rise in production to higher levels even than exists today, is ridiculous.

At the beginning of the existing boom in Britain there were about 5.2 million people in the armed forces. Today the number is only 1.2 million, besides which about a million women left employment after the end of the war. This means that about 4 million served as a reserve of labour power. Germain forgets this. But even if this reserve did not exist, the boom in Britain would not have been impossible.

### The Rate of Profit and the Boom

Germain writes:

'We have limited ourselves to these four points, but it is obvious that the boom has still other characteristics that one only needs to take the trouble to look up in the works of Marx. Let us note this essential point: *It is the movement of the average rate of profit . . . which determines the unfolding of the cycle of capitalist production.'* (Germain's emphasis.)

Of the four characteristics given by Germain as the *sine qua non* of the boom at least three, we have seen, were wrong. It is the point which he adds here about the rate of profit which is really the factor which characterises the boom. Since the profit motive is the driving force of capitalism, there cannot be a boom without a high rate of profit. The extraction of surplus value and its transformation into capital, are thus necessary attributes of a capitalist boom. They are, in fact, its basis. If, therefore, it could have been proved either that the rate of profit in Britain is low, or that the rate of accumulation is low, then we may have said with certainty that there is no boom in Britain. As usual, Germain finds it sufficient to *assert* whatever comes into his head, without adducing any facts. He writes:

'The average rate of profit (in Britain – TC) is kept to such a low level and the new investments bring such little hope of immediate and abundant profit that an enormous mass of capital *refuses* to converge towards industry – exactly the opposite phenomenon to that which is produced during a period of boom.' (Germain's emphasis.)

What abysmal ignorance! That the rate of profit is very high, and the rate of investment extraordinarily high, will become only too clear from a few cold facts. Of the total national income in 1947, according to the Government White Paper 'Economic Survey of 1947', 20 per cent will be devoted to capital equipment and maintenance, or 13 per cent to capital equipment alone. This will be the highest investment *in volume* to be made in the last hundred years. (See Colin Clark, *op cit,* p. 396.) This represents the tremendous sum of £1,700,000,000 against which about £600,000,000 must be set off for depreciation and maintenance, leaving a new net capital formation of £1,100,000,000. As against this, the annual investments in Britain in 1860–69 were on the average £150 million; in 1907, £248 million; in 1924, £327 million; in 1929, £314 million; in 1932, £29 million; in 1935, £325 million; in 1937, £354 million (including £60 million in armament production).

Taking into account the price changes that have occurred, there is no doubt that British investments today are the highest *in volume* for the past hundred years. (See Colin Clark, *op cit,* p. 396.)

*A Few More Weeds from Germain's Garden*

Germain poses the question: 'Is there a "feverish push of production in all the branches of industry" (Marx) in Britain?'

He answers simply: In Britain today 'there is nothing which resembles' this. It is difficult to comprehend what Germain understands in this reference from Marx. Is almost full employment a sign of such a 'feverish push of production in all the branches of industry'? Are tremendous investments a sign of it? Is a rapid increase in the productivity of labour a proof of it? One is driven to reiterate once again, Comrade Germain, that pontifical declarations do not suffice.

The lack of gold and hard foreign currency also is not, as Germain thinks, proof that there is not a boom in England. We need only mention the boom in Germany in the years 1924–29 in which equilibrium could not have been achieved in her balance of payments if not for the American loans.

The difficulties Britain is experiencing in attaining her balance of payments are neither proof nor refutation of a boom. Let us recollect that at the beginning of the crisis of 1929–33 Britain's balance of payments turned against her, being a reflection of the tremendous rise in imports due to the readiness of the foreign producers to flood the British market with goods at the cheapest prices. After a while, however, and especially after leaving the gold standard, the conditions of slump reflected themselves in a change in the terms of trade to Britain's benefit and a greater ease in gaining equilibrium in her balance of payments. From Britain's difficulties in attaining equilibrium today, therefore, nobody with any knowledge of economics would assert that this is proof that there is not a boom.

One could go on pulling the weeds out of Germain's garden. But I am afraid that were this to be done, nothing would remain at all.

### Germain's Analysis of the Cycle of Production under Conditions of Decadent Capitalism

After showing such a lamentable lack of understanding of the theory of cycles, Germain tries to apply it to the conditions of declining capitalism. He gives four characteristics. The first is almost entirely a quotation from Trotsky, and is, therefore, correct. All the rest are based on a mechanical interpretation of the ABC of Marxism, and on a complete misunderstanding of the realities of capitalism in decline.

He writes:

'The world market ceases to expand *globally*. *There is no more boom on a world scale*. The splitting up of the world market or the violent destruction of a competitor alone allows for the development of feverish booms *in certain capitalist countries*.' (Germain's emphasis.)

It is difficult to imagine the concentration of more mistakes in so few words. Instead of explaining that the decline of capitalism means that historically the productive forces expand more rapidly than the market, that, while not standing still, they lag far behind the potential productive possibilities, that more and more productive capacity is left unused, that production is ever further diverted from the production of means of production and means of consumption to the production of means of destruction – instead Germain puts forward the above-quoted vulgarisation of Marxism. A few simple facts will prove how careless he was in writing.

Let us begin by comparing industrial production on a world scale from the peak of one cycle to the peak of the next.

| World Industrial Production (1913 : 100) | |
|---|---|
| 1891 | 33 |
| 1900 | 51 |
| 1906 | 73 |
| 1913 | 100 |
| 1920 | 102 |
| 1928 | 148 |

(**Weltproduktion und Welthandel in den letzten 100 Jahren** by Jurgen Kuczynski, Libau, 1935, pp. 20–21).

While immediately after the First World War and certainly after the Second World War European production was lower than before the war, there is no question but that on a world scale production today, as against the situation after the First World War, is considerably higher than before the war. In 1929 all the countries of Europe except Britain overreached the level of production of the peak year, 1913. It would be wrong even to say that the world market shrinks *absolutely* during the whole period of the decline of capitalism. As the accumulation of capital determines the market, builds it, limits it, and undermines it, to speak about an absolute decline of the world market as a permanent phenomenon, and not as a stage in a cycle, is tantamount to declaring that the accumulation of capital ceases to take place in the period of the decline of capitalism. Such a theory can take its place not among revolutionary Marxists, but among IKDers, with their 'theory of retrogression'.

Let us bring a few facts about the development of world trade from the time of the transition of rising industrial capitalism to decadent monopoly capitalism until today.

*Volume of World Trade (in milliard Swiss francs, 1913 prices)*

| | |
|------|-------|
| 1870 | 45.5 |
| 1880 | 68.8 |
| 1890 | 94.2 |
| 1900 | 118.7 |
| 1913 | 197.8 |
| 1920 | 193.3 |
| 1929 | 261.7 |

*(Ibid)*

During the cycle of 1929–37 world trade declined tremendously at the beginning but then rose, not however, reaching the 1929 volume even at its peak; it was 4 per cent lower. There are no statistics as regards world trade today.

Germain writes:

'There is no more all-round development of productive forces on a national scale. Even during the period of "prosperity" certain branches develop only at the expense of other branches. Advances in technology are no longer or are only very partially incorporated in production.'

If we understand this to be relative, and not as Germain considers it, to be absolute, it is correct. It simply repeats in other words what Lenin wrote in **Imperialism**: 'It would be a mistake to believe that this tendency to decay precludes the possibility of the rapid growth of capitalism. It does not. In the epoch of imperialism, certain branches of industry, certain strata of the bourgeoisie and certain countries betray, to a more or less degree, one or another of these tendencies. On the whole, capitalism is growing far more rapidly than before. But this growth is not only becoming more and more uneven in general; its unevenness also manifests itself, in particular, in the decay of the countries which are richest in capital (such as England).' (**Little Lenin Library,** p. 109).

From this no one, except perhaps Germain, would conclude that technological developments are only partially, or not at all, incorporated in industry today. That this is not so, will be clear from a comparison of the changes in the productivity of labour in England in the fifty years before the Second World War, when this country showed traits of decadence to a much greater extent than any other capitalist country. These are the facts.

Productivity per Worker per Hour
(1913    :    100)

| Trade Cycle | Productivity per Worker per Hour |
|-------------|----------------------------------|
| 1880–86 | 71 |
| 1887–95 | 75 |
| 1895–1903 | 80 |
| 1904–08 | 87 |
| 1909–14 | 93 |
| 1924–32 | 105 |
| 1933–39 | 119 |

(Jurgen Kuczynski, **A Short History of Labour Conditions in Great Britain and the Empire to the Present Day**, London, 1942, p. 96.)

A summing up of Germain's conception of the rise and decline of capitalism, can best be illustrated by drawing the following graphs:

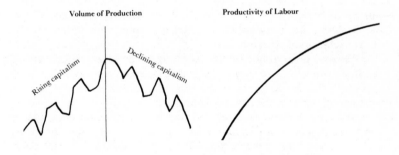

In reality the graphs should look something like this:

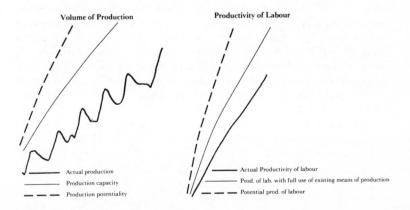

*The Standard of Living of the Masses in the Period of the Decline of
Capitalism*

Germain writes:

'There is no more all-round amelioration of the standard of
living of the industrial workers from one revival to another.'

Ascendant capitalism did not yield a general improvement in
the living standards of the workers from one boom to another. Proof
of this is to be found in the pages of the first volume of **Capital**,
which describes the labour conditions in this period and points not
only to the relative impoverishment of the working class, but also to
its absolute impoverishment, not only to the decline of the workers'
portion of the total product, but also to the absolute decline of real
wages. Excellent proof of this is also to be found in Engels' **The
Condition of the Working Class in 1844**, written in a year of boom.
The connection between the general economic situation and the
standards of living of the working class is determined by many
different factors: by the tempo of accumulation of capital; by the
relationship between the increase of production and the rise of the
productivity of labour which influences employment; by the extent
of the proletarisation of petty bourgeois strata (peasants, artisans
and others) following upon industrialisation, which influences the
supply of labour; by the general price structure influenced by
national and international factors, etc., etc.; and, most important of
all, the relation of class forces.

Whereas until about the 60s and 70s of the nineteenth century
the living standards of the working class declined, there is no doubt
that in all the developed countries during the last few decades of the
nineteenth century the absolute standards of living of the workers
rose. Now, with capitalism in decline, the general and continuous
rise that took place for these few decades not only stopped but was
even reversed for a certain period in some countries. To proceed
from this to the oversimplified conclusion of Germain would be no
less mistaken than to infer that throughout the rise of capitalism
there was a general and continuous improvement in the living
standards of the workers. It is most important to guard against
underestimating the influence of the class relationship of forces in
determining the value and price of labour power. To demonstrate
that the decline of British capitalism has not yet been accompanied
by a decline in the standard of living of the workers between the
peaks of the cycles, let us look at some figures given by A. L. Bowley
in **Wages and Income in the United Kingdom since 1860**, (London,
1937):

*Real Wages in Britain*
*(1914 : 100)*

| | |
|------|-----|
| 1880 | 69 |
| 1890 | 93 |
| 1900 | 103 |
| 1914 | 100 |
| 1924 | 111 |
| 1929 | 118 (p. 30) |

This rise in real wages, of course, does not preclude a decline in wages relative to total production, i.e. an increase in the rate of exploitation. Thus relative wages in Britain were:

| (1900 | : | 100) |
|---|---|---|
| Cycle | | Relative Wages |
| 1859–68 | | 124 |
| 1869–79 | | 111 |
| 1880–86 | | 96 |
| 1887–95 | | 95 |
| 1895–1903 | | 94 |
| 1904–08 | | 91 |
| 1909–14 | | 88 |
| 1924–32 | | 76 |

(Kuczynski, *ibid,* pp. 64,101)

Germain writes that although 'There is no more all-round amelioration of the standard of living of the industrial workers from one revival to another', this 'does not exclude either a relative "amelioration" between the crisis and the revival, or a relative amelioration of the position of unemployed or peasants, etc., transformed during the "revival" into industrial workers.'

We have already explained that an amelioration of the standard of living of the workers between two revivals even in the period of the decline of capitalism, is not excluded. It is even not excluded that the position of the unemployed *during the depression* will not be worse than the position of the unemployed in a previous depression, or indeed even than the position of the employed workers in a previous boom.

Colin Clark, who made excellent statistical investigations into the British national income and its distribution, points out: 'During recent years of low food prices, it has been about true to say that an unemployed man with a wife and two children drawing benefits has been better off than an unskilled labourer in full work in 1913.' (**National Income and Outlay**, London, 1937, p. 270.)[5]

These few facts are a warning to us not to interpret mechanically and in the spirit of the 'Third Period' the words of Trotsky when he said that in the '. . . epoch of decaying capitalism . . . in general, there can be no discussion of systematic social reforms and the raising of the masses' living standards . . . every serious demand of the proletariat and even every serious demand of the petty bourgeoisie inevitably reaches beyond the limits of capitalist property relations and of the bourgeois state.' (Transitional Programme.)

Although the nineteenth century was the century of reforms, this did not prevent the short-lived Paris Commune from coming into existence. In the same way, the fact that the twentieth century is the century of socialist revolution, does not exclude the possibility of certain reforms or semi-reforms being introduced. But these reforms cannot be of a general and lasting nature; necessarily, they must be very meagre as against the vast potentialities of production.[6]

### A Few Remarks in Conclusion

It is outside the scope of this article to make an exhaustive analysis and elaboration of the Marxist theory of crises. Nor does it attempt to show how the theory of crises applies to world capitalism in general, and Britain in particular; or to attempt to analyse the influence of the war on the economic cycle. Nevertheless, if it succeeds in throwing some light on these questions it will have accomplished what it set out to do.

In view of the fact that Comrade Germain writes extensively and prolifically on many theoretical and political subjects requiring considerable study, it is very necessary for the well-being of the Fourth International, that he prepares his writings with scientific conscientiousness. The analysis of his article under review proves that sweeping confidence and pontifical declarations regarding facts and theoretical generalisations are no substitute for really scientific work. And this holds good not only for current reading, but also for the ABC.

---

1. *Capital, I,* Trans. Samuel Moore & Edward Aveling, Modern Library, p. 495.
   *Capital, I,* Trans. Samuel Moore & Edward Aveling, Swan Sonnenschein & Co. Ltd, p. 455.
   *Capital, I,* Trans. Eden and Cedar Paul, Everyman's Library, p. 486.
2. Germain's juggling with words makes up such an important part of his article that, although we do not intend to weed out every error he makes, this particular one deserves mention, even if only in the form of a note.

   He says that there are 'two terms by which Marx characterises the period that we call "boom": the term "upswing" (essor) and the term "production at high pressure".' He arrives at this conclusion after citing two quotations from Marx describing the cycle. Even if the passage from Marx was not wrongly quoted, the way Germain derives his definitions from them is absolutely arbitrary.

   In the first passage (wrongly quoted) the cycle is divided into six sub-sections: moderate activity, prosperity, upswing, over-production, crisis and stagnation. In the second, it is divided into four sub-sections: moderate activity, production at high pressure, crisis and stagnation.

   Now, by eliminating the common terms in these two formulations, we would be left in the first formulation with: *prosperity, upswing and over-production.* In the second we are left with *production at high pressure.* If production at high pressure is, for Germain, identical with boom, why does he exclude Marx's terms of prosperity and over-production from being part of the boom?
3. The implication that the comrades of the RCP Majority consider the coal shortage to be 'a result of the boom' is readily shattered by an analysis of their resolutions for several years and especially by the article to which Germain pens his reply.
4. It would be possible to establish the same facts as regards other industrial countries also, but let this one example suffice.
5. In the light of the above-quoted figures of real wages, and of a comparison of the existing conditions in Britain today, with those described by people living before the First World War, it is clear that the writers of the editorial in the *Fourth International* of March 1947, were not very well informed when they wrote: 'The prospects in England are dimmer and dimmer for a return to the living levels of 1939, let alone the levels achieved before 1914.' According to this the standard of the British worker today is lower than in 1939, and in 1939 it was lower than in 1913!

6. In order to prevent any misunderstanding, it is necessary to point out: while Germain is wrong when he speaks of the inevitability of the standard of life decreasing from one peak of a cycle to another in the period of decadent capitalism, it does not follow that every boom must bring a standard of life to the masses higher than in the preceding boom. No, definitely not. Marxist economic laws are not of this schematical character. If the RCP majority perspectives speak about reforms and semi-reforms at the present time, they could not derive this prognosis from the fact that Britain is in a period of economic boom alone. There were many booms not accompanied by a rise in the standard of life of the masses. The RCP perspectives were conditioned, and must be conditioned by three factors: one, the existence of a boom; two, the prevailing relation of forces in Britain; three, an American Loan which will bridge the big deficit in the balance of foreign trade. As Trotsky formulated it: 'Every historical prognosis is always conditional, and the more concrete the prognosis, the more conditional it is.'

# On the class nature of the people's democracies

IN THE FOURTH International the supporters of the position that Russia is a degenerated workers' state are divided into two basic groups in their evaluation of the class nature of the 'People's Democracies':

(1) Those who declare that they are capitalist states;
(2) Those who declare that they are workers' states.

We are convinced that if the first of these groups brought their ideas to their logical conclusion they would realise that Russia is a state capitalist country; the other point of view leads directly to Stalinism.

## I. If the 'People's Democracies' are Capitalist Countries, what Conclusion can we draw about Russia?

In all the 'People's Democracies' industry is almost completely state-owned.

In Poland, according to a speech of Roman Zambrowski, Secretary of the Stalinist Party, delivered on 12 July 1948, 85% of industry was in the hands of the state and co-operatives (the latter having not more than 5%), the same percentage of communications and 100% of banking. Since 1948 state ownership has extended even further.

In Czechoslovakia on 1 November 1946, 60.4% of industry, according to the number employed, was state-owned, 11.6% state-administered (later in nearly all cases declared state property), 3.6% owned by co-operatives and municipalities, and only 24.4% privately owned. After the February coup the proportion of industry privately owned was cut even further, to 7%, according to the number employed. Today it is not more than 2.6% (speech of Gottwald, 24 February 1950). All banks and insurance companies, and nearly all transport, have been state-owned since 1945.

In Yugoslavia the percentage of state-owned industry was estimated at 70–80% by the **Economist** of 19 January 1946, and since then it has risen to over 90%.

In Hungary a law of 25 March 1948 put 78% of industry into the hands of the state. Another law of 28 December 1949 made all enterprises employing more than ten workers state property, and also all enterprises owned by foreign capital (Russian excluded, of course). Thus today more than 90% of Hungarian industry is state-owned, 100% of banks, insurance companies and communications.

In Bulgaria a law of 23 December 1947 transferred 93% of industry into state hands (while 2% was owned by co-operatives and 5% remained private property) and 100% of banks and insurance.

In Rumania, also, more than 90% of industry is state-owned (in this is included Russian state-ownership).

In the Soviet Zone of Germany a minority of industry is privately owned. Here there are three main owners of industry: Russia, which owns 'Soviet Shareholding Companies' (SAG's), the Local German States which own *Landseigene Betriebe* (LEB), and private people. The proportion of these three groups in the total industrial production was as follows (percentages):

| | SAG's | LEB | Private enterprises |
|---|---|---|---|
| 1947 | 27–30 | 35 | 35–38 |
| 1948 | 30–33 | 40 | 27–30 |

(**Wirtschaftsprobleme Der Besatzungszonen,** Berlin 1948, p235)

Without the SAG's the nationalised enterprises do not comprise the majority of industry. The SAG's importance is even greater than appears from the table, first of all as nearly all the large-scale enterprises are owned by them. Every SAG employs on the average 2,400 workers, as against 139–146 in the LEB's and about ten in the private industries. Their importance will be even clearer if we take into account that they control heavy industry entirely. Since 1948 the proportion of private industry declined even further and today it does not make up a fifth of all industry in the Soviet Zone.

Banks and transport in the 'People's Democracies' are completely state-owned. Trade is in the hands of the state at least to the same extent as it was in USSR during the NEP period. Foreign trade is 100% in the hands of the state. The majority of wholesale trade is likewise in its hands: Czechoslovakia 100%, Yugoslavia 100%, Poland (state and co-operatives run by the state) 95.6%, Bulgaria 64%. The position of retail trade is different. In Poland (July 1948) the state had only 25–30% of retail trade in its hands; in the Czech lands of Czechoslovakia it had 66.5%; in Bulgaria (31 October 1948) it had 22.3%; in Yugoslavia (31 March 1948) it had 39.9%, and co-operatives had 58.31%.

That on the whole the proportion of private ownership in industry, banking, transport, wholesale and retail trade in the 'People's Democracies' is not larger than it was in USSR during the NEP period is clear if we compare the above figures with the corresponding figures for Russia during the NEP. Trotsky wrote in **The Real Situation in Russia** (1927): 'Altogether, the production of the non-state industries constitutes more than a fifth of the whole production of goods, and about 40% of the commodities in the general market' (p. 27). According to **International Press Correspondence** of 20 October 1927, the percentage of private industry in the total industrial production of Russia in 1926–27 was 18.1%. The proportion of wholesale trade in private hands in 1924–25 was 9.3% of the turnover and of retail trade 42.6%. (In 1927–28 the figures were respectively 1.5% and 27.0%).

Only as regards land is there less state-ownership in the 'People's Democracies' than in the USSR during the NEP period. The land in the USSR was nationalised, while that in the 'People's Democracies' is privately owned. Faced by the experience of forced 'collectivisation' in Russia, where nationalisation was the point of departure legalising this enforced 'collectivisation', the Stalinist leaders in the 'People's Democracies' had to fight very hard against the accusation that they also intend to enforce 'collectivisation'. But in substance, if not in form, there is no great difference between the legal position as regards land in the 'People's Democracies' and that in Russia before the big drive towards 'collectivisation'; in the 'People's Democracies' the peasant owns his land, but the basic characteristic of private ownership – the right of contract, of buying and selling, of leasing and renting – is denied him. There are far more state and co-operative farms in the 'People's Democracies' than in Russia during the NEP period. As late as October 1929 – twelve years after the October revolution – only 4.1% of peasants were in Kolkhozes. As against this, in Yugoslavia today 23% of agriculture is in state and co-operative farms; in Bulgaria in January 1950, 7.2% of land was in the hands of co-operative farms, and the target for 1953 is 60% (probably an exaggerated target which will not be reached); in Hungary state and co-operative farms on 1 November 1949 made up 7% of all cultivated land; in Poland state farms produced about 7.9% of gross agricultural output in 1949.

Together with state ownership there is state planning. here, no doubt, the plans of the 'People's Democracies' are far more ambitious than those of Russia during the NEP period, and in a number of them the plans even exceed the achievements of Russia in the First Five-Year Plan. The current plans in the 'People's Democracies' fix, as their production targets, an annual increase in the gross national product of 8% in Czechoslovakia, 10% in

Hungary and Poland, 12% in Poland, 13% in Hungary, 17% in Bulgaria and 37% in Yugoslavia. In Russia in 1928 industrial production was only 19.6% higher than in 1913, and the First Five-Year Plan aimed at an annual increase of 20.6%.

If an economy based on state ownership with economic planning (with a monopoly of foreign trade as its concomitant) in which the bourgeoisie has a tiny and dwindling part, is nevertheless a capitalist economy, which the 'People's Democracies' represent, how is it possible to argue against the conception of state capitalism and the definition of Russia herself as a state capitalist country?

Only inertia and conservatism can explain why people like E. Germain and John G. Wright define the 'People's Democracies as capitalist countries while clinging to the definition of Russia as a workers' state.

In trying to find some economic argument for their case, they point to three things:

(1) The existence of enterprises in the satellites which are not owned by the states of these countries, but by the Russian state;

(2) The greater dependence of the economies of the 'People's Democracies' on the Western world markets than that of the USSR at any time;

(3) The prevalence of capitalist production in agriculture (which point has already been dealt with, showing that in reality the absence of the right to buy and sell cuts across private ownership in land, and as regards 'collectivisation' it is more advanced in the 'People's Democracies' today than it was in Russia in 1929).

On the first point John G. Wright writes:

'Inside the USSR the Stalinists have been and remain a monstrous parasitic growth on the social system that emerged from October. Even today they have no juridical basis for their power and privileges; even today they play no independent role in Soviet economic life.

'But what is their position in Eastern Europe? Do their power and privileges have a juridical basis there? Does their position provide them with an independent role in the economic life of these countries?

'The answer is of course, yes! To deny it is to blind oneself to the full enormity of the counter-revolutionary crimes of Stalinism and of the counter-revolutionary regimes they have been trying to sustain in almost half of Europe.

'In Bulgaria, Rumania, Hungary and Eastern Germany – leaving aside Finland and Austria – they have the status of conquerors of belligerent states. This status is sealed by treaties and underwritten by the Western imperialists. It is paid for in indemnities, reparations, special trade treaties, not to mention outright pillage. One can scarcely use the term parasitism for what they have perpetrated there. They have exploited the masses and economies of Eastern Europe in a way which differs in degree but not in substance from the imperialist brigands. In relation to the other countries – Poland, Czechoslovakia, Albania – they pose as "liberators". But here, too, they played and still play the role of ruthless conquerors. These countries too are subject nations who are likewise being oppressed and exploited. What is the gist of the Yugoslav charges and revelations if not the exposure of precisely such ruthless exploitation?'

Believing that the character of the exploitation of the peoples of the 'People's Democracies' by the Russian bureaucracy throws the clearest light on the capitalist relations of production prevailing between the workers of these countries and the Russian bureaucracy on the one hand, and on the relations of production in Russia herself on the other, we shall give some facts about this.

We have already mentioned the SAG's whose production made up 30–33% of the industrial production of the Soviet Zone of Germany in 1948. In addition to this portion taken by Russia as her property, she also took the products of other industries as reparations. The products of the SAG's are not included as reparations, as the SAG's themselves are declared non-German property. (Their value was originally included in the reparations account.) The Two-Year Plan (1949–50) fixes the reparations deliveries from current production at 17% of the net output of industry plus 8% for the upkeep of the Occupation Forces, making a total of 25%. If to this is added the output of the SAG's, the Russian bureaucracy appropriates 55–58% of the total output of the industrial workers of Eastern Germany. It is difficult to find a colony of a Western imperialist country where a higher proportion of the industrial product is taken as a surplus value by the capitalists of the 'mother' country.

Rumania and Hungary also had to pay very high reparations. Not to overburden the text with figures, just one thing need be said about the amount of these reparations: measured in relation to the national income, to the Government budget or to foreign trade, the amount of reparations Rumania and Hungary had to pay to Russia was much greater than what Germany paid to the Western imperialist Powers after World War I. In addition to the reparations there are the Mixed Companies, in which Russia owns 50%, but which in reality are completely under her control. These companies are particularly important to Rumania. Mention must first be made of the Sovrom Petrol Company, which controls the richest oil fields in Rumania. Then there are Sovrom companies for shipping, air communications, timber, chemicals, tractor production, steel, engineering, coal mining, the exploitation of natural gas deposits, building, glass; Sovrom Banco (where the Russians have a share larger than half) which controls nearly all the light industries; a Sovrom insurance company – all in all making up far more than half the industries, transport, banking and insurance of Rumania.

In Hungary the importance of the Soviet-Hungarian companies is very much smaller.

A telling characterisation of these companies was given by **The World Today**, the monthly journal of the Royal Institute of International Affairs (January 1949), describing the position of Sovrom Petrol:

'. . . the only capitalist in Rumanian industry is Communist Russia. Only the Russian Government has the right to own private shares, and only the company in which Soviet Russia has private shares is allowed to make profits and distribute them to the shareholders. Sovrom Petrol has now the best fields and concessions and the right to export in free currency areas. It is also officially subsidised by the Rumanian Government in the event of loss. Thus it can be seen that Sovrom Petrol has the best of the bargain. The second sector belongs in principle to the Rumanian State. Its task will be to prospect for, and explore, new fields as well as to exploit the exhausted wells left by the expropriated companies. Its personnel is untrained. Its trade will be limited to the adverse one with Soviet Russia and the other satellites. Therefore, while both sectors are working for the benefit of Soviet Russia, it is not difficult to guess which has the best chance of successful working, which is doomed to failure.'

While one cannot but agree with John G. Wright that there is no difference 'in substance' between the exploitation of, let us say, oil workers in Sovrom Petrol by the Russian bureaucracy, and the exploitation of Iranian workers in the Anglo-Iranian Company, this begs the question of what difference there is between these and the relations between the Russian bureaucracy and the Ukrainian, or for that matter the Russian, workers. If the fact that Russia owns 30–33% of industry in her zone of Germany makes the relations in this zone capitalist (as John G. Wright argues) and makes this zone a state capitalist country, would an increase of Russian ownership to 100%, as in Ukraine or Uzbekistan, have made any difference to the relations between Russia and the Soviet Zone, or, for that matter, within Russia herself?

And if we take the trade relations between Russia and the 'People's Democracies' as a proof that the 'People's Democracies' are capitalist countries subordinate to the laws of capitalist exploitation, as John G. Wright tells us, the argument applies no less to the internal relations in Russia herself.

Since the Tito-Stalin conflict, the Yugoslav leaders have dealt at great length with the question of the sharp trade practices used by Russia in her dealings with the 'People's Democracies'. They cite many statistics to prove that Russia sells her products to them at prices far higher than those prevailing on the world market, while she buys their products for very low prices. The leaders of Yugoslavia also proved, basing themselves on the Marxian theory of value, that even if the prices Russia demanded were those prevailing on the world market, there would still have been *capitalist* exploitation of those 'People's Democracies' which are more backward industrially.

Particularly important in the analysis of this problem is the pamphlet of M. Popovich, Deputy Finance Minister, **On Economic Relations among Socialist States**. He argues that industries with a high organic composition of capital, i.e. with a great deal of capital compared with living labour, get part of the surplus value which workers in industries with a lower organic composition of capital produce. This applies also in international trade between more developed and less developed countries, i.e. countries which have relatively more capital and those which have less. He quotes Marx to support this: the 'favoured country obtains in such an exchange more labour in return for less labour'. Thus, even under conditions of free competition, the toilers of the poor countries produce surplus value which is appropriated by the rich countries. Popovich argues that this exploitation increases where the latter, for one reason or another, has a monopoly position as against the former.

If we accept the Titoist assertions that capitalist exploitation prevails in the relations between Russia and her satellites, it of necessity puts certain conclusions as regards the economic relations within Russia herself, or within each of her satellites. The assumption of Marxism that foreign policy is a continuation of internal policy is as true for trade as for other aspects of policy. If it is true that the country with a lot of capital gets surplus value produced by workers in the countries with relatively less capital, and these relations are capitalist relations of exploitation, then certainly the Russian workers who own no capital at all are exploited, *capitalistically*, by the bureaucracy which owns all the capital. And if, with her monopoly position, Russia tries to sell her products as dearly as possible to her satellites and tries to buy their products as cheaply as possible, this applies no less to the relations between the bureaucracy and the workers in the USSR when labour power is bought and sold. In the absence of any possibility of choosing their employer and of any political rights, the Stalinist state confronts them as an absolute monopolist.

Thus if we draw the Titoist arguments to their logical conclusions, the capitalist exploitation of Yugoslavia by Russia is only one *facet* of the capitalist exploitation of all workers in Stalin's Empire by the Russian bureaucracy. The fact that Tito does not draw this conclusion, but stops midway, is because it will reflect on the regime in Yugoslavia herself (this we shall deal with elsewhere). In a similar manner Gandhi attacked the imperialist exploitation of India *without showing the connection between this and the class rule of the British bourgeoisie. But for the Marxist it is clear that capitalist relations of exploitation between 'nations' is only a facet of capitalist exploitation prevailing in the ruling nation itself. The capitalist exploitation of the toilers of the 'People's Democracies' by Russia, exposed by the Titoists, is a facet of the capitalist exploitation in Russia herself.*

The second argument of an economic character put forward by the comrades who claim that the USSR is a workers' state while the 'People's Democracies' are capitalist countries, is that the latter are much more dependent on trade with the Western capitalist countries than Russia ever was. This argument is quite wrong. The trade of some of the 'People's Democracies' with the West is relatively no greater than that of Russia during the First Five-Year Plan; in the case of four of them incomparably smaller, smaller even than Russia's dependence on trade with the West after the First Five-Year Plan. These countries are Bulgaria, Albania, Rumania and Hungary; it was also the case in Yugoslavia until the rift. The position of Poland and Czechoslovakia is different, but the tendency of their foreign trade is more and more towards trade with the USSR and the other 'People's Democracies'. If reparations and the products of the SAG's is taken into account, the Soviet Zone of Germany trades much less with the West than Czechoslovakia or Poland or even Hungary. The trend of the external trade of the 'People's Democracies' can be shown from the following calculation (which excludes the Soviet Zone of Germany):

*East European Countries' Foreign Trade   (millions of dollars in 1938 prices)*

|  | Import | | | Export | | |
|---|---|---|---|---|---|---|
|  | 1938 | 1947 | 1948 | 1938 | 1947 | 1948 |
| Trade among themselves and with the USSR | 154 | 184* | 355* | 161 | 162* | 314* |
| Trade with other countries | 750 | 458† | 411† | 920 | 276† | 384† |
| Total | 904 | 642 | 766 | 1,081 | 438 | 698 |
| And in percentages: |  |  |  |  |  |  |
| Trade among themselves and with the USSR | 17.0 | 28.6 | 46.3 | 14.9 | 37.0 | 45.0 |
| Trade with other countries | 83.0 | 71.4 | 53.7 | 85.1 | 63.0 | 55.0 |
| Total | 100.0 | 100.0 | 100.0 | 100.0 | 100.0 | 100.0 |

*excluding trade between Germany and Yugoslavia †excluding Yugoslavia

(Calculated from the table on pp66–7 of **United Nations Economic Survey of Europe in 1948**, Geneva 1949.)

As Yugoslavia did not publish figures of foreign trade for the years 1947 and 1948 it was not possible to take them into consideration in drawing up this table. Otherwise the tendency of these countries to trade mainly among themselves and with Russia and to constrict relations with countries independent of Russia would have been even more pronounced. (For the general tendency of Stalinist state capitalism to economic autarchy, see T. Cliff, **The Nature of Stalinist Russia**, p. 99.)

No scholastic argument will succeed in convincing anyone that the 'People's Democracies' with state ownership, a monopoly of foreign trade, planned economy, the increasing collectivisation of agriculture, are capitalist countries, while Russia, the motive force behind the development of all these traits in the 'People's Democracies' is a workers' state. In time the position of Germain and John G. Wright will become less and less tenable, and its main danger is not so much in itself, as its absurdity will become manifest, but that by preventing people from thinking it out to its logical conclusion, it can drive them to the other alternative, namely that if Russia is a workers' state, then the 'People's Democracies' are also workers' states. This position forces us to drop our definitions of Stalinism in general as counter-revolutionary (a point we deal with afterwards). At the same time the Germain-Wright position, by its internal contradictions, also opens the way to a correct restatement of the question of Stalinism in general: the economic relations between the 'People's Democracies' are not different in substance from the relations between the satellites and colonies of traditional capitalist countries and their 'mother' countries, because the economic relations in Russia are basically similar to those in the Western imperialist Powers – they are capitalist relations of production. Supporters of Germain and John G. Wright will therefore have to choose between rallying to the position of those who say that Russia as well as the 'People's Democracies' are workers' states, or to the position of those (like the present writer) who think that Russia is a state capitalist country.

## II. Were there Victorious Proletarian Revolutions in Eastern Europe?

The above arguments on the economic relations between the USSR and the 'People's Democracies', and the conclusions derived from them regarding the *internal* relations of production prevailing in the Stalinist countries, are a challenge to those comrades who claim that the 'People's Democracies' are workers' states. Besides those aspects which come into the orbit of political economy, these comrades will have to tackle a number of questions that are connected with the basic tenets of historical materialism, and first of all the Marxist-Leninist theory of the state. They must prove that a social revolution took place in these countries. E. R. Frank thinks that he does this by putting two incontrovertible facts side by side:

(1) That in E. Europe key positions of the economy are statified while formerly they were privately owned;

(2) That with the crumbling of German militarism a revolutionary wave swept Eastern Europe.

Here he stops. But it must be shown that the former was the result of the latter, that it was the *revolutionary activity of the masses* that brought about the statification of the means of production, which for E. R. Frank is decisive as the criterion of a workers' state. By paying no attention to dates, his article gives the impression that the nationalisation was the culmination of the revolutionary wave, that all the other protagonists of the theory do the same. The theory must stand the test of the Marxian assumption that the working class cannot take hold of the bureaucratic and militaristic state machine of the bourgeoisie, but must smash it and institute in its place the working class organised as the ruling class.

Let us check the facts.

### Rumania, Hungary and Bulgaria

The defeat of German militarism was followed by a big revolutionary wave in Bulgaria, a much smaller one in Hungary, and a still smaller one in Rumania. This wave reached its summit in the last months of 1944 and the first few months of 1945. After it, 'order' was restored not less ruthlessly, but indeed much more so, than ever the Stalinists in collaboration with the bourgeoisie had succeeded in doing in Western Europe. No large-scale nationalisation was carried out in these countries until another three years had passed by. Thus the countries were capitalist, if private property is the criterion. In the three countries, the bureaucratic militarist state machine was not smashed, but was taken hold of, captured by the Stalinists. Let us look at some facts to prove this.

The revolutionary wave in Bulgaria was described by the **Economist** on 7 October 1944 in these words:

'Reports on the Bulgarian forces of occupation in Western Thrace and Macedonia vividly recall the picture of the Russian army in 1917. Soldiers' councils have been set up, officers have been degraded, red flags hoisted, and normal saluting has been abolished. Molotov hastened to intervene, declaring: "If certain communists continue their present conduct we will bring them to reason. Bulgaria will remain with her democratic government and her present order . . . You must retain all valuable army officers from before the *coup d'état*. You should reinstate in service all officers who have been dismissed for various reasons.' (**New York Times**, 16 January 1945.)

And earlier, on 21 September 1944, the **New York Times** correspondent in Sofia reported that 'Communist leaders are doing everything they can to stop extremists in the party from agitating for Sovietization of the country'. As regards the 'Red Army', we are told: 'On several occasions when local Communists in the provinces tried to displace city officials and take matters into their own hands they were ordered by the Russian military authorities to return the jobs to the old officials until orders were received from the Fatherland Front Government in Sofia.' The Fatherland Front Government hastened to establish 'order'.

As regards the restoration of 'order' in the Bulgarian Army, the same article in the **Economist** states:

'M. Volchev [Minister of War in the Fatherland Front Government – TC] has issued a stern order to the troops to return immediately to normal discipline, to abolish Soldiers' Councils and to hoist no more red flags. Now Sofia reports that the

Bulgarian army has been placed under the supreme command of Marshal Tolbukhin. Apparently, the Soviet commander has no patience with Balkan repetitions of 1917 . . .'

The Bulgarian Stalinist leaders declared very emphatically that they stood for the social *status quo* and for the maintenance of private property. Thus, for instance, Yugov, Minister of the Interior, declared:

'This government, of which I am a member and on whose behalf I speak, categorically denies that it has any intention of establishing a Communist regime in Bulgaria. There is no truth in rumours that the government intends to nationalize any private enterprise in the country.' (**New York Times**, 22 September 1944.)

A few months later, at the National Congress of the Fatherland Front in March 1945, another Stalinist leader declared: 'We are building a democratic country based on private property and private initiative.' A few years later Dimitrov declared: 'The immediate task is neither the realisation of Socialism nor the introduction of the Soviet system but the consolidation of a truly democratic and Parliamentarian system.'

The Fatherland Front Government was headed from September 1944 to October 1946 by General Kimon Georgiev, who not only played a leading part in the military, semi-fascist *coup d'etat* of Tsankov in 1923, as a result of which tens of thousands of workers and peasants were massacred, but was also the author of the military coup of 1934 which led to the immediate dismissal of Parliament, the terrible persecution of Communists, Socialists, Agrarians, and, for the first time in Bulgarian history, the dissolution of the trade unions and their illegalisation. Georgiev's supporters wielded such power in the Fatherland Front Government that **The Observer** of 10 September 1944 could remark: 'The composition of the Government suggests that the group that has now taken over Sofia is the famous Military League which took power by a *coup d'etat* in 1934.'

The fact that because of the geographical position of Bulgaria the bourgeoisie hoped to switch from the side of Germany not to that of Russia, but to that of England and the USA, made it necessary for the Stalinists to carry a large-scale purge through the law courts.

That the Bulgarian people were successfully 'kept quiet' is illustrated by the fact that until April 1948 the Stalinists did not consider it necessary to hold even sham elections to the local authorities; mayors and members of the local councils were appointed by the Minister of the Interior.

The policy of the Stalinists in Bulgaria, therefore, was no different from that of the Stalinists during the Spanish Civil War. In Spain the Soldiers' Councils and the militia were abolished, and the regular army with its officers and hierarchical organisation reinstated in their place. The right of private property and the defence of the *status quo* was vehemently proclaimed, the coalition with the bourgeoisie was upheld as the programme for the present and the future. In Spain, as in Bulgaria, the Stalinists took over the key Ministry of the Interior, infiltrated into the Army and police, making up a considerable proportion of the commanding personnel. In Spain the Franco uprising brought about a situation where in the Republican area only tiny remnants remained of the old militarist bureaucratic state machine and the Stalinists had to build up the new bureaucratic military state machine almost from scratch. In Bulgaria, on the other hand, the old state machine remained almost intact and the Stalinists simply infiltrated into positions in it. The 'progress' that Stalinism made between Spain 1936–38 and Bulgaria 1944–50 is symbolised in the 'progressiveness' of the ex-fascist Kimon Georgiev compared with the Liberal Azana.

The Stalinists followed the same pattern in Rumania as they did in Bulgaria. For three years the Stalinists were in a coalition government with Georges Tatarescu and four of his friends, a number equal to that of the Stalinists. The **Economist** rightly characterised this government as 'a queer coalition of the local Darlans and the parties of the Left' (30 December 1944). Tatarescu has an even worse record than Georgiev, if this is possible. In December 1927 he organised anti-Semitic pogroms. After the rise of Hitler he belonged, as the Comintern paper **International Press Correspondence** formulated it, to 'the right, pro-Hitler wing of the National Liberal Party'. He was the main actor in the transference of Rumania into the Axis orbit. Now for three years he was the vice-Premier of the 'People's Front' Government. The Prime Minister himself, who is still at the head of the government, Groza, was a very rich man, an owner of factories and large hotels, with wide banking interests. He had been a minister in two extreme right-wing, anti-Soviet governments under General Averescu (1920–21, 1926–27).

Premier Groza declared on 26 September 1945 that his government 'did not intend to apply either collectivisation of land or nationalisation of banks or industries'. Radio Bucharest reported that in a description of his talks with Stalin, Groza said that Stalin had advised him to 'keep a system of private enterprise and private property'. Even as regards foreign capital Groza was not unfriendly, declaring: 'The government and the parliament will make every effort possible in order to realise a fruitful field of collaboration for foreign capital' (**International News**, Bucharest, 8 January 1947). This was more than three years after the establishment of the People's Front Government! The Stalinist Minister of Justice, Patrascanu, went so far as to point out that Nazi collaborators were far more leniently dealt with in Rumania than, for instance, in France. The **New York Times** correspondent reported on 17 March 1945:

'Industrialists, businessmen and bankers will escape punishment as war criminals under a law being drawn up by Lucretsiu Patrascanu, Minister of Justice and Communist member of the Government, it was learned today. Rumania could not afford to lose the services of merchants and industrialists, M. Patrascanu said. He expressed the opinion that the country would pursue a more liberal policy toward this class than the French have.'

The bureaucratic and militarist character of the Rumanian state was not altered, and even its personnel remained very largely the same. Of the legal system Patrascanu could say:

'The procedures, methods, traditions, and structure of Rumanian jurisprudence have remained unchanged since a Communist became Minister of Justice. No more than 20 new judges out of 2,000 have been appointed. About a quarter of the old staff have been purged or pensioned.'

It is symbolical that the president of the Military Tribunal that tried Maniu was the war-time Director General of prisons and concentration camps in Rumania.

The structure of the army remained hierarchical, with complete subordination of the soldiers to their officers, and no soldiers' committees. For three years even the composition of its personnel showed marked continuity with the past. Thus, for instance, Lieutenant-Colonel Nicolas Cambrea, commander of the Rumanian units fighting against Russia at Stalingrad, was promoted by the Groza Government to the rank of General, and appointed Assistant Chief of Staff. Major Popescu-Argetoia, a prominent fascist in the past, was put at the head of the secret police. General Vasiliu Rascanu, Chief of Military Police during the war against Russia, was appointed Minister of War. Another old general, Pretorian, was appointed Chief of Staff at the same time. General Lascar, Brigadier-General in the anti-Soviet front of 1941, who received the Knight Cross of the Iron Cross from Hitler, was, after joining the Communist Party, considered 'loyal' enough to be appointed Minister of War.

The enthusiasm of the Stalinists for 'law and order' is illustrated by their ardour for the monarchy. On 3 November 1946, Premier Groza declared: 'The King, the Church, the Army, the people and the Government are one.' A few days later at the Stalinist-controlled front organisation, the National Democratic Bloc, meeting, vice-Premier Tatarescu said:

'From Gheorghiu Dej [leader of the CP] to myself we shall all fight together for the consolidation of the Monarchy, because we are convinced that the King is the strongest factor that rallies all Rumanians. We shall fight for the consolidation of the National Church and of private property, the source of all creative enterprise.'

On 8 November, King Michael's birthday, the Stalinist daily **Era Noua** said: 'The people of Rumania have faith in their King.'

In the election demonstrations of the Communist-controlled front organisation, the National Democratic Bloc, a constantly repeated slogan was *Traiasca Regele!* – Long live the King! The monarchist enthusiasm of the Stalinist Party reached such heights that they attacked Maniu as . . . anti-monarchist. Thus **Era Noua** of 3 December 1946 referred to the withdrawal of Maniu and his followers from parliament, and suggested that 'in fact Maniu's unparliamentary attitude is only a guise for his anti-dynastic policy. Maniu has already tried his first obstructive move in King Michael's reign . . . Neither Ferdinand nor King Carol were exempt from Maniu's political tactics.'(!)

In Hungary the policy of the Stalinists was basically the same as their policy in Bulgaria and Rumania. It is therefore unnecessary to describe it, but the following quotation from the report of Nagy Imre, member of the Political Bureau of the Party, to its Congress in September 1946 is typical of many declarations: 'While the war was still being fought, we have determined, and this is one of the basic principles, that in Hungary this is not the time for transition from capitalism to socialism, for struggle between the two social systems, but for uprooting the powerful remnants of feudalism. It is not a question then of struggle between the two social systems but of the struggle between democracy and reaction within capitalism.'

After the latter months of 1944 and the first few months of 1945, Bulgaria, Rumania and Hungary did not experience any wide revolutionary activity on the part of the workers. Since then the state machine remained unchanged – except for its increased bureaucratisation and militarisation.

When the Stalinist leaders decided to carry out large-scale statifications in these countries – December 1947 in Bulgaria, March 1948 in Hungary, and June 1948 in Rumania – they had no need to rely on the *independent* activity of the masses, or any mass activity at all, however deformed, but they carried out the statification purely through the bureaucratic state machine. The bureaucratic character of the statification is clear from the following facts.

In Hungary and Rumania Russia's demands for reparations and her schemes for the building of Mixed Companies which would give her direct control of certain key positions in their economies, resulted in the postponement of any statification until the requisitioning, dismantling, etc., was finished, the reparations payments nearly completed, and nearly all the Mixed Companies established. Then, in the first half of 1948, the statification was carried out. That it was carried out only when it was in the interests of the Stalinist bureaucracy to do so is clear from the following facts: after the big defeat of the Stalinists in the general elections of November 1945, when, in spite of the pressure they applied, their tremendous wealth and control over the majority of the press, the direct and indirect intervention of the Russian Occupation Army, the falsification at the polls, they got only 17% of the votes, the Hungarian bourgeoisie felt self-confident, and the Government, headed by the bourgeois Smallholders' Party, tried to delay agreement to the establishment of the Mixed Companies. Suddenly, quite out of the blue, the Stalinists began an intensive campaign for the nationalisation of industry on a large scale. Rakosi, in a speech over Radio Budapest on 4 March 1946, demanded the nationalisation of *precisely* those industries in which Russia demanded the establishment of Mixed Companies. When the Hungarian Government gave way and the Mixed Companies were established, the Stalinists reverted for another two years to their previous policy of foregoing any demand for the nationalisation of industry. Even when they decided to carry out the nationalisation, they did so in a most cynical and bureaucratic fashion. Easter Monday 1948 was declared a holiday, and when the workers were not in the factories, state officials came and took them over. Next day the workers came and found the new boss.

In Rumania the first major step towards the nationalisation of industry was taken on 11 June 1948, when quite unexpectedly the government introduced a law which was passed after only three hours' discussion, providing for the nationalisation of the over-whelming majority of industry. At the Congress of the CP (21–23 February 1948) which had to decide on the policy for the near future, no word had been said about planning the nationalisation of industry.

In Bulgaria the statification was carried out in no less bureau-cratic a fashion.

Anyone who says that Bulgaria, Rumania and Hungary are workers' states, must choose between two distinct alternatives:

(1) That they were workers' states from 1944, although for more than three years their economies were based entirely on private property, workers' states headed by coalition governments, in one case a monarchical workers' state (Rumania), workers' states where the workers were 'put in their places'; they were workers' states simply because the Stalinists took control of key ministries, with or without mass support (being very popular in Bulgaria, much less so in Hungary – where the Social Democrats were much stronger – and in Rumania a negligible factor);

(2) That they became workers' states only when the nationalisa-tion of industry took place long after the revolutionary wave died out. In no way is it possible to demonstrate that the statifications were the culmination of the activities, no matter how deformed, of the working class.

If Bulgaria, Rumania and Hungary are workers' states, it is simply because the Stalinists took hold of the old state machine. Hence, contrary to Marx, the proletarian revolution must not smash the bureaucratic military state machine of the bourgeoisie, but simply take hold of it: if the Ministers of War and the Interior (which controls the police) and all the commanding staff of army and police are members or sympathisers of bourgeois parties, the state is capitalist; if the positions are held by Stalinists or their allies – of the type of General Lascar and General Georgiev – it is a workers' state. To use this criterion, the Spanish Republic was a workers' state *par excellence*.*

## Czechoslovakia

In Czechoslovakia the statification of the majority of industry – all the banks and insurance companies as well as transport – took place at the same time as the country passed through a revolutionary crisis – May 1945. In this case it would seem, at first sight, that the statification was really the result of the class activities of the proletariat. However, almost the only enterprises to be statified were German enterprises, and practically no Czech or Slovak capitalists were expropriated. The expropriation of the German capitalists was part and parcel of the expulsion of the entire German population, rich and poor. Before the war 40% of the industry of Czechoslovakia belonged to German citizens of the country. German capital continued to infiltrate during the war, so that the proportion of German capital must have been not less than 60% in industry and nearly 100% in financial institutions (banks, insurance companies, etc.). As Benes explained (**Manchester Guardian**, 15 December 1945):

> 'The Germans simply took control of all main industries, main banks. If they did not nationalise them directly, they put them in the hands of big German concerns . . . In this way they automatically prepared the economic and financial capital of our country for nationalisation. To return the property and the banks to the hands of Czech individuals, or to consolidate them without considerable state assistance and new financial guarantees, was simply impossible.'

For the first two years after the downfall of the German military machine, what characterised the Stalinist agitation in Czechoslovakia was the hysterical, racial propaganda of Slavs against Teutons, unabated by even formal homage to internationalism, the class struggle, etc. As a high UNRRA official said: 'The familiar terminology of class struggle is conspicuous by its absence from Communist writings and speeches.' To exemplify the extreme racial propaganda which accompanied the expropriation of the Germans and thus the statification of the key industries, let us give some quotations.

On 12 May 1945, Gottwald declared:

> 'The new Republic will be a Slav state, a Republic of the

---

*By the way, de facto, the industry of Republican Spain was to a major extent in the hands of the state, because of the defection of the overwhelming majority of the bourgeoisie – especially the big bourgeoisie – to the side of Franco – as was the case in Rumania, Bulgaria and Hungary *after* the first statification laws of 1947–48. The industries in Spain were managed by bureaucrats, while the CP promised that private property would not be touched.

Czechs and the Slovaks. We will deprive the Germans and the Hungarians, who have so heavily sinned against our peoples and the Republic, of their citizenship and severely punish them.'

The Stalinist Minister of Information, Kopecky, speaking over Radio Prague on 25 May 1945, said:

'The Czechoslovak army is already prepared for the purification of the border area of the Republic from Germans and Hungarians, and for the restoration of the wealth of these old Slav areas into the hands of the Czechs and the Slovaks.'

In a speech at Liberec (Reichenberg) he said:

'We will clear Liberec of the German enemies, and we will do it so thoroughly that there will remain not the smallest place where the German seed could grow once more. We shall expel all the Germans, we shall confiscate their property, we shall de-Germanize not only the town but the whole area . . . so that the victorious spirit of Slavdom shall permeate the country from the frontier ranges to the interior.'

The Stalinist Minister of Education, Nejedly, expressed the same 'Slav' spirit, saying:

'Consider Middle Europe – there are Hungarians. What can they do? Then the Rumanians – what can they do? And what can the Germans do? They have no future anywhere. *We are greater than all of them:* with our culture we can stand up to all of them. And they will see that they in their hopeless situation will be happy only to follow our leadership. How many composers are there in Europe who are the equal of Smetana? How many painters of the rank of Mánes and Ales? How many historians the equal of Palacky? How many scientists the greatness of Purkyne? . . . Our culture must be national . . . Nothing but cultural ruins surround us . . . We will first of all carry our civilization to the border regions, and there will plant our national cultural ideal.'

In the competition of chauvinism, the Stalinists outdid the bourgeois parties, while the latter did their best to prove that they were not less anti-German than the CP. Thus, for instance, Dr Ivor Duchacek of the Catholic People's Party said in the National Assembly, March 1946:

'I regard as a downright falsification of history and as a building up of legends, which I do not hesitate to call pre-election legends, if the Communists, of all parties, assert that the credit for the transfer of the Germans from our country is due mainly to them, or almost alone to them.'

Nevertheless in this competition the Stalinists gained the upper hand. Firstly they could point to the fact that nowhere except in Russian-controlled territories were Germans evicted *en masse.* Secondly, and of greater importance, the direct organisation and carrying out of the expulsion was in the hands of members of the CP themselves. A Stalinist Minister of the Interior, Nosek, organised the expulsion and redistribution of the German property. (In Poland, too, the CP was in charge of the expulsion of the Germans from the Western territories, and the settlement of Poles in their place. There Gomulka, then General Secretary of the Party, was responsible.) The Security Corps which carried out the physical expulsion was also headed by members of the CP.

Owing to the fact that in the eyes of the people the CP bore the greatest responsibility for the expulsion, the new Czech settlers in the Sudeten areas contained a much higher proportion of CP supporters than the people in any other part of the country, even than those in the big towns with large concentrations of workers. In the 1946 general elections, in the districts of Jablonec and Turnot they polled 70% of the votes, in Kadan 62%, in Falknov 59%, in As over 50%, and so on.

Although the workers of Czechoslovakia did not have any revolutionary party to lead them, although they suffered years of miseducation in 'Slav brotherhood', here and there Czech and German workers instinctively showed international class solidarity expressed in open fraternisation. Thus, for instance, a number of rank-and-file CP members in Bodenbach began the publication of a daily paper in Czech and German immediately after the overthrow of the Hitlerite army. It was called **Rudy Prapor – Rote Fahne** (Red Flag). This enterprise was short-lived, as Nosek immediately prohibited the publication of any German paper, or any paper in two languages one of which was German.

The expulsion of the Sudeten Germans was a criminal act outdone only by Hitler's atrocities against the Jews. The number of Germans in Czechoslovakia was 3.2 million in 1930. Some of the small countries of Europe do not have bigger populations: Norway has 2.8 million, Finland 3.6 million, Denmark 3.7 million, Switzerland 4.1 million. The percentage of workers in the German population was bigger than among the Czechs, and much bigger than among the Slovaks. The Sudeten Germans had a long socialist tradition, Sudetenland being one of the first and strongest socialist centres in the Austro-Hungarian empire. Before the Nazi victory they had trade unions which were much stronger than those of Switzerland. Now these millions were compelled to leave the country, were robbed of everything they had, thousands of women were raped, tens of thousands of children died of starvation and epidemics, thousands were shot out of hand, others tortured in the worst Gestapo fashion in concentration camps. Some tens of thousands of Germans who were indispensible skilled workers, and therefore retained, were kept in conditions similar to those in which compulsory foreign labour was recruited by Hitler: they had to work at least twelve hours a day, and if the employer thought it necessary, fifteen hours; they were put under the jurisdiction of the National Committees which prohibited them from belonging to trade unions, did not allow them to derive benefit from the social services, allowed them no holidays, prohibited their children from receiving any public education; a quarter of their wages was taken by the state as reparations.

The fate of the Hungarians was a little better, but their plight was none the less unenviable. On 14 August 1946 the Hungarian Foreign Minister in the Paris Peace Conference made the following declaration which the representative of Czechoslovakia did not deny:

'650,000 Hungarians who live in Slovakia were deprived of their most elementary rights. Their property has been confiscated. No Hungarian may undertake any manual or intellectual work. He may not claim justice, he may not become a member of a trade union, he may not exercise his civic rights. The use of Hungarian in offices and even in churches and in public places is prohibited and subject to penalties. No newspaper or periodical in Hungarian may be published in Czechoslovakia, nor is it allowed to speak over the telephone or send wires in Hungarian. Hungarians may not own radio receivers. All Hungarian schools are closed, and even tuition in Hungarian is subject to penalties. The Czechoslovak authorities have dismissed all civil servants and private employees of Hungarian descent, and they have suspended payment of their pensions. Disabled servicemen, war-widows, and orphans do not receive their relief allocations.'

The Hungarian press, in particular the CP papers, pointed out that many of the Hungarians expelled from Czechoslovakia had been sent by the Nazis to Dachau and had been awarded high Czech decorations for this. Many were members of the Hungarian CP. Joseph Révai, editor of the Hungarian Stalinist daily, **Szabad Nép,** asked: 'Does it make no difference to the Czecho-Slovaks whether they establish a democratic or reactionary state, as long as it is a national state?' (15 July 1945). On the same day Rakosi condemned the expulsion of Hungarians from Czechoslovakia and the 'excesses resembling the old fascist methods'. (He was tactful enough to put the blame on the local officials.) On another occasion he attacked *all* the parties of Czechoslovakia (this includes the CP); on 26 May 1946 he said:

'We had a feeling that every Czecho-Slovak Party wanted to bake its own electoral cake by the fire of its treatment of the Hungarians. Let us hope that now the elections are over the Hungarians in Slovakia will at last be treated in a way becoming a democratic country.'

The brutal treatment of the Hungarians, however, continued. Even in the days of the *coup d'etat* in February 1948, the Czechoslovak Government did not omit to issue instructions prohibiting Hungarians, even if they were citizens of Czechoslovakia, and had excellent records in the anti-Nazi struggle, from being members of the Action Committees. (This policy changed later: on 21 October 1948 a Bill was passed giving civil rights to Hungarians in Czechoslovakia.)

We wish to make it quite clear that the expulsion of the Germans was *identical* with the statification of the means of production carried out in 1945, which left in the hands of the bourgeoisie only 24.4% of industry, no banks, no insurance companies and no transport. A year after the statification of the means of production, the Two-Year Plan was established. If state ownership and planning are identical with a workers' state, the chauvinistic struggle of 'Slavs against Teutons' is *identical* with the proletarian revolution.

To speak of the February events as the proletarian revolution (as Haston did in his outrageous article in the **Socialist Appeal**) is nonsense. Before the February event only 24.4% of industry was privately owned, after it 7%. Why does 24.4% private ownership make a country capitalist and 7% a workers' state? The February events showed most openly the subordination of the workers by the Stalinists to the bureaucratic and militarist state machine. The immediate cause of the political crisis was a move of the bourgeois and Social Democratic ministers to step Nosek from further increasing the hold of the Stalinists over the police. The question under discussion was what proportion of the commanding positions in the police would be in the hands of the Stalinists. The solution of the crisis was a foretold conclusion. The Stalinists had, besides the majority of the police, nearly all the political police, a majority of the press (through the Minister of Propaganda), control over the radio, and much greater wealth than the bourgeoisie (as they managed the nationalised industries). In the February 'revolution' the masses were manipulated as an auxiliary to the Security Police who were armed with sub-machine guns and met no serious opposition.*

The popular demonstrations were needed simply as a camouflage for the ominpotent bureaucratic state machine which was in no way different from that existing before 1945, and was to a large extent, even in its personnel, a continuation of it. The real aim of the February coup was to put the state beyond any popular control by abolishing parliamentary elections, and eliminating the few democratic rights held by the people. Faced with the move of the Social Democrats away from a united front with the Stalinists (the crypto-Stalinist Fierlinger being routed in the November 1947 Conference of the Social Democrats), the increasing disappointment of the workers in the bureaucratically managed state industries and the exploitation of the country by Russia (expressed in a growing number of defeats of the Stalinist lists in factory elections in the

---

*H. Seton Watson, the prominent expert on Eastern Europe, wrote in the *Manchester Guardian* on 4 August 1949: 'The Communists conquered Czechoslovakia not by smashing the State machine but by taking it over from above after careful penetration.'

winter of 1947–48), the Stalinists were rightly afraid of the approaching elections of May 1948.

They therefore hastened to tighten their hold over the police and used the first opportunity to launch the coup. After the coup, of course, the elections were held in the usual Stalinist manner, one list being put up which was nominated by the Stalinist bureaucrats. If a parallel to the February 'revolution' were sought, it would not be found in the October revolution, but, *mutatis mutandis*, in the 'March on Rome'. The generals and police agents were not going to be pushed aside by the masses, but were omnipotent, and intended to secure their omnipotence with the help, as an auxiliary factor, of a well-manipulated 'mass movement'.

*Poland*

To save space we shall only say a few words about Poland. A big part of industry – at least half the total, and the majority of the statified (the most important) industries – became state property as an accompaniment of the expulsion of eight million Germans, the overwhelming majority of them workers, from the part of Eastern Germany annexed to Poland. In Poland the working class in general did not support the Stalinist government, not even critically or hesitantly, but was in more or less open opposition to it. The independent activity of the workers had culminated in the Warsaw uprising of August–September 1944, where an advanced programme of nationalisation with workers' control and management was proposed by the Polish Socialist Party (PPS). The Russian army allowed 200,000 of the Warsaw people to be massacred, and 600,000 to be taken prisoner by the Germans.

After the Russians occupied Poland they were not successful in gaining mass support. To take only one example: in the elections to shop committees held at the end of 1945 in the largest industrial district of Poland, the Stalinists gained 21%, the PPS 64%. In spite of all the pressure they could apply, at the November 1945 Congress of the TUC, the Stalinists did not succeed in preventing the PPS from gaining two-thirds of all the delegates, and Rusinek, of the PPS, from being elected general secretary of the new Central Committee of the trade unions. The fact that afterwards the Stalinists did not suffer such open defeats was due to their abolition of elections altogether and their use of the police as the main weapon. To speak of statification in Poland as a result of the revolutionary activity of the people is a blatant misrepresentation, as in Poland the revolutionary activity was smashed with the occupation of the country by the Stalinists, and the Stalinists never succeeded in gaining the support of the basic sections of the working class. If they carried out a revolution in Poland, it was not only without the revolutionary activity of the masses, but even without any sympathy for them on the part of the working class.

*The Soviet Zone of Germany*

We shall restrict ourselves to a few words in dealing with this country too. Many of the arguments given above also apply here. We shall sum up by saying: if state ownership and a planned economy are the criteria of a workers' state, the Soviet Zone must be characterised as one, and we shall have to argue that the social revolution was carried out by the Stalinists, who were a small minority of the workers and carried out the revolution openly in the interests of the exploitation of Germany by the Russian bureaucracy.

We shall deal at length with Yugoslavia below.

### The Stalinist 'Social Revolution' and the Marxist-Leninist Theory of the State

Scores of times Marx repeated the idea that the political supremacy of the working class is a *prerequisite* for its economic supremacy. The workers cannot own the means of production collectively – i.e. be the ruling class economically – unless the state which owns the means of production is in their hands; in other words, the proletariat has political power. In this the proletariat as a ruling class is *fundamentally* different from the bourgeoisie. The bourgeoisie has a direct relation of ownership over wealth; therefore, whatever the form of government, so long as the bourgeoisie is not expropriated, it does not cease to be the ruling class: a capitalist can own his property in a feudal monarchy, in a bourgeois republic, in a fascist dictatorship, under military rule, under Robespierre, Hitler, Churchill or Attlee. As against this, where the state, which is the repository of the means of production, is totally alienated from the working class, by this very fact of political alienation the workers are separated from the means of production, they are wage slaves. Hence, Marx emphasised: firstly, the political rule of the working class is a *prerequisite* for its economic rule; secondly, it demands that there be no alienation of the working class from political power, i.e. that the workers' state, the dictatorship of the proletariat, have no bureaucracy and standing army; thirdly, that the first act of the revolutionary proletariat, therefore, be the smashing of the bourgeois-bureaucratic and militarist state machine.

We shall bring a few quotations from the great Marxist teachers on these points. The **Communist Manifesto** declares:

'. . . the first step in the revolution by the working class is to raise the proletariat to the position of ruling class, to win the battle for democracy.

'The proletariat will use its political supremacy to wrest, by degrees, all capital from the bourgeoisie, to centralise all instruments of production in the hands of the state, i.e. the proletariat organised as the ruling class . . .'

The proletarian revolution – the victory of 'the battle of democracy': workers' state – 'the proletariat organised as the ruling class'.

Forty years after the publication of the **Communist Manifesto**,

Engels wrote:

'If anything is certain, it is that our party and the working class can only come to power under the form of a democratic republic. Precisely this is the specific form for the dictatorship of the proletariat, as the Great French Revolution has already shown.'

Lenin in 1917: 'We all know that the political form of the "state" at that time [after the proletarian revolution – TC] is the most complete democracy.' (**State and Revolution**).

Lenin defines the dictatorship of the proletariat as 'a state that is democratic *in a new way* (for the proletariat and the propertyless in general) and dictatorial *in a new way* (against the bourgeoisie)'. *(Ibid)*.

In 1872 Marx and Engels wrote: 'One thing especially was proved by the Commune, viz. that "the working class cannot simply lay hold of the ready-made state machinery and wield it for its own purposes".'

Marx and Engels at that time confined their conclusions about the necessity of smashing the state machine to the Continent. Lenin explains this thus:

'This was natural in 1871, when England was still the model of a purely capitalist country, but without militarism and, to a considerable degree, without a bureaucracy.

[And he adds] 'Today, in 1917, in the epoch of the first great imperialist war, Marx's exception is no longer valid. Both England and America, the greatest and last representatives of the Anglo-Saxon "liberty", in the sense that militarism and bureaucracy are absent, have today plunged headlong into the all-European filthy, bloody morass of bureaucratic-military institutions to which everything is subordinated and which trample everything underfoot. Today, both in England and America, the "essential" thing for "every real people's revolution" is the *smashing*, the *destruction* of the "ready-made state machinery" . . . ' *(Ibid)*

In emphasising that the dictatorship of the proletariat will mean the most complete democracy with no bureaucracy or standing army, Marx hailed the Paris Commune as the model:

'The first decree of the Commune . . . was the suppression of the standing army, and the substitution for it of the armed people . . . The Commune was formed of the municipal councillors, chosen by universal suffrage in the various wards of the town, responsible and revocable at short terms. The majority of its members were naturally working men, or acknowledged representatives of the working class . . . Instead of continuing to be the agent of the Central Government, the police was at once stripped of its political attributes, and turned into the responsible and at all times revocable agent of the Commune. So were the officials of all the other branches of the administration.

From the members of the Commune downwards, the public service had to be done at *workmen's wages*. The vested interests and the representation allowances of the high dignitaries of state disappeared along with the high dignitaries themselves . . .' The judicial functionaries were to be divested of sham independence. Like the rest of public servants, magistrates and judges were to be elective, responsible and revocable. (**The Civil War in France.**)

[Further,] '. . . against transformation of the state and the organs of the state from servants of society into masters of society – an inevitable transformation in all previous states – the Commune made use of two infallible expedients. In the first place it filled all posts – administrative, judicial and educational – by election on the basis of universal suffrage of all concerned, with the right of the same electors to recall their delegate at any time. And, in the second place, all officials, high or low, were paid only the wages received by other workers . . . In this way, an effective barrier to place-hunting and careerism was set up, even apart from the binding mandates to delegates to representative bodies which were also added in profusion.'

The result of all these measures is that totally new relations came into being between the people and the government, relations in which the people are the master and the government the servant: '. . . universal suffrage was to serve the people, constituted in Communes, as individual suffrage serves every other employer in search for the workmen and managers in his business.'

Now, the 'revolution' that took place in Eastern Europe and the regime of the 'People's Democracies' is not a *partial* contradiction, not a *deformation* of what Marx taught about the revolution and the dictatorship of the proletariat; it is its *total negation*. The 'People's Democracies' entirely conform to Marx's characterisation of the *capitalist state*:

'. . . executive power with its monstrous bureaucratic and military organisation, with its artificial state machinery embracing wide strata . . . this appalling parasitic growth, which enmeshes the body of . . . society like a net and chokes all its pores [and] threaten to devour the whole of society.

*The Stalinist 'Socialist Revolution' and the Marxist Conception of the Role of Proletarian Class Consciousness*

Marx repeated hundreds of times that the proletarian revolution is the conscious act of the working class itself. Now certainly no member of the Fourth International will say that 'Slavism' – hatred of Germans and Hungarians, and the ideology of 'national unity' – including the Tatarescus, Georgievs and Lascars, are elements of proletarian class consciousness. Therefore, if we accept that the 'People's Democracies' are workers' states, what Marx and Engels said about the socialist revolution being 'history conscious of itself' is refuted. Refuted is Engels' statement:

'It is only from this point [the socialist revolution – TC] that men, with full consciousness, will fashion their own history; it is only from this point that the social causes set in motion by men will have, predominantly and in constantly increasing measure, the effects willed by men. It is humanity's leap from the realm of necessity into the realm of freedom. (**Anti-Duhring**.)

Rosa Luxemburg, too, must have spoken nonsense in her summing up of what all the Marxist teachers wrote about the place of proletarian consciousness in a revolution:

'In all the class struggles of the past, carried through in the interests of minorities, and in which, to use the words of Marx, "all development took place in opposition to the great masses of the people", one of the essential conditions of action was the ignorance of these masses with regard to the real aims of the struggle, its material content, and its limits. This discrepancy was, in fact, the specific historical basis of the "leading role" of the "enlightened" bourgeoisie, which corresponded with the role of the masses as docile followers. But, as Marx wrote as early as 1845, "as the historical action deepens, the number of masses engaged in it must increase". The class struggle of the proletar-iat is the "deepest" of all historical actions up to our day, it embraces the whole of the lower layers of the people, and, from the moment that society became divided into classes, it is the *first* movement which is in accordance with the *real* interests of the masses. That is why the enlightenment of the masses with regard to their tasks and methods is an indispensable historical condition for socialist action, just as in former periods the ignorance of the masses was the condition for the action of the dominant classes.'

*Is Staliniam Socially Counter-revolutionary?*

Those who believe that the 'People's Democracies' are workers' states, and after 'diplomatic' avoidance of the issue will in due course say that Mao-tse Tung's China is also a workers' state, claim that this is not 'undermining our position on Stalinism and the consistency of our world programme', any more than the social revolution (according to Trotsky) brought about in Eastern Poland and the Baltic countries in 1939–40 did. (Trotsky did not cease to call Stalin the 'grave-digger' of the socialist revolution', and Stalinism a socially counter-revolutionary force, in spite of the transformation of Eastern Poland and the Baltic countries into workers' states.) They say that this argument is as good today as it was then, even though it leads to the assumption that half Europe and half Asia have been transformed into workers' states by Stalin. This is simply nonsense, and contrary to the basic law of dialectics about the change of quantity into quality. Let us examine the argument more closely.

Trotsky analysed the transformation brought about by Stalin in 1939–40 in the newly occupied areas against the following background: first his idea that the bureaucracy pushes towards the restoration of private property in Russia herself:

'it [the bureaucracy – TC] continues to preserve state property only to the extent that it fears the proletariat. [Hence] in case of a protracted war accompanied by the passivity of the world proletariat the internal social contradictions in the USSR not only might lead but would have to lead to a *bourgeois-Bonapartist* counter-revolution.'

As the **Transitional Programme** declares, under conditions of war an increasing part of the bureaucracy (the Butenko wing) would strive to restore private property, which for Trotsky was identical with capitalism. In **In Defence of Marxism**, where Trotsky explains his view of the social revolution carried out by Stalin in the areas newly occupied by the Russian army, he is no less emphatic in declaring that the Stalinist bureaucracy leads towards the restoration of capitalism. It was only a question of years, at the most, possibly of months, before the inevitable downfall of Stalin.

On such assumptions, and only on such assumptions, it is logical to call Stalin the grave-digger of the social revolution. On the other hand, the explicit or implicit assumptions of those comrades who today declare the 'People's Democracies' to be workers' states are: capitalism cannot exist without private property; the Stalinist bureaucracy in Russia does not lead to the restoration of private property; outside Russia Stalinism led to a social revolution on a much bigger scale than the October revolution; in a few years half of Europe and half of Asia underwent a social revolution brought about by Stalinism. If this evaluation were correct it would be necessary to describe Stalinism as the organisation of the social revolution and not its grave-digger, at least in these areas. At the same time the Fourth International would have had to declare itself as the organisation not of the social revolution in these areas, but at best of the political revolution which will take place after Stalin has carried out the social revolution.

A number of comrades who hold the view that the 'People's Democracies' are workers' states put forward as an analogy to the revolution that took place in Eastern Europe and Bismarckian path of capitalist development in Germany. These comrades think that they thus prove that the social revolution of the proletariat can be carried out not by the revolutionary action of the proletariat itself, but by a state bureaucracy, with 'a momentum of its own'. This idea, if thought out, leads to the most shocking conclusions. It is true that the bourgeoisie took power in many and various ways. As a matter of fact it was only in one case that they carried through to the end a revolutionary struggle against feudalism – this was in France. In the case of England they compromised with the feudal landowners. In Germany and Italy, Poland and Russia, China and

South America, they came to power without a revolutionary struggle. In the USA the almost complete non-existence of feudal remnants enabled the bourgeoisie to avoid an anti-feudal revolutionary struggle.

The 'Bismarckian' path was not the exception for the bourgeoisie, but the rule, The exception was the French revolution. If the proletarian revolution can be carried out not necessarily through the activity of the working class itself but by a state bureaucracy, then the Russian revolution would inevitably be the exception while the 'Bismarckian' path would be the rule. The rise of the bourgeoisie was based on the deception of the masses, whether the French sansculottes or the soldiers of Bismarck. If a proletarian revolution can be carried out without an independent revolutionary leadership there is no reason at all for this leadership to appear. The law of lesser resistance will lead history to choose the path of revolution carried out by small minorities deceiving the big majorities.

### The Basic Contradiction

Members of the FI day in and day out repeat the basic Marxist conceptions: the liberation of the working class can be carried out only by the working class itself, class conscious and led by a revolutionary party, that it cannot lay hold of the bourgeois state machine but must smash it and establish in its place a state of a new type, a state of proletarian democracy (Soviets, etc.). How to explain the fact that nevertheless many call the 'People's Democracies' workers' states?

The reason is to be found in the conception of Russia as a degenerated workers' state. If Russia is a workers' state even though the workers are separated from the means of production, have no say in running the economy and state, are subordinated to the most monstrous bureaucratic and militarist state machine, which does its best not only to terrorise the workers, but also to blunt their class-consciousness and mislead them with lies, there is no reason why workers' revolutions establishing *new workers' states* should not be carried out without the independent, class-conscious activity of the working class, without smashing the existing bureaucratic and militarist state machines. It is enough for the bureaucracy to be able to expropriate the bourgeoisie while keeping the workers 'in their place' for the transition from capitalism to a workers' state to be accomplished. If the revolutionary intervention of the masses is not essential to the existing workers' state, there is no reason why it should be an essential condition for the establishment of a workers' state, for the social revolution. The intervention of the masses in the socialist revolution can to some extent help the bureaucracy which leads this revolution; this is the case where the military-police strength of the bureaucracy is not enough to expropriate the bourgeoisie. But whatever the case, the revolutionary intervention of the masses is an auxiliary subordinate to the Stalinist bureaucratic revolutionary transformation of society.

The fact the bureaucratic and revolutionary is a contradiction in terms is only one element of this conception. The essence of the proletarian revolution becomes the change in the form of property, whether after the change the workers are oppressed and exploited or not; whether they are the subject running the economy or the object; whether the change is achieved through the nationalistic struggle of 'Slavs against Teutons', or through the internationalist struggle of the workers as a class; whether through Soviets which smash the old state machine or through a military, bureaucratic state machine; whether through the masses acting under the leadership of a revolutionary party or through a military-police bureaucracy isolated and hated by the workers; whether it is in the interests of the people of the country or in those of a foreign bureaucracy – all these are only variants of the same social revolution.

The Marxist-Leninist theory of the state is turned upside down: while the proletarian revolution can use the old state machine without needing to smash it, the 'political revolution' of the proletariat against 'their' bureaucracy must smash the state machine.

■■■■■■■■■■■■■

### III. On the Attitude to Tito

In formulating their attitude to the Tito regime the IS (International Secretariat) showed the most unprincipled approach possible. Unashamedly they changed overnight from calling the regime a capitalist regime with an 'extreme form of Bonapartism' to an all-out uncritical evaluation of Yugoslavia as a workers' state, without even the reservation 'degenerated'. Tito's past and present are rewritten.

#### Tito's Stalinist Past

The moment Stalin conflicted with Tito, all the Stalinist hacks began to rewrite Tito's past, making out that he had always been an enemy of Moscow. Conversely, the IS, until the excommunication of Tito, repeatedly exposed him as a Stalinist *par excellence*, the most damning example of counter-revolutionary Stalinism; but they have now forgotten all this, and it seems that since the Partisan war against Germany, or even perhaps earlier, Tito has not been a fully-fledged Stalinist. Let us try to keep the record clear. Tito became the General Secretary of the CP of Yugoslavia in 1937, at the height of the Moscow Trials, when thousands of foreign Communists in Russia were executed. Tito became the Secretary of the Party because of the execution of Gorkich, the former General Secretary, as well as the majority of the Central Committee, by Stalin. The leading layer of the present CPY not only condoned the murder of all oppositionists in the Yugoslav CP, but passed through the school of the Spanish GPU murders of Trotskyists, POUM'ists, etc. On coming back from the International Brigade to Yugoslavia, their readiness to murder all oppositionists did not abate. As proof we may see the boast of Tito at the Fifth Congress of the CPY in 1948, that he and his friends knew how to tackle 'Trotskyist-fascists' by bringing them before the People's Courts and making them pay the supreme penalty. As **Borba** of 4 July 1948 puts it: '. . . a handful of Trotskyists, who showed their true faces in the war as collaborators and agents of the invaders, ended shamefully before the People's Courts.' **The Militant** of 5 July 1948 correctly wrote:

'Tito knows no other school of politics than Stalinism. The hands of this shady adventurer drip with the blood of hundreds of Yugoslav Trotskyists and other militants whom he murdered during the civil war in Yugoslavia. He began his service as a purger of Stalin's political opponents as far back as 1928 . . . Everywhere his speciality was purging "Trotskyists". It was precisely in this capacity as an unquestioning and willing tool of the GPU that Tito was permitted to rise to the top.'

During the Partisan war against Germany, Tito's policy was that of the Stalinist 'People's Front'. The social programme he put forward was exactly the same as that of the Spanish Stalinists, standing for the social *status quo*. Thus the Anti-Fascist Council of National Liberation (AVNOJ) – the Partisans' parliament – at its first meeting in Bihach on 26 November 1942 declared for a six-point programme, two points of which were:

(2) The inviolability of private property and the providing of every possibility for individual initiative in industry, trade and agriculture.

(3) No radical changes whatsoever in the social life and activities of the people except for the replacement of reactionary village authorities and gendarmes who may have gone over to the service of the invaders by popularly elected representatives truly democratic and popular in character. All the most important questions of social life and State organisation will be settled by the people themselves through representatives who will be properly elected by the people after the end of the war.

These aims were constantly reiterated by the Partisans' press and radio during the whole war.

There was some opposition to this policy in the ranks of the CPY. An uprising in July 1941 in Montenegro raised the banner of 'Soviet Montenegro'. Similarly, the Party organisations in Herzegovina deviated from the Party line, calling forth the harsh criticism of Rankovich. (**Proleter**, December 1942.) In spite of some leftist deviations, however, the Bihach programme was consistently implemented until the liberation of all Yugoslavia from Germans. Even after that, the Yugoslav leaders continued to insist that they intended sticking to the Bihach programme. Thus on 14 February 1945, vice-Premier Kardel stated in a broadcast that the economic structure in Yugoslavia had not abandoned and would not abandon the general framework of capitalism. A similar statement was made by Tito on 13 November 1945 in an interview with the special correspondent of **The Times**.

To emphasise the conservatism of their programme, a confessor or chaplain (vjerski referent) was attached to all the large military units, and a religious oath was made compulsory. Thus every Croat volunteer had to take the following oath:

'I swear by God Almighty and by all I hold dear that on my word of honour I shall always be true to the traditions of my ancestors, I will always fulfil my trust towards the Croat people and will defend with my blood my national home from the German, Italian and Hungarian oppressors, and the traitors of my people. So help me God.' (Radio Free Yugoslavia, 13 June 1943.)

As in Spain, one of the first and most important tasks of the Stalinists was to abolish the plebeian democratic character of the armed forces and transform it into a regular army hierarchically organised, with ranks, medals, etc. On 1 May 1943 the ranks of officers and non-commissioned officers were introduced, and in the next four months about 5,000 officers and generals were created, and Tito was raised to the rank of marshal. These higher layers of the Tito army took the commanding positions in state administration and economy when at the end of 1944 Belgrade, Zagreb and the other important towns were liberated from the Germans.

The policy of national unity with (to use Trotsky's own words about Spain) the 'shadow of the bourgeoisie' and the raising of a hierarchical bureaucracy behind the façade of the 'People's Front' which would be ready to take control in the interests of the Stalinist bureaucracy, was mor easily carried out in Yugoslavia that in Spain; first of all because the Yugoslav CP was incomparably stronger than the Spanish CP, and was not confronted with any organised opposition, no matter how muddled, centrist and reformist, like the POUM, the Anarchists, and the Socialists; secondly, the Yugoslav Stalinists had the advantage of not having to begin by tackling an industrial working class like that of Barcelona or Madrid.

For three years the Partisans were far away from the industrial centres of Yugoslavia, and limited to the most backward, poverty-stricken parts of the country. Hence the workers fulfilled a very small role in the Partisan movement. As Bogdan Raditsa, a former press service director for the Tito government, put it: 'The working class was far from being a vital factor in the resistance, as the Communists allege in their propaganda. For the workers remained in the big-city factories or were sent into Hitler's labour camps' (**New Republic**, 16 September 1946).

The fact that in these backward, mountainous regions of Yugoslavia, landed property was divided more or less equally before the war (the main land reform after World War II being carried out in the Danube area in the north) made it even easier for the Yugoslav Stalinists to impose the conservative Bihach programme as a screen behind which, in the name of national unity, a bureaucratic, hierarchical administration arose. No flight of imagination could succeed in presenting Tito's policy in Yugoslavia during the war as more revolutionary and progressive than the policy of Pasionaria during the Spanish Civil War.

The policy of Tito on the national question during the war is a chapter on its own. Seeing that the German invasion broke Yugoslavia up into different national units, and that no one nation had an absolute majority, it was essential for the Stalinists to put forward a programme of national equality, and this they did. Hence they built up military units of Italians, Hungarians, Czechs, and even Germans (of the minority living in Yugoslavia – *Volksdeutsche*). But after the successes on the military front, and with the increasing 'Slav' propaganda from Moscow, Belgrade becoming the centre of the Pan-Slav World organisation, Tito abruptly changed his policy towards the Germans. The whole German minority in Yugoslavia, of about half a million, were expelled from the country. Instead of trying to win over German POW's to the side of the Partisans, Tito put forward a new line: 'One German officer, for interrogation purposes,' he said, 'was enough of prisoners.' The fate of the rest is clear. When at the end of the war scores of thousands of German POW's fell into the hands of the Yugoslav army, their exploitation was very harsh. 85,000 of them were put to work barefooted, very badly nourished and treated, and not allowed to be visited by the Red Cross.

The religious policy followed the same pattern as that of Russia. We have seen that Tito had a more than benevolent attitude to religion in the Partisan Army. After the war, when the Stalinists waged their struggle against the Catholic hierarchies (and in one case – Bulgaria – the Protestant hierarchy) but did not touch the Greek Orthodox Churches, whose eyes are turned towards the Patriarch in Moscow, Tito did the same, condemning Stepinac, the Catholic Archbishop, to sixteen years' imprisonment, while embracing Patriarch Gavrilo, head of the Serbian Orthodox Church, whose activities under the dictatorship of Alexander and Peter were notorious.

*On which Side of the Dividing Line between Stalinism and Trotskyism does Tito stand?*

Any serious thought must, inevitably, lead to the conclusion that on every important issue on which Trotsky fought Stalin, Tito in the past stood and today stands on the same side as Stalin.

Everyone knows that the fundamental dividing line, the question of life and death, which separated Trotsky and Stalin, was the question of 'socialism in one country'. The central theme of the propaganda of Tito and his associates is the possibility of building socialism in one country, and Yugoslavia at that. They thus out-Herod Herod: in a country with a population less than 10% of that of Russia, an area much smaller even than that, with natural wealth which cannot compare with Russia's riches, it is possible to establish socialism! It would demand the worst type of Stalinist double-thinking to proclaim Stalin's theory of 'socialism in one country' as an out-and-out betrayal of socialism, an out-and-out counter-revolutionary conception, and overlook Tito's conception of 'socialism in one country', or at best propose friendly criticism of this conception.

As regards the political regime in Russia herself, Trotsky declared the Stalin Constitution of 1936 to be a plebiscitary, Bonapartist regime, legalising the one-party-bureaucracy rule behind the façade of general elections where only one list is allowed. As a counter to this, Trotsky put forward the slogan of the legalisation of all Soviet parties. The Yugoslav Constitution is a copy, almost word for word, of the Stalinist Constitution of 1936, as may be seen by a comparison article by article. In the Yugoslav elections the *one list* of candidates (26 March 1950) got 94.2% of the votes (the comparative figures in the Czechoslovakian elections were 89.2%, in Hungary 95.6%, Bulgaria 97.66%). The fact that legally people were allowed to put other candidates to the one list exposes even more clearly the plebiscitary character of the regime. Every hundred citizens, according to the law, are allowed to put up a candidate of their own (the comparative figure in Bulgaria is every ten citizens). But among the many million Yugoslavs not a hundred Cominform supporters, Socialist Party supporters or Peasant Party supporters could be found to do this. At the same time we are told that 5.8% of the electorate, or 613,125 people, voted against the government. Why did they not put up any candidate? It cannot be explained otherwise than the fact that 300,000 people in the USSR voted against the Government in the last general elections, but put up no independent candidate even though by law they are allowed to do so, as in Yugoslavia.

As regards the Party, the central fight between Trotsky and Stalin was round the question of the right to build factions. On this question Tito certainly stands with Stalin against Trotsky; he put forward as an axiom 'that every factionalist is not far from being a provocator or similar enemy of the working class'. (Quoted in **Fourth International**, October 1949.) We are told by Tito to believe that there is unanimous, voluntary support of the leadership of the CP of Yugoslavia, as we are told to believe that there is unanimous, voluntary support of the Stalin leadership in the CPUS. Consider that 468,000 Party members are educated day and night to believe that Stalin played a revolutionary role as leader and teacher of the international working class; now with the Cominform-Tito rift, no paper published a single letter of these Party members justifying the

Cominform or casting doubt on Tito's line in the conflict. The six Congresses that took palce immediately after the Cominform resolution unanimously passed all the resolutions put forward by Tito condemning the Cominform. In the Congress of the CPY the Prime Minister of Croatia said that among the 82,000 members of the Party in Croatia three opposed the line of the leaders. A list can be made of many more than three Croatian leaders who were arrested at the time, and of more than a hundred rank-and-file members whose arrests were mentioned in the press.

The IS knows very well that on these two vital issues (the legalisation of all Soviet parties, and the right of factions inside the CP) Tito stands squarely with Stalin in the agelong fight against Trotsky. They therefore do not even propose to ask for the right of having a Trotskyist faction inside the CPY. They think, it seems, that it is not tactful, but it can be not tactful only if Tito is as firmly opposed to democracy as Stalin is. Therefore to avoid putting forward the two central political demands of the Bolshevik-Leninist Opposition is tantamount to cowardice before calling things by their right names, to capitulation before a bureaucracy.

In the fight between Trotskyism and Stalinism, Trotsky was emphatic in saying that the leader-cult is not an accidental aberration of a healthy democratic regime, but the summit of a bureaucratic, Bonapartist dictatorship. Where does Tito stand on the question of the leader-cult? The answer is clear to anyone who looks into the Yugoslav press, who reads reports of conferences and meetings, which always reach their climax in prolonged applause for Tito, at which time he himself stands up and applauds – the same habit Stalin cultivated. The Marshal's pictures are as prominent today in Yugoslavia as the Generalissimo's were in Russia years after he was firmly established. Stalin has his Stalingrad; Tito has his Titograd.

Trotsky emphasised that 'lying is a weapon of reaction'. Stalin perfected the lie machine, presenting every opponent as a 'fascist'. Where does Tito stand in the choice of weapons to fight his opponents? The record of the Titoists in the last two years is damning. No 1 pro-Stalin leader of the CPY was Hebrang. Tito did not hesitate to call him an *Utashi* (a quisling Croatian fascist) and police spy. The fact that Hebrang spent twelve-and-a-half years in fascist prisons as a member and leader of the CPY, that after 1942 he occupied one of the highest positions in the Partisan army and the Government, does not deter Tito from making such an accusation.

Or to take the case of Kostov: Stalin's agents 'proved' that he was a 'police spy' – since he opposed the national subjugation of Bulgaria. At the same time Tito, who was opposed by Kostov on the question of the ways and means of federating Bulgaria and Yugoslavia, also accused him of being a 'police spy'.

Djilas, head of the agitation and propaganda departments of

the CPY, said in a speech on 1 September 1948 that all the supporters of the Cominform in Yugoslavia 'who have fled to the other People's Democracies and to the USSR' were 'traitors to socialism, opportunists, Trotskyists, malcontents with unlimited ambitions'. Such cynical demagogy, coming on the morrow of devoted friendship, would not be swallowed by its hearers unless the people were thoroughly terrorised. This being the case, Djilas was applauded.

Soon after the publication of the Cominform Resolution, 233 students were expelled from the University of Belgrade and technical institutes on charges ranging from criticism of the authorities to spy work, collaboration with the enemy during the war, stealing public property, speculation, and so on. What an amalgam!

In his report to the Third Congress of the People's Front of Yugoslavia (9 April 1949), Tito attacks Yugoslav supporters of the Cominform Resolution. One, he says, 'was Nedich's district police officer during the Occupation and . . . tortured patriots. He succeeded in covering up his past and smuggling himself into our party.' Another was 'Pavelich's district chief of police', another a 'Gestapo agent', and so forth. To sum up: 'In the case of at least 95% of them you will find that either they have a marked record [have been police spies – TC] or that they are people of ambition, cowards and weaklings, class enemies, kulak's sons or Chetniks and Ustashi elements, White Guards, etc.' – in short, 'human rubbish'. To crown the amalgam Tito says in the same speech that in Prague a 'well-known Trotskyist was attacking Yugoslavia on behalf of the Cominform'.

Tito says that the Cominform supporters in Trieste collaborate with the Italian fascists and 'have the wholehearted support of the Anglo-American Occupation Authorities'. This was in protest against a 'calumnious article' published in the Polish daily **Tribuna Ludu** (13 February 1939) entitled 'The Anglo-American Forces of Occupation Support Tito's Clique in Trieste'.

**Borba** said:

'The Bulgarian Communist regime is rife with civilians and officers who committed war crimes in Yugoslavia during the Bulgarian occupation in parts of Serbia and Macedonia. Some of the officers received promotions, others got pensions and some of the civilians hold important posts in the Bulgarian Communist Party.

'The Budapest Communist regime is employing Hungarian war criminals and former spies of the pro-German Hungarian Army.

'Former Gestapo members are active in the Rumanian Communist police.'

If all this is true, one may ask, why was it not mentioned in the years between the establishment of the 'People's Democracies' and

Tito's rift with Stalin?

Or take the attitude of the Titoists to Dimitrov. As long as he was alive, Dimitrov was one of the main targets of their attack, accused of being a pan-Bulgarian chauvinist, fostering the oppression of the Macedonians in Bulgaria, etc. Especially articulate in this campaign was Mosa Pijade. As soon as Dimitrov died, the same Pijade declared that Dimitrov was the best friend of the CPY and that he told the Yugoslav leaders to be adamant in their stand against the Cominform.

If the IS protests against Tito's, Kostov's and Rajk's being called 'fascists, police spies, etc., by the Stalinists, do they not think that it is as much their duty to protest against Hebrang's, Kostov's and other anti-Titoists being called 'fascists, police spies', etc., by the Titoists?

In choosing methods of struggle against the political opposition Tito stands squarely with Stalin and against Trotsky.

Besides covering his opponents with mud, Stalin also finds it necessary to use extreme methods of terror. It is true that if the Yugoslavs had to choose between Tito and Stalin, the overwhelming majority of them would freely choose the former, so that Tito has not so far found it necessary to use terror on a very large scale. Nevertheless, in fighting his Cominform opponents, he makes use of the old terroristic NKVD methods. Let us give a few examples. **The Times** correspondent wrote from Trieste on 22 August 1948:

'In the Yugoslav zone of the Free Territory Yugoslav police have been breaking up meetings of Italian Communists, and several Italian Communist leaders who have attempted to voice their criticism of the Tito regime have been placed under arrest.'

On 2 December 1949, the Ljubljana District Court charged two men with distributing pro-Cominform leaflets. One was sentenced to twelve years' hard labour, the other to eight. On 11 March 1949, **The Times** correspondent wrote from Belgrade:

'Sentence of death has been passed by the District Court of Osijek on four employees of a state farm at Josipindvor, Slavonia, for poisoning pigs. The men, according to the Belgrade press, were members of an underground group formed last July [i.e. immediately after the Cominform excommunication of Tito – TC] to carry out economic sabotage and later to take armed action against the State.'

When an attempt is made to study the economic conditions of the people, the difficulties met with are not smaller than those connected with such a study of Russia. Yugoslav statistics are comparable to Russian in their efforts to cover up the facts. There are no statistics as regards the division of the national product between workers, factory managers, high government dignitaries, etc. Even the achievements of the Plan are given in percentual form, which makes any check very difficult. No index of the cost of living is published. Even foreign trade is kept like a military secret (and the only way to study Yugoslav trade is to find out from the countries which do publish their trade figures their trade with Yugoslavia).

Nevertheless some facts showing the real economic position of the people do come to light.

First of all there is the regimentation of labour. An advance over Russia's Labour Book is the Yugoslav Karakteristika: each citizen has a *sealed* book in which his political reliability is recorded, and he has to show this when he takes on any job; he is never allowed to know its contents, so that he cannot appeal against what is written in it.

As regards the freedom of workers to change their place of labour: on 16 April 1948 a law was passed prohibiting any state employee from leaving his place of work without permission from a special government commission.

As in the other 'People's Democracies' the Yugoslav Constitution does not include the right of strike. The explanation was put in a nutshell by the spokesman of the Yugoslav Government when replying to a proposal to include 'freedom to strike' in the Constitution: 'Now, when our Constitution fully guarantees the rights of the working class such a proposal is outright reactionary and anti-national' (20 January 1946). Like Russia since 1928, Yugoslavia since Tito's rule has not had a single strike.

In denying another freedom to the people of Yugoslavia, Tito again copied Stalin: the law of 22 April 1948 prohibits marriage between Yugoslav citizens and foreigners unless special permission is granted by the authorities.

If slave labour does not exist to any great extent in Yugoslavia, while it does exist in Russia, we must not forget that it does not exist in any of the other 'People's Democracies' (increasing industrialisation and 'collectivisation' together with a surplus agricultural population and lack of capital are necessary conditions for a wide use of this sort of labour, which is very unproductive and wasteful).

Like the Russian Government, the Yugoslav Government inflicts the severest penalties for theft, reminding one of the punishments meted out to thieves at the time of 'primitive accumulation of capital' in England. To quote one example: Reuter reported from Belgrade on 30 December 1948: 'A Zagreb court has sentenced two officials to death by shooting for stealing clothing coupons, fourteen others charged with economic sabotage by stealing clothing coupons and selling them on the black market, received prison sentences ranging from two to twenty years.'

That Yugoslavia is one of the hungriest, if not the hungriest, countries in Europe is testified to by all correspondents, even those who have no reason to hold Yugoslavia in disfavour as against the other 'People's Democracies'. Under such conditions, nevertheless, the bureaucracy, it seems, does not suffer at all. We give a few quotations from the press. A banquet given by Tito, which lacked none of the brilliant characteristic of those given by Stalin, was described thus by a Swiss paper:

'In a great hall 300 generals waited, covered from head to foot with gold and sliver braid and decorations. With them were women in gorgeous evening gowns. The waiters were in snow-white, gold-trimmed dress-coats. You felt you were in a Hollywood fairyland. The tables groaned under the weight of huge gold and silver dishes laden with food. Eighty different kinds of hors d'oeuvres were served. There was an abundance of Tokay, Bordeaux, Frascati and, of course, champagne.' (**Er und Sie**, 29 February 1949.)

Another correspondent described the position three years earlier thus:

'Frequently, in city hotels, I felt ashamed to eat magnificent meals of goose or duck, caviare or filleted salmon, chicken or veal, when I remembered the "diet" of men, women and the few miraculously surviving children in the forgotton villages of distraught Bosnia . . .' (**The Contemporary Review**, February 1946.)

And Vernon Bartlett wrote as late as 25 April 1949 from Belgrade:

'Here, as in Moscow during the war, I am shocked that leaders who boast so much of the dictatorship of the proletariat, should enjoy privileges that are relatively far greater than those enjoyed by any privileged class in Britain or in most of the other countries condemned by Moscow as fascist and imperialist. (**News Chronicle**, 26 April 1949, 'Tito has Special Luxury Shops for Friends, Workers are Barred'.)

That the Yugoslav propaganda agencies are doing their best to hide the abyss between the position of the toilers and that of the bureaucracy (no less than the agencies of the other 'People's Democracies' and Russia) is clear. To bring only one interesting fact illuminating Titoist hypocrisy on the question: the letter of Tito and Kardelj to Stalin and Molotov of 13 April 1948 claimed that the salaries of Russian experts – colonels, generals, etc. – were much higher than the salaries of Yugoslav experts (and therefore Yugoslavia had to reduce the number of Russian experts in the country); the answer of the CC of the Russian Party (4 May 1948) says on this point: 'But the Yugoslav generals, apart from drawing salaries, are provided with apartments, servants, food, etc.' This the Yugoslav letters did not deny, but as the fact must be hidden from the public, the Yugoslav publication of the correspondence between the CC of the CPY and the CC of the CPSU wrote, instead of 'apartments, servants, food, etc.': 'a flat, food, and similar things'. A small correction: the servants are hidden from the public eye!

Russia's efforts to industrialise, because of her economic and cultural backwardness, inevitably pushed her to capitalist relations of production which raised the bureaucarcy to be the ruling class. Yugoslavia is even more isolated than Russia. She is much poorer in natural resources and population, and her point of departure was not the rule of the Soviet system, of a Bolshevik Party with an internally democratic life, with workers' control and management of industry, but a totalitarian, oligarchic bureaucracy. That such a regime, making efforts at industrialisation, at 'fighting barbarism with barbaric methods', could develop into something different in kind from Russia, can be believed only by shallow impressionists.

Here we must come back to the question of Tito's 'socialism in one country'. Trotsky emphasised that the source of Stalin's 'theory' of socialism in one country was not in his faulty understanding, but in the material interests of the Russian bureaucracy. Does this not apply also to Tito's 'socialism in one country'? That it does is clear also from Tito's foreign policy.

Marxism teaches us that the foreign policy of a country is a continuation of its internal policy. Hence we showed that the foreign policy of Russia – towards the League of Nations, her secret diplomacy, etc. – are in themselves condemnations of the internal policy of her bureaucracy. The accessibility to information on foreign policy, which by its very nature is much greater than accessibility to information on internal policy, so well veiled in Russia, has made this connection an important element in our arsenal of weapons against Stalinism. What is the nature of Tito's foreign policy? The Titoists are even more enthusiastic about UNO than ever Stalin was about the League of Nations. And if Stalin proclaimed that socialism and capitalism can live together peaceably, the Titoists go even further and proclaim that it is not true that capitalism leads to wars, that generally the question of war and imperialism has nothing to do with the social regime, but are the result of 'hegemonistic tendencies among the rulers'. This is an example of the crude way in which the Titoists, like Stalin, are ready to create *ad hoc* 'theories' to justify the immediate interests of Yugoslav foreign policy. It has even less to do with Marxism, if this is possible, than Stalin's one-time formulation that it is not capitalism that leads to war, but only fascism.

### The 'Democratisation of Yugoslavia' and the Perspectives of the FI

The 1948 World Conference defined the 'People's Democracies' (including Yugoslavia) as 'an extreme form of Bonapartism'. Trotsky considered it impossible to remove Bonapartist rulers by way of reforms, without a revolution. Now there is no mention whatsoever of the Bonapartist character of the Tito regime by the IS. The idea of the need to remove the Titoist leadership by revolution is shunned, and instead a friendly attitude, at the most watery criticism of this leadership, is adopted. Declarations of the Yugoslav leaders about democratic elections taking place in Yugoslavia are printed in the press of the FI without any mention that these elections are Bonapartist plebiscites, but they are taken at their face value.*

If this attitude really corresponded with the facts, if a Bonapartist police regime of yesterday could be transformed by evolutionary development into a more or less democratic regime, then Trotsky's line of argument would have to be totally reversed. When he declared the Russian regime to be Bonapartist, he said that the way to reform was closed. Two conclusions followed from this: in Russia the political revolution had to be carried out, and on a world scale a new international had to be built. The only conclusion from the IS position on Yugoslavia must be that till 1948 a revolution and the building of a party in opposition to the CP of Yugoslavia were necessary, but that afterwards no more than reform was needed, and there was no place for an independent Trotskyist party. If it is true that a Bonapartist regime which had existed for a number of years in a small and backward country could in the space of a few months become more and more humane and transform itself into a democracy, there is no ground at all to assume that the Stalinist Bonapartist dictatorship will not transform itself into a democracy when the pressure of the capitalist Western world becomes lighter relatively to the internal strength of the country. In other words, if it is accepted that in Tito's Yugoslavia the Bonapartist regime dies a natural death with no uprising of the working class against it – in a country more backward than Russia and more exposed to world economy – there is no ground at all for excluding the same possibility for the Stalinist regime. If we accept the idyllic descriptions given by the FI leadership of Yugoslavia today, we shall have to deny to the FI even the function of carrying out the political revolution after the Stalinists carried out the so-called 'social revolution'.

---

*To quote one example: In May 1950 Comrade Pablo tried to prove the existence of real plebian democratic committees in Yugoslavia by quoting Article 6 of the Constitution: 'The people exercise their authority through the medium of the freely elected representative bodies of the state power, etc.' He forgets to mention that this article is copied almost word for word from Stalin's Constitution of 1936 and is to be found in all the Constitutions of the 'People's Democracies'. Furthermore, Article 6, adopted on 31 January 1946, did not prevent Comrade Pablo from voting for the Resolution of the Second World Congress of the FI (April 1948) which states that Yugoslavia was *'an extreme form of Bonapartism'*.

Each of the Constitutions proclaims the freedom of press, association, the duty of every official elected to report back to his electors and the right of the electors to recall him. The Russian press, as well as that of the 'People's Democracies', is full of proclamations against bureaucratism, for popular iniative, for criticism and self-criticism, etc. It is full of criticism of local officials, factory managers, etc. But in *no* case is any leader criticised, or the Party as such, or the Party line; the 'criticism' of the lower officials makes them scapegoats and creates a target for mass dissatisfaction. All this propaganda waits for a Pablo to 'prove' from it that democracy exists in the 'People's Democracies' or in Russia.

The practice, now becoming a habit in the FI press, of whitewashing Tito's regime by quoting his attacks on Stalin's regime, is no better. It is not more legitimate than to draw the conclusion that there is no exploitation and oppression in Russia from Stalin's attacks on the exploitation and oppression prevailing in the USA.

### The Correct Attitude to the Tito-Stalin Conflict

The first duty of socialist-internationalists is to fight for the independence of Yugoslavia; for the defence of Yugoslavia from Russian aggression. It is necessary to expose the barrage of lies spread by Moscow and its agents about Yugoslavia. This exposure will be helped on by the fact that the inventions and exaggerations the Stalinist bureaucracy, so accustomed to totalitarianism and absolute control, naturally makes use of, are readily refuted by the Yugoslav reality (through reports of Youth Brigades visiting Yugoslavia, through reading the propaganda literature spread by the Yugoslav Government, etc.). The exposure of Moscow lies about Yugoslavia will help to expose other lies spread by the Kremlin, as, for instance, the Moscow Trials which created a wall of prejudices insulating the CP rank and file from our influence.

Titoism causes a breach in the front of monolithism so long preserved by the Kremlin. It brings into question the omniscience of Stalin. For this it is not at all necessary that the Tito regime be different from Stalin's. Even if the two are basically the same, and at the same time in bitter conflict, it exposes Stalinism very clearly.

What impresses anyone who reads what the Titoists say about their regime is the similarity with what the other 'People's Democracies' and Russia say about theirs. When a rank-and-file member of the CP compares the **Yugoslav Fortnightly** with **Moscow News**, **Free Bulgaria**, **Polish Facts and Figures**, **Rumanian News**, etc., he finds out that in all of them there is news of tremendous material and cultural achievements, a great rise in the standard of living of the people (expressed in the nebulous form of percentages), in all of them everybody is happy – there are pictures of smiling men, women and children – in all of them complete democracy prevails, etc. etc. The similarity readily leads to a disbelief in all of them, a disbelief in the omniscience of absolute authority.

The fact that two 'infallible' Popes now preach the same thing, brings into doubt the authority of the Popes as such. An historical precedent reveals this. The appearance side by side between 1378 and 1417 of a number of Catholic Popes, each attached to a national monarchy, did great damage to Catholicism as such. When Henry VIII quarrelled with Rome and decided to cut the connection between the Church in England and the Pope without greatly modifying the religious rites and dogmas, he opened the door to nonconformism: if each secular imposes his truth as the absolute and only one, conformity as such is exposed.

With the deep contradictions in Stalinist reality and the contradictions between the theory and practice of Stalinism, only iron totalitarian discipline can keep the system together. Titoism breaks this discipline, and at the same time exposes in practice the false basic psychological assumption of the whole edifice – that there is a choice only between Moscow and Washington, that there is no place for small independent nations which think and decide for themselves, that in every nation there is no place for more than one party, faction and opinion. However unpalatable those conclusions are, not only for Stalin, but also for Tito, they are inevitable as long as Yugoslavia does not revert to the private ownership of industry, come into the United States orbit or become a dependency of Russia. When Henry VIII burnt heretics in Smithfield, many of them Catholics, he did not put an end to heresy, but prepared the ground for the abolition of the national 'Inquisition' headed by an English king, and the international Inquisition headed by the Pope of Rome. The persecution of Cominform 'dissenters' by Tito, and the persecution of Titoist 'dissenters' by Stalin, will prepare the ground for the really consistent dissenters, the revolutionary Marxists.

Titoism can help to expose the rapacious, exploitative, aggressive character of Russian imperialism. When explaining the motives of capitalist Britain in the conquest of India, let us say, the Marxists showed that it was because the British ruling class found cheap sources of raw materials there, good markets for British products, and a good field for exploitation by establishing British-owned enterprises. The Titoists prove, by a wealth of facts, that Russia *capitalistically* exploits the 'People's Democracies', first of all, by buying their products very cheaply.

To give two examples. The Russo-Polish agreement dated 16 August 1945 stipulated that from 1946 onwards, Poland was to deliver to Russia at a special price (said to be two dollars per ton) the following quantities of coal: 1946, 8 million tons; from 1947–50, 13 million tons each year; and subsequently 12 million tons annually as long as the occupation of Germany goes on. This coal is not to be paid for by Russian products, but by reparations taken from Germany by Russia. As far as is known, Poland did not get anything on this account. Anyhow, 12–13 million tons of coal at two dollars a ton, when the price of coal in the world market is 12–16 dollars a ton, gives a net profit to Russia of 10–14 dollars a ton, or altogether 120–180 million dollars a year (a sum comparable with the maximum annual profits of British capitalists from their investments in India).

**Borba** of 31 March 1919 writes that a ton of molybdenum, an essential ingredient of steel, that cost Yugoslavia 500,000 dinars to produce, was sold to the USSR for 45,000 dinars. Examples of cases in which the 'People's Democracies' are capitalistically exploited by Russia as the seller are also cited in plenty. Thus, for instance, in 1948 when, because of the drought, Czechoslovakia had to buy 600,000 tons of grain from Russia, she paid more than £1 a bushel, when the world market price was only 12s 6d. As regards the ownership of enterprises and the capitalist exploitation of the workers in them, we have already given some facts about the SAG's and the Mixed Companies; the Titoists again supply an abundance of information on this.

The gist of all the Titoist explanations of the conflict with Russia is that they did not want Yugoslavia to be an exploited colony. To gloss over this basic aspect of the conflict between Tito and Stalin, and to speak in general terms like 'a struggle for national independence', etc., without showing the *material* content of the national struggle, does not benefit Marxists. To show the economic drive behind the Tito-Stalin conflict, to expose the capitalist-imperialist exploitation of the 'People's Democracies' by the Russian bureaucracy, is to expose its aggressive aims, to show up its 'peace campaign', just as its 'democracy' or 'socialism', for the fraud it is. The Titoists claim that Russia wanted to establish many Mixed Companies in Yugoslavia which would have served to exploit the Yugoslav toilers by Russia, and they, the Yugoslav rulers, refused. Now Russia directly owns a third of all German industry in her zone, controls more than half Rumanian industry, an important part of Hungarian industry, etc. What is more natural than that the Stalinist bureaucracy would strive to conquer new territories, new fields for state-exploitation? This is the real motive behind what Tito calls 'Russian expansionism and aggression', 'Russian war-mongering'. When laying bare the motives of Russian expansions, the Titoists cannot but speak of Russia as a power endangering world peace by her exploitive, aggressive actions and designs. This is an excellent weapon to explain Stalinist Power politics in the last decade or so, and an indispensible weapon in exposing Stalinism as a reactionary force.*

In fighting Moscow, Tito will probably try to build Titoist parties outside Yugoslavia. He would try in this way to strengthen his political influence over the people of Yugoslavia, pointing out to them that he is not isolated, and counteracting the Moscow accusation that his only allies are the US and British imperialists. That is why such prominence is given to visits of Rogge, vice-President of the American Progressive Party (Wallace) and Zilliacus to Belgrade. A Titoist party outside Yugoslavia will definitely have to deny the liberatory role of the Russian Army and to emphasise that 'the working class of every country can liberate itself', that small countries can think and act for themselves. This in addition to

---

*The supporters of the conception that Russia is a degenerated workers' state of course gloss over all the Titoist information regarding the capitalist exploitation of the 'People's Democracies', regarding the fight for Yugoslavia against this exploitation as the *basic cause* for the Tito-Stalin rift. They also fail to quote Yugoslavia's accusation that Russia is actively pushing towards imperialist expansion and war. If not for this oversight, these members would have to state their policy of defence of Russia thus: in case of war, it is the duty of every worker to help Russia to achieve military victory over the USA (with Yugoslavia as the USA's ally?), so that the SAG's will exist not only in Eastern Germany, but also in Western Germany and other Western countries. And the justification for this policy, as Comrade Grant will have to say, is that Russia will 'develop the productive forces' in the West – a justification coming fifty years after Lenin, Luxemburg and Trotsky have taught us that the productive forces in Western Europe are sufficiently mature for building socialism!

the internal logic of fighting against the existing high-handed CP bureaucracy will give 'a momentum of its own' to the *rank and file* of the Titoist party against any bureaucratism. On the other hand the dependence of the Titoist party on a ruling bureaucracy will condemn it to the twists and turns of foreign policy, the inculcation of half-truths, etc., of which the experience of the Comintern headed by the CPSU is a grim warning. The necessary double character of a Titoist party outside Yugoslavia will give the Trotskyists the possibility of using it as a step forward in the building up of the revolutionary party. For this the Trotskyists must, while being tactically flexible (under certain conditions not excluding entry into a Titoist party as a faction), stick firmly to their principles: against 'Socialism in one country' as a counter-revolutionary conception, for Soviet democracy, etc. etc.

## APPENDIX

### Theoretical Bankruptcy and Political Dishonesty – The Record of the International Secretariat (IS) on the 'People's Democracies'

The first big document written by a member of the IS dealing with the 'People's Democracies', officially declared to 'express in its entirety the leading opinion of the IS', was E. Germain's 'The Soviet Union after the War' (September 1946). Here Germain tells us, first of all, that all the 'People's Democracies', Yugoslavia included, are capitalist countries. He proves that their states are bourgeois thus:

'This structure (hierarchical and centralised administration, apparatus of repression, etc.) is preserved everywhere, with the same officials still functioning, since the "purge" touched only the smallest fraction of them. The only exception is Yugoslavia, and to a lesser degree Poland. In these countries the people who made up the former state apparatus have almost completely disappeared as a result of certain historical factors. Further proof of the bourgeois character of the state is the fact that the new state apparatus makes use of roughly the same structure as the previous apparatus did.'

We are told that the Stalinists did not bring about a revolution in Eastern Europe, but a *counter-revolution*. To quote only what is said about Yugoslavia (and Albania):

'In these two countries, the Soviet bureaucracy did not have to carry on any consistent counter-revolutionary activity; the native Stalinists took this upon themselves.
[In both countries, the Stalinists constructed] '. . . a new bourgeois state apparatus.'

On the question of whether the Stalinist bureaucracy can smash capitalism in these countries. or whether there must be revolutionary activity on the part of the proletariat, Germain is unambiguous:

'. . . in the last analysis only the revolutionary action of the proletariat can determine the final crushing of capitalism in the buffer countries.'

In the same document Germain calls to task the ex-Trotskyist, Leblanc, who put forward the 'theory' that the Stalinists did carry out the proletarian revolution in Eastern Europe. He says:

'This theory is a complete petty bourgeois revision of the Marxist-Leninist concept both of the state and of the proletarian revolution.

'. . . Leblanc's thesis completely revises the Trotskyist conception of the objectively counter-revolutionary role of the Stalinist bureaucracy both in Russia and in other countries . . . The whole struggle of the Bolshevik-Leninists against Stalinism has been based on the fact that its role is that of grave-digger of the world revolution, and grave-digger of the USSR. And now suddenly this grave-digger is offered to us as the one who will "objectively carry through the proletarian revolution". From the conclusions which Leblanc draws in his thesis it is clear that what we have here is a capitulation under the pressure of Stalinism – a very powerful pressure among the French intelligentsia – a capitulation resulting both from disillusionment in the absence of a victorious revolutionary movement and from complete lack of confidence in the revolutionary potentialities of the world proletariat.'

On 15 November 1946, E. Germain wrote ('The Conflict in Poland', **Fourth International**, February 1947):

'No one can doubt for a moment that in Finland, in Hungary, in Rumania or in Bulgaria . . . *capitalism* continues. [And then:] Does he [Shachtman – TC] really think that the Stalinist bureaucracy has succeeded in overthrowing capitalism in half of our continent? Shachtman again finds himself in this hardly enviable condition of having to share his views with the Stalinists! . . . It is precisely because the Polish Stalinists, like the Spanish Stalinists, want to force the workers to remain within the limits of a bourgeois society and state that we accuse them of betrayal . . . That is why we fight against Stalinism!'

The Resolution of the Second World Congress of the Fourth International, April 1948 (**Fourth International**, June 1948), says on the class nature of the 'People's Democracies', Yugoslavia included:

'. . . these countries retain their fundamentally capitalist structure. [The] mixed corporations, Soviet-owned stock companies, preferential trade treaties, etc. [are] forms of capitalist exploitation . . . The nationalised sector itself continues to retain a capitalist structure (individual profit balance, role of money, individual management and accounting, and so on).'

(The Resolution, by the way, forgot to mention that the 'individual profit balance, role of money, individual management and accounting' apply not only to the 'nationalised sector' of the 'People's Democracies', but also to the whole of the Russian economy.)

The same Resolution tells us about the nature of the States in the 'People's Democracies', Yugoslavia included:

'. . . In the "buffer" countries the state remains bourgeois: a) because the state structure remains bourgeois . . . b) Because the *function* of the state remains bourgeois. Whereas the workers' state defends the collective ownership of the means of production, arising from a victorious socialist revolution, the state of the "buffer" countries defends property which, despite its diverse and hybrid forms, remains fundamentally bourgeois in character . . .

'Thus, while maintaining bourgeois function and structure, the state of the "buffer" countries represents at the same time *an extreme form of Bonapartism* . . .

'From the bourgeois character of the state in the "buffer" countries results the necessity for the violent destruction of its bureaucratic machine as an essential condition for the victory of the socialist revolution in these countries.'

We are told again about 'the bourgeois function and structure of the state': 'Its destruction is impossible without a revolutionary mobilization of the masses.' We are assured that up to then (April 1948) this did not happen anywhere, and as an illustration of how the Stalinist bureaucracy maintained the bourgeoisie states we are referred to the February coup in Czechoslovakia:

'Wherever it is forced to undertake a limited mobilisation of the masses in potential organs of dual power (e.g. Action Committees in Czechoslovakia) it insists both in action and propaganda that these organs are not intended to replace the state organs but merely to supplement them.'

From all this the Congress drew the inevitable conclusion as regards the attitude to be taken in case of a war between, let us say, capitalist USA and capitalist Czechoslovakia or Yugoslavia: 'The capitalist nature of these countries imposes the necessity of the strictest revolutionary defeatism in war time.'

What is more natural after this than that the IS should severely attack the new edition of Leblanc – Haston's declarations (three years after his French fellow-thinker) that the Stalinists carried out the proletarian revolution in Czechoslovakia!

Thus in April 1948 we are told that the 'People's Democracies' are capitalist countries with 'extreme forms of Bonapartism', 'police dictatorships', etc., that the destruction of capitalism can be carried out only by the 'revolutionary action of the masses' which was not yet a fact, that a revolution demands the 'violent destruction of the bureaucratic state machine', that you cannot defend any of these states but must observe the 'strictest revolutionary defeatism'. And we are assured all along that anyone who says that the Stalinists did carry out a proletarian revolution in these countries is 'capitulating to Stalinism'.

There came the Tito-Stalin conflict, and the IS wrote an 'Open Letter to the Congress, Central Committee and members of the Yugoslav Communist Party'. Not a word is said about the capitalist character of the regime, about thē 'extreme forms of Bonapartism', the necessity for 'violent destruction of the bureaucratic state machine'. Not a word about why it was necessary to observe the 'strictest revolutionary defeatism' in Yugoslavia in case of a war with capitalist US, and thus ten times more so in case of a conflict with the workers' state of Russia.

To avoid the unpleasant duty of self-criticism, the IS does not tell us that the position it held as regards the 'People's Democracies' in the years 1945–48 was *totally* wrong. Thus the International Executive Committee's Seventh Plenum (April 1949) finds the temerity to declare: '. . . the tasks of the Fourth International in these countries ['People's Democracies' including Yugoslavia – TC] remain, in a general way, those enumerated by the Second World Congress' (i.e. 'strictest revolutionary defeatism').

In the last few months we are told, firstly that Yugoslavia is a workers' state (without the reservation 'degenerated'), secondly that Poland, Czechoslovakia, Hungary, Rumania and Bulgaria are also workers' states. It is only a question of time till Eastern Germany and China will also be included among the workers' states.

What a picture of the IS years after the 'People's Democracies' were established, after the proletarian revolution took place in half Europe and half Asia (according to the new IS version) they told us that these countries were capitalist, with the most reactionary Bonapartist police dictatorships. Now, suddenly, they have discovered that the leadership of the world revolutionary organisation succeeded in finding a series of proletarian revolutions carried out years back. If people cannot distinguish easily between the two extreme opposites – capitalist state and workers' state – something must be amiss in the conceptions of these people as regards what constitutes the one or the other. The IS, by missing a series of proletarian revolutions and finding them only years after they assumedly broke out, as if they were needles in a haystack, expose themselves as completely bankrupt theoretically.

To match the theoretical bankruptcy now comes political dishonesty. The IS does not make a balance sheet which will include at least the answer to these questions: If there were proletarian revolutions in Eastern Europe, how did they happen to miss the sight of the IS? Was the IS right to attack Leblanc and Haston as capitulators to Stalinism when they said that the Stalinists did carry out the proletarian revolution in Eastern Europe? Was the IS right in declaring Stalin counter-revolutionary? Was the IS right in declaring – in the steps of Marx, Lenin and Trotsky – that the bourgeois state machine must be smashed by the 'revolutionary action of the masses', etc. etc.?

Instead of self-criticism we have total amnesia. Caliban hates to look into the mirror!

# The theory of bureaucratic collectivism: A critique

## 1. Introduction

FOR OBVIOUS reasons, discussion of the nature of Soviet society was central to the thinking of most socialists of the last generation.

The conception of Russia under Stalin and his heirs as socialism, or a deformed kind of socialism ('degenerated workers' state' in the language of dogmatic 'orthodox' Trotskyists), has met two kinds of critique by Marxists. The first, to which the present writer subscribes, defines the Stalinist regime as state capitalist. The second sees it as neither socialism of any sort – nor capitalism. This last school of thought coined a special term for the Stalinist regime – Bureaucratic Collectivism. The first writer to coin this term was the Italian Marxist, Bruno R, in his book **La Bureaucratisation du Monde** (Paris 1939). The same term was adopted and the idea developed (without acknowledgement of the work of Bruno R) by the American socialist, Max Shachtman.

The subject of the present article is an evaluation and criticism of this thesis.

It is difficult to make a critique of Bureaucratic Collectivism because the authors never actually published a developed account of the theory. It is true that Shachtman wrote hundreds of pages of criticism of the theory that Stalinist Russia was a socialist country or a workers' state of any sort (he dismissed the theory of state capitalism in a sentence or two). But he wrote scarcely a paragraph on the laws of motion of the 'Bureaucratic Collectivist' economy, and made no analysis at all of the *specific* character of the class struggle within it. The place of Bureaucratic Collectivist society in

Duplicated document 1948. Reprinted International Socialism (1) No 32 the chain of historical development is not clearly stated, and, in any case, Shachtman's account is often inconsistent.

A central thesis of the present article is that the theoretical poverty of the theory of Bureaucratic Collectivism is not accidental. We will try to show that the theory of Bureaucratic Collectivism is only *negative*; it is thus empty, abstract, and therefore arbitrary.

Criticism of the theory will suggest a number of characteristics that are common – implicitly at least – to other conceptions of Stalinism – from that of the apologists to that of George Orwell's **1984**. In criticising the theory, the strength or weakness of the alternative theory of Stalinist Russia – as state capitalist – will emerge.

## 2. The Place of Bureaucratic Collectivism in History

At first glance what is more plausible than describing Stalinist Russia as neither a capitalist nor a workers' state? But this simplification is of little value, for it tells us little about the regime; feudalism too was neither capitalism nor socialism, similarly slave society, and any other regime that has not existed but is created by our imagination. Spinoza was right when he said that 'definition is negation', but not all negations are definitions. The statement that the Stalinist regime was neither capitalist nor socialist left the latter's historical identity undetermined. Hence Shachtman could say on one occasion that Bureaucratic Collectivism was more progressive than capitalism (however unprogressive it was, compared with socialism), and, a few years later, that it was more reactionary than capitalism.

Shachtman first called Russia a Bureaucratic Collectivist state in 1941. A resolution on the Russian question passed at the 1941 Convention of his organisation, the now-defunct Workers' Party, stated:

'From the standpoint of socialism, the bureaucratic collectivist state is a reactionary social order; in relation to the capitalist world, it is on an historically more progressive plane.'

On the basis of this, a policy of 'conditional defensism' was adopted. The Resolution states:

'The revolutionary proletariat can consider a revolutionary (that is, a critical, entirely independent, class) defensist position with regard to the Stalinist regime only under conditions where the decisive issue in the war is the attempt by a hostile force to restore capitalism in Russia, where this issue is not subordinated to other, more dominant, issues. Thus, in case of a civil war in which one section of the bureaucracy seeks to restore capitalist private property, it is possible for the revolutionary vanguard to fight with the army of the Stalinist regime against the army of capitalist restoration. Thus, in case of a war by which world imperialism seeks to subdue the Soviet Union and acquire a new lease of life by reducing Russia to an imperialist colony, it is possible for the proletariat to take a revolutionary defensist position in Russia. Thus, in case of civil war organised against the existing regime by an army basing itself on "popular discontent" but actually on the capitalist and semi-capitalist elements still existing in the country, and aspiring to the restoration of capitalism, it is again possible that the proletariat would fight in the army of Stalin against the army of capitalist reaction. In all those or similar cases, the critical support of the proletariat is possible only if the proletariat is not yet prepared itself to overthrow the Stalinist regime.'

In logic, when, a few months after this Convention, Hitler's Germany attacked Russia, Shachtman and his followers should have come to the defence of Russia, as it was 'on an historically more progressive plane'.

The argument Shachtman put now was that, even though Russia was more progressive than capitalist Germany, her war was nevertheless only a subordinate part of the total war, the basic character of which was a struggle between two capitalist imperialist camps. He wrote:

'The character of the war, the conduct of the war and (for the present) the outcome of the war, are determined by the two couples of imperialist titans which dominate each camp respectively, the United States and Great Britain, and Germany and Japan. (Within each of the two, in turn, there is a senior and a junior partner!) *All* the other countries in the two great coalitions are reduced to vassalage to the giants which differs in each case only in degree. This vassalage is determined by the economic (industrial-technical), and therefore the financial, and therefore the political, and therefore the military, domination of the war by the two great "power-couples". Italy is less dependent upon the masters of its coalition than Hungary, and Hungary less than Slovakia. But these facts do not alter the state of the vassalage – they only determine its degree. Stalinist Russia is less dependent upon the masters of its coalition than China (it would lead us too far afield to show in what sense, however, it is even more dependent upon US-England than China), and China less than the Philippines. But again, these facts only determine the degree of their vassalage. Except, therefore, for inconsequential cranks and special pleaders in the bourgeois world, everyone in it understands the total nature of the war as a whole; the total nature of each coalition; the relative position and weight of each sector of the coalition; the mutual interdependence of all fronts.'[1]

Thus, although Bureaucratic Collectivism is more progressive than capitalism, a defeatist position was adopted because of Russia's vassalage to Anglo-American imperialism. The **New International** of September 1941 emphasised the point:

'Stalin has lost the last vestige of independence . . . Soviet diplomacy is already dictated in London.'

We shall not dwell on the factual mistakes. These are less serious than the method by which Shachtman arrives at his conclusions. Marxism demands that from sociological definitions we draw political conclusions. When the course of the war contradicted his judgement of Russia as a vassal state, Shachtman should have rejected his previous defeatist position, for Bureaucratic Collectivism, he said, is more progressive than capitalism. Instead, he held to the political conclusion of defeatism and altered the sociological basis. Bureaucratic Collectivism now came to be called the new barbarism, the decline of civilisation, etc. Yet in no document did he give any new analysis of the Russian economy after the Resolution of the 1941 Convention.

The only two constant elements in the theory have been: first, the conclusion that in any concrete conditions, Stalinist Russia must not be defended (no matter that the concrete conditions change all the time); second, that the name of the Stalinist regime is Bureaucratic Collectivism.

With regard to the first element, serious Marxists, while seeking to hold consistently to the same principles, often change their tactics, as tactics must change with changing circumstances. Marxists should not decide on one tactic and hold to it when the justification for it is proved incorrect. This is eclecticism, impressionism. But exactly this approach was adopted by Shachtman. He draws the same conclusion from two opposite and mutually exclusive assumptions, the one that Bureaucratic Collectivism is more progressive than capitalism, the other that it is the image of barbarism, more reactionary. Defeatism is the tactic. Why? Once because Russia was not the main power, but only a vassal of Anglo-American imperialism, now because Russia is a major imperialist power which threatens to conquer the world.

As for the name, we might well repeat Marx's apt criticism of Proudhon, who used to invent lofty words, thinking in this way to advance science. Marx quoted the following: 'wo Begriffe felhen Da stellt zur rechten Zeit ein Wort sich ein.' (Where there is a lack of ideas, an empty phrase will do.)

In Marx's and Engels' analysis of capitalism, the fundamentals – the place of capitalism in history, its internal contradictions, etc. – remained constant from their first approach to the problem until the end of their lives. Their later years brought only elaborations of and additions to the basic theme. The theory of Bureaucratic Collectivism in its short history has had a much less happy fate. Shachtman first considered Bureaucratic Collectivism more progressive than capitalism, and then as 'totalitarian barbarism'. Another proponent of the theory, Bruno R, *at one and the same time* considers it both a slave society and the threshold of a peaceful transition to communism.

### 3. Bruno R on Bureaucratic Collectivism

Bruno R differs from Shachtman in many fundamentals. His analysis of the genesis of Bureaucratic Collectivism, for instance, is basically different from Shachtman's. They agree on the genesis of the system in Russia. But when they step beyond its borders, they are at variance. While the Resolution of the Workers' Party Convention of 1941 maintained that 'bureaucratic collectivism is a nationally-limited phenomenon, appearing in history in the course of a single conjuncture of circumstances', Bruno R saw it as a society which would replace capitalism on a world scale through the expropriation of the bourgeoisie by the Stalinist bureaucracy and the fascist bureaucracy. However, on the characterisation, description, and analysis of Bureaucratic Collectivism *as such* – as a social order – they are in entire agreement.

In his book **La Bureaucratisation du Monde** (Paris 1939), Bruno R writes:

'In our opinion, the USSR represents a new type of society led by a new social class: that is our conclusion. Collectivised property actually belongs to this class which has introduced a new – and superior – system of production. Exploitation is transferred from the individual to the class.[2]

'In our opinion, the Stalinist regime is an intermediary regime; it eliminates outdated capitalism, but does not rule out Socialism for the future. It is a new social form based on class property and class exploitation.[3]

'In our opinion, in the USSR, the property owners are the bureaucrats, for it is they who hold force in their hands. It is they who direct the economy as was usual amongst the bourgeoisie; it is they who appropriate the profits to themselves, as was usual amongst all exploiting classes, and it is they who fix wages and the prices of goods: once again, it is the bureaucrats.'[4]

What is the character of the ruled class? Does there exist a Russian proletariat, or, just as the bourgeoisie was substituted by a new exploiting class, is the proletariat substituted by a new exploited class? Bruno R answers thus:

'Exploitation occurs exactly as in a society based on slavery: the subject of the State works for the one master who has bought him, he becomes a part of his master's capital, he represents the livestock which must be cared for and housed and whose reproduction is a matter of great importance for the master. The payment of a so-called wage, consisting partly of State services and goods, should not induce us into error and lead us to suppose the existence of a Socialist form of remuneration: for indeed, it only means the upkeep of a slave! The sole fundamental difference is that in ancient times the slaves did not have the honour of carrying arms, whilst the modern slaves are skilfully trained in the art of war . . . The Russian working class are no longer proletarians; they are merely slaves. It is a class of slaves in its economic substance and in its social manifestations. It kneels as the "little Father" passes by and deifies him, it assumes all the characteristics of servility and allows itself to be tossed about from one end of the immense empire to the other. It digs canals, builds roads and railways, just as in ancient times this same class erected the Pyramids or the Coliseum.

'A small part of this class have not yet lost themselves in complete agnosticism; retaining their faith, they meet in caves for purposes of discussion, as of old, the Christians praying in the catacombs. From time to time the Pretorians organise a raid and round everybody up. "Monster" trials are staged, in the style of Nero, and the accused, instead of defending themselves, say "mea culpa". The Russian workers differ completely from the proletarians in every respect, they have become State subjects and have acquired all the characteristics of slaves.

'They no longer have anything in common with free workers except the sweat on their brow. The Marxists will truly need Diogenes' lamp if they intend to find any proletarians in the Soviet towns.'[5]

Even though Bruno R describes Stalinist Russia as the renewal of slavery (with all the historical retrogression connected with it), he nevertheless says that this regime is more progressive than capitalism, and, further, that it leads directly, without leaps or struggles, to communist society. He says:

'We believe that the new society will lead directly to Socialism, because of the enormous volume attained by production.

'The leaders (so will now be called those whom we have contemptuously labelled bureaucrats and the new class will be called leading class), having satisfied their material, intellectual and moral needs, may of course find a pleasurable occupation in the constant material, intellectual and moral elevation of the working class.[6]

'The totalitarian State should not impress the Marxists. For the time being, it is totalitarian rather in the political than in the economic sense. These factors will be reversed in the course of the forthcoming and normal social developments. The totalitarian State will more and more lose its political characteristics and retain only its administrative characteristics. At the end of this process we will have a classless society and Socialism.'[7]

A new 'withering away' – of 'collective slavery', of 'totalitarian bureaucratic collectivism', in communism! And this development Bruno R proudly proclaims '*the triumph of historical materialism*'! (See particularly the chapter in his book under this name.)

Bruno R's Bureaucratic Collectivism leads directly, automatically, to communism. It is undoubtedly a materialist conception, but it is not dialectical; it is a mechanical, fatalist approach to history which denies the class struggle of the oppressed as the necessary motive force.

### 4. The Stalinist Regime – Barbarism?

Shachtman writes about the Stalinist regime:

'It is the cruel realisation of the prediction made by all the great socialist scientists, from Marx and Engels onward, that capitalism must collapse out of an inability to solve its own contradictions and that the alternatives facing mankind are not so much capitalism or socialism as they are: *socialism or barbarism.* Stalinism is that new barbarism.'[8]

If the Stalinist regime denotes the decline of civilisation, the reactionary negation of capitalism, then, of course, it is more reactionary than the latter. Capitalism has to be defended from Stalinist barbarism.

But Shachtman ties himself in knots.

When Marx spoke of the 'common ruin of the contending classes' – as in Rome after slave society disintegrated – it was associated with a general decline of the productive forces. The Stalinist regime, with its dynamic development of the productive forces, certainly does not fit this description.

Barbarism in Marx's concept meant the death of the embryo of the future in the womb of the old society. The embryo of socialism in the body of capitalism is social, collective, large-scale production, and associated with it, the working class. The Stalinist regime not only did not weaken these elements, but spurred them on.

### 5. The Motive for Exploitation in Bureaucratic Collectivist Society

Shachtman explains the motive for exploitation in Bureaucratic Collectivist society thus: 'In the Stalinist State, production is carried on and extended for the satisfaction of the needs of the bureaucracy, for the increasing of its wealth, its privileges, its power.'

Now if the motive for exploitation under Bureaucratic Collectivism was simply the needs of the rulers, how does this relate to the general historical roots of exploitation in different social systems?

Engels explains why, in the past, society was divided into exploiters and exploited:

'The division of society into an exploiting and an exploited class, a ruling and an oppressed class, was the necessary outcome of the low development of production hitherto. So long as the sum of social labour yielded a product which only slightly exceeded what was necessary for the bare existence of all; so long, therefore, *as all or almost all the time of the great majority of the members of society was absorbed in labour, so long was society necessarily divided into classes.* Alongside of this great majority exclusively absorbed in labour, there developed a class, freed from direct productive labour, which managed the general business of society: the direction of labour, affairs of state, justice, science, art and so forth.'[9]

In an economy in which the motive for production is the production of use values for the rulers, there are certain limits to the extent of exploitation. Thus, for instance, in feudal society, village and town alike were subjugated to the feudal lords' need for consumption goods, and so long as the produce which the serfs gave to their lord was not widely marketed, 'the walls of his stomach set the limits to his exploitation of the peasant' (Marx). This does not explain the existence of exploitation under capitalism. The walls of the capitalist's stomach are undoubtedly much wider than those of the feudal lord of the Middle Ages, but, at the same time, the productive capacity of capitalism is incomparably greater than that of feudalism. We should therefore be quite mistaken if we explained the increase in the exploitation of the mass of workers as the result of the widening of the walls of the bourgeoisie's stomach.

The need for capital accumulation, dictated by the anarchic competition between capitals, is the motivation for exploitation under capitalism.

Actually, if the Bureaucratic Collectivist economy is geared to the 'needs of the bureaucracy' – is not subordinated to capital accumulation – there is no reason why the rate of exploitation should not decrease in time, and as the productive forces in the modern world are dynamic – this will lead, willy-nilly, to the 'withering away of exploitation'.

With the dynamism of highly developed productive forces, an economy based on gratifying the needs of the rulers can be arbitrarily described as leading to the millenium or to 1984. Bruno R's dream and George Orwell's nightmare – and anything in between – are possible under such a system. The Bureaucratic Collectivist theory is thus entirely capricious and arbitrary in defining the limitation and direction of exploitation under the regime it presumes to define.

## 6. Class Relations under Bureaucratic Collectivism

The essence of Shachtman's position is summed up in the statement that the rulers of Russia under Stalin were neither workers nor private owners of capital. What is decisive, according to the Marxist method, in defining the class nature of any society? As the history of all class society is the history of the class struggle, it is clear that what does determine the place of any regime in the chain of historical development are these factors which determine the character of the class struggle in it. Now, the character, the methods and the aims of the class struggle of the oppressed class are dependent on the nature of the oppressed class itself: the position it has in the process of production, the relation between its members in this process, and its relation to the owners of the means of production. These are *not* determined by the mode of appropriation or mode of recruitment of the *ruling* class. A few examples will explain this.

We know that in the Middle Ages the feudal lord had the right to bequeath his feudal rights to his heirs; on the other hand the bishop did not have this right, nor even that of raising a family. The feudal lord was the son of a feudal lord, a nobleman; the bishops were recruited from different classes and layers of society, often from the peasantry. (Engels pointed to the plebian origin of the upper hierarchy of the Church – and even of a number of Popes – as one of the causes for the stability of the Church in the Middle Ages.) Thus the mode of recruitment of the bishops was *different* from that of the private feudal lords. As regards the form of appropriation, the difference was equally great: the feudal lord, as an owner, was entitled to all the rent he could collect from his serfs, while the bishop was legally propertyless and, as such, entitled only to a 'salary'. But did these differences between the mode of appropriation and the mode of recruitment of the feudal lords and the upper hierarchy of the Church make any *basic* difference to the class struggle of the serfs on Church land, or on the lord's land? Of course not. The peasant with his primitive means of production, with the individualistic mode of production, had the same relation to other peasants, the same relation to the means of production (primarily the land), and the same relation to his exploiter, whether he was a feudal lord or a collective exploiter – the upper clergy (or as Kautsky calls them in a book, highly recommended by Engels, the 'Papacy Class').

Similarly, in slave society there was besides the private ownership of slaves, collective state ownership, as in Sparta.[10]

From the standpoint of the exploiters the question of their mode of appropriation and recruitment is of prime importance. Thus, for instance, Kautsky, in **Thomas More and his Utopia**, says:

'It looked as if the Church aspired to become the sole landed proprietor in Christendom. But the mightiest were to be curbed. The nobles were always hostile to the Church; when the latter acquired too much land, the king turned to the nobles for assistance in setting limits to the pretensions of the Church. Moreover, the Church was weakened by the invasion of Heathen tribes and the Mohammedans.'[11]

The Church acquired, not without a struggle (in which one of the weapons it used was the forging of deeds of gift), about a third of all the land in Europe as a whole, in some countries the majority share of the land (e.g. Hungary, Bohemia). Perhaps, therefore, the nobles considered the differences between themselves and the upper clergy – in their origin, and mode of appropriation – of importance.

But from the standpoint of the class struggle of the serfs or the rising bourgeoisie against feudalism, these differences were of quite *secondary* importance. It would not be correct to say that they were of no importance, as the differences in the composition of the ruling class to some extent conditioned the struggle of the serfs or the rising bourgeoisie. Thus, for instance, the concentration of the means of production in the hands of the Church made the struggle of the serfs against the Church much more difficult than their struggle against individual landlords; the ideological justification of feudal ownership was different in form when blue blood and coats of arms were presented than when religious phrases were quoted in Latin. And the fact that while Church property was officially called 'patrimonium pauperum' (the inheritance of the poor), private feudal property was not endowed with this exalted title, helps to show that these judicial differences were not unimportant. But from the standpoint of the historical process as a whole, i.e. from the standpoint of the class struggle, all the differences in the mode of appropriation and method of recruitment of the different groups are only secondary.

Shachtman and Bruno R (as well as 'orthodox' Trotskyists) forget Marx's statement of a century ago: that the form of property considered independently of the laws of motion of the economy, from the relations of production, is a metaphysical abstraction.

Thus the big differences between the mode of appropriation and recruitment of the Russian bureaucrats and that of the bourgeoisie, in itself, does not at all prove that Russia represents a non-capitalist society, a new class society of Bureaucratic Collectivism. To prove this, it is necessary to show that the *nature* of the ruled class – its conditions of life and struggle – is fundamentally different in Russia from what exists, even for Shachtman, in capitalism. And this is exactly what Bruno R, and later Shachtman, tried to do.

## 7. The Nature of the Working Class in Russia

On the question of whether the workers in Russia are proletarians, the proponents of the theory of Bureaucratic Collectivism answer, and must answer, that they are not. They compare the Russian with the classical worker who was 'free' of the means of production and also free of any legal impediments to selling his labour power. It is true that there often were legal impediments to the movement of Russian workers from one enterprise to another. But is this a sufficient reason to say that the Russian worker was not a proletarian? If so, there is no doubt that the German worker under Hitler was also not a proletarian. Or, at the other extreme, workers in power are also not proletarians inasmuch as they are not 'free' as a collective from the means of production. No doubt an American worker is very different from an indentured girl in a Japanese factory who is under contract for a number of years and must live in

the company's barracks for that time. But basically they are
members of one and the same class. They were born together with
the most dynamic form of production history has every known, they
are united by the process of social production, they are in actuality
the antithesis of capital, and in potentiality socialism itself (because
of the dynamics of a modern economy, no legal impediments in fact
put an end *altogether* to the movement of workers from one enterprise
to another under Stalin's regime).

Hilferding, Bruno R, and Dwight MacDonald were consistent
and maintained that just as they did not consider a Russian worker
to be a proletarian, so they did not consider a worker in Hitler's
Germany to be a proletarian. The Shachtmanites tried to avoid this
conclusion. In so doing they were led to falsify facts. For instance,
they claim that the German workers under Hitler were freer to move
than the Russian, that they were freer to bargain with their
employers, and that slave labour was never as widespread in
Germany as in Russia. Thus Iriving Howe, one of Shachtman's
followers at the time, wrote:

'The Nazis did not use slave labor to the extent that Stalinist
Russia has; under the Hitler regime, slave labor never became
as indispensable a part of Germany's national economy as it has
become for Russia under Stalin . . . industry under Hitler was
still largely based on "free labor" (in the Marxist sense; that is,
free from ownership of the means of production and thereby
forced to sell labor power, but also possessing the freedom to
decide whether or not to sell this labor power). For all of the
Hitlerite restrictions, there was considerable bargaining between
the capitalist and proletarian, as well as between capitalists for
workers during labor shortages.'[12]

In reality the Russian worker, notwithstanding all restrictions,
moves from one factory to another *much more* than the German
worker, or, for that matter, than any other worker in the whole
world. As early as September 1930, workers were prohibited from
changing their place of work without special permission, and year
after year brought new prohibitions. Despite this, the rate of
turnover was tremendous. In 1928, as against 100 workers employed
in industry 92.4 leavings were registered; in 1929, 115.2; 1930,
152.4; 1931, 136.8; 1932, 135.3; 1933, 122.4; 1934, 96.7; 1935, 86.1.
In later years figures were not published, but it is clear that the large
turnover continued, to which the frequent declamations in the press
bear witness. Even the war did not put an end to it. The German
administration was incomparably more efficient in combating the
free movement of labour under Hitler. This, in addition to other
factors (especially the relatively much greater dynamism of the
Russian economy), made the labour turnover in Germany much
lower than in Russia.

What about the slave camps in Stalin's Russia? Shachtman
tried to suggest that slave labour was the basic factor of production

in Russia. But this is absolutely wrong. The labour of prisoners is suitable only for manual work where modern technique is not used. It is therefore employed in the construction of factories, roads, etc. Despite its cheapness, it is necessarily only of secondary importance to the labour of workers, as 'unfree' labour is always relatively unproductive. If not for the fact that slave labour were an impediment to the rise of the productivity of labour, the decline of Roman society would not have taken place. Likewise, although in different circumstances, slavery would not have been abolished in the United States. In the face of special circumstances – the lack of means of production and the abundance of labour power – it is explicable that the Stalinist bureaucracy should introduce and use slave labour on a large scale. But it is clear that the main historical tendency is in an opposite direction. All the factories in Russia producing tanks and aeroplanes, machinery, etc., were run on wage labour. During the war Hitler's Germany found it expedient to use twelve million foreign workers, most of whom had been recruited as prisoners and forced labourers.

Marx maintained that the historical tendency towards the degradation of the *proletariat*, its increased oppression by capital, is fundamental to capitalism, whereas the substitution of the proletariat by a new, or rather, ancient, class of slaves is quite contrary to the general tendency of history. As we have said, only a lack of means of production and an abundance of labour power can explain the widespread use of prison labour in Stalin's Russia. Hence its almost complete disappearance since the death of Stalin, since Russia reached industrial maturity.

Shachtman's theory of Bureaucratic Collectivism must lead to its logical conclusion. If the Russian worker is not a proletarian, the German worker under Hitler was not a proletarian, and in Hitler's Germany there was not a wage labour system, but a system of 'collective slavery'. Accordingly, the ruling class in Hitler's Germany could not be called a capitalist class, as capitalists are exploiters of proletarians. Bruno R, Dwight MacDonald and Hilferding, at least, have the merit of consistency. They drew these conclusions and were therefore justified in calling Hitler's Germany Bureaucratic Collectivist (Bruno R and Dwight MacDonald) or a 'Totalitarian State Economy' (Hilferding).

If we accepted that workers employed by the Stalinist state are not proletarians, we should have to come to the absurd conclusion that in the Western Powers' zones of Berlin the workers are proletarians, but in the Russian zone those employed in the nationalised German enterprises are not proletarians, while those employed in the Russian zone by private industry are proletarians!

Again, we should have to come to the absurd conclusion that non-workers under Stalin have been gradually transformed after his death into proletarians.

Above all, if Shachtman is right and there is no proletariat in the Stalinist regime, Marxism as a method, as a guide for the proletariat as the subject of historical change, becomes superfluous, meaningless. To speak about Marxism in a society without a proletariat, is to make of Marxism a supra-historical theory.

## 8. Historical Limitations of Bureaucratic Collectivism

If one accepts the state capitalist nature of the Stalinist regime, one not only accepts its laws of motion – the accumulation of capital as dictated by the pressure of world capitalism – but also the historical limitations of its role. Once capital is amassed and the working class is massive, the ground is undermined beneath the feet of the bureaucracy.

For a Marxist who thinks Russia is state capitalist, the historical mission of the bourgeoisie is the socialisation of labour and the concentration of the means of production. On a world scale this task had already been fulfilled. In Russia the revolution removed the impediments to the development of the productive forces, put an end to the remnants of feudalism, built up a monopoly of foreign trade which defends the development of the productive forces of the country from the devastating pressure of world capitalism, and also gave a tremendous lever to the development of the productive forces in the form of state ownership of the means of production. Under such conditions, all the impediments to the historical mission of capitalism – the socialisation of labour and the concentration of the means of production which are necessary prerequisites for the establishment of socialism, and which the bourgeoisie was not able to fulfil – are abolished. *Post-October Russia stood before the fulfilment of the historical mission of the bourgeoisie,* which Lenin summed up in two postulates: 'increase in the productive forces of social labour and the socialisation of labour.'

Once the Stalinist bureaucracy created a massive working class and massive concentrated capital, the objective prerequisites for the overthrow of the bureaucracy had been laid. The Stalinist bureaucracy thus created its own grave-digger (hence the post-Stalin convulsions in Russia and Eastern Europe).

The theory of bureaucratic Collectivism is inherently incapable of saying anything about the historical role and limitations of the Stalinist bureaucracy. Hence socialism also appears simply as a Utopian dream, not a necessary solution to contradictions inherent in the Stalinist regime itself. Abstracted from the contradictions of capitalism, the urge towards socialism becomes merely an idealistic chimera.

## 9. Attitude to the Stalinist Parties

From the assumption that Bureaucratic Collectivism is more reactionary than capitalism, Shachtman draws the conclusion that if a choice has to be made between Social Democratic Parties which support capitalism and Communist Parties – agents of Bureaucratic Collectivism – a socialist should side with the former against the latter.

Thus Shachtman wrote in September 1948:

*'Stalinism is a reactionary, totalitarian, anti-bourgeois and anti-proletarian current IN the labor movement but not OF the labor movement.*

. . . where, as is the general rule nowadays, the militants are not yet strong enough to fight for leadership directly; where the fight for control of the labor movement is, in effect, between the reformists and the Stalinists, it would be absurd for the militants to proclaim their "neutrality" and fatal for them to support the Stalinists. Without any hesitation, they should follow the general line, inside the labor movement, of support-ing the reformist officialdom against the Stalinist officialdom. In other words, where it is not yet possible to win the unions for the leadership of revolutionary militants, we forthrightly prefer the leadership of reformists who aim in their own way to maintain a labor movement, to the leadership of the Stalinist totalitarians who aim to exterminate it . . . while the revolution-ists are not the equal of the reformists and the reformists are not the equal of the revolutionists, the two are now necessary and proper allies against Stalinism. The scores that have to be settled with reformism – those will be settled on a working-class basis and in a working-class way, and not under the leadership or in alliance with totalitarian reaction.'[13]

Again there is a lack of historical perspective, of real analysis of social forces, an oversimplification. The dual role of the Communist Parties in the West – as agents of Moscow and as a collection of fighting individual militants, strangled by the same bureaucracy – is completely overlooked. Shachtman's attitude to the Communist Parties, if adopted by any socialists in the West, would: firstly, strengthen the right-wing Social Democratic Parties; and, secondly, strengthen the hold of the Communist Party leadership on their rank and file. It is a sure way to liquidate any independent working-class tendency.

### In Conclusion

The theory of Bureaucratic Collectivism is supra-historical, negative and abstract. It does not define the economic laws of motion of the system, explain its inherent contradictions and the motivation of the class struggle. It is completely arbitrary. Hence it does not give a perspective, nor can it serve as a basis for a strategy for socialists.

1. 'China in the World War', *New International*, June 1942.
2. *La Bureaucratisation du Monde*, p31.
3. *Ibid*, p95.
4. *Ibid*, p56.
5. *Ibid*, pp72–4.
6. *Ibid*, p283.
7. *Ibid*, p284.
8. Max Shachtman, *The Bureaucratic Revolution*, New York 1962, p32.
9. Engels, 'Socialism Utopian and Scientific', in Marx/Engels, *Selected Works*, Vol I, p183. My emphasis – TC.
10. Kautsky describes this regime: 'The Spartans made up the minority, perhaps a tenth of the population. Their state was based on real War Communism, the barrack communism of the ruling class. Plato drew his ideal of the State from it. The ideal differed from real Sparta only in that it was not the military chiefs but the "philosophers", that is, the intellectuals, who directed the war communism.' *Die Materialistische Geschichtauffassung*, Zweiten Band, Berlin 1927, pp132–3.
11. Karl Kautsky, *Thomas More and his Utopia*, p38.
12. *New International*, December 1947.
13. Max Shachtman, *op cit*, pp306, 308–9. A by-product of this hysterical anti-Stalinism is softness, even idealisation, of Social Democracy: 'In most of the countries of Europe west of the barbed-wire frontiers, the socialist parties not only represent the sole serious alternative to the futile and futureless parties of the *status quo* but are the political instrument of the democratic working class.'

# Perspectives for the permanent war economy

THE ECONOMIC level of society, the level its productive forces have reached, is the decisive factor in the organisation of its armies. As Marx said: 'Our theory that the organisation of labour is conditioned by the means of production, is, it seems, nowhere as brilliantly corroborated as in the "human slaughter industry".'

In the early period of capitalism the backwardness of the economy made it impossible to feed and arm large armies. Compared with the mass armies mobilized during the first and second world wars, the armies of early, rising capitalism were very small.

Even during the Napoleonic Wars, France, ruler of practically the whole of Europe, did not at any time have more than half a million troops. The British armed forces at the time were less than a tenth of those of France.

All this changed with the First World War. Then France, whose population was only some 10 million more people than during Napeolonic times (40 million against 30), mobilized as many as five million soldiers. The other belligerent countries showed similar increases.

Together with the tremendous increase in the size of the armies during the last half century, there came a change in the role of the military sector in the national economy.

Frederick the Great declared of the wars of the eighteenth century: 'The peaceful citizen should not even notice that his country is at war.' Even during the wars of the nineteenth century, the Napoleonic Wars, the Opium Wars, the Crimean War, etc., the life of the belligerent nations was on the whole hardly affected.

### 1914 – The turning point

However, during the First World War, with a significant proportion of the population mobilized and a major portion of the economy harnessed to the service of war, not only the soldiers engaged in battle, but also millions of industrial workers, peasants, etc. – in fact, the whole civilian population – felt the impact.

Before the First World War, although the imperialist Powers were to some extent prepared for the struggle, it was usual for the economy to be hardly geared to armament production at all. It was only *after* the outbreak of the war that it was accommodated to the situation it was now squarely faced with – Guns or Butter.

Up to the First World War, therefore, it was possible to analyse the development of capitalism without paying much attention to wars or preparations for them, as they played a minor role in economic development.

Immediately after the First World War the military sector of the economy again dwindled: the large armies were to a major extent demobilized and armament production was drastically cut.

However, in the wake of the great slump of the thirties and Hitler's rise to power, a powerful peacetime military sector appeared for the first time in history. The Western capitalist powers – Britain, France and the United States – were slow to enter the armaments race. And although the industries of these countries did get some benefit from war orders, even at the outbreak of the war the war sector of the economy was not decisive: thus there were 11 million unemployed in the United States and $1\frac{1}{2}$ million in Britain: the index of industrial output in the United States in 1939 had not yet reached the level of 1929. It was not until a few years later that the Western Powers harnessed their countries fully to the waging of the war.

Between 1939 and 1944 the production of munitions multiplied in Germany 5 times, in Japan 10 times, in Britain 25 times, and in the United States, 50 times. (F. Sternberg, **Capitalism and Socialism on Trial,** London, 1951, p. 438).

### The War Economy

| | Germany Milliard marks | | Britain Million pounds | | United States Million dollars | |
|---|---|---|---|---|---|---|
| | 1939 | 1943 | 1938 | 1943 | 1939/40 | 1944/45 |
| I National income | 88.0* | 125.0* | 5.2 | 9.5 | 88.6* | 186.6* |
| II Government expenditure (Mainly arms) | 60.0* | 100.0* | 1.0 | 5.8 | 16 | 95.3 |
| II as % of I | 68 | 80 | 19.2 | 61.1 | 18 | 51 |

* Approximate figures.

Whereas after the First World War there was a period of about a decade and a half in which no advanced country had a relatively large war sector, after the Second World War there was no such break. Soon after its end the armaments race was once again on.

*It is clear that even with the present level of labour productivity no economy can allow half or more of its gross output to be devoted to war over a long period. The war sector had, as a matter of fact, eaten into the national capital of all the belligerent countries; factories and their equipment had worn out and not been maintained or replaced, housing had been neglected, cars, furniture, clothing, etc. had hardly been replaced.*

On the whole, even during prosperous periods of capitalism, some 80 per cent of the national income has been consumed by the civilian population, and at most 20 per cent or so devoted to capital accumulation. The following figures show the rate of accumulation in the national income in the past: Britain: 1860–9, 16.6 per cent; 1900–10, 12.2 per cent; 1919–24, 8.1 per cent; 1925–30, 7.6 per cent; 1934–7, 7.0 per cent. United States: 1900–10, 14.3 per cent; 1919–24, 12.2 per cent; 1925–30, 10.9 per cent; 1934–7, 5.0 per cent. France: 1870–9, 6.0 per cent; 1900–10, 9.0 per cent; 1913, 12.5 per cent; 1925–30, 11.2 per cent. Germany: 1900–10, 19.1 per cent; 1925–30, 7.7 per cent; 1934–7, 11.8 per cent. Japan: 1919–24, 21.9 per cent; 1925–30, 19.8 per cent; 1934–7, 21.9 per cent (Colin Clark, **The Conditions of Economic Progress,** First Edition, London, 1940, p. 406).

If, even with the present level of technique, 20 per cent of the national income were spent on armaments for any length of time, there would be scarcely any resources left for capital accumulation, in other words, the economy would stagnate.

Even if the military sector makes up, let us say, 10 per cent of the national economy of the capitalist countries, its effect on the economy in general is *fundamental.* Let us see how this comes about.

### Arms, boom and slump

For more than a century capitalism has gone through a rhythmical cycle of prosperity and slump. Slumps occurred more or less regularly every ten years. But since the advent of a permanent war economy the cycle has somehow been broken. Twenty-four years have passed since the low point in the slump of the thirties – 1933. Even since mass unemployment has gone from the major Western capitalist countries, some eighteen years have passed.

To understand how this has come about, how a military sector of some 10 per cent or less of the national economy could prevent a general slump, we should first shortly sum up the cause of slumps under capitalism.

### Cause of crises

The basic cause of capitalist crises of overproduction is the relatively low purchasing power of the masses compared with the production capacity of industry. As Marx said: 'The last cause of all real crises always remains the poverty and restricted consumption of the masses as compared to the tendency of capitalist production to develop the productive forces in such a way, that only the absolute

power of consumption of the entire society would be their limit.'
(Karl Marx, **Capital,** Vol. III, p. 568).

In the *final* analysis, the cause of the capitalist crisis is that a
greater and greater part of the income of society falls into the hands
of the capitalist class and a greater and greater part of this is
directed not towards buying means of consumption, but, instead,
means of production, that is, it is directed towards the accumulation
of capital. But, as all means of production are *potentially* means of
consumption – that is, after a certain lapse of time, the value of the
means of production becomes incorporated in means of consumption – the relative increase in the part of the national income
directed to accumulation compared with the part directed towards
consumption must lead to overproduction. And this is a cumulative
process. The increase in accumulation is accompanied by rationalization, resulting in an increased rate of exploitation. The greater the
rate of exploitation, the greater is the fund from which accumulation is drawn as compared with the wages of the workers and the
revenue of the capitalist. Accumulation breeds accumulation.

### Effect of arms budget

Now the armament economy has very great influence on the
level of popular purchasing power, the level of real capital
accumulation, and the amount of goods seeking a market.

Let us assume that there are a million people seeking employment in a certain country. Further, that 10 per cent of them are
employed by the Government in producing arms – some 100,000
people. Their purchasing power would bring about the employment
of more people elsewhere. The numerical relation between the size of
the first group and the second is called by the great bourgeois
economist Keynes, the Multiplier. For brevity this term can usefully
be borrowed. If the Multiplier is 2 the employment of 100,000
workers by the State will increase general employment by 200,000.
If the Multiplier is 3, the increase will be 300,000, and so on.

Hence there is no doubt that the cumulative effect of an arms
budget of 10 per cent of the national income can be quite out of
proportion to its size in increasing the purchasing power of the
masses.

### Guns and Butter

Again, when 10 per cent of the national income goes to arms,
the capital resources seeking investment are drastically cut: in our
example, from 20 per cent of the national income to 10 per cent.
And the increasing purchasing power of the people, together with
the new State demands for arms, army clothing, barracks, etc., gives
greater openings for capital investment.

In addition, the war economy naturally has a big effect on the
rate of increase of the supply of non-military goods seeking civilian
purchasers.

With the possibilities of employment increasing, wages may well rise. But this, paradoxically, does not deny the possibility of increasing profits: capital is working more fully than otherwise, there is much less capital working at a loss, its turnover is greater. Thus, for instance, in the years 1937–42 total wages in United States industry rose by 70 per cent, profits by 400!

With the stupendous productive forces available to society at present, the increase in the armaments burden does not necessarily and always lead to a cut in civilian consumption. This was shown most clearly in the richest capitalist country in the world – the United States – during the Second World War. Although in 1943 the United States spent the huge sum of 83.7 milliard dollars on the war, civilian consumption did not fall, but was actually higher than before the war, rising from 61.7 milliard dollars in 1939 to 70.8 milliard in 1943 (expressed in 1939 prices), i.e. an increase of 14.7 per cent. The consumption of food rose by 70 dollars per head of the population, expenditure on housing and repairs by 12 dollars, purchases of clothing by 25 dollars. Spending on other goods, with the exception of cars, also rose. So long as armaments do not consume beyond a certain limit, the increased production of guns does not exclude an increased production of butter.

*Why arms alone*

Let us see what are the basic characteristics which distinguish the armament economy as a great stabilising factor for capitalist prosperity.

To succeed as a stabiliser, the 'Public Works' undertaken by the state must have the following basic characteristics:

*(1) That they do not compete with private interests which produce in the same field. Thus, a state factory producing, let us say, shoes and competing with private shoe producers, would not decrease the danger of over-production of shoes, but increase it. But in the field of, say, barrack building, the state stands alone.*

*(2) That they employ the industries which are generally most affected by slumps – capital goods industries, heavy industry, industries whose weight in the economy is increasing and whose chiefs are predominant in the ruling class.*

Seeing that whatever 'Public Works' are undertaken, some sections of the capitalist class will benefit, such as, for instance, the producers of building materials, these sections will be quite ready to support such a programme. Other sections which benefit less but have to foot the bill through taxation, may well oppose or try to curtail it. Only if the main sections of the ruling class – those in heavy industry, the monopolists and the bankers – have a direct interest in the 'Public Works' proposed, can these be carried out on a scale wide enough to prevent a slump.

*(3) That they do not add much – in preference should subtract from – the productive capacity of capitalism and should, as far as possible, slow down the growth of social capital.*

*(4) That they do not add much, if at all, to the output of mass consumer goods and thus are not dependent on higher wages for an increasing market.*

*(5) That, while not adding to the national productive capital, the capitalist class should consider them an important factor in defence of its wealth and even a weapon for enlarging its prospective markets, in which case the capitalists would be quite happy to accept them.* Thus, for instance, the American capitalists who had been very angry with Roosevelt for incurring an annual budget deficit of 2–4 milliard dollars (1934, 3.6 milliard, 1935, 3.0; 1936, 4.3; 1937, 2.7) did not mind a deficit of 59 milliard in 1941–2.

*(6) That all major countries indulge in these 'Public Works' to an extent corresponding to their level of national output and wealth. If only one or a few countries were to do so, they would have less resources for capital accumulation, would suffer more than others from inflation, would be defeated in competition on the world market. Only if ALL major countries indulge in them, will each dare to do so.*

*Only armaments fit these necessary six characteristics of prosperity-stabilising 'Public Works'.*

### Arms breed difficulties

There are three kinds of basic contradictions into which the permanent war economy may fall.

*First, although on the whole there is conformity between the productive forces of society and the technique of the 'slaughter machine', the conformity is far from absolute.* The burden of armaments may grow much quicker than the national output. Armaments can so cut into workers' standards of living as to cause great social upheavals, and even a socialist revolution. Thus they could lead not to the prosperity of capitalism, but to its overthrow.

*Secondly, although armaments may eat up a large portion of the national surplus value seeking investment, and thus weaken the forces leading to over production and slump, they may encourage a big advance in general technique and with it increasing pressure towards a slump.* (Thus automation was, in part, the child of war industry). Under such conditions, to keep capitalist prosperity going, instead of 10 per cent of the national income devoted to military ends, 20, 40 per cent or more will have to be devoted. This may create strong opposition among workers and lower middle class people, and perhaps mild opposition even among sectors of the capitalist class who would not benefit directly from the armament drive.

### Competitive disarmament

*Thirdly, the Powers may compete so fiercely on the world market that each, in order to strengthen its position, would start to cut arms expenditure.* We are at present witnessing Britain's being pushed to cut her 'Defence Budget' through competition with Germany, and deterioration of her international balance of payments. Up to now no country has been able to match the United States, force her to abandon the arms race and start competing on 'who cuts the arms budget quickest'. She can afford the greatest military budget in the world and the greatest absolute investment in industry. But with the huge strides of Russian industry, it is possible that in another 10 or 20 years, she may, even if she does not reach the absolute level of United States industry, at least challenge the United States on the world market in certain branches – those of heavy industry. Then the United States may learn from Sandys and Macmillan how to cut the defence budget in order to circumvent defeat on the world market. The war economy may thus less and less serve as a cure for over production, a stabiliser of capitalist prosperity. When the war economy becomes expendable, the knell of the capitalist boom will surely toll.*

---

*Of course, certain capitalist countries may face great economic upheavals and hardships even during the era of American prosperity. Thus capitalist Britain and France suffer from balance of payments crises caused by the general, military-induced, world prosperity. They are also affected gravely by the national uprisings of the colonial peoples. But in all probability, so long as the United States (with some half of the world industrial output) continues to prosper, the life-belt will be thrown to the European junior partners of United States imperialism. Britain, France and Germany may well become more and more dependent on the United States. But as long as Uncle Sam is prosperous, he will not stop dishing out the dole.

# Economic roots of reformism

WE LIVE IN a critical period for civilisation. During the last half century humanity has suffered two terrible wars and is now living in the shadow of total annihilation. The present generation has witnessed mass unemployment and hunger, fascism and the gas chamber, barbarous murders of colonial peoples in Kenya and Malaya, Algeria and Korea.

However, in the midst of these terrible convulsions, the working class in a number of countries in the West – the United States, Britain, Canada, Norway, Sweden, Holland, Demnark, Germany and others – show a stubborn adherence to Reformism, a belief in the possibility of major improvement in conditions under capitalism, and a rejection of the revolutionary overthrow of capitalism. Why is this so? Why the general political apathy and rejection of revolutionary changes in society, when humanity as a whole is in the grip of life and death struggles?

Only if we find the correct answer to this question can we answer a further one: For how long can Reformism push aside revolutionary aspirations in the working class? There can scarcely be a question more vital for Socialists in the West and hence for the world Socialist movement. The present article is an attempt to contribute something towards the clarification of these problems.

### Lenin's theory

The most important Marxist to define the roots of Reformism was Lenin.

In 1915, in an article entitled **The Collapse of the International**, Lenin explained Reformism, or to use the term he coined, Opportunism, thus: 'The period of imperialism is the period in which the distribution of the world amongst the "great" and privileged nations, by whom all other nations are oppressed, is completed. Scraps of the booty enjoyed by the privileged as a result of this oppression undoubtedly fall to the lot of certain sections of the petty-bourgeoisie and the aristocracy and bureaucracy of the working class.'

How big was the section of the working class which received these 'scraps of booty'? Lenin says: '. . . these sections . . . represent an infinitesimal minority of the proletariat and the working masses.'

And in line with this analysis Lenin defines Reformism as 'the adherence of a section of the working class with the bourgeoisie against the mass of the proletariat.'

The economic foundation of the small 'aristocracy of labour' is to be found, according to Lenin, in imperialism and its super-profits. He writes in a preface dated 6 July, 1920, to his book **Imperialism, the Highest Stage of Capitalism**:

'Obviously, out of such enormous *super-profits* (since they are obtained over and above the profits which capitalists squeeze out of the workers of their "own" country) *it is possible to bribe* their labour leaders and an upper stratum of the labour aristocracy. And the capitalists of the "advanced" countries do bribe them: they bribe them in a thousand different ways, direct and indirect, overt and covert.

'This stratum of bourgeoisified workers or "labour aristocracy", who have become completely petty-bourgeois in their mode of life, in the amount of their earnings, and in their point of view, serve as the main support of the Second International and, in our day, the principal *social* (not military) *support of the bourgeoisie*. They are the real *agents of the bourgeoisie in the labour movement,* the labour lieutenants of the capitalist class, the real carriers of reformism and chauvinism.'

### Conclusion vs. facts

An inevitable conclusion following upon Lenin's analysis of Reformism is that a small thin crust of conservatism hides the revolutionary urges of the mass of the workers. Any break through this crust would reveal a surging revolutionary lava. The role of the revolutionary party is simply to show the mass of the workers that their interests are betrayed by the 'infinitesimal minority' of 'aristocracy of labour'.

This conclusion, however, is not confirmed by the history of Reformism in Britain, the United States and elsewhere over the past half century: its solidity, its spread *throughout* the working class, frustrating and largely isolating all revolutionary minorities, makes it abundantly clear that the economic, social roots of Reformism are not in 'an infinitesimal minority of the proletariat and the working masses' as Lenin argued.

Showing where Lenin's analysis went wrong will help us to see more clearly the real economic, social and historical foundations of Reformism.

### How to throw crumbs

The first question one has to ask in tackling Lenin's analysis is this: How did the super-profits of, say, British companies in the colonies, lead to the 'throwing of crumbs' to the 'aristocracy of labour' in Britain? The answer to this question invalidates the whole of Lenin's analysis of Reformism.

To take an example, the Anglo-Iranian Oil Company has been drawing magnificent super-profits over decades. How does this lead to crumbs being thrown to the aristocracy of Labour? First of all, this company employs only a small number of workers in Britain. And even these are certainly not given higher wages simply because its rate of profit is high. No capitalist says to the workers: 'I have made high profits this year, so I am ready to give you higher wages.'

*Imperialism, and the export of capital, can of course greatly affect the wages level in the industrial country by giving employment to many workers who produce the machines, rails, locomotives, etc., which make up the real content of the capital exported. This influence on the level of employment, obviously affects the wages level generally. But why should it affect only the real wages of an 'infinitesimal minority'? Does the increase of employment possibilities, and decline in unemployment, lead to the rise of a small 'aristocracy of labour' while the conditions of the mass of the working class is hardly affected at all? Are conditions of more or less full employment conducive to increasing differentials between skilled and unskilled workers? They are certainly not.*

One may argue that the high super-profits of the capitalists on their investments in the colonies led to a rise of wages in another way: that the capitalists do not oppose labour laws defending workers' conditions as strongly as they would do if profits were low. This is so. But these laws cannot be said to lead to an increasing differentiation of living standards between the different layers of the working class.

### We go up together

Look at simple examples like the prohibition of child labour or limitations on female labour in certain industries. This does not affect the supply, and hence wages, in the skilled labour market more than in the unskilled. The limitation of the workday also does not affect the skilled labour market more than the unskilled. Indeed, everything that raises the standard of living of the mass of the workers, unskilled and semi-skilled, *diminishes* the difference between their standards and those of the skilled workers. The higher the general standard of living, including the educational level, the easier is it for unskilled workers to become semi-skilled or skilled. The financial burden of apprenticeship is more easily borne by better-off workers. And the easier it is for workers to learn a skill, the smaller is the wage differential between skilled and unskilled workers.

Again, one can argue that imperialism throws 'crumbs' to workers through the fact that it gets foodstuffs (and raw materials) extremely cheaply from the backward, colonial countries. But this factor, again, affects the standard of living not only of a minority of 'aristocracy of labour' but the whole of the working class of the industrial countries. To this extent, by raising general living standards, it *diminishes* differences between sections of this same working class.

The effect of trade unions and the political activity of the labour movement on the whole is similar. The better the general conditions of the workers the less is the income differentiation between its sections. (This was only partly counteracted when the trade unions consisted only of skilled workers.)

In fact, all historical experience testifies that the fewer the workers' rights and the more downtrodden they are, the greater are the differentials especially between skilled and unskilled workers. This is clearly illustrated by the following table comparing the wages of skilled and unskilled workers between the two world wars in an economically advanced country like Britain and a backward one like Rumania:

Skilled Wages as Percentage of Unskilled

|  | Pattern Makers | Fitters & Turners | Iron Moulders | Plumbers | Electricians | Carpenters | Painters |
|---|---|---|---|---|---|---|---|
| Britain | 131 | 127 | 130 | 147 | 152 | 147 | 146 |
| Rumania | 200 | 210 | 252 | 300 | 182 | 223 | 275 |

(Clark, **Conditions of Economic Progress**, London, 1950, p460.)

Or to take another example: '. . . a locomotive engineer of ordinary length of service and rating receives 3.3 times the wages of an unskilled man of ordinary length of service in Spain, while in New Zealand the ratio is only 1:2.' (*Ibid*, p. 461.)

It can be shown statistically that in the last century the differentiation in the working class of Britain (as well as in many other industrial countries) has become smaller, and that not only an 'infinitesimal minority', but the whole of the working class, benefited from increasing living standards. To prove this one last point, one need but compare present conditions in Britain with the conditions of the workers described in 1845 by Engels in **The Conditions of the Working Class in England**.

### Where we came from

This is his description of typical housing conditions:
'In the parishes of St. John and St. Margaret there lived in

1840, according to the **Journal of the Statistical Society**, 5,366
working-men's families in 5,294 "dwellings" (if they deserve the
name!), men, women, and children thrown together without
distinction of age or sex, 26,830 persons all told; and of these
families three-fourths possessed but one room.'

'They who have some kind of shelter are fortunate, fortunate in
comparison with the utterly homeless. In London fifty thousand
human beings get up every morning, not knowing where they
are to lay their heads at night. The luckiest of this multitude,
those who succeed in keeping a penny or two until evening,
enter a lodging-house, such as abound in every great city, where
they find a bed. But what a bed! These houses are filled with
beds from cellar to garret, four, five, six beds in a room: as many
as can be crowded in. Into every bed four, five, or six human
beings are piled, as many as can be packed in, sick and well,
young and old, drunk and sober, men and women, just as they
come, indiscriminately. Then come strife, blows, wounds, or if
these bedfellows agree, so much the worse; thefts are arranged
and things done which our language, grown more humane than
our deeds, refuses to record. And those who cannot pay for such
a refuge? They sleep where they find a place, in passages,
arcades, in corners where the police and the owners leave them
undisturbed.'

Health, clothing, sanitation, education were all of the same
standard. One scarcely needs further proof that the conditions of the
working class *as a whole*, and not only of a small minority, have
improved radically under capitalism this last century.

■■■■■■■■■■■■■■■■
### Imperialism and reformism

As we have seen, there has been a close connection between the
imperialist expansion of capitalism and the rise of Reformism.
Risking some repetition, we think it is worth while summing up the
connection between the two.

■ The markets of the backward colonial countries, by increasing demand for goods from the industrial countries, weaken the
tendency for over-production there, decrease the reserve army of
unemployed, and so bring about an improvement in the wages of
workers in the industrial countries.

■ The increase in wages brought about in this way has a
cumulative effect. By increasing the internal market in the industrial countries, the tendency for over-production is weakened,
unemployment decreases, wages rise.

■ The export of capital adds to the prosperity of the industrial
countries as it creates a market for their goods – at least temporarily.
The export of cotton goods from Britain to India pre-supposes that
India is able to pay for it straight away, by exporting cotton, for
instance. On the other hand, the export of capital for the building of

a railway presupposes an export of goods – rails, locomotives, etc. – beyond the immediate purchasing power, or exporting power, of India. In other words, *for a time*, the export of capital is an important factor in enlarging markets for the industries of the advanced countries.

## Boomerang effect

However, in time, this factor turns into its opposite: capital once exported puts the brake on the export of goods from the 'mother' country after the colonial countries start to pay profit or interest on it. In order to pay a profit of £10 million to Britain (on British capital invested in India), India has to import less than it exports, and thus save the money needed to the tune of £10 million. In other words, the act of exporting capital from Britain to India expands the market for British goods: the payment of interest and profit on existing British capital in India restricts the markets for British goods.

*Hence the existence of great British capital investments abroad does not at all exclude over-production and mass unemployment in Britain. Contrary to Lenin's view, the high profit from capital invested abroad may well be not a concomitant of capitalist prosperity and stabilisation in the Imperialist country, but a factor of mass unemployment and depression.*

■ The export of capital to the colonies affects the whole capital market in the Imperialist country. Even if the surplus of capital looking vainly for investment were very small, its cumulative influence could be tremendous, as it would create pressure in the capital markets, and strengthen the downward trend of the rate of profit. This in turn would have a cumulative effect of its own of the activity of capital, on the entire economic activity, on employment, and so on the purchasing power of the masses, and so again in a vicious circle, on the markets.

*The export of surplus capital can obviate these difficulties and can thus be of great importance to the whole capitalist prosperity, and thus to Reformism.*

■ By thus relieving pressure in capital markets the export of capital diminishes competition between different enterprises, and so diminishes the need of each to rationalise and modernise its equipment. (This to some extent explains the technical backwardness of British industry, the pioneer of the industrial revolution, as compared with that of Germany today, for example.) This weakens the tendencies to over-production and unemployment, wage cuts, etc. (Of course, in changed circumstances, in which Britain has ceased to have a virtual monopoly in the industrial world, this factor may well cause the defeat of British industry in the world market, unemployment and cuts in wages.)

Buying cheap raw materials and foodstuffs in the colonies allows real wages in the industrial countries to be increased without cutting into the rate of profit. This increase of wages means widened domestic markets *without* a decrease in the rate and amount of profit, i.e. without weakening the motive power of capitalist production.

The period during which the agrarian colonial countries serve to broaden markets for the industrial countries will be longer in proportion to (a) the size of the colonial world compared with the productive power of the advanced industrial countries, and (b) the extent that the industrialisation of the former is postponed.

### Vested interest in nationalism

*All the beneficial effects of Imperialism on capitalist prosperity would disappear if there were no national boundaries between the industrial Imperialist countries and their colonies.*

Britain exported goods and capital to India and imported cheap raw materials and foodstuffs, but it did not let the unemployed of India – increased by the invasion of British capitalism – enter Britain's labour market. If not for the barrier (a financial one) to mass Indian immigration into Britain, wages in Britain would not have risen throughout the last century. The crisis of capitalism would have got deeper and deeper. Reformism would not have been able to replace revolutionary Chartism.

Here again the weakness of Lenin's theory of the aristocracy of labour is shown clearly. According to Lenin, Reformism is a creature of the period of what he called 'the highest stage of capitalism' – the period of the export of capital which earns a high rate of profit and allows for crumbs from this profit to fall into the hands of the 'aristocracy of labour'. This period of big export of capital began in Britain in the last decade or so of the nineteenth century.

### Wages rise before Empire

As a matter of fact a tremendous rise in workers' wages took place long before: in 1890 real wages of industrial workers in Britain were some 66 per cent higher than in 1850 (Layton and Crowther, **A Study of Prices**). The reason was quite obvious: the most important factor in improving real wages in Britain was the expansion of work opportunities – the expansion of production – based on an enlargement of the market for the industrial goods. And this took place long before the period of export of capital.

To put it roughly, between 1750 and 1850, when the expanding output of British industry was accompanied by the ruin of many British artisans and Irish peasants, these went into the British labour market and so kept wages very low. But since the middle of the nineteenth century, British artisans and, after the 'Hungry Forties', the surplus agricultural population of Ireland, were either absorbed into British industry, or emigrated. From then on it was the Indian artisan and peasant who were ruined by the competition of British industry – but they did not enter the British labour market to depress wages.

That the turning point in the British wages trend took place long before the end of the nineteenth century, and actually at the time when indigenous unemployed artisans and peasants were already absorbed into industry while the colonial unemployed were prevented from entering the British labour market, i.e. during the '30s and '50s of the nineteenth century, is clear from the following interesting table:

Real Wages, 1759 to 1903
(1900  :  100)

| Decades and Trade Cycles | Index |
|---|---|
| 1759–68 | 62 |
| 1769–78 | 60 |
| 1779–88 | 60 |
| 1789–98 | 58 |
| 1799–1808 | 50 |
| 1809–18 | 43 |
| 1819–28 | 47 |
| 1820–26 | 47 |
| 1827–32 | 48 |
| 1833–42 | 51 |
| 1843–49 | 53 |
| 1849–58 | 57 |
| 1859–68 | 63 |
| 1869–79 | 74 |
| 1880–86 | 80 |
| 1887–95 | 91 |
| 1895–1903 | 99 |

(J. Kuczynski, **A Short History of Labour Conditions in Great Britain 1750 to the Present Day**, London, 1947, p54.)

■ The effects of Imperialism on capitalist prosperity, and thus on Reformism, do not limit themselves to the Imperialist Powers proper, but spread to a greater or lesser degree into all developed capitalist countries. Thus a prosperous Britain, for instance, can offer a wide market to Danish butter, and so spread the benefits derived by British capitalism from the exploitation of the Empire to Danish capitalism.

### Economic basis of the Right

■ The expansion of capitalism through imperialism made it possible for the trade unions and Labour Parties to wrest concessions for the workers from capitalism without overthrowing it. This gives rise to a large Reformist bureaucracy which in its turn becomes a brake on the revolutionary development of the working class. The major function of this bureaucracy is to serve as a go-between the workers and the bosses, to mediate, negotiate agreements between them, and 'keep the peace' between the classes.

This bureaucracy aims at prosperous capitalism, not its over-throw. It wants the workers' organisations to be not a revolutionary force, but Reformist pressure groups. This bureaucracy is a major disciplinary officer of the working class in the interests of capitalism. It is a major conservative force in modern capitalism.

*But the trade union and Labour Party bureaucracy are effective in disciplining the working class in the long run only to the extent that the economic conditions of the workers themselves are tolerable. In the final analysis the base of Reformism is in capitalist prosperity.*

### Labour imperialism

■ If Reformism is rooted in Imperialism, it becomes also an important shield for it, supporting its 'own' national Imperialism against its Imperialist competitors and against the rising colonial movements.

*Reformism reflects the immediate, day-to-day, narrow national interests of the whole of the working class in Western capitalist countries under conditions of general economic prosperity. These immediate interests are in contradiction with the historical and international interests of the working class, of Socialism.*

As capitalist prosperity, together with relatively favourable conditions in the labour market, can be helped by Imperialist expansion, by the exploitation of the colonies, Reformism has been to a large extent the expression of the Imperialist domination over backward countries.

As, however, prosperity with more or less full employment and relatively tolerable wages, may be induced at least for a time by the conditions of the permanent war economy (see my article 'Perspectives of the Permanent War Economy', **Socialist Review**, May, 1957), Reformism has economic roots also where the Imperialist war economy takes the place of Imperialist expansion.

### The war economy

During the thirties, in face of the deep world slump, unemployment and Fascism, it looked as if the foundations of Reformism were undermined for good. Writing in that period and prognosticating the future, Trotsky wrote: 'in (the) epoch of decaying capitalism, in general, there can be no discussion of systematic social reforms and the raising of the masses' living standards, when every serious demand of the proletariat and even every serious demand of the petty bourgeoisie inevitably reaches beyond the limits of capitalist property relations and of the bourgeois state.' **The Death Agony of Capitalism.**

If serious reforms are no longer possible under capitalism, then the knell of bourgeois parliamentary democracy is sounded and the end of Reformism is at hand.

The war, as a sharpener of contradictions in capitalism, would lead to the acceleration of these processes, according to Trotsky.

However, Trotsky's prognosis was belied by life. The war, and the permanent war economy gave a new lease of life to capitalism and hence to Reformism in many of the Western capitalist countries.

In itself, the increasing dependence of Reformism on the permanent war economy shows its bankruptcy and the need for a revolutionary overthrow of capitalism with its twins – the permanent war economy and Reformism. However, this bankruptcy of Reformism is not yet apparent to every worker through his daily experience. As I tried to show in my article in the May issue of **Socialist Review**, it will be a matter of some years till the permanent war economy leads to a big deterioration of workers' conditions, and thus to a withering away of the roots of Reformism.

For this to happen it is not necessary, of course, that the standard of living of workers should be cut to the bone. An American worker would react very strongly to a threat to his car and television set, even if workers elsewhere look at these things as undreamt-of luxuries. To the extent that past reforms are accepted as necessities, a series of new reforms becomes the expected course of events. With the eating comes the appetite. When capitalism, however, decays to the extent that any serious demands of the working class reach beyond its limits, the bell will toll for Reformism.

A realistic understanding of the foundations of Reformism, its strength and depth, as well as the factors undermining it, is necessary to an understanding of the future of the Socialist movement. As Engels put it more than a hundred years ago: 'The condition of the working class is the real basis and point of departure of all social movements at present . . . A knowledge of proletarian conditions is absolutely necessary to be able to provide solid ground for socialist theories . . .' (Preface to **The Condition of the Working Class in England**.)

Of course, even when the economic roots of Reformism wither away, Reformism will not die by itself. Many an idea lingers on long after the disappearance of the material conditions which brought it forth. The overthrow of Reformism will be brought about by conscious revolutionary action, by the propaganda and agitation of consistent Socialists. Their job will be facilitated by a future sharpening of the contradictions in capitalism.

*Every struggle of the working class, however limited it may be, by increasing its self-confidence and education, undermines Reformism. 'In every strike one sees the hydra head of the Revolution.' The main task of real, consistent Socialists is to unite and generalise the lessons drawn from the day-to-day struggles. Thus can it fight Reformism.*

# The future of the Russian empire: Reform or revolution?

## 1. A Page from History

In 1855 Tsar Alexander II succeeded to the throne of Russia on the death of his father, Nikolai I. One of his first pronouncements was a declaration of his intention to abolish serfdom, which in 1861 he duly carried out.

Two main factors impelled the tsar along this path.

First, serfdom had become a serious impediment to the development of the economy, and the big landowners, especially those in the South, whose crops were beginning to enter the field of international trade and bring in handsome profits, had become more and more convinced that serf labour was inefficient and inferior to that of wage-workers.

That this actually was so became apparent after emancipation had been in force some years. At the end of the forties, a few years before emancipation, the average annual yield of four principal crops (wheat, rye, barley and oats) was some 430 million cwts; after it, in the seventies, it was 630 million cwts. The great Marxist historian M. N. Pokrovsky stated that without doubt 'free labour did prove far more productive than forced labour.' (**Brief History of Russia**, London, 1933, Vol. I, p. 116.)

The second main cause for the emancipation was a steady rise in the number of outbreaks of localised but violent peasant revolts.

There were 400 in the ten years 1845–55 and 400 more in the five years 1955–60. Fearful of the outcome, the tsar, at a meeting of Moscow nobility, uttered his startling and famous phrase: 'It is better to abolish serfdom from above than to wait until the serfs begin to liberate themselves from below.'

However, the emancipation of the serfs was carried out halfheartedly, and it did not turn them into really free wage-workers, but in fact left the peasants with less land and a heavier economic burden to bear.

Following upon the emancipation of the serfs, Alexander implemented some other reforms.

■ On 1 January, 1864 he granted local government to the provinces and districts of European Russia.

■ On 20 November, 1864, he reformed the judicial institutions: trial by jury was introduced for all criminal cases and court proceedings were made public. (And there is no doubt that freedom of expression in the court-room and the publicity given to trials helped greatly in the formation of democratic anti-tsarist public opinion.)

■ 6 April, 1865 saw the partial abolition of preventive censorship. (One of the results of this was the legal publication in Russian a few years later of Marx's **Capital**.)

That all these democratic reforms were very restricted was soon made quite clear. Thus, for instance, while the press was freed from preventive censorship, it was not allowed to publish accounts of any meetings of societies and clubs without special permission from the Provincial Governors; the Ministry of the Interior was empowered to inform editors of papers what subjects were 'unsuitable' and were of 'State significance'.

The tsarist police soon showed its iron hand. Many a radical was incarcerated. Thus in July 1862 N. G. Chernichevsky was arrested and condemned to prison and eventually exiled for life to Siberia. He remained there until 1883, and was not allowed to return to his home town of Seratov until 1889, where he died a few months later.

### Deutscher's Ancestors

In the first flush of Alexander II's promises of reform, many were eager to believe in his words. Thus the two leaders of Russian radicalism, the moderate Alexander Herzen and the revolutionary democratic socialist Chernichevsky, in 1857–58 praised the tsar when he announced his intention of abolishing serfdom. Herzen went so far as to write letters full of admiration to the tsar.

Both suffered a rude shock a few years later when the terms of the emancipation of the serfs were made known. But the political conclusions that they drew from the new situation were poles apart.

Herzen, whose following had dwindled to nothing, continued to believe in the reforming zeal of the tsar and to place his faith in the desire and ability of the 'enlightened nobility' to persuade the tsar to carry his reforms further. (Was he a Deutscher?) Chernichevsky and his increasing number of followers concluded that the tsar was, in fact, the chief representative of the exploiting landowners, and that only the overthrow of tsarism could clear the road for social and political progress.

The rude awakening led a number of radicals to issue illegal anti-tsarist leaflets. Thus one of them entitled 'To Young Russia' (May 1862) called for an 'immediate revolution, a bloody and merciless revolution, which must radically change everything, all the foundations of society without exception'. It ended with the words: 'Long live the social and democratic Republic of Russia!' (Pokrovsky, page 178.)

But the tsar 'Liberator' showed himself most vicious in his attitude to the Poles.

Tsar Nikolai's brutality, his method of governing by means of the rod, had earned him the hatred of the Poles. His son, who was not a fool, realised this and started his rule wooing Polish public opinion. He mitigated the severity of Russian rule over Poland, and curtailed somewhat the powers of the tsarist viceroy in Warsaw. He even replaced him with a new 'liberal' face.

But it was obvious, even in the early days of his reign, that Alexander II intended to curb his 'reforming zeal' even more strenuously in Poland than in Russia. He made it quite clear when he said laconically to representatives of the Polish gentry and bourgeoisie at their first meeting in 1856: 'No dreams!'

### How Reforms waken Revolution

Yet the reforms carried out by the tsar, however shadowy they were, inspired many a Pole, and their dreams of liberty grew wings. The people in the Polish towns, who had attained a far higher degree of political consciousness than in Russia, could not but hope to see in this first ray of light piercing the black clouds of tsarist oppression the approach of a new dawn.

More and more societies were founded in Poland, illegal leaflets were issued, and demonstrations took place. And immediately the Cossack's *nagaika* and gun played their usual part. Already in February and March 1861 mass demonstrations in Warsaw were shot down.

Two years later, in January 1863, a Polish national insurrection broke out. The insurrection was doomed to defeat.

The Poles did not possess a regular army and the whole of the country was garrisoned by Russian troops. But even more serious for the fate of the insurrection was the fact that only a minority of Poles supported it actively: the Polish peasants were quite indifferent to a movement led by the nobility. Out of a population of some five million persons, only ten thousand badly armed and inexperienced insurgents joined the armed struggle.

The rebels managed to hold on for eighteen months in a guerilla war. This was partly due to the lack of enthusiasm that many of the Russian garrisons showed for their job of killing. A number of officers expressed sympathy with the Poles, and were court-martialled; others escaped to the insurgents and even assumed command over their detachments.

Again the 'revolutionary contagion' spread, even if not very widely, beyond the borders of Poland. In March 1864 insurrection spread to Lithuania, and the same year saw an incipient rising in Russia, near the Volga – but this was nipped in the bud.

Alarmed, the government made some concessions. It granted the serfs in the so-called Northern Provinces – Lithuania, Latvia and Estonia – exclusive property rights in the land they held.

The Polish national revolution ended in defeat. But the blood of Poland did not flow in vain. Two years after the defeat of the insurrection, on 4 April, 1866, the first revolutionary attempt on the life of the tsar was made, by the Russian student Karakozov. He failed and was executed, but his was the first act in a revolutionary drama that ended with the overthrow of tsarism, half a century later.

Even this brief historical outline shows quite clearly that under autocracy reforms from above necessarily tend to waken revolution from below.

One cannot cross the abyss separating autocracy from democracy in a number of small steps. (Of course the autocracy does not want to make that crossing.) Any concession from the top, instead of averting the revolution from below, kindles the flame of liberty; and in the final analysis armed autocracy has to face the armed insurgent people.

The similarity between the first years of rule of the 'Tsar Liberator' Alexander II and those of the First Secretary 'Democratiser' Khrushchev is indeed great. And one can learn a number of important lessons from a comparison of the two.

The analogy, however, must not be pursued too far:

■ Russia of the horse age moved far more slowly than Russia of the jet age.

■ Poland of the nobility was a weakling compared to the mighty Polish mass peoples' movement.

■ The different oppressed nationalities, isolated from each other geographically, economically and spiritually, in the past, are now bound closely to one another.

■ The social content of the revolt against autocracy in the twentieth century differs enormously from that of the nineteenth century.

■ The mighty working class of all the nationalities oppressed by the Russian autocracy (and above all the Russian working class) is a waking giant which is bursting asunder the chains of social and national oppression.

## 2. The Post-Stalin Reforms

Stalin's method of approach to each new failure or difficulty was to increase pressure and terrorism. But this rigid method became not only more and more inhuman but also more and more inefficient. Each new crack of the whip increased the stubborn, even if mute, resistance of the people.

Where serfdom under Tsar Nikolai hampered the productive forces in agriculture, rigid Stalinist oppression became a brake on all modern agricultural and industrial progress.

Two and a half decades after the inauguration of the forced collectivisation, it became clear that Russian agriculture was stagnating.

Nothing could highlight this crisis better than Khrushchev's report to the plenary meeting of the Central Committee of the Communist Party of the Soviet Union delivered on 3 September, 1953. He painted the situation in sombre colours.

He stated that while in 1916 there were 28.8 million cows, in 1953 there were only 24.3 million. At the time of the tsar there had been six persons for every one cow; in 1953 – nine!

Khrushchev went on to say that 'districts which had long been famous as butter suppliers are now producing less butter than before. Siberia, for instance, produced 75,000 tons of butter in 1913 and only 65,000 tons in 1952.'

Vegetable farming, another intensive branch of agriculture, shows the same trend.

Agriculture in the satellites fared no better. The cause is not to be sought in the lack of agriculture machinery or fertilisers.

Indeed, the mechanisation of agriculture and supply of fertilisers was sharply stepped up: Thus the number of tractors in Poland rose from 15.5 thousand in 1949 to 49.3 thousand in 1954; in Hungary from 9.2 thousand to 15.4 thousand; the other satellites showed similar rises. (UN, **Economic Survey of Europe in 1954**, Geneva, 1955, p. 273.)

The amount of fertilisers supplied per hectare of land in Poland in 1948-9 was 17.7 kg (of pure content); in 1953-4 – 30.8 kg; in Czechoslovakia – 31.1 kg in 1948-9 and 51.0 kg in 1952-3; and so on (*Ibid*, p. 274).

In spite of the better supply of machines and fertilisers, grain output in *every* one of the Eastern European satellites has not risen, but has declined since the beginning of collectivisation.

In the 1934-8 period they produced 42.8 million tons of grain annually; in 1951-3 they produced only 37.5 million tons (*Ibid*, p. 120), a decline of 12.4 per cent.

Eastern Europe, which was a big exporter of grain, has become a net importer.

The very low level of productivity in Russian agriculture is clear from the following facts: it was estimated that in April 1956 not less than 56.6 per cent of the Russian population lived in the countryside (**The National Economy of USSR**, Russian, Moscow, 1956, p. 17), nearly all – i.e. practically half the total population – engaged in agriculture. And this half hardly manages to produce sufficient food to feed both itself and the urban population.

As against this, in the United States only 13 per cent of the population is engaged in agriculture and it supplies enough food not only for the whole of the American people, whose level of consumption is much higher than that of the Russian, but also for export. In Britain the farming population makes up only 5 per cent of the total population, but it supplies half the food consumed in the country.

### Crisis on the Land

The low productivity of agriculture alarms the Kremlin for three basic reasons:

■ First, it impedes the rise of productivity in industry – hungry workers cannot be expected to work well.

■ Secondly, it makes it impossible to syphon off labour power from the countryside to the town. (The loss directly and indirectly of some 30–40 million lives during the Second World War makes such syphoning particularly difficult.)

■ Thirdly, the low productivity combined with the state's pillaging of the kilkhozniks lowers the morale of the rural population, a corroding influence which is liable to spread throughout the land.

It was not accidental that the crisis in agriculture came to a head just after the post-war rehabilitation of the Russian economy.

During the thirties Russian agriculture was mechanised on a large scale; this made possible, if not an increase in the absolute size of agricultural output (a development sabotaged by the passive resistance of the peasantry), at least a decrease in the number of people employed in agriculture. The number of people in the countryside declined from 121 million in 1926 to 115 million in 1939. The 6 million so released, plus the natural increase in population was syphoned off into the towns, where the peasants, and especially their sons and daughters, were turned into industrial workers.

With the annexation in 1940 of Lithuania, Latvia, Estonia and Western Ukraine and Byelorussia, the actual population of the USSR increased by 21 million – which gave further opportunities for mechanising agriculture in the new areas and syphoning off millions of people from the countryside to the towns.

During all this period agriculture was in stagnation if not in decline. As **Pravda** of 4 October, 1955 had to admit:

'A total of 5 per cent fewer grain crops were planted on the collective farms in 1953 than in 1940. This reduction was even greater for individual crops: 11 per cent for winter rye, 35 per cent for millet, and 6 per cent for corn. At the same time the proportion of grain crops for forage dropped. These crops accounted for 29.6 per cent of the total area under cultivation in 1913, for 24.1 per cent in 1940 and for only 19.0 per cent in 1954.'

With agriculture stagnating, and without the annexation of new areas with a large population (not to speak of the tremendous loss of life during the war) and with the added crisis of agriculture in the satellites, where output was considerably lower than before the war, the agricultural crisis reached alarming proportions. (Perhaps the Lysenko sleight-of-hand, and the much trumpeted but now totally forgotten 'Stalin Plan for the Transformation of Nature,' were but opiates to calm the nerves of the Russian rulers.)

### Crisis in the Factories

The industrial workers in Russia and her satellites do not show any greater enthusiasm for production than the peasantry. The best proof is the fact that the productivity of labour in industry lags far behind the technical level of its equipment.

Russian industry, being quite new and built in very large units, has equipment which on the whole does not fall short of the level of American industry if indeed it does not surpass it, and certainly is far more advanced than that of the countries of Western Europe. Despite this, the productivity of labour in Russian industry in 1950 was calculated to be only 40 per cent of that in the United States industry or about the same as that in Britain and Western Germany. (W. Galenson, **Labour Productivity in Soviet and American Industry**, New York, 1955, p. 236.)

To raise labour productivity in industry, great efforts have been made to improve the skill of the workers through better technical education. But the more cultured and skilled the worker, the greater is the feeling of frustration and resentment against the exploiting bureaucracy and the poverty and drabness of his life. How oppressed must an engineer engaged on building jet planes feel when he returns from work to the one-room 'apartment' in which he and his family live!

The longer the time since the industrial revolution the longer the worker is 'cooked in the factory', and the greater his skill, the more resentful, if not rebellious, does he become.

### Bureaucrats vs. the Kremlin

The third largest class after the peasants and workers in the Russian empire is the bureaucracy.

One of the paradoxes of the Stalinist regime is that even the socially privileged bureaucrats are not at one with it. Of course they are glad to know that the Kremlin protects them. But alas, too often the MVD, besides arresting workers and peasants, also lays its hand on the exalted bureaucrat himself! (Thus it was estimated that in 1938–40 some 24 per cent of the technical specialists were imprisoned or physically eliminated – see N. De Witt, **Soviet Professional Manpower**, Washington, 1955, p. 231.)

The less zeal the toilers show in labour, and the greater the desire of the Kremlin to push production forward, the more does the whip lash at the individual bureaucrat who has to make the former carry out the wish of the latter.

Towards the end of Russia's industrial revolution, from 1936 to 1938, the vast mass purges were carried out. Then came the war with its terrible destruction. At the end of the period of reconstruction, in 1949, the campaign against 'cosmopolitanism' was launched, directed mainly against members of the ruling class; the 'Titoist' show trials took place, which culminated in the 'discovery' of the 'Doctors' Plot' and the stage was set for an unparalleled mass purge. Stalin was just about to crown his life's work, when he died.

Many sons of the tsarist nobility rebelled against the tsar, a number of them turning to terrorism to overthrow him. Many a bureaucrat and his children must have become embittered against the later tsar, Stalin. Stalin was certainly the most hated man in his empire.

### Tension in the Satellites

In the satellites during the later years of Stalin's rule, the tensions became even more acute than in Russia herself. A number of factors contributed to this.

First, national oppression was added to social. One aspect of this is the economic exploitation of the satellites by the Russian states.

Thus, for instance, the Polish-Russian agreement dated 16 August, 1945 stipulated that from 1946 onward Poland was to deliver to the USSR at a special price the following quantities of coal: 1946 – 8 million tons; from 1947 to 1950 – 13 million tons each year; and subsequently, 12 million tons annually as long as the occupation of Germany continued. This coal was to be paid for not by Russian products but by reparations taken from Germany by Russia and transferred to Poland.

According to Professor W. J. Rose, the price agreed on was said to be $2 per ton. (**Poland, Old and New**, London, 1948, p. 290.) As far as is known, Poland did not get anything on this account.

Anyhow, 12–13 million tons of coal at $2 a ton was extremely cheap. At the time of the signing of the Polish-Russian agreement, Denmark and Sweden were offering Poland $12 per ton, subsequently to be raised to $16.

The robbery of Poland through this transaction alone amounted to over $100 million a year. (To get some idea of this amount, it is worth mentioning that British capitalists never got such a large annual profit out of their investments in India.)

In 1948 Russia cut her demands for Polish coal to 7 million tons a year; even so, this is a heavy commitment for Poland. (Y. Gluckstein, **Stalin's Satellites in Europe**, London, 1952, pp. 66–67.)

The presence of Russian garrisons in the satellite states could certainly not help to foster a love of Moscow. Moreover, some of the satellites at least had higher living standards than those existing in Russia, and therefore could not take happily to Russian rule.

In addition, whereas in Russia Stalin had to deal mainly with a backward peasantry and new raw workers at the beginning of his rule, some of the Eastern European countries – mainly Eastern Germany, Czechoslovakia, Hungary and Poland – had a relatively large and not so raw working class, with its own socialist traditions.

The social and national tensions in the satellites became unbearable. A distorted expression of this was the anti-'Titoist' purges.

### 3. In Fear of Revolution

To meet the economic, social and national difficulties, Stalin's heirs carried out a number of reforms.

For lack of space we will not describe the reforms from above carried out in the different parts of the Russian empire. In general, it can safely be said that the reforms went further in the peripheral provinces than in its centre.

Also in the different satellites the extent of the reforms varied. In Poland and Hungary they went further than in Czechoslovakia, Bulgaria and Rumania.

This is probably mainly because the Communist Parties in these two countries are very weak and unpopular, having risen to power on the ruin of the considerably stronger socialist parties; under such circumstances the local Stalinist rulers had to make greater efforts to ingratiate themselves with the people.

However, the reform has its own logic.

The more concessions given, the greater becomes the pressure of the people for new ones. The rulers who were formerly hated and feared are now not feared so much as despised. This is especially the case with the quislings leading the satellites.

Hence after the concessions are given from above, an attempt is made from below to wring more. The further the rulers go on this path the more difficult they find it to withstand the popular ire. The process is cumulative.

#### The People demand More

A few examples from Poland will demonstrate this process.

A short while after the death of Stalin, the Polish leaders made it clear that the Plan was exceeding the country's resources, over-taxing its capacity and depressing the standard of living. The first step was a small cut in the rate of capital investment.

While in 1949 21.8 per cent of the national income was invested, the rate rose to 26.9 per cent and it was expected to reach 28.0 per cent in the last year of the Plan (1955). Actually the rate was cut in 1953 to 25.1 per cent, in 1954 to 21.2 per cent, and in 1955 to 19.8 per cent. (Bierut's Report to the Central Committee, 29–30 October, 1953, **For a Lasting Peace, For a People's Democracy!**, 20 November, 1953.)

Whether this cut was enough to satisfy the people is another question: after all in 1938 the rate was only 12.7 per cent (Institut National de la Statistique et des Etudes Economiques, **La Pologne**, Paris, 1954, p. 214).

The original Six-Year Plan imposed by Moscow had provided that of all the capital invested in industry 76 per cent should be devoted to the means-of-production industries, and only 24 per cent to the consumer-goods industries. (H. Minc, 'The Six-Year Plan for Economic Expansion and for the Laying of the Foundations of Socialism in Poland', **Nowe Drogi**, July-August, 1950.) But shortly after the death of Stalin, Bronislaw Minc (brother of the vice-premier) stated: 'There must not be too great a discrepancy between the manufacture of producers' goods and consumers' goods.' (**Gospordarka Planowa**, March 1953.)

The Six-Year Plan provided that in 1955 producers' goods would make up 63.5 per cent of all industrial output. (H. Minc in **Nowe Drogi**, July-August 1950.) In November 1953 the Central Committee of the Unified Polish Workers' Party (the name of the Communist Party) announced that they had revised the target of the Plan so that in 1955 only 50 per cent of all capital invested in industry would go to the producers' goods sector. (**Trybuna Ludu**, 4–5 November, 1953.)

On 14 November, 1953 and in May 1954 two price cuts were announced on certain industrial articles and food products. Promises were made that by the end of 1955 real wages should rise by 15–20 per cent above the 1953 level. Again, on 6 April, 1956 Edward Ochab, First Secretary of the Party, declared that from 1 May, 1955 the minimum wage would be raised from 364 zlotys per month to 500 zlotys, some 37 per cent. (**Polish Facts and Figures**, issued by the Polish Embassy in London, 14 April, 1956.)

While on the one hand promises became greater and greater, on the other hand the frantic efforts to shed the responsibility for the present suffering of the people impel increasingly frank admissions that all the promises and declarations of the past meant little or nothing.

For instance, we quote two versions of what happened to the standard of living of the people:

(1) On 23 December, 1955 Vice-Premier Minc stated that in the six years 1949–55 real wages rose by 27.6 per cent. (**Trybuna Ludu**, 23 February, 1956.)

(2) In July 1956, after the mass workers' strikes and demonstrations in Poznan, First Secretary Ochab admitted in a speech to the Central Committee that there had been a rise of only 13 per cent in real wages in the five years 1951 to 1955 and that an 'important part of the working population is no better off than in 1949!' (**Trybuna Ludu**, 20 July, 1956.)

But promises alone, or even recantations of past mistakes, are not enough. If the concessions in the economic field and the increasingly glowing promises of future reforms are to carry any weight, the rulers of the satellites must clothe the iron fist in a kid glove.

As late as April 1955, five Jehovah's Witnesses were accused in court in Warsaw of 'Opposing conscription' and spreading 'propaganda for a third world war'. Three of them were condemned to 12 years imprisonment, one to 8 years, and one to 6. (**Polish Facts and Figures**, April 9, 1955.) A year later after the Poznan riots, the condemned got a maximum of $4\frac{1}{2}$ years. A few weeks later a general amnesty to Poznan 'rioters' – excluding those connected with murder and robbery – was announced.

With every breath of air, the lungs demand more!

### New Heads for Old

As the pressure of the people increases so that it can no longer be contained in the channels of concessions, promises and recantations, the regime, in a last attempt to divert the stream (before resorting to armed force) changes its figurehead. 'New chiefs for old' becomes the slogan of the day.

When Alexander II came to the throne, he was known as the Tsar Liberator. Following this pattern why should not Gomulka or Nagy assume the laurel wreaths of Liberators? They are ideally placed, as for many years these persons were not responsible for running the country, nor for all the exploitation, terror and suffering.

Were not they themselves among the ranks of the persecuted? Thus Gomulka, after five years of imprisonment by Stalin's gaolers, can surround himself with the aura of martyrdom.

'After all, Stalin and his agents are the enemies. Gomulka was Stalin's enemy. Hence he is our friend. The enemy of our enemy is our friend!'

While such illusions about Gomulka and his ilk exist, they must quickly disappear under his rule. Indeed, such illusions can scarcely be spread at all, as Gomulka has a past which is not calculated to endear him to the people. And the Eastern European peoples, especially the Polish people with their centuries of struggle against Russian oppression, have good memories.

When Gomulka lost power in 1948, Poland was already a totalitarian one-party state, and Gomulka had played an important role in bringing this about.

Gomulka did not protest at, and actually benefited from, the purges of the leadership of the Communist Party of Poland carried out by Stalin. As Poland lay on the Russian border and the Polish Communist Party was illegal, the most important leaders of the party were usually in the USSR, and were thus involved in the big purges of the thirties. Many of them were executed or perished in forced-labour camps – Domski, Sofia Unschlicht, Warski-Warszawski, Kostrzewa-Koszutska, Prochniak, Huberman (brother of the violinist), Winiarski, Sochacki, Lenski, Rval, Zarski, Wandurski and Jasienski.

Apparently the purge so decimated the Polish Communist Party leadership that the Russians found it necessarily officially to dissolve the party (1938), using as an excuse the 'infiltration of Troskyites and police agents into the party.' It was this purge which opened the door to the rise of Gomulka (an obscure trade union official who was also practically unknown in the party) to the Central Committee. (The killing by the Nazis of the Secretary General Merceli Nowotko and his successor Paul Finder hastened Gomulka along the road to supreme power in the party.)

### They Remember his Record

Again, during the Warsaw uprising, one of the most magnificent chapters in the history of the Polish people, Gomulka showed himself to be a traitor and a Russian quisling.

On 30 July, 1944 the Russian army under the command of Marshal Rokossovsky came to within 10 kms of Warsaw. Next day mobile patrols of the Russian army had advanced as far as Praga, a suburb of Warsaw on the eastern bank of the Vistula. German troops began to be evacuated en masse from the city and its environs. Radio Moscow called upon the people of Warsaw to take to arms. But when the people of Warsaw, organised and led in the main by the Polish Socialist Party (PPS), rose up in arms against the German Army of Occupation, the Russian troops stopped their advance and waited on the eastern side of the Vistula until, after 63 days of struggle, Warsaw was in ruins, 240,000 of its inhabitants were killed and 630,000 deported by the Germans.

Gomulka, as First Secretary, that is, chief of the Polish Communist Party, never raised his voice against Stalin for this murder and did not hesitate to smear the Warsaw insurgents.

Finally, it will not be easy to forget that Gomulka played a leading part in the liquidation of the Polish Peasant Party and the Socialist Party.

The people of Poland will remember Gomulka's past.

### 4. On the Razor's Edge

Eight years ago, in 1948, Tito broke with Moscow. In the process of defending the national independence of the country from outside, while preserving the rule of his own bureaucracy inside, he was pushed into carrying out a number of reforms.

The logic of the struggle against the domination of Moscow, which compelled the Yugoslav leaders more and more openly to expose the real character of Stalin's regime, forced them to renounce, or at least to pretend to renounce, its more obnoxious features. The struggle, by making it a question of life and death for the Yugoslav government to enlarge its mass support, forced it to 'liberalise' the dictatorship. The economic difficulties connected with the isolation of Yugoslavia from the Russian bloc of countries, and even more, the very severe drought of 1950, pushed the government in the same direction.

As a counter to Stalin's 'bureaucratic centralism', Tito attempted to implement 'socialist democracy'. The administration was decentralised, beginning with the economy. The federal ministries of Electricity and Mines were abolished by a decree of 17 February, 1950, and responsibility for the management of these branches of the economy handed over to the governments of the component republics of Yugoslavia. On 11 April, another six ministries of the central government were abolished – agriculture, forestry, light industries, commerce and supply, and state supplies. At the federal level the departments are headed by councils, and the decrees grant wide autonomy to the governments of the republics.

On 26 June, 1950 the Yugoslav Federal Assembly passed the 'Basic Law on Management of State Economic Enterprises and Higher Economic Associations by the Workers' Collectives'.

The Yugoslav leaders do not try to explain how decentralisation of the administration can be compatible with the existence of a monolithic, highly centralised, one-party system, managed by the Political Bureau; nor how 'workers' management' of an enterprise can be compatible with a central economic plan determined by the same nine people in the centre of political power.

What autonomy can a workers' council have when it is elected from a list of candidates put forward by the trade union, which is centralistic and controlled by the party?

Again, what autonomy can it have when the economy is planned and the vital decisions on production, such as real wages (the amount of consumers' goods to be produced and distributed nationally) are made by a central government independent of the people?

How can there be genuine local self-government in a situation where everything, from factories to papers, from people to machines, is in the hands of the centralised, bureaucratic party?

### The Limits of Titoism

To illustrate the limited rights the Yugoslav worker has in 'his' factory, it need but be mentioned that not a single strike took place either before or after the law on workers' management of 26 June, 1950; that the labour-book (the *karakteristika*, a sealed record of the workers' political reliability which has to be shown every time he takes on a new job) continues to exist; and that the most severe punishments are meted out to workers who break discipline or pilfer, even if they do so only to ease their hunger.

This last point shows clearly the contradiction between the outward form – 'the workers own the factories' – and the real social content, and it will therefore be relevant to give an instance. The **Manchester Guardian** of 19 August, 1950 gave the following report under the heading 'Death Sentence in Workshop for Stealing':

'The novel procedure of trying offenders in their place of work instead of a courtroom was introduced in Belgrade a few days ago. Seventeen workers were tried in a big workshop of an engineering works for having committed numerous thefts. One man was sentenced to death and 16 to penal servitude ranging from two months to twenty years. The whole staff of the works had to attend the trial that was designed to serve as a warning.

'It is small wonder that Yugoslav workers resort to stealing and have to be warned off by spectacular methods. Rations are small and the government finds it hard to honour them. Prices on the free market are extremely high . . .'

One other characteristic of Titoism, interwoven with its nationalism, was its soft-peddling of collectivisation by agriculture.

Tito's cautious attitude toward this has been determined by economic-political considerations. He knew that in Russia 'collectivisation' so isolated and weakened the state that its very existence was in the balance. He could not conduct a war on two fronts, externally against Russia and internally against the peasantry, and any attempt at large-scale and compulsory 'collectivisation' would have put him at the mercy of Stalin.

As a result, while in Bulgaria in June 1953, 51.7 per cent of all arable land was in collective farms, in Czechoslovakia 40 per cent was; in Hungary (March 1953) 26 per cent was; in Rumania 12 per cent was (UN, **Economic Survey of Europe, 1954**, *op cit*, p. 61), and in Yugoslavia only 9.5 per cent was. (**Satellite Agriculture in Crisis**, New York, 1954, p. 62.)

Notwithstanding the basic similarity of the Stalinist and Titoist regime, there is one big difference between the two. Stalin's regime became more and more tyrannical while becoming less and less efficient, these two aspects mutually strengthening each other. Under the policy in Yugoslavia the regime, although totalitarian, has not led to increasing convulsions. No opposition parties are allowed, and in the party no oppositional voice may be raised (see the case of Djilas and Dedijer), class differences continue, and the bureaucracy rules supreme. However, there are no bloody trials, no bloody 'collectivisation' and no increasingly draconic labour laws.

### Can Gomulka do a Tito?

There can be no doubt that Gomulka, Nagy and the other rulers of the satellites are making attempts to follow the Yugoslav model. The first steps in this process – decentralisation of the administration, 'democratic management of industrial enterprises', and back-pedalling on the collectivisation of agriculture – have already been taken in Poland and Hungary.

But one cannot simply presume that the satellites will be able to copy Tito and stabilise their regime as 'enlightened totalitarianism'. This is so for a number of reasons.

First of all, there are economic reasons which make this impossible. The 'liberality' of the Titoist regime is dependent on the modesty of the industrial targets it sets out to achieve. It does not set its sights very high, thus avoiding overtaxing its capacity and exceeding its resources.

As a matter of fact the rate of growth in industry in Yugoslavia since the 1950 reforms is very low indeed. It is much lower than the rate of growth of industry in the satellites, in Russia, or even in the countries of Western Europe, as can be seen from the following table:

*Percentage Growth of Gross Output of Industry, 1950–1953*

| | | | |
|---|---|---|---|
| Yugoslavia | 6% | Rumania | 76% |
| Russia | 46% | United Kingdom | 6% |
| Czechoslovakia | 52% | France | 9% |
| Bulgaria | 57% | Belgium | 12% |
| Eastern Germany | 60% | Austria | 17% |
| Poland | 75% | Western Germany | 39% |

(Sources: for Russia, **The National Economy of the USSR**, *op cit*, p. 47; for all other countries, UN, **Economic Survey of Europe in 1954**, pp. 72, 199.)

The avoidance of forced mass collectivisation in Yugoslavia is integrally bound up with its extremely slow industrial advance: without syphoning off surpluses from agriculture, the sources of capital accumulation must be quite small.

(Apologists of Stalinism in its different variants, who praise Russia and her satellites for their speedy industrial advance and Yugoslavia for its 'democratic' political regime, will have to choose: either they argue for industrial advance paid for by vicious oppression, or for more 'democracy' paid for by relative economic stagnation.)

A fall in the Russian rate of industrial development to the Yugoslav level would entail a drastic curtailment of the armaments drive; it would force China, now seeking aid for industrialisation, to gravitate toward the US and the Western European capitalist powers; it would demand the surrender of any ideas of world supremacy.

And it must be remembered that even the modest rate of growth of Yugoslav industry was made possible by fairly lavish American economic aid to bolster her up against mighty Russia. But will US imperialism grant the same support for all the satellites, especially since Russia will obviously be weakened, as the shock of their defection takes effect? Or can one expect US imperialism to give economic aid on a large scale to Russia?

### From Titoism to Revolution

Above all, Gomulka and Nagy are not, as is Tito, masters in their own homes. Unlike the other leaders of the 'People's Democracies', Tito and his friends came to power without the support of the Russian army. And while there are no Russian troops on Yugoslav soil, Poland, Hungary, Eastern Germany, and Rumania are heavily garrisoned by them.

Again, while Yugoslavia is so situated geographically that it can get military aid from the West and so balance between Russia and America, no other 'People's Democracy' (except Eastern Germany and Albania) is as advantageously situated.

Furthermore, unlike the case of Yugoslavia, the Communist Party leaders on coming to power had mass support only in Czechoslovakia and Bulgaria; and even in these countries, where the support had not been forged through years of heroic struggle in a war of national liberation, it was much weaker than in Yugoslavia. The relative popularity of the Party plays a significant role in the extent of the stability of the regime.

In the last analysis it is clear that to do a Tito, Gomulka & Co. will have to wage a revolutionary struggle against the Russian army, a struggle which can only attain a victorious conclusion if the whole people is mobilised. And what the people have achieved in bitter struggle they will not surrender to local bureaucrats, turncoat quislings.

The Gomulkas are balancing between the workers, peasants and intellectuals of their own country on the one hand, and Russian imperialism on the other. They try to use the pressure of the one in order to wring concessions from the other.

Turning to the Russians, Gomulka says in so many words: 'Unless you retreat and give Poland greater freedom, the people will rise in arms against you.' To the Polish people Gomulka says: 'If you go too far, the Russian troops will intervene, and the Polish people will bleed to death.'

Without the Russian garrisons Gomulka, Nagy & Co. will be swept aside by the popular masses. Without the mass movement, they will be the helpless slaves of Russia.

*Revolution is Contagious*

But balancing on a razor's edge is a difficult trick and it can not continue indefinitely.

The outbreak of the French Revolution in 1830 and the revolt in Belgium ignited the great Polish rising of the same year. In 1848 the French and German revolutions sparked off the Hungarian revolution, in which many Polish volunteers aided the struggle against the Russian troops that had come to crush the revolution. French and Belgian, German, Polish and Hungarian blood together watered the tree of liberty.

In 1864, after the collapse of the recent Polish uprising, a socialist delegation from France came to London, and at a meeting which it called to protest against the cruel suppression of the Polish national revolution, it was decided to found the 'International Workingmen's Association', the First International. In it Polish and Russian, French and British, Italian and German socialists and workers joined hands to struggle for the emancipation of humanity.

Whether the fighters of Warsaw and Budapest win their present battle or not, the international working class will remember them as the glorious harbingers of the new world, the world of revolutionary democratic socialism. Stalinism will have earned eternal loathing and contempt.

In victory or in defeat the Eastern European revolution will have blazed the trail for the new consolidation and spreading of the ideas of independent, revolutionary and democratic socialism.

# Mao Tse-Tung and Stalin

During recent events in Hungary the Chinese press came out firmly in support of Moscow's oppressive policy. Thus, for instance, the editorial for 5 November in Peking's **People's Daily**, entitled 'Celebrate the Great Victory of the Hungarian People', stated: 'The joyful news has arrived that the Hungarian people . . . with the support of the Soviet armed forces have overthrown the reactionary Nagy Government which betrayed the Hungarian people and the Hungarian nation.' Every victory of Russian arms in Hungary was applauded in ever more glowing terms.

On 29 December, 1956, the **People's Daily** published a major pronouncement entitled 'More on the Historical Experience of the Dictatorship of the Proletariat'. This approved the general course of Moscow's policy, in the main justified Stalin's career, supported Russia's policy in Hungary and reproved Tito. It emphasized the 'leading role of the Soviet Union in the Socialist camp'. Chou En-lai again and again harped on the same theme throughout his tour of Moscow, Warsaw and Budapest in January this year. It was indicative that Chou applauded the loudest after Khruschev had said 'All of us Communists . . . consider it a matter of pride for us to be as true to Marxism-Leninism as was Stalin himself.' (**Manchester Guardian**, 18 January, 1957).

## Not unexpected

To many a sincere Communist, suffering under the profound illusion that Mao and his regime are not Stalinist, this must have come as a great shock. However, to anyone using the Marxist method of analysis, which looks at the economic foundation of politics, Mao's extreme Stalinism is not unexpected.

*To understand Mao's policies one must bear in mind the main historical task facing the Chinese bureaucracy, the task of industrialising the country. The Chinese bourgeoisie proved incapable of accomplishing this. The Chinese working class, after the defeat of the 1925–27 revolution, the world slump and the Japanese invasion, being pulverised and leaderless, has not played an active, decisive role for the last three decades. The task of industrialising an extremely backward country when it cannot rely on the aid of industrially advanced socialist centres is extremely difficult. It demands that the people tighten their belts in order to make quick capital accumulation possible. A considerable tightening of the belt cannot be done democratically for any length of time. Hence the more backward the country and the greater the drive towards quick industrialisation, the more harsh and totalitarian the regime has to be. The rulers of such a regime, while being the guardians of capital accumulation, will not, of course, forget themselves; they accordingly derive increasing privileges from their position of absolute control over the economy, society and State.*

### China's poverty

China is extremely backward economically. Thus, for instance, steel consumption per head of population in 1950 was 2 lbs, as against 11 in India, 111 in Japan, 278 in Russia, 556 in Britain, and 1,130 in the United States. (W. S. Woytinsky and E. S. Woytinsky, **World Population and Production**, New York, 1953, p. 1124.) The output of electricity in 1950 was 3,500 million kwh in China, as against 5,063 million in India and Pakistan (whose population is two-thirds of China's), 38,840 million in Japan and 91,200 million in Russia. (*Ibid*, p. 967.) The number of spindles in China in 1951 was 4 million as against 10.8 million in India. (*Ibid*, p. 1067.) Chinese transport is also extremely backward. It was estimated that prior to the second world war there was 1 km of railways per 25,300 people in China, as against 1 per 6,878 in India. (UN, **Economic Survey of Asia and the Far East, 1947**, Shanghai, 1948, p. 113.) In motor transport China was even more backward relatively to India.

As a result of economic backwardness, China's national income is extremely low. Colin Clark estimates that the net income produced per head of population in China (1933–5) was 138 International Units (he defines the Unit as 'the amount of goods and services which one dollar would produce in USA over the average of the period 1925–34); in India (1944–45), 246; USSR (1937), 379; Hungary (1938–39), 408; Poland (1938), 508; Japan (1940), 600; Britain (1947), 1,383; USA (1947), 2,566 (C. Clark, **Conditions of Economic Progress**, First Edition, London, 1940, and Second Edition, London, 1951).

## The plans

The rate of industrial growth aimed at by Mao in his first Five-Year Plan is quite ambitious, although it falls short of Russia's aims in her first Five-Year Plan (see Table 1).

So meagre are China's initial resources that even after her first Five-Year Plan she will be far behind Russia's level of production not only after its first Five-Year Plan, but even before it was started. This can be seen clearly from Table 2. China will need a number of Five-Year Plans to reach the level Russia reached even prior to her Plan era.

China's First Five-Year Plan shows an even greater emphasis on heavy industry than Russia's First Five-Year Plan. According to the plan, of all gross capital investment in industry, 88.8 per cent will be devoted to means of production industries, and only 11.2 per cent to light industries (Li Fu-chun, **Report on the First Five-Year Plan, Peking**, 1955, p. 34). In Russia the corresponding figures were 85.9 and 14.1.

*Table 1*

| | China | | Russia | |
|---|---|---|---|---|
| | *Index for 1957 (1952 : 100)* | *Yearly Rate of increase* | *Index for 1932 (1928 : 100)* | *Yearly Rate of increase* |
| Value of gross industrial output | 198.3 | 14.7 | 202.0 | 19.3 |
| Output of large-scale industry | 207.0 | 15.7 | 230.0 | 23.2 |

(Yang Chien-pai, 'A Comparative Analysis of China's First Five-Year Plan and the Soviet Union's First Five-Year Plan', **Statistical Work Bulletin** (Chinese), Peking, August 1955.)

*Table 2: Per Capita Output of Different Goods in China and Russia*

| | | China | | Russia | |
|---|---|---|---|---|---|
| | *Unit* | *1952* | *1957 (target)* | *1928* | *1932* |
| Power supply | kwh | 12.71 | 25.20 | 32.50 | 81.70 |
| Cotton cloth | kh | 2.36 | 6.54 | 27.60 | 35.80 |
| Steel | metres | 6.70 | 8.85 | 18.00 | 16.30 |
| Grain | kg | 286.95 | 305.74 | 475.20 | 421.50 |

*(Ibid.)*

## Consumption bows to investment

The subordination of consumer goods industries to the needs of capital goods is shown in the fact that while the amount of profits of light industries in the years 1952–1955 was some 10.8 milliard yuan larger than the amounts invested in these same industries, this sum went mainly to capitalise heavy industry. (**Statistical Bulletin** (Chinese), Peking, 14 November, 1956.)

With the national income very low, capital investment takes up a big portion of the national income. It has been stated that gross capital investment in 1952 made up 15.7 per cent of the national income; in 1953 it was 18.3 per cent; in 1954, 21.6 per cent; in 1955, 20.5 per cent; in 1956, 22.8 per cent. (**Jen Min Jih Pao, [People's Daily]**, 20 September, 1956.) This rate is only a little lower than in Russia during her first Five-Year Plan, but seeing that in absolute terms the level of income in China is some three times lower than in Russia at the time, a rate of 20 per cent accumulation is a much greater burden than a rate of even 30 per cent would have been in Russia.

In absolute terms, however, the capital accumulation in China is quite small. Thus the average annual investment rate during the five years 1953–7, was planned to be 8,548 million People's Dollars, or, at the official rate of exchange, some 3,650 million US dollars.

In Canada, with a population one-fortieth of China's population in 1956, capital investment reached 7,900 million US dollars. (Even if we consider possible differences in price levels between the two countries, the picture would not alter radically.)

### The burden of arms

The military budget of China made up 18.1 per cent of the national income in 1952; in 1953, 15.9 per cent; in 1954, 15.2 per cent; and in 1955, 16.2 per cent. (Calculated from Wang Tzu-ying, 'On Public Finance', **Ta Kung Pao**, Tientsin, 29 January, 1955.) These figures compare with the military budget of Russia in 1928, which made up only 2 per cent of the gross national product of the country.

With a high rate of capital accumulation and with the great burden of the military budget, workers' wages naturally lag far behind their output, that is, the rate of exploitation is high – and is rising.

This was underlined by a **People's Daily** editorial, which stated: 'In 1952, the workers of State-operated enterprises produced a yearly average rate of 100 million People's Dollars per worker. Of this, except for 500 thousand dollars as the average monthly wage for each worker, 94 per cent directly represented capital created for the State.' (**People's Daily**, 13 December, 1953.) The above figures probably exaggerate the rate of exploitation of the workers, but there is no doubt that it is extreme.

### Growing exploitation

As time goes by the rate of exploitation is increasing, as can be seen clearly from the lag of wages behind labour productivity. This was the situation according to the **People's Daily**:

|      | Labour Productivity Increase (%) | Wage Increase (%) |
|------|------|------|
| 1953 | 13 | 5 |
| 1954 | 15 | 2.6 |
| 1955 | 10 | 0.6   19 June, 1956) |

(For reasons that cannot be dealt with in the present article, it can be proved that it is doubtful if real wages showed even the rise mentioned in this table.)

The exploitation of the peasantry is even more extreme than that of the industrial workers. For lack of space we shall mention only a few facts to show this.

Vice-Premier Chen Yun stated that in the year July, 1954, to June, 1955, the State acquired in the form of grain tax and compulsory deliveries of produce, a total of 52 million tons of grain, or some 30 per cent of the total grain output of the country. (**New China News Agency**, 30 April, 1955.) This figure is not far behind that taken by the Russian State as taxation in compulsory deliveries: in 1938 it was some 33 per cent. (A. Arina, 'Kolkhozes in 1938', **Sotsialisticheskoe Selskokhozyaistvo**, Moscow, December, 1939.)

The figure for China exceeds what the peasantry used to pay as rent under the Kuomintang regime – some '30 million tons of grain'. (Chen Han-seng 'Industrialisation Begins,' **China Reconstructs**, Peking, January-February, 1953.)

---

### Forced labour

Capital being so very scarce and human labour so very plentiful and cheap, the natural result is the widespread use of forced labour – including prisoners, or slave labourers.

Unlike Moscow, Peking is not shy about giving information on forced labour. Thus, for instance, in a 'Report on the Work of the Kwangtung Provincial Government during the Past Ten Months', given by Ku Tats'un, its Vice-Chairman, on 15 September, 1951, it was stated that in the province of Kwangtung alone during 10 months, a total of 89,701 counter revolutionaries were arrested, 28,332 were executed, while 'those whose crimes were punishable by death, but who did not incur the intense hatred of the public were sentenced to death, but had their execution delayed for two years, during which time they were made to undertake forced labour to give them a chance to reform themselves.' (Canton, **Nan Fang Jih Pao**, 18 September, 1951.) If some 60,000 people were condemned to slave labour in only one of China's 27 provinces in a matter of 10 months, the size of the slave labour force in the country as a whole must be huge. Po I-po, at the time Minister of Finance, claimed that in three years 'more than two million bandits' were liquidated (**New China's Economic Achievements**, 1949–52, Peking, 1952, p. 152), the majority, presumably, not being killed, but put to work.

A milder form of forced labour is the compulsory conscription of peasants to public works. Thus, Fu Tsoyi, Minister of Water Conservancy, stated on 28 October, 1951: 'During the two years (October, 1949 – October, 1951) a total labour force of 10,370,000 workers was mobilised for various conservancy projects . . . '

(**People's Daily**, 30 October, 1951). The average pay for this kind of work was some 2–3 catties of rice for a 12-hour workday. (Calculated from the book of the Stalinist, W. G. Burchett, **China's Feet Unbound**, London, 1952, p. 157.) Under the Kuomintang in the years 1929–33, the average daily wage of agricultural workers was equal to 14 catties of rice. (J. L. Buck, **Land Utilisation in China**, Shanghai, 1937, pp. 305–6.)

The low level of the productive forces at the disposal of the Chinese bureaucracy makes for an even harsher political regime than in Russia. Space allows for only a few points to be dealt with in this connection.

### Police dictatorship

As in Russia so in China, there is also a system of internal passports, the obligation to register with the police any change of address, etc. (See the decree of the Ministry of State Security, *Provisional Regulations Governing Urban Population, New China News Agency*, Peking, 16 July, 1951; Ministry of State Security, *Provisional Rules for Control of Hotels and Lodging Houses, New China News Agency*, Peking, 4 August, 1951; State Council, *Directive Concerning the Establishment of a Permanent System for Registration of Persons, New China News Agency*, Peking, 2 July, 1955.)

To control the population three sets of regulations were issued. First, *Organic Regulations of Urban Inhabitants' Committees;* secondly, *Organic Regulations of Urban Street Offices;* and thirdly, *Organic Regulations of Public Security Sub-stations.* All three were adopted by the Standing Committee of the National People's Congress on 31 December, 1954.

To strengthen these organisations, special *Denunciation Rooms* and *Denunciation Post-Boxes* were set up all over the country.

### Sons against fathers

Nothing shows the extreme of totalitarianism reached in China more than the demand that children should denounce their own 'counter-revolutionary' parents. To give one example: The **China Youth Journal** published an open letter by a student called Lu Ch'eng-hsu, accusing her father of being an agent of Chiang Kai-shek. The letter opens with these words:

'Lu Hsu,

'When I write out this stinking name of yours, I feel ashamed and intolerably insulted. In the past I looked upon you as my father, but now I have seen your true face: you are a cannibal with your teeth bared in madness and your paws whipping about in the air.'

It ends with these words:

'Now, I am a member of the New Democratic Youth League, and you are the people's enemy, forever unpardonable. Between us there is nothing in common now. I would rather be a daughter of the people than the slave of a special agent. It is our sworn principle that we will never co-exist with our enemy. So no matter where you hide yourself, we will get you in the end. You just wait and see.' (**China Youth Journal** (Chinese), Peking, 8 May, 1951.)

Such a level of depravity imposed by the totalitarian state was not surpassed, indeed not even reached, by Stalinist Russia.

### Cult of the individual

The cult of Mao is, in a way, even more extreme and nauseating than the former cult of Stalin. Portraits of Mao hang everywhere. Five storeys high, they adorn Shanghai and other cities. Trains carry portraits of Mao over the boiler. In many peasant houses his picture replaces the former kitchen god, and a kind of grace is said before meals by the household: 'Thank Chairman Mao for our good food.' His pictures occupy the tiny household shrines where formerly clay images were kept. A report of the Peking Municipal People's Government quotes a peasant approvingly: 'Formerly we worshipped Kuan Kung, who was said to be omnipotent. Where is his omnipotence? Whom shall we worship? To my mind, we should worship Chairman Mao.' (**General Report of Peking Municipal People's Government on Agrarian Reform in Peking Suburban Areas**, approved by Government Administrative Council on 21 November, 1950.)

Special obeisance is made to Mao at all public meetings. A description of a mass trial ran: 'The meeting opened with the singing of the national anthem. Then everybody took off their hats and bowed to the national flag and to the portrait of Chairman Mao,' (Hsiao Ch'ien, **How the Tillers Win Back their Land**, Peking, 1954, p. 72), just as they had formerly done to the landlord as he was borne past them.

Not to be outdone, Wa-ch-mu-chi, Governor of the Yi Nationality Autonomous *chou* in Lianshen (Sikang) sang the following hymn of praise at the National People's Congress: 'The sun shines only in the day, the moon shines only at night. Only Chairman Mao is the sun that never sets.' (**New China News Agency**, Peking, 26 July, 1953.) Practically the same words were used about Stalin: 'I would have compared him to the shining moon, but the moon shines at midnight, not at noon. I would have compared him to the brilliant sun, but the sun radiates at noon, not at midnight.' (**Znamya**, Soviet Authors' Union Monthly, October, 1946.)

### China's Stalinism

The basic facts of the Stalinist regime are the subordination of consumption to the needs of quick capital accumulation, the bureaucratic management of industry, the limitation of workers'

legal rights, the enforced 'collectivisation' of agriculture, the differentiation of society into privileged and pariahs and the totalitarian
police dictatorship. All these traits are to be found in Mao's China.
Being a relatively late comer and rising on extremely backward
productive forces, the oppressive facets of the system are even more
accentuated in Mao's China than they were in Stalin's Russia. The
historical function of the bureaucracy is the accumulation of capital
on the one hand and the creating of a working class on the other (a
function fulfilled by the bourgeoisie in the West). The less capital a
country is endowed with and the smaller its working class, the
deeper are the roots of bureaucratic state capitalism and the longer
its span of life, if taken in isolation.

*To put it differently, as the backwardness of China is so much greater than
that of Russia, not to speak of the European satellites, the working class so
small in size and so lacking in cohesion and culture, the forces compelling the
bureaucracy to give concessions and even threatening to explode the regime in
revolution are much weaker in China than in Russia, not to speak of Eastern
Europe. In all probability, if not for the influence of revolutionary events
elsewhere, China will have to go through a whole generation, or perhaps two,
until its working class becomes a strong enough power to challenge the rule of
the bureaucracy. In isolation the present regime in China will probably surpass
in harshness as well as in length of life its Russian Stalinist precursor. In this
we find one reason why Peking did not take kindly to the 'reformers' in Eastern
Europe and why it applauded the defeat of 'reactionary Nagy'.*

There is another reason, connected with the above, for Mao's
support for 'Stalinist' policies, and – if there is a split in the Kremlin
– for the 'Stalinist' faction. Being interested in China's rapid rise to
be a giant industrial and military world power, Mao cannot but
oppose any weakening or softening of the austere regime in Russia
and Eastern Europe, a regimen that makes for emphasis on heavy
industry at the expense of popular consumption. Mao prefers to get
steel, machine tools, turbines, etc., rather than that the Russian or
Hungarian people should get better housing, food and clothing.

Mao's China is a tremendous rock on which probably many
revolutionary anti-Stalinist waves will break. However, in the long
run, probably after a few decades, this rock will begin to crumble
not only, or perhaps even mainly, through the effect of anti-Stalinist
revolutions in Europe, but through revolutionary events in China
itself.

# Crisis in China

### 1. In Stalin's Footsteps:
### Everything Subordinated to Heavy Industry

TO UNDERSTAND THE forces behind the Cultural Revolution, one must start by analysing the socio-economic problems with which China is wrestling.

Up to 1957, the end of the First Five-Year Plan, China followed Stalin's model of economic advance: the emphasis was on heavy industry to the detriment of light industry and agriculture. Thus, for instance, during the First FYP, agriculture received only 6.2 per cent of State investment, while industry's share was 61.8 per cent. Of the amount invested in industry, only 11.2 per cent was scheduled for light industry (even lower than in Russia during her First FYP when the corresponding figure was 14.1 per cent).[1] As the figures refer to **gross** investment, that is, without taking into account depreciation of existing capital, it is doubtful if the Plan envisaged **any** net investment at all in light industry.

There can be no doubt that one of the main factors behind the very high rate of industrial growth in the USSR was the fact that a very large portion of the capital invested in industry went into capital-goods rather than consumer-goods industries. A machine to produce machines plays a greater role in capital-formation than a machine producing, say, shoes for the people to wear.

There is an intimate connection between the neglect of light industry and the neglect of agriculture in both Russia's and China's first Five-Year Plans. If the light industry which supplies the needs of the peasants is neglected, the peasants have little incentive to increase agricultural output. In Russia the springboards for the fantastic achievements of industry under Stalin were forced collectivisation and the enforced syphoning off of grain to the towns to feed the newly-recruited industrial working class that was engaged primarily in heavy industry.

Alas, as early as towards the end of the First FYP, it became clear that Mao simply could not follow in Stalin's footsteps, that the Soviet model of development could not be transferred effectively to China. First of all, the industrial base from which Mao started was much narrower than that from which Stalin launched his industrialisation drive. Even in absolute terms, China's industrial output in almost every sector lagged well behind that of Russia in 1913. Per head of population China was still worse off, her population being four times as big as Russia's at that time. Second, however swiftly China developed industrially (and during the First FYP her advance was very impressive – a 14 per cent annual rate of growth!), the growth of employment possibilities lagged far behind the growth of population. Thus, non-agricultural employment rose from 36.5 millions in 1953 to 40.9 millions in 1957, or by 4.4 millions. The average annual increase in employment outside agriculture was, therefore, 880,000. The population of working age increased during the same period by an annual average of 4 millions (a figure that probably rose to 5 millions in the years 1958–62 and to 7 millions in the years 1963–7). The result was that the agricultural labour force did not decline – as happened in Russia under Stalin – but rose by 75 million from 222 million in 1952 to 297 million in 1957.[2] A third cause for anxiety at the time was the way that agriculture threatened to lag behind the multiplying population. One must remember that China, prior to Mao's coming to power and for more than two generations, had been a net importer of grain (unlike Russia which prior to the Revolution, was a granary for Western Europe). Any deterioration in her precarious grain balance – either a decline in the productivity of agriculture, or even a failure to keep pace with the increase in population – would wreak havoc, given the infinitesimal margin of output above the absolute minimum needed to avoid famine.

With the lagging of agricultural output behind population growth and especially with the **rise** in the size of the agricultural population, Mao found it more and more difficult to get hold of agricultural surpluses to feed the towns and for exporting abroad to get the wherewithal to import machinery and the like. State procurements and taxation in kind, which in the agricultural year 1953–4 together amounted to 29.12 per cent of all grain produced, declined to 25.15 in the year 1956–7.[3]

But above all, there were, and are, other fundamental reasons why the methods of forced syphoning off of agricultural output from the countryside could not work as effectively in China as in Russia. The failure of forced deliveries in China was forecast in

1957:

'In Russia, State control over the Machine Tractor Stations guarantees that a big portion of whatever the peasants produce will go into the State treasury to provide capital for industrialisation. In China the role of the machine tractor stations – even in the few places where they do exist – could not be as commanding, as intensive agriculture, especially garden cultivation is not, and could not be, as dependent upon mechanisation. The converse of this greater importance of human labour is that the will to work, care and zeal in production play a much greater role in China's agriculture than in Russia's. Forced deliveries, together with the emphasis on heavy industry, inevitably pour cold water on the peasant's desire to increase production: not only is he prevented from eating more but no consumer goods are offered to induce him to sell his surplus output. And without inducement, increased output from intensive agriculture is most unlikely.

'The conclusion that the pattern of Russian collectivisation is likely to prove a false guide to China gains support from the economic history of the two countries . . . ever since Chinese agriculture became dependent on irrigation, serfdom gave place to a peasant economy based on private property. However exploited and oppressed the peasant may have been, it was not the whip which urged him to work. As against this, serfdom and the feudal whip were the salient features of rural society in Russia, with its extensive agriculture, for a thousand years.'[4]

In 1958, Mao tried to break out of the above contradictions by a new forced march.

## 2. 'Walking on Both Feet'

The People's Communes and the Great Leap Forward had as their slogan 'Walking on both feet' – agriculture to keep pace with industry. The aims of the Great Leap Forward can be summarised thus:

(1) To increase agricultural output and radically redistribute it in order to syphon off large surpluses;

(2) To widen employment opportunities, not only in large-scale industry, but also in agriculture, in construction work in the countryside, and in small industry and handicrafts;

(3) To syphon off agricultural products for the 'surplus' population – who were to be in visible proximity to the peasants, engaged on work that was obviously contributing to their income – by having the peasants feed them directly: this was intended to help overcome the difficulty of getting the food to follow those who migrated from the countryside into the towns.

In a gallant and heroic effort to accomplish these great tasks the unique experiment of the People's Commune was launched. Millions were mobilised in the countryside to work on water conservancy. In the three years 1949–52, 'about 20 million people took part in water conservancy work,'[5] but for 1957 and 1958 it was reported by Vice-Premier Po I-po (in February 1958): 'At present nearly 100 million men and women are going out every day in China to work on irrigation work,' each working for an average of 100 days.[6] Millions were mobilised to build steel ovens, and 60 million were engaged in iron smelting and steel-refining furnaces.[7]

However, the Great Leap Forward ended in disarray.*

### 3. Third Turn: Priority to Agriculture

Once again Peking had to change course. That the Great Leap Forward ended in a shambles is clear from the Chinese authorities' complete silence since 1959 on the subject of actual output or even planned output expressed in physical terms. When one compares this statistical blackout with Peking's eagerness to publish a multitude of statistics beforehand – even on the number of flies eliminated – one may be sure that the production figures were not favourable.

The first clear hint of the coming Third Turn was given in the Report of Li Fu-ch'un to the National People's Congress in March 1960. He put forward the idea that agriculture should be regarded as the foundation, with industry taking the lead in economic development.[8] But no indication was given yet that the basic policy of giving priority to the development of heavy industry had been changed. It was in the autumn of 1960, when the harvest turned out to be much worse than expected, that a new policy turn became apparent. In late September a movement of 'all people to agriculture and food grains' was brought to a peak by cadres all over the country.[9] This represented a complete turnabout from the nationwide movement of 'all people to iron and steel' that had taken place in the late summer of 1958.

In January 1961 Li Fu-ch'un, in his report to the 8th Plenum of the Central Committee, admitted that the planned agricultural output for 1960 had not been attained because of 'severe natural calamities in 1959', and 'natural calamities in 1960 that were unprecedented in 100 years'. This led the Plenum to reaffirm the movement of 'all the party and all people to agriculture and food grains'. The Plenum decided further that 'since there had been tremendous development in heavy industry in the last three years – its output of major products already far in excess of the planned level for 1961 and 1962 – the scale of basic construction should therefore be appropriately reduced.' The general industrial policy

---

*One important sidelight: it has been estimated that the value added in the iron-smelting and steel-making Communes sector was actually negative – the product was of lesser value than the materials used in the manufacture. (See Wu Yuan-li, *The Steel Industry in Communist China*, New York, 1965, Chapter IV.)

was to be that of 'readjustment, consolidation, reinforcement and improvement.'[10]

Chou En-lai's report to the National People's Congress on 27 March 1962, entitled 'The Work of Readjusting the National Economy and Our Immediate Tasks', put forward 10 immediate tasks, three of which were of direct concern to industry:

'Task 3. Contract further the basic construction front, and redirect the materials, equipment and manpower to the most urgent areas.

'Task 4. Properly reduce urban population and workers and functionaries, the first move being to send those workers and functionaries who came from the rural districts back to take part in agricultural production, so as to strengthen the agricultural front.

'Task 10. Improve further the work in planning and try to attain a comprehensive balance among different sectors in the national economy in accordance with the (declining priority) order of agriculture, light industry and heavy industry.'[11]

That a great shift from industry to agriculture in the balance of the economy probably did take place after the retreat from the Great Leap Forward is clear from the following estimate of the Gross National Product of China and its composition:[12]

|  | Gross National Product of China (1952 prices) | | |
|---|---|---|---|
|  | 1957 | 1959 | 1962 |
| Aggregate in million yuan | 95.2 | 110.5 | 82.7 |
|  |  | Percentages | |
| 1. Agriculture | 39.2 | 32.2 | 47.1 |
| 2. Modern industry | 20.3 | 29.5 | 14.5 |
| 3. Handicrafts | 5.7 | 5.3 | 6.4 |
| 4. Others | 34.8 | 33.0 | 32.0 |

## 4. Relaxation in Agriculture

After the end of the Great Leap Forward there was a marked relaxation of State control in agriculture. The People's Communes have in many places become empty shells, while the small production teams and peasants' private plot are the important factors of production.

In 1958, all the Chinese peasants were organised in 24,000 Communes with an average of over 20,000 people per Commune. All land and other means of production, such as livestock and ploughs, were declared the common property of the Commune, which, besides managing agriculture, was to own and manage industrial undertakings and educational and other social institutions such as schools, nurseries and hospitals. All members of the Commune were to be fed in a number of common mess-halls. The Commune was also declared to be a political-military unit of the State and Party.

The Commune ownership of practically all means of production was only a transition stage to State ownership, 'the completion of which may take less time – three or four years – in some places, and longer – five or six years or even longer – elsewhere.'[13] The transition to complete communism in China as a whole was on the horizon.

'. . . the People's Communes are the best form of organisation for the attainment of socialism and gradual transition to communism. They will develop into the basic social units in communist society . . . It seems that the attainment of communism in China is no longer a remote future event. We should actively use the form of the People's Communes to explore the practical road of transition to communism.'[14]

In tightening the control over peasants, an end was put to the elements of private property that still existed in the agricultural producer co-operatives.

To realise the Great Leap, a big effort was made to raise the rate of capital accumulation in the Communes. Thus, the **People's Daily** recommended that 30–40 per cent of the net income of Communes should be put to reserves 'over the following several years'.[15] However, the high tide of Commune building lasted only a few short months; then came the ebb. A turning point was reached in August 1959 at a Plenum of the Central Committee, which criticised the Commune movement for 'tendencies to over-centralisation, to egalitarianism and extravagance.'[16] The production-team of some 10 to 20 families was now to become the basic accounting and production unit.

There was no more talk of the imminent transfer of Commune property to full State ownership. In the high fever of Commune building, all garden plots, livestock and other property had been expropriated on the promise that all needs would be satisfied by the Commune. In the about-face, individual initiative and work were to play a significant role. Small plots of land were returned to individual householders for private cultivation. In addition, 'the Commune members should be enabled to utilise their spare time to grow some food grains, melons, vegetables, and fruit trees, and raise some small domestic animals and domestic poultry on vacant plots and land and waste land.'[17]

As a result, **individual** farming was now going to play quite a considerable role in the life of the peasantry. It was found, for example, in P'enghsing Commune, Hupeh Province, that the share of individual farming in the general income of production-brigade members was: one brigade, 36.38 per cent; a second brigade, 28 per cent; a third brigade, 19.76 per cent.[18] In Hsiaokang People's Commune, Hupeh, peasants individually raised 65 per cent of all pigs sold and 95 per cent of all chickens and eggs sold.[19] One paper noted, in 1965, that 70 per cent of subsidiary production in agriculture was on private plots.[20] As the income from subsidiary production makes up over 60 per cent of the total income from agriculture,[21] it is to be concluded that income from private plots constitutes as much as 40 per cent of the total income from agricultural production.

Peasants were now no longer obliged to work on Commune enterprises. Thus, for instance, the Kwangtung Provincial Committee of the Communist Party decided that 'the enterprises of the Communes (including those in the categories of industry, communications, forestry, animal husbandry, subsidiary production and fishery) are as a rule not allowed to draft more that 8 per cent of the labour power of the production-brigades.'[22]

Production brigades were now allowed to deduct only up to 3 per cent of their income for accumulation.[23] The hullabaloo about Commune-run industry subsided completely. Now we are informed:

'To initiate Commune industry, rural People's Communes should depend mainly on the profits of Commune enterprises and Commune reserve funds and may not expect funds either from above (the State) or from below (brigades). Under present conditions, Commune industry should generally not take up more than two per cent of the total number of labourers in production brigades.'[24]

At the time of the Great Leap Forward, we were informed that the building of the People's Communes helped the Party to keep the countryside under its control. 'Why do we say that with the setting up of People's Communes the Party leadership will be strengthened? . . . a large-scale, highly-centralised organisation is naturally easier to lead than a small-scale, scattered organisation.'[25]

Now, with the great retreat, a relaxation of Party control over the countryside took place.

## 5. Relaxation of Control over Industrial Management

During the Great Leap Forward, the authority of Party Committees at the local and enterprise levels was enhanced. A system of 'close co-ordination among management, workers, technical personnel and administrative staff under the leadership of the enterprise's Party committee' was inaugurated.[26] The secretary of the Party Committee became, to all intents and purposes, the chief executive of the enterprise. The emphasis was, as the press put it at the time, on 'redness' not 'expertness'.

However, when the Great Leap Forward met with reverses, the policy had to change. In April 1959, the weather-cock, Chou En-lai, put it thus: 'Every industrial enterprise must carry through the system of the manager taking full responsibility under the Party Committee's leadership.'[27] However, some time later, at the end of 1960, the manager re-emerged as the recognised 'head of enterprise'.[28] Thus the balance tilted in favour of the 'professionals' at the expense of the Party.

Later, on 10 August 1961, Marshal Ch'en Yi, the Foreign Minister, made the emphasis on 'expertness', not 'redness', even plainer:

'At present we should stress specialised studies because failure to do so will keep our country perpetually backward in science and culture. In the early years of the liberation, it was completely necessary for the Party and the Government to stress political study . . . There is a need for us . . . to train a large number of specialists . . .

'To make efforts in the study of his special field is the political task of the student . . . the students . . . should devote most of their time and efforts to specialised studies. Of course these students should also study politics to equip themselves with a certain degree of political consciousness . . .'[29]

After 1961, all aspects of 'independent managerial authority' were stressed, and it was made clear that it was up to the enterprise manager to make the correct economic decisions with the capital granted him and the task the State assigned him.[30] The Party sphere of influence shrank radically and the morale of the Party cadres suffered correspondingly.

## 6. Intellectual Relaxation and Mao's Withdrawal

Not only did the intellectuals take advantage of the limited liberalisation of 1960–62 to criticise the Party and its policies of the Great Leap Forward, but they resisted subsequent efforts to reform them. Mao himself was moved to comment on their obstinacy. In 1963, it is now revealed, he said that in the cultural field ' . . . very little had been achieved so far in socialist transformation . . . Wasn't it absurd that many communists showed enthusiasm in advancing feudal and capitalist art, but no zeal in promoting socialist art.' In 1964 Mao complained that most of the associations of literary and art workers and their publications ' . . . had not carried out the policies of the Party and had acted as high and mighty bureaucrats, had not gone to the workers, peasants and soldiers and had not reflected the socialist revolution and construction. In recent years they had even slid to the verge of revisionism. If serious steps were not taken to remould them, they were bound at some future date to become groups like the Hungarian Petofi Club.'[31]

One significant expression of the general relaxation of Party control over agriculture, industry and the intellectuals was Mao's relinquishing of the chairmanship of the People's Republic of China. He kept his other job, as chairman of the Central Committee of the Party, the first job going to Liu Shao-ch'i. The extent of the Party's retreat, the loss of self-confidence and nerve, can be seen also in the fact that for a number of years the Central Committee had held no Plenary session: the 10th Plenary Session of the 8th Central Committee was held in September 1962, while the 11th Session took place in August 1966, some four years later. (Article 33 of the 1945 Party Constitution provides that regular sessions of the Central Committee should take place every six months!)

### 7. Bukharinism Raises its Head

In many ways the period after the Great Leap Forward was similar to the NEP period in Soviet history. In the years 1924–28 a remarkable debate on economic policies took place in Russia. (An excellent account of this can be found in Erlich's book.[32]) One of the main protagonists was Nikolai Bukharin, by far the best educated economist of the Party. His arguments have been repeated, practically word for word, by Chinese economists since 1961 (though it is very doubtful if there has been any direct influence of the former over the latter).

Bukharin argued that the key problem facing the Soviet economy of the mid-twenties revolved around the relation between agriculture and industry, and that the development of the latter was dependent on that of the former. Agricultural production should be encouraged by incentives: by lowering the prices of industrial goods supplied to the peasants, and relatively improving the prices paid for the farm produce. He vehemently opposed turning the terms of trade against the farm as a means of syphoning off resources from agriculture into industry. This method was suggested by Preobrazhensky, Bukharin's most consistent opponent. Preobrazhensky called this 'the primitive accumulation of capital,' which he defined as:

'the accumulation in the hands of the State of material resources obtained chiefly from sources lying outside the State economic system. This accumulation will, necessarily, in a backward agrarian country, play a colossal role . . . Primitive accumulation will predominate during the period of industrialisation . . . We must, therefore, term this whole stage as the period of primitive or preparatory socialist accumulation.'[33]

Bukharin argued that if the terms of trade turned against agriculture, there was a danger that the peasantry would turn away from the market, cut supplies to the towns, and indulge in self-sufficiency. It was in this context that Bukharin disinterred Guizot's famous 'enrichissez-vous' which was later to haunt him for years: 'We have to tell the whole peasantry, all its strata: get rich, accumulate, develop your economy.'[34]

To the extent that industry developed, the emphasis, Bukharin argued, should be on light industry, not heavy industry:

'We believe that the formula which calls for a maximum of investments in heavy industry is not quite correct, or rather, quite incorrect. If we have to put the main emphasis on the development of the means of production, we must combine this development with a corresponding expansion of light industry which has a quicker turnover and repays within a shorter time the amounts spent on it. We must attempt to get the optimal combination of both.'[35]

After all, 'Our economy,' Bukharin declared, 'exists for the consumer, and not the consumer for the economy.'[36]

If the speed of industrialisation is dictated by its subordination to the pace of advance of agriculture, while heavy industry is subordinated to light industry, it is just too bad if industry crawls forward. This is unavoidable: 'We have come to the conclusion that we can build socialism even on this wretched technological level . . . that we shall move at a snail's pace, but that we shall be building socialism and that we shall build it.'[37]

It is really uncanny how Bukharin's arguments have been resurrected in China after 1962 in practically every detail. First of all a number of Chinese economists made it clear that industrial development should be dictated by the development of agriculture:

'As the foundation of the national economy, agriculture demands that all production departments including those of industry, all construction units and all cultural and educational undertakings develop themselves with the actual conditions of agricultural production as the starting point and give due consideration to the quantities of commodity grain and industrial raw materials and to the sizes of the market and the labour force which agriculture can supply. In other words, all social undertakings cannot separate themselves from these conditions which agriculture provides . . . Agriculture plays a decisive role in influencing and restraining the national economy and the whole social life . . . It is only after agricultural production has been rehabilitated and expanded and after agriculture, the foundation of the national economy, has been consolidated that industry, communications and transport, and cultural and educational undertakings can be better developed . . . National economic plans should be formulated in the order of agriculture, light industry and heavy industry.'[38]

The Chinese economists went much further than Bukharin did in subordinating industrial advance to agriculture. Some of them argued that for a long time **industrial advance should help release labour power from the towns to the countryside,** instead of leading to the more common, opposite direction of population movement:

'Productivity of labour in industrial and mining enterprises must be raised, labour must be saved, **the number of workers and employees must be reduced and the population of the cities must be decreased. In this way, more people will go back to the countryside to increase the labour force there and greatly strengthen the agricultural front and hasten the development of agriculture.'**[39]

The terms of trade, which have historically been against farming, have to be radically changed in its favour.

While Preobrazhensky recommended the syphoning off of capital surpluses from agriculture to industry and Bukharin aimed at industry and agriculture travelling on parallel rails, Chinese economists went further and argued for **capital transfer from industry to agriculture:**

'Under the present conditions in our country, so far as the source of accumulation is concerned, the accumulation from industry will increase at a faster rate than that from agriculture, because the rate of growth of industry and the rise of its labour productivity are faster than those of agriculture. So far as the allocation of accumulation is concerned, **the accumulation used for agriculture will increase at a faster rate than that used for industry,** because the production level of our agriculture is still very low at present and so is its labour productivity, and the State must place the emphasis of its economic work on agriculture and invest heavily in agriculture and give it massive material support, so as to change the backward aspect of agriculture as soon as possible and enable it to meet the needs of the development of all branches of the national economy.'*[40]

Practically repeating Bukharin's words that 'the economy exists for the consumer and not the consumer for the economy' and the need to subordinate heavy to light industry, one Chinese economist wrote:

'Under ordinary conditions, should arrangements be made first for the necessary consumption of the people throughout the country and then, if circumstances permit, for accumulation? Or, should arrangements be made after accumulation has been guaranteed? According to the basic aim of socialist production, it should be the former and not the latter.'[41]

## 8. Mao Does Not Like Bukharinism

The Chinese neo-NEP widened the gap between rich and poor, advanced and backward areas and villages, and increased the

---

*Once the concept that industry will not get resources from agriculture is accepted, more care must be given to cost-accounting, as the profit of the industrial plant is the source of capital accumulation. (During forced industrialisation, with the emphasis on heavy industry and the exploitation of farming, the **gross volume** of Industrial output was accepted as the criterion of success). On 19 July 1962, the *People's Daily* published an article by two economists who are generally identified with the less liberal wing, in which the following statement occurs:

'Cost accounting is the foundation of economic accounting of enterprises . . . we believe that we should principally use the cost target and the profit target for the evaluation of the economic results of the enterprises, the two being equally important . . . In spite of the fact that there are defects to the profit target, it is, after all, the quality target for the whole work of enterprises. It includes results that cannot be reflected by the cost target, and it is also the principal basis for the calculation of accumulation for the State because the realisation of the financial budget of the State if represented by the profits that have been paid to the Government.' (Yang Jun-jui and Li Hsün, *'A Tentative Discussion on Economic Accounting of Industrial Enterprises,' JMJP,* 19 July 1962. *SCMP* 2817.)

earnings of factory managers, technicians and better-off peasants.

Yet it is fraught with the greatest dangers to a large section of the bureaucracy. It weakens Party control and could in the long run undermine its monolithism, threatening to fracture the Party under the pressure of sectional interests. Its continuation would also put an end to any grand nationalist ambitions for the quick transformation of China into a country of heavy industry and a mighty military-industrial establishment.

The alternative to Bukharinism, i.e. the continuation of NEP, has been supplied by the history of Russia – when Stalin broke with Bukharin and carried out forced industrialisation and collectivisation, enforcing the severe regimentation of workers and peasants. But in trying to follow the same path, Mao is hampered by much greater obstacles than Stalin was (and one should not forget how tough the going was in Russia). First, there are the objective factors mentioned above (the much narrower industrial base from which Mao has to launch his industrialisation than Stalin had; the lower agricultural output; the greater population pressure; the difficulty of State control of intensive rice farming, etc.). Further obstacles accrue from the fact that the administrative set-up in China is not conducive to easy victory of the Centre over centrifugal tendencies.

Because the Communists came to power in the different provinces at the head of marching armies, there has not been the wide, even if not complete, separation of the personnel of the Party, Army, Police and State administration that existed in Russia.

Prior to 1949 it was difficult to distinguish between Party and military leaders, because of the widespread practice whereby the same people held military, Party and State offices at the same time. After 1949, this practice continued in the military and administrative committees. Practically all Party leaders have a military rank: General Mao Tse-tung, General Chou En-lai, General Teng Hsiao-p'ing (General Secretary of the Party), Marshal Ch'en Yi (Foreign Minister), etc. The regional military commanders show an impressive continuity if one examines their military careers after Liberation and before the establishment of the regions in 1954.

'Ten out of the thirteen commanders in the period 1954–58 (of whom eight are still in office either as commander or political commissar) had held leading military positions within the region after Liberation. Thus Huang Yung-sheng, commander of Canton until 1958 and again after 1962, had been deputy commander and then commander of Kwangsi military district until 1954, Ch'en Tsai-tao, commander of Wuhan since 1954, had commanded the Honan military district from 1950 onwards. Two more, Teng Hua (Shenyang) and Hsieh Fu-chih (Kunming) were appointed to their military regions after service in Korea. Only one of the thirteen original commanders, Wang Hsint'ing (Tsinan), was moved directly from one part of China to another (from Szechwan to Shantung) . . . Information on political commissars is less revealing. It seems that in many cases until 1958 the posts of commander and commissar were held concurrently, and that their functions were separated and the deputy commissar promoted to full commissar at the time of the Great Leap Forward. (In Inner Mongolia and Sinkiang the posts are still concurrent.) In general, most leading military officers in the field have remained almost stationary within their particular region since the early fifties.'[42]

There is a large overlap in the jobs of Political Commissar of the Army and First Secretary of the Provincial Party Committees.

'Out of fifteen commissarships identified in or around 1960, nine were held by the first secretary of the province. The commissars of Peking and Shanghai garrisons were also ranking Party secretaries. All these appointments appear to date from the Great Leap Forward and the increasing attempts at that time to establish more effective Party control over the Army. On a much smaller scale, this trend can also be noted in the military regions, where the most recent appointment to the post of political commissar (Tsinan region, 1964) was given to the first Party secretary of Shantung, T'an Chi-lung. Earlier, T'ao Chu, the first secretary of Kwantung province, became political commissar of Canton region, relinquishing the post again in 1962. In the key defence areas of Inner Mongolia, Sinkiang and Foochow, the commander and/or commissar since 1954 has also been the Party secretary (Wu Lan-fu, Wang En-mao and Yeh Fei).'[43]

The tie-in between the Security Service and the Party machine is probably also quite close, although for obvious reasons this cannot be documented.

Stalin used one arm of the bureaucracy against another; if need be, he used the Secret Police against the Party; and when he wanted to purge the Secret Police itself (as when he got rid of its chief Yagoda in 1936 and, subsequently, his successor, Yezhov, in 1938) he used his own private security organisation, headed by the sinister General Alexander Poskrebyshev. Mao cannot use the same weapons in the same swift and effective way.

A further obstacle to smooth centralised control is the fantastic size of China: in area it is larger than the whole of Europe, but it has a minute railway system, only two thirds the length of Britain's, or a third of India's!

Central sway is also hampered by the fact that a very large proportion of industry is under local administrative control. During the Great Leap Forward the control of industry was decentralised, and this has not been reversed. The changes during those years show clearly in the following figures (percentages):[44]

|  | 1957 | 1958 | 1959 |
| --- | --- | --- | --- |
| Central control | 46.0 | 27.0 | 26.0 |
| Local control | 54.0 | 73.0 | 74.0 |

The increasing dispersal of industry must also strengthen the centrifugal tendencies.

Another factor strengthening the centrifugal tendencies is the impact of neo-NEP conditions – trade and speculation* – on farming. There is a great divide between the southern provinces (above all Szechwan Province) which have a grain surplus and the northern provinces which are always grain deficient.

### 9. On Whom Can Mao Rely?

One of the most striking aspects of the 'Cultural Revolution' is that Mao **did not** mobilise the Party with its more than 20 million members, nor the Young Communist League and the Pioneers with their 150 million members. Instead he created a new body, the **Red Guards** . . . The movement started its own paper, **Red Guard**, on 1 September 1966 soon after the disappearance of **China Youth** on 16 August and **China Youth News**, the daily paper of the Central Committee of the YCL, on 20 August. Since then little has been heard of the YCL, but posters in Peking attacked Hu Yao-pang, First Secretary of the YCL, and other former YCL leaders, who were accused of seeking to 'convert the YCL into a low, popular Komsomol of the Soviet type.'

Why does Mao look to the students for his main support? First, the students are fairly privileged compared with the overwhelming majority of the people. As one professor put it:

'The State provides very favourable conditions for university students to study – annual expenditure for one university student is equivalent to the fruit of labour of six to seven peasants toiling through the entire year.'[45]

Second, the students are not yet integrated into the ruling bureaucracy, and hence are less affected by the moods of those bureaucrats who mellowed under the neo-NEP.

Third, on the whole, students see themselves as a non-specialised section of society, and in a manner of speaking they represent the interests of the 'nation' as against conflicting sectional interests. Students are also most sensitive to the technical lag of their country behind the advanced countries. Participating in the scientific and technical world of the twentieth century, they are stifled by the backwardness of their own country. They aspire to industrialisation and modernisation so as to leap from medievalism to the nuclear age.

Fourth, having passed through a radical, revolutionary change

---

*For some time in 1961 the official retail price of rice in Nanking was 0.13 yuan per shih catty (1.1 lb) while the free market price was 3 yuan. The official price of cooking oil in Shanghai was 0.61 yuan per catty while the free market price was 30 yuan (*JMJP*, 14 March 1961. Yuan-li Wu, *The Economy of Communist China*, London, 1965, p96). The scarcity conditions with the lag of agricultural output behind population growth explain these huge differences.

in knowledge through their own lifetime – especially if they come from peasant or workers' families – the sky is the limit for them, and Mao's voluntarism strikes a willing chord.*

There is also a purely technical reason why Mao finds it so convenient to use the students in his 'Cultural Revolution'. Students' demonstrations are quite easy to organise centrally: by simply closing the schools, or part of them as need be, by fiat. As one English teacher who worked in China for a year described the 'spontaneous' demonstrations:

'If it is a 250,000-man demonstration . . . then a third of every class will go. If it is a 500,000-man demonstration . . . then two-thirds will go, but if it is a million-man demonstration, the whole college will be out for the whole day.'[46]

Closing schools for some nine months is one thing; to close factories – for any length of time – is a totally different business.

Besides the student body, another instrument Mao used is the Army. As early as 1960 Lin Piao, the Minister of Defence, had begun to move into the 'cultural struggle'. He founded an Arts Institute in the People's Liberation Army which graduated its first class in 1965. Writers were one of the first groups in 1964 directed to display the revolutionary tradition of the PLA in their work. A novel by a member of a PLA drama troupe, **The Song of Ouyang Hai,** the story of a PLA squad leader, was the most important literary event of the first half of the 1960s. Members of the PLA became authoritative critics of the arts, film, theatre, and literature. When the 'Cultural Revolution' unfolded, key Army people grasped complete control over propaganda and agitation: T'ao Chu, former head of the Army Political Department of the Fourth Army, became the new head of propaganda, and Lieutenant-General Hsiao Wang-tung became acting Minister of Culture. Actually, **Liberation Army Daily** made the running in the 'Cultural Revolution' from its inception. It played an incomparably greater role than the Party paper, the **People's Daily.** Again and again the PLA has been set up as a revolutionary model for the whole country. There was a frequent coupling of Lin Piao's name with that of Mao, attributing to him, as to no other leader, the distinction of 'creatively' applying Mao's ideas.

At the first mass rally of the 'Cultural Revolution' – 18 August – Mao, as well as his wife, Chiang Ch'ing, appeared wearing army uniforms. (Next day the **Liberation Army Daily** published an editorial stressing the great significance of Mao's wearing his military uniform.) Speaking to the rally, Chou En-lai called on the Red Guards to observe the PLA's 'three main rules of discipline and eight points of attention,' adding: 'The Red Guards must be built into a highly organised and disciplined militant army with a high

---

*These generalisations are very schematic. It must be borne in mind that students are not an island separated from the rest of society, hence they do not constitute a homogeneous body which supports Mao completely in the 'Cultural Revolution'.

level of political consciousness and become the reliable reserve force of the Liberation Army.' Many of those present at the rally wore army-style uniforms and were transported in Army lorries.

Since then at every stage of the 'Cultural Revolution' – which for lack of space cannot be described here – and especially its latest stage, that of establishing new authorities (the so-called 'Three-Way Alliance'), the PLA played a central role. There are a number of reasons why the PLA on the whole – notwithstanding provincial and regional centrifugal tendencies – sides with Mao. First of all, the Army rises above society. It is identified with national grandeur and above all with the development of a heavy-industry-military establishment.

One notion quite widespread in the West, about the egalitarian nature of the PLA, is completely unfounded. The PLA officers are a privileged group. It is true that originally and for many years, the prevailing system provided both officers and men with food and small allowances in lieu of salaries. However in 1955 the system was replaced by cash payments. 'The present scale of pay – which ranges from US$2.50 per month for a private to $192–236 for a full general'[47] is indicative of the differentials. The stratification in the PLA is reflected in privates' cotton uniforms, officers' gaberdine; in privates' fourth-class travel in trains, officers' – from captain upwards – first-class fares.

Above all, Mao must know that if political loyalties cannot be imposed on the army with its advantages of military discipline and total control of personnel, there is no hope at all of regimenting civilian life.

## 10. Voluntarism Gone Mad

The greater the objective impediments – including popular resistance – to the dictates of a centralised State capitalist bureaucracy, the greater the emphasis on voluntarism, on the omnipotence of the will of the righteous people, i.e. of those who blindly follow the Leader. Maoist voluntarism by far surpasses its Stalinist precursor. Stalin tried to pull Russia up by her bootstraps industrially-militarily; Mao tries to do the same to a country without boots and without straps. Stalin repeated again and again that 'there is nothing that Bolsheviks cannot do' – but he always made it clear that this was by using German techniques or, in later years, American techniques. Mao's whole ideology is the omnipotence of sheer will.

It is this that explains why Mao found it necessary in the midst of the 'Cultural Revolution' to swim nearly 15 kilometres in the Yangtse in just over one hour!*

---

*Incidentally, this achievement was so staggering that the President of the World Professional Marathon Swimming Federation, Senor Carlos Larriera, invited Mao to enter two ten-mile swimming races in Canada since his reported time was almost four times as fast as the world record for 10 miles.

This extreme voluntarism of Mao bestows superhuman qualities on him. The cult of Mao far surpasses that of Stalin. To quote a few examples, selected at random: an article entitled 'Chairman Mao, You are the Red Sun in our Hearts', in the theoretical organ of the Central Committee, **Hung Ch'i (Red Flag)**[48] ends like this:

'The seas may dry up, the mountains may rot. The red hearts of us hundreds of militia men who are loyal to you will never change. Whoever opposes you is also removing our hearts and taking our lives. To defend you we are willing to go up mountains of knives, descend into seas of fire. Let our hearts roll and let our hot blood flow.'

'O, most beloved chairman Mao, you are the Red Sun in our hearts. We cheer every day and sing every day. There are many intimate words we want to say to you. There are many songs we want to sing to you from the bottoms of our hearts. All words of praise in the world may be exhausted, but they cannot do full justice to your wisdom and greatness. All hymns in the world may be exhausted, but they cannot do full justice to your abundant merits and great achievements. I can't help jumping and shouting at the top of my voice a thousand times, ten thousand times: Long live, long live, long live the great teacher, great leader, great commander, great commander and great helmsman, Chairman Mao!'

A paper called **New Sports**, of 19 May 1966, had an article entitled 'A Talk on the Philosophical Problem of Selling Watermelons in a Large City'. The conclusion of the article was that Mao's teachings are the main inspirer for selling watermelons. The **People's Daily** shows a picture of a mother and son reading Mao Tse-tung's book. The title is 'Parents are not so dear as Chairman Mao. Nothing is so good as Chairman Mao's writings.'[49]

New China News Agency quotes a Chinese seaman saying,

'If the water in all seas were ink, it would not suffice for us to write about our warm love for Chairman Mao, nor are thousands of songs adequate to express our gratitude to Chairman Mao.' (NCNA, 10 January 1967.)

One mass meeting of commanders and privates of the PLA sent a message to Mao stating:

'Respected and beloved Chairman Mao, if all the trees in the world were pens and all its waters ink we still could not say enough about your love and concern for our upbringing. You are our greatest teacher, leader, supreme commander and helmsman.'

## 11. Extreme Zhdanovism

To assume that the 'Thoughts of Mao Tse-tung' are omnipotent, one must accept that not only the Leader but also his cultural aides-de-camp – the writers, poets, artists, etc. – are 'human engineers', 'engineers of the soul'. It demands a rejection of the validity of any artistic creation or tradition taken from the past, as these reflect the limitations of the individual. In 'socialist realism' there are no Hamlets or Othellos – in the real world they are all too common. Zhdanovism is the necessary price of bureaucratic omnipotence. In China, recently, during the 'Cultural Revolution', Zhdanovism reached depths even lower than did its Russian archetype. To quote only a few examples of cultural nihilism:

Yang Hen-sheng, former vice-chairman of the All-China Federation of Literary and Art Circles, was denounced for extolling such bourgeois literary men as Shakespeare, Molière, and Ibsen.[50]

Chou Yang, who translated Chernyshevsky and Tolstoy into Chinese, was accused in **Red Flag** of the crime of praising the 'foreigners' (this word is actually used in the accusation) Belinksy, Chernyshevsky and Dobrolubov.[51] Chou Yang 'stubbornly announced' that 'in aesthetics he was a faithful follower of Chernyshevsky.'[52]

Chao Feng, formerly secretary of the Secretariat of the Association of Chinese Musicians and Vice President of the Central Conservatory of Music, was accused of having 'produced Beethoven's Ninth Symphony which proclaimed "love of mankind".' (i.e. Khrushchevite Revisionist ideology – TC).* He also 'extolled **Swan Lake.**'[53]

For some 30 years Mao, and his mouthpiece on literary affairs, Chou Yang, had accepted, if critically, the Chinese literary tradition. Yet in the summer of 1966 all the culture of the past – even such classics as **The Dean of the Red Chamber** – was labelled feudal and rejected. All this nihilism in the name of Culture!

## 12. A New Stage in the 'Cultural Revolution'

At the time of writing, the 'Cultural Revolution' has reached a new stage: with the bureaucracy split from top to bottom, the industrial working class has stepped into the arena. For the first time since the Revolution of 1925–27, mass strikes took place in China, in December 1966 and January 1967.

The only source of information regarding the strikes has been the official declarations from the Maoist authorities who opposed them. Hence we cannot be sure of the actual breadth of the strike movement. But that the strikes have been very widespread is clear from the statements of the authorities themselves, who certainly would have liked to conceal them.

A preliminary remark is necessary. The Maoist press explains the strikes as the work of a 'handful of persons in authority within the party who were taking the capitalist road'. This is repeated

---

*The Maoists, it seems, have not noticed that Karl Marx had a lifelong admiration for Shakespeare, that Lenin loved Beethoven and that Chernyshevsky had a decisive formative influence on Lenin!

hundreds of times. It is very doubtful if there is any more truth in this kind of explanation than there is in the usual explanation in the Western capitalist press, of strikes in the West as the handiwork of a 'handful of troublemakers'.

A strike of stevedores and dockers in Shanghai port went on for nearly a fortnight.[54] Strikes paralysed railway traffic between Shanghai and Hangchow and between Shanghai and Nanking for 12 days, from 30 December to 10 January 1967.[55] Workers also stopped work at the Yangshupu Power Plant.[56] In Nanking, in the Urban Transport Company, supporters of Mao 'set out to gain control over the company's finances and stopped paying a bonus which had originally been issued to sap the fighting will of the revolutionary workers.'[57] In the Taching Oil Field, the 'handful' used 'material incentives to lure large numbers of workers to leave their production posts.' They were 'using State money to sabotage production'.[58]

Similar stories come from a number of factories: '. . . a large number of workers at the Shanghai No. 17 Textile Mill were taken in and deserted their posts.'[59] In the Shanghai Glassmaking Machinery Factory, the 'handful' deceived a number of workers, including heads of work teams, technical personnel and other cadres in the basic production units, and incited them to desert their production posts. Some of them 'hid blueprints and other technical data, left their posts and of course affected production.'[60] In Shanghai No. 2 Camera Plant, as a result of a strike 'only 9.2 per cent of the (production) target was completed in the first 14 days of January.'[61] Peking's No. 2 Machine-Tool Plant fulfilled 'in the first 18 days of January . . . only one third of the month's production target.'[62] 750 workers of the National Cotton Mill No. 31 of Shanghai, incited by 'bad elements', left the factory.[63] Similarly, 'a large number of workers at the Shanghai No. 17 Textile Mill were taken in and deserted their posts.'[64]

One of the most interesting phenomena is that throughout the 'Cultural Revolution' the trade unions and their daily paper **Kung Jen Jih Pao** was **not once** quoted as playing any role at all.

## 13. A Missing Link

The similarities and differences between the problems facing contemporary China and Russia at the time of her industrialisation drive have been the central themes of the present article. One factor that played a key role in Russia on the eve of her industrialisation and collectivisation drive was the Marxist-Leninist Opposition – the Trotskyist Left Opposition. This, or a tendency similar to it, is completely missing in China.

On the face of it, there is a formal similarity between the Trotskyist programme of the years 1923–8 and the policy of Stalin after 1928. Trotsky, in opposition to the Stalin-Bukharin bloc, advocated economic planning, accelerated industrialisation and the collectivisation of agriculture. Stalin opposed this policy, saying in his usual crude way that the peasant needed a cow; 'he needs Dnieproskroy like he needs a gramophone.'

With Stalin's launching of the FYP in 1928, and subsequently, it seemed as if Stalin simply stole Trotsky's clothes. Many of Trotsky's followers (Preobrazhensky, Radek, Smilga, Smirnov, and so on) believed this to be the case, and decided to join Stalin's bandwagon. With hindsight it is easy to see that there was only a purely formal similarity between Trotskyism and Stalinism.

For Stalin, the workers were the object of industrialisation and planning. They were to be planned, regimented by industrialisation. Collectivisation was to do the same to the peasantry. The workers had to be completely disenfranchised, politically and economically.

For Trotsky, the working class was the **subject** of history, whose self-emancipation – improvement in material and cultural conditions, extended democratic control over all levers of power – were the rungs on the ladder to socialism and communism. To cite at random a few extracts from Trotsky: in November 1928, Trotsky stated that the 'criterion of socialist upswing is constant improvement of labour standards,' and wages 'must become the main criterion for measuring the success of socialist revolution'. The 1927 Platform of the Left Opposition called for 'a consistent development of workers' democracy in the party, the trade unions and the Soviets.'[65]

> 'Workers' democracy means freedom to judge openly all party life, free discussion on it, and also election of the responsible governing personnel and the collegiums from top to bottom.'[66]
> 'The work of the trade unions should be judged primarily by the degree to which it defends the economic and cultural interests of the workers.'[67]
> 'The absolute independence of the shop committee and local committees from the organs of management must be guaranteed.'[68]
> Trotsky in 1931: 'The standard of living of the workers and their role in the State is the highest criterion of socialist success.[69]

If it was axiomatic for Trotsky that the active creator of socialism was the working class, it was also axiomatic that the arena for the establishment of socialism must be international. 'Socialism in one country' is nothing but prostration before the pressures of world capitalism. As long as world capitalism is stronger than the workers' State in one country, and especially in a backward country, its pressures must lead to distortions in the workers' State and finally to its degeneration and collapse.*

While there is without doubt a 'Bukharinist' wing in the Chinese Communist Party, and a Stalinist (Maoist) wing – even though there are differences between them and their precursors, in their different national and international environments – there is **not** a Trotskyist or Left-Oppositionist wing.

The Left Opposition in Russia represented the continuation of the traditions of the working class which came to power in 1917. The Chinese urban working class played no role at all in the rise to power of Mao. Hence there is no Left Opposition inheritance. The workers' strikes in China, therefore, do not yet find political expression.

However, without indulging in crystal gazing, one may be quite optimistic about the future development of a revolutionary working-class movement in China. First, the Chinese working class, in absolute terms, is much bigger than was the Russian in the 1920s – four or five times bigger. Second, while working-class activity was quite low in Russia during the years of struggle of the Left Opposition,[†] in China the movement is rising very stormily. Third, while the 1920s, and even more so the 1930s, were years of working-class defeat in one country after another, today the international scene is much more favourable. Last, and most important, the crisis in the Russian economic development of the 1920s could be overcome by sheer Stalinist brute force. In China the impediments to development are much greater, and hence the crisis is much deeper and more prolonged, and it is bound to effect deep cleavages in the bureaucratic structure. The crisis from above may also spur on a new, revolutionary working-class political movement below.

---

*Bukharin was **formally** further away from Trotsky than Stalin – both Stalin and Trotsky suggested planning, accelerated industrialisation and collectivisation, while Bukharin did not. But in content Bukharin was much nearer to Trotsky. He still represented a wing of Bolshevism. He reflected the pressure of factory managers and trade-union bureaucrats on Bolshevism, but did not, like Stalin, repudiate all the aspirations of Bolshevism, did not aim at the total expropriation of the political and economic rights of the workers. The fact, too, that the supporters of both Trotsky and Bukharin were massacred by Stalin suggests the degree of basic agreement between both and Bolshevism.

† The number of workers involved in strikes in State-owned enterprises in Russia was: 1922, 192,000; 1923, 165,000; 1924, 43,000; 1925, 34,000; 1926, 32,900; 1927, 20,000.

1. Li Fu-chun, *Report on the First Five Year Plan for Development of the National Economy of the People's Republic of China in 1953-57,* Peking, 1955, p47.
2. Shigeru Ishikawa, *Long-term Projections of Mainland China's Economy: 1957-1982,* Tokyo, 1965, p32.
3. *Ibid,* p36.
4. Y Gluckstein, *Mao's China,* London, 1957, pp171-2.
5. *New China's Economic Achievements, 1949-52,* Peking, 1952, p196.
6. *New China News Agency (NCNA),* 13 February 1958.
7. *Ibid,* 19 November 1958.
8. *Jen-min Jih-pao (JMJP, People's Daily),* 31 March 1960.
9. *Ibid,* 27 September 1960.

10. Kung Hsiang-cheng, 'Produce More and Better Light Industrial Products for Daily Use', *Hung-ch'i (Red Flag)*, 10 February 1962.
11. *JMJP*, 17 April 1962.
12. Y L Wu, F P Hoeber and M M Rockwell, *The Economic Potential of Communist China*, 1963; quoted in Choh-ming, 'China's Industrial Development, 1958–63', *China Quarterly*, No. 17, p18.
13. *People's Communes in China*, Peking, 1958, p7.
14. *Ibid*, p8.
15. *JMJP*, 31 October 1958; *Survey of the Chinese Mainland Press (SCMP)* 1961.
16. *NCNA*, 26 August 1958.
17. *Chung-kuo Ch'ing-nien Pao (China Youth News)*, 8 July 1959; *SCMP*, 2086.
18. *JMJP*, 24 August 1959; *SCMP* 2092.
19. *Ibid.*
20. *Ta-kung Pao*, 2 June 1965; *SCMP* 3490.
21. *JMJP*, 19 July 1965; *SCMP* 3520.
22. *JMJP*, 11 July 1960; *SCMP* 2301.
23. *Kung Jen Jih Pao*, Peking, 21 July 1961; *Current Background (CB)* 669, Hong Kong.
24. *Ibid*, 28 July 1961; *CB* 669.
25. *Che Hsueh Yen Chiu (Philosophical Study)*, No. 5, 10 September 1958; *Extracts from China Mainland Magazines (ECMM)*, 149.
26. Liu Shao-ch'i, 'The triumph of Marxism-Leninism in China,' *JMJP*, 1 October 1959.
27. *JMJP*, 19 April 1959.
28. Hsu Hsin hsueh, 'Strengthen Further the System of Responsibility in Industrial Enterprises,' *Hung-ch'i*, 16 October 1961.
29. *Chung-kuo, Ch'ing-nien Pao*, 1 September 1961.
30. Chin Li, 'Discussions in the Very Recent Period by our Country's Economists on Problems of Socialist Economic Accounting', *Ching-chi Yen-chiu (Economic Research)*, 11 November 1962, pp66–67.
31. 'Raise High the Great Red Banner of Mao Tse-Tung's Thought and Carry the Great Proletarian Cultural Revolution to the End', *Op cit*, pp18, 17.
32. A Erlich, *The Soviet Industrialisation Debate, 1924–1928*, Cambridge, Mass., 1960.
33. E A Preobrazhensky, 'The Law of Primitive Socialist Accumulation,' article published in 1924 and then included as a chapter in his *New Economics* (Russian), Moscow, 1926, Vol I, Part 1, pp57–58; published in English as *The New Economics*, Oxford, 1965.
34. Erlich, *Op cit*, p16.
35. *Ibid*, pp81–82.
36. *Ibid*, p79.
37. *Ibid*, p78.
38. Lu Hsu'n and Li Yün, 'On the Practice of Economy,' *JMJP*, 21 August 1962; *SCMP*, 2817.
39. Sun Meng-ming, 'On the Proportional Relationship between Industry and Agriculture', *Ta-kung Pao*, 15 June 1962; *SCMP*, 2882. My emphasis, TC.
40. Ouyang Ch'eng, 'Concerning the Question of Harmony or Disharmony in the Proportional Relationship between Industry and Agriculture,' *Ta-kung Pao*, 22 October 1962; *SCMP*, 2863. My emphasis, TC.
41. Yang Ch'i-hsien, 'On the Need to Arrange National Economic Plans in the Order of Agriculture, Light Industry and Heavy Industry', *Ta-kung Pao*, 11 December 1961; *SCMP*, 2649.
42. J Gittings, 'Military Control and Leadership, 1949–1964', *China Quarterly*, No. 26, p95.
43. *Ibid*, pp99–100.
44. Choh-ming Li, 'China's Industrial Development, 1958–63', *China Quarterly*, No. 17, p16.
45. *Chung-kuo Ch'ing-nien Pao*, 21 July 1962; *SCMP*, 2795.
46. Diana Lowry, 'Teaching English in China', *China Quarterly*, No. 24, p7.
47. Edgar Snow, *The Other Side of the River: Red China Today*, New York, 1962, p289.
48. 1 October 1966.

49. *JMJP*, 22 September 1966.
50. *Kuang-ming Jih-pao*, 27 December 1966; *SCMP*, 3681.
51. *Hung-ch'i*, 1 January 1967.
52. *Ibid.*
53. *Kuang-ming Jih-pao*, 22 January 1967; *SCMP*, 3872.
54. *Hung-ch'i*, 1 February 1967; *SCMM*, 564.
55. *NCNA*, 9 February 1967.
56. *Ibid*, 16 January 1967.
57. *Ibid*, 14 January 1967.
58. *Ibid*, 15 January 1967.
59. *Ibid*, 9 January 1967.
60. *Ibid*, 15 January 1967.
61. *Ibid*, 17 February 1967.
62. *JMJP*, 2 February 1967; *SCMP*, 3881.
63. *NCNA*, 28 January 1967.
64. *Ibid*, 9 January 1967.
65. Leon Trotsky, *The Real Situation in Russia*, London, p100.
66. *Ibid*, p129.
67. *Ibid*, p56.
68. *Ibid*, p57.
69. Leon Trotsky, *Problems of the Development of the USSR*, New York, 1931, p40.

# The end of the road: Deutscher's capitulation to Stalinism

Among the most distinguished writers on the Russian revolution and its aftermath is Isaac Deutscher. His careful and exhaustive collation of sources and documents, together with his majestic style, lend great significance to his writings. Against a background of poverty in Marxist scholarship over the last generation his work stands out in sharp relief. With the appearance of the last volume of his trilogy on Trotsky, the time for appraisal of his work has come. The present article will deal with his theoretical and political views.[1]

## Deutscher's Predecessor – Otto Bauer

A QUARTER of a century before Deutscher Otto Bauer expressed views which use the same categories of analysis and the same theoretical vocabulary as does Deutscher. Bauer, as one of the foremost theoreticians of Austrian and international social democracy, achieved a unique accommodation of reformist practice, as a minister in a bourgeois government, to apparently radical theory.

In 1931 he foretold what he took to be the inexorable evolution of the totalitarian Stalinist regime. The key to this he found in the interrelation of industrialisation, economic rationality, and that rationality in society as a whole, whose political expression is democracy:

'Rationalization advances a style of thought appropriate to engineers, a matter-of-fact, positivistic, relativistic style of thought which reckons in terms of measurable results, seeking to reach desired goals at the least possible cost. This style of thought avoids everything that cannot be calculated; it shuns every risk, every uncertain adventure. Therefore it will always attempt to bring about social change only if and only to the extent that the majority of the people, 'public opinion', can be won over and only as long as such support is maintained. Modern democracy is rooted in this style of thought.'[2]

Any economic or social violation of rationality, such as occurred at the beginning of the industrial revolution in England or in Stalinist Russia, is transitional.

'The terroristic dictatorship will be overcome and will be dismantled to the degree that the standard of living of the masses is improved. The Soviet regime can be democratised. If the dictatorship which controls the state-owned machinery of production is replaced by a system of democratic control by the workers, there will emerge from dictatorial state capitalism, a socialist order of society.'[3]

(Bauer's view of the basic incompatibility of an industrialised society and political dictatorship prevented him from visualising the rise of Nazism, and led him to define the 1929 crash as only a passing 'crisis of rationalisation'.)

Some five years later, just on the eve of the Moscow trials, he elaborated further the perspectives of democratic evolution in Russia.

'. . . the further the Soviet Union develops away from the period of the greatest difficulty, and the more it can improve the standard of living of the workers, the easier it will be, using methods of education and persuasion, to create a real, genuine agreement between the Government and the people.'[4]

'Admittedly the dictatorship of the proletariat has become something quite different to what was intended originally by its founders. It is not a dictatorship of freely elected soviets. It is not the 'higher type of democracy' intended by Lenin, without bureaucracy, police or standing army. It is not the free self-determination of the working masses, who exercise their rule over the exploiting classes. It has become the dictatorship of an all-powerful party bureaucracy, which has suppressed all free expression of opinion and formation of opinion even within the party, and rules the people by means of the powerful machinery of the State and economic bureaucracy, the police and standing army. This development was inevitable.'[5]

But this is past tense.

'The successes of the dictatorship are winning it ever wider mass support.' The old generation 'is being replaced by a new generation, educated in the schools, youth organisations and army of the Soviet State, and filled with socialist thoughts and desires . . . the Soviet Union is approaching a stage in which it no longer needs a rule of force over the people, because the majority of the people is giving support willingly to the new system of developing socialism. But if this development makes the democratisation of the Soviet Constitution possible, it also makes it necessary.'[6]

'. . . the gradually continuing democratisation of the Soviet constitution becomes possible, inasmuch as the living standards of the masses in town and country rise with increasing productivity . . . The gradual democratisation of the Soviet constitution is becoming necessary as the people of the Soviet Union, in a rapid cultural development, become self-conscious civilised men, who are not willing to obey any bureaucratic absolutism, and who demand personal freedom, intellectual freedom, self-determination and self-government. The decision of the Soviet Congress of November 1934, to set about the democratisation of the constitution of the Soviet Union with the democratisation of the franchise for the soviets . . . in fact . . . was the first sign of the development that was beginning.'[7]

(Poor Bauer, the Moscow Trials were just around the corner.)

## Summary of Deutscher's Views on the Self-liquidation of the Bureaucracy in Russia

Deutscher's literary brilliance contrasts sharply with his theoretical poverty. He nowhere sets out his own conception of the development of Stalinism in systematic fashion, and his views have to be pieced together from a variety of widely scattered and ambiguously worded statements.

It seems impossible that Otto Bauer's ideas should have had **no** influence on Deutscher. Bauer was, after all, one of the most influential socialist theorists in Central Europe during the period in which Deutscher became a Marxist, Deutscher's views agree completely with Bauer's in the already quoted statements about the future of the Stalinist regime – even though they refer to different decades. Yet Deutscher never acknowledges even a nodding acquaintance with Bauer's views.

Just as Bauer saw a functional connection between industrialisation and democracy, so also does Deutscher.

'It is a truism that modern forms of democratic life have developed mainly in industrialised nations and have, as a rule, failed to develop in nations that have remained on the pre-industrial, semi-feudal level of civilisation. But what is accepted as a truism in the modern and contemporary history of the non-communist world is, in the eyes of our critics, totally inapplicable to the Soviet Union: there it is simply preposterous to expect that massive industrialisation, urbanisation, and educational progress may foster any democratic trends and tendencies.'[8]

Scarcities caused the rise of the bureaucracy; a rise in production will bring abundance, and with it equality.

'. . . with the growth of productive forces, which makes possible an alleviation of the still existing poverty in consumer goods, a reduction of inequality becomes possible, desirable, and even necessary for the further development of the nation's wealth and civilisation. Such a reduction need not take place primarily or mainly through the lowering of the standards of living of the privileged minority, but through the raising of standards of the majority. In a stagnant society, living on a national income the size of which remains stationary over the years, the standard of living of the broad masses cannot be improved otherwise than at the expense of the privileged groups, who therefore resist any attempt at such improvement. But in a society living on a rapidly growing national income, the privileged groups need not pay, or need not pay heavily for the rise in the well-being of the working masses; and so they need not necessarily oppose the rise.

'The privileged minority in the USSR has no **absolute** interest – it may still have a relative and temporary one – in perpetuating the economic discrepancies and social antagonisms that were inevitable at a lower level of economic development. Nor need they cling to a political regime designed to suppress and conceal those antagonisms behind a "monolithic" facade.'[9]

'In the early phases of primitive accumulation the upkeep of the Stalinist oligarchy represented probably a considerable *faux frais* in the general balance of national expenditure; but it seems to me doubtful whether this can amount now to more than a marginal item of "wasteful consumption".'[10]

Education of the masses, says Deutscher, also leads to democratisation.

'There is undoubtedly an important core of truth in Soviet claims that the Soviet method of mass education is narrowing the gulf between manual labour and brain work. It was in the abysmal depth of that gulf that the Russian bureaucratic absolutism – and Stalinism – had been rooted; and one can foresee that the narrowing and bridging of the gulf will render obsolete and impossible even the milder, the Kruschevite form of bureaucratic dictatorship.'[11]

And who will execute the reforms? As the *yezhovshchina* had eliminated any Party opposition or even potential opposition '. . . the reform of the most anachronistic features of the Stalinist regime could be undertaken only from above, by Stalin's former underlings and accomplices,'[12] or as Deutscher put it some ten years earlier, Malenkov carried out Trotsky's policy:

'In the 1930s Trotsky advocated a "limited political revolution" against Stalinism. He saw it not as a fully fledged social upheaval but as an "administrative operation" directed against the chiefs of the political police and a small clique terrorising the nation. As so often, Trotsky was tragically ahead of his time and prophetic in his vision of the future, although he could not imagine that Stalin's closest associates would act in accordance with his scheme. What Malenkov's government is carrying out now is precisely the "limited revolution" envisaged by Trotsky.'[13]

The locus of all reform is in the CPSU:

'The process by which the nation may relearn to form and express its opinions may at first be slow and difficult. It can start only from inside the Communist Party. The regime will, either from self-preservation or from inertia, continue as a single party system for years to come. This need not be an important obstacle to democratic evolution as long as party members are permitted to speak their minds on all matters of policy. All politically minded and active elements of the nation are, anyhow, in the ranks of the Communist Party, if only because there has been no other party to turn to.'[14]

While Trotsky again and again called for revolution against the Stalinist bureaucracy, Deutscher speaks only in terms of reforms, and reforms from above at that: 'Unlike their predecessors, however, the Belinskys of contemporary Russia, if they exist, can be only reformers, not revolutionaries.'[15]

Let us sum up Deutscher's (and Bauer's) conclusions regarding the future of the Stalinist regime:

■ Industrialisation has been associated in the past with the rise of democracy, and this will be the case in Russia.

■ Increasing economic production must lead towards egalitarianism.

■ Massive educational achievements must narrow the gulf between different social strata and hence lead to equality and democracy.

■ Planning means economic rationality, and must lead to general political rationality, i.e. democracy.

■ The international spread of communism must undermine the factors which have caused the rise of the Stalinist bureaucracy, and hence will lead to greater equality and democracy.

■ The regime will be reformed from above; the locus of democratic change is in the CPSU; there is no place in the scheme of things for popular revolutions from below.

Let us deal with each point in turn.

### Must Industrialisation lead to Democracy?

On this point, one has the feeling that both Bauer and Deutscher have more in common with progressive nineteenth century bourgeois liberalism than with revolutionary socialism, with Herbert Spencer than with Karl Marx. For Marx human progress is not a harmonious process in which the advance of the productive forces is accompanied by the general enrichment of all society. The age of humanism – of the Renaissance – was utterly inhumane. Queen Elizabeth's reign, which produced a Shakespeare, also witnessed the hanging and maltreatment of thousands of vagabonds.

Marx tried to use the specific content of historical movements to explain events and to analyse trends, and he opposed the presentation of the laws of history as metaphysical, supra-historical ideas. So, for example, he argued that the accumulation of wealth and the emergence of free proletarians could lead in certain circumstances not to capitalism and a flourishing economy, but – as they did in Rome – to the opposite:

> 'Thus events strikingly analogous but taking place in different historic surroundings led to totally different results. By studying each of these forms of evolution separately and then comparing them one can easily find the clue to this phenomenon, but one will never arrive there by the universal passport of a general historico-philosophical theory, the supreme virtue of which consists in being super-historical.'[16]

Only if social content is abstracted, can it apparently be shown that there is a functional relationship between industrialisation and democracy. It was in similar fashion that Immanuel Kant drew the now obviously ridiculous conclusion that when all countries were ruled by republican governments, eternal peace would be guaranteed. (Unfortunately, the actual social content of the French republic did not anaesthetise its imperialist aggressiveness.)

To return to the question of the interrelationship between industry and democracy, we can see that the association of industrialism with democracy in nineteenth-century Britain was produced by a number of factors. One important cause was that the then small, rising capitalist class had to fight the landed aristocracy for the control of political power. Another factor was the desire of the industrialists throughout the period from Adam Smith to Bright and Cobden to get 'cheap government', whose main function was to be the 'night-watchman', intervening as little as possible in economic affairs. With the atomisation of economic power, parliamentary democracy seemed to be the most suitable form of rule for the bourgeoisie as a whole.

In the twentieth century the national and international context of industrialisation is radically different. Now large-scale centralised industry faces the state on equal terms; industry progressively integrates itself with the state; the trends towards bureaucratisation and state capitalism become more and more decisive (even in young industrial countries not ruled by a Communist Party, such as Nkrumah's Ghana or Nasser's Egypt). In the 1940s Manchuria and Japan witnessed a fantastic rate of industrial growth – comparable to that of the USSR – but this did not lead to democratisation. And of course Nazi Germany was an advanced industrial country . . .

## Must Increased Industrial Output Lead to Equality?

Here again Bauer and Deutscher abstract one element – growth of the productive forces – from the organic whole of the Stalinist social order and its international context. The first problem to investigate is how far relative scarcities are likely to disappear, however phenomenal the increase in production. We shall start with the division of total production between production directed towards capital accumulation and the production of consumer goods. The facts cannot but lead to the conclusion that under Stalin's heirs the subordination of consumption to accumulation have not relaxed. The pattern of capital investment, as between light and heavy industry, has in fact not changed at all between Stalin's era and Kruschev's. Thus, the share of the light and food industries in state capital investment in industry was, during the First Five-Year Plan (1928–32), 16.0 per cent; Second Plan (1933–37), 17.5 per cent; Third Plan (the $3\frac{1}{2}$ years 1938–41), 15.9 per cent; Fourth Plan (1946–50), 12.3 per cent; Fifth Plan (1951–55), 9.6 per cent; Sixth Plan (1956–60) (target), 9.8 per cent; Seven-Year Plan (1959–65) (target), 8.5–9 per cent. The share of consumer goods in industrial output continues to be low, and is even declining, although at a much slower rate than under Stalin. It cannot indeed, decline beyond a certain point without threatening labour incentives and even the viability of the regime.

|  | Division of Gross output of industry into Means of Production and Means of Consumption (in percentage) | | | | |
|---|---|---|---|---|---|
|  | 1913 | 1928 | 1950 | 1959 | 1960 (Plan) |
| Means of Consumption | 66.7 | 60.5 | 31.2 | 27.8 | 27.3 |
| Means of Production | 33.3 | 39.5 | 68.8 | 72.2 | 72.7 |

That relative scarcities of a pressing nature are bound to continue is made clear by perusing the figures for the expansion of the production of consumer goods over the planning period.

|  | First Plan targets (1932) | 1961 actual output |
|---|---|---|
| Cotton goods (milliard metres) | 4.7 | 4.9 |
| Woollen goods (million metres) | 270 | 455 |
| Linen goods (million metres) | 500 | 493 |
| Shoes (million pairs) | 80 | 442 |

At the same time, between 1932 and 1961 the population of Russia rose by more than a third, and the town population – whose standards of consumption everywhere are much higher than in the countryside – trebled.[17]

The picture for food production is even worse. In speeches in Leningrad and Moscow on 21 May and 2 June 1957, Kruschev came out with a plan to overtake the United States in per capita meat output by 1960, or at the latest 1961 (speech in Leningrad) or 1962 (speech in Moscow). To achieve this the USSR should produce 20 million tons of carcass meat. Instead in 1961 meat output was 8.8 million tons (**Pravda**, 6 March, 1962), or with the correction necessary for comparison with US statistics, some 7.3 million tons. Meat (and milk and butter and grain) are far from becoming 'free goods'! (One result of the scarcities, *pace* Deutscher, is the harshness of the law against economic crimes. Thus in 1961 the net of the death sentence was cast wider: on 5 May it took in the theft of state and public property and forgery, on 18 May revolts in prisons, and on 1 July violation of foreign currency regulations.[18])

Although the achievements in housing over the last few years have been impressive, housing scarcities are still pressing. The number of persons per room in towns, 2.60 in 1923, rose to 3.91 in 1940, and then declined to 3.43 in 1950, and 3.04 in 1960.[19] It has been calculated that it would take the USSR until 1980 to achieve a living space of 7.38 square metres per person – a figure which still represents only 82 per cent of the minimum Soviet health standard.[20] This is about half the Belgian standard or a third of the French or Swedish. Thus housing too is far from being a 'free gift'!

In the framework of international economic and military competition, the subordination of consumption to accumulation, when accompanied by inequality and a 'revolution of rising expectation', brings in its wake social tensions, not harmony. A single but dramatic example of existing inequalities must suffice: a deputy to the Supreme Soviet gets a salary of 1,200 rubles for a sitting of usually four days a year (he has of course other sources of income: he may be the director of a factory, a government or Party official, an artist); a charwoman gets 45 kopeks an hour or 14.8 rubles for 4 days![21] How different reality looks from the abstract picture drawn by Deutscher and Bauer of plenty leading to equality.

Actually the basic assumption that once a cause disappears the effect also disappears – if scarcities cause inequality, then the disappearance of scarcities will cause the disappearance of inequality – is founded not on a causal but a teleological concept of development. The human appendix served certain biological needs millions of years ago, but if you want to get rid of it now it must be cut out. Many a social phenomenon continues to exist long after its *raison d'etre* is no more.

### Must massive educational achievements lead to Equality and Democracy?

More education does not mean increasing equality of educational opportunity. Actually the educational ladder is very steep in Russia and has become even steeper since Stalin's death. Thus at the end of 1958 the number of persons enrolled in the different grades was as follows:[22]

| | |
|---|---|
| Grades 1–4 | 19.0 million |
| Grades 5–7 | 6.2 million |
| Grades 8–10 | 3.5 million |
| Graduates from 10th year | 1.4 million |
| Admitted to Institutes of higher education | 0.24 million |

A further narrowing of the opening to higher education was made in December 1958 with the retreat from the hitherto declared aim of 10 years' compulsory education. The 19th Congress of the CPSU (1952) originally stated the aim of 10 years' compulsory education, and the 20th Congress (1956) reiterated it. Kruschev in his report to the Congress, stated that this would be fully implemented by the end of 1960.[23]

However, from 1958 only 8 years was to be compulsory, after which most youths, at the age of 15 or 16, were to start working in factories, mines, construction works, and the like. Further schooling was to be on a part-time basis, through evening classes or correspondence courses, for example. The minority, who showed greater talent, would go to a three-year secondary school – grades 9 to 11 – so called a 'general polytechnical school with production training.' This school was to be more selective than were grades 8 to 10 hitherto. Exceptionally gifted pupils (and those with parental connections?) were to proceed directly to higher education without prior employment.[24]

In 1958 only 1.6 per cent of the population had university education! And with the 1958 'reform' the proportion will not rise much in the future. Education is not the great leveller.

███████████████████████████████████████

### 'Planning means Economic Rationality which must lead to General Political Rationality, i.e., Democracy'

This argument was advanced forcefully by Bauer and runs through Deutscher's thought. Two assumptions are implicit in it: 1. there is such a thing as planning which is independent of the people who plan; 2. Stalinist irrationality appears in the political and cultural superstructure and is not inherent in the economic system itself; it is an external abscess that can be removed without damage to the body social.

To begin with, it must be categorically stated that there can be no planning apart from planners, any more than there can be thought without thinkers. Secondly, the irrationality of the Stalinist regime – of bureaucratic state capitalism – is inherent. It is not confined to the surface phenomena of Russian society. Let us elaborate this point. The organisational structure of Soviet industry under Stalin was hierarchical and centralised in the extreme. Moving from base to summit, it consisted of: brigade, shop, department (comprising several shops), firm, trust, chief subdivision (glavk), Ministry, Economic Council of Ministers.

Intertwined with these chains of administration were a number of other apparatuses, criss-crossing at different levels. There were inspectors of the Ministry of Finance, agents of the District Prosecutors, agents of the State Planning Commission, agents of the Ministry of State Control, 'special sections' of the Secret Police, the Party apparatus in the factory. The result was economic irrationality, administrative discord, tensions in the factory. The multiplicity and different degrees of efficiency of the control systems lead in themselves to increasing arbitrariness and wastage, and thus recreate the very conditions that make strict and multitudinous controls necessary.

Unable to rely on the self-activity of the people, prohibiting any working-class democracy, the Kremlin has to rely on bureaucrats to control other bureaucrats. The hydra of bureaucratic anarchy and its concomitant, bureaucratic control flourishes in the sea of workers' alienation from the means of production and their exploitation.

With the extreme centralisation of the administration, and the consequent mountains of paper work, the number of administrative workers is clearly very large. Thus, for instance, the Georgian Oil Trust 'has three oil fields and 12 offices to serve them. There is one official for every four or five employees. It is not surprising, therefore, that the administrative expenses alone for one ton of oil drilled by the Trust total 60 rubles, while in certain areas the full cost of drilling one ton of oil amounts to only 22 rubles.'[25] Again, in the Moldavian Fishing Industry Trust 'there are 112 officials as against 163 workers at the fisheries, of which only 98 are employed in catching fish.'[26] A **Pravda** editorial pointed out that in the Ministry of Building Materials 16,700 people, or 26 per cent of all administrative personnel are busy with accounts and records. In addition, other 'employees, technicians and foremen are taken from work to complete all sorts of reports.'[27] The organ of heavy industry, **Industriya**, compared two coal mines, that of the Pittsburgh Coal Company in Pennsylvania and the Lenin Mine of the Kizel Trust in the Urals. Production in the former was three times as great as in the latter. However, the Russian mine had 165 administrative and technical personnel, compared with 15 in the US mine, and there were 8 office workers in the US mine, compared with 67 employed in the Russian mine. The number of actual miners was only **twice** as big in the Russian mine as in the American.[28]

Again, **Voprosi Ekonomiki** compared the United States Steel Corporation mill in Pittsburgh with a similar Soviet mill (not mentioned by name) which was one of the largest, most recently built and smoothest running mills. While the output of the American mill was some one-and-a-half times that of the Russian, the latter employed four times as large a managerial staff, and four times as many technicians.[29]

A major cause of irrationality in the economy was the irrationality of the price mechanism. Lacking a price criterion for the success of a factory, the authorities placed all their emphasis on the physical **volume** of production. Hence for many years Russian agricultural machinery weighed considerably more than similar machinery produced elsewhere. For instance, the diesel tractor,

Belarus, weighs 3 tons, whereas the similar British Fordson-Major 1951 model weighs only 2 tons. Premier Bulganin remarked that '. . . the greater the weight of the metal, the heavier the structure, the more "profitable" ' for the factory directors.[30]

The topsy-turvy price position leads to a situation where, to take an example, a cab-man in Moscow may earn more by travelling without a fare than with a fare. His bonus on the mileage and petrol saved – assured on a long drive along a quiet road without stopping and starting – could be larger than the bonus on the same drive derived from his share in a fare.

Another fantastic example of irrationality comes from heavy engineering. According to official prices, wages made up 10.9 per cent of total costs; according to calculations made by a competent Soviet economist, they made 39.2 per cent.[31] The Polish Vice-Premier, Jarosewicz, summed up the situation:

'The economic system which has prevailed hitherto is an abracadabra about prices, costs and wages. No wise man can tell what is profitable or what is not.'[32]

The net result of all the irrationalities corroding the bureaucratic state capitalist regime is that until now, the productivity of labour in Russian industry has lagged far behind the technical level of its equipment. While new equipment comes up to American standards, and is more advanced than that of Western European countries, labour productivity is only about half the American. In 1955, the number of industrial workers in the USSR was a little larger than the number in USA, while the gross industrial output of the former was only some 48 per cent of the latter.[33]

The role of the bureaucracy in agriculture is even more dubious. One need but quote Kruschev's report of December 1958 in which he said that 'In actual fact, as regards grain production the country remained for a long time (up to Stalin's death – TC) at the level of pre-revolutionary Russia.' The meat, butter, and vegetable production were lower in 1953 than in 1916 – and 1916, remember, was the third year of the war, when herds were depleted and the population was some 50 million less than in 1953! Kruschev went on to state that the labour time expended in a Soviet *kolkhoz* in 1956–7 was, for grain, 7.3 times more per unit than on an American farm (1956); potatoes, 5.1 times; beetroot, 6.2; cotton, 2.3; milk, 3.1; weight cattle, 14.2; weight pig, 16.3.[34] In 1956, 43 per cent of the population of USSR was engaged in agriculture, while in the United States only 9 per cent were so engaged (1960). The US produces a surplus of agricultural output, the USSR not even enough to make up the meagre consumption levels of Russia.

Above all, the irrationality of the whole system is inherent in the alienation of the toilers. The more science concentrates at the top of the pyramid, the more apathy, resentment and resistance spread below. Hence the numerous complaints in the Soviet press that workers do not work hard enough!

The concept of 'rationalisation' goes back to Marx (and Hegel), and along with it the notions of 'alienation', 'reification', and the 'fetishism of commodities', all of which express the thought that in a class-dominated society man becomes a 'thing', an object manipulated by forces above him, instead of being a subject who makes and remakes life according to his own wishes.

It is characteristic of Deutscher (and Bauer) to speak of the plan in isolation from its subject – the bureaucracy – and its object, the victims of the plan – the toilers. The word 'alienation' – inherent in rationalisation in a class society – is completely alien to these two authors.

## Must the Spread of world Communism Lead to the Undermining of the International Factors that encourage the rise of the bureaucracy and so lead to greater Equality and Democracy?

Even if the international environment has so changed over the last generation as to put an end to the causes that produced Stalinism, it is incorrect to assume that an end to the cause puts an end to its effects. But in fact has the international environment really changed to such an extent as to abolish the original causes of the rise of Stalinism?

The Stalinist bureaucracy arose as a result of the backwardness of Russia in the framework of world capitalist encirclement; the industrial revolution, requiring the primitive accumulation of capital, therefore took on an extremely harsh form. The spread of Stalinism over the last two decades has been in the main in areas even more backward than Russia in 1917, with a considerably larger population, and hence with even more hurdles on the path of industrialisation. Under such circumstances, the following conclusions, drawn in 1956 regarding China, were realistic:

'. . . the following may safely be said of China's general role in world Communism: that it will be the strongest and most impregnable citadel of Stalinism. As China's backwardness is so much greater than Russia's – not to speak of Russia's European satellites – her working class so small, and lacking in cohesion and culture, the forces compelling the bureaucracy to grant concessions, perhaps even threatening to blow up the regime through revolutionary explosions, are much weaker in China than in Russia, and even more, than in Eastern Europe. In all probability, if revolutionary events elsewhere do not cause China's course to be steered along a different path, she will have to pass through a generation, perhaps two, before the rule of the bureaucracy is threatened. The present regime in China, if she is kept in isolation, will probably make its Russian Stalinist precursor seem mild by comparison.

'Mao's China is and will be an important factor strengthening

Stalinist exploitation, oppression and rigidity in the "Socialist Third of the World".'[35]

The Maoist adulation of Stalin is not accidental (notwithstanding the arguments of the various Fourth Internationals). The eastward spread of Stalinism has given it a new lease of life. Only where Stalinism has spread westward has it faced any serious threat (the break of Yugoslavia with Moscow in 1948, the East German uprising of 1953, the Hungarian and Polish revolutions of October 1956).

### Is the CPSU the Locus of Evolution towards Democracy and Equality?

In stating that the Party is the locus of change towards egalitarianism and democracy, Deutscher, as is his wont, does not appraise the Party as an organic whole intertwined with the body, economic and social, of Russia, but as an abstract entity. The CPSU is however in fact a **bureaucratic club**, and hence cannot but defend the privileges of the bureaucracy.

While among the population as a whole Party membership makes up some four per cent, among the three million odd specialists, Party membership reached 2,300,000 in 1959.[36] Among Army officers the percentage of Party members was 90 (in 1962).[37] Practically all factory managers are Party members.[38]

The higher one rises in the Party hierarchy, the scarcer are workers and collective farmers. Thus, for instance, in the Kirghiz Republic, 81 per cent of the Secretaries of the *kolkhoz* party organisations and 85 per cent of the secretaries of the *raion* committees,[39] and in the Moldavian Republic in 1960, 92 per cent of the personnel working in the offices of the Central Committee had some sort of higher education, and 50 per cent of the secretaries of the *raion* committees had a higher education.[40] In Ukraine 93 per cent of the secretaries of the *raion* committees had a higher or an incomplete higher education.[41]

The social composition of Party Congresses brings out the same bias. Thus for instance, at the 18th Congress of the Communist Party of Georgia, January 1958, there were 813 delegates, of whom 175 were Party officials, 154 state officials, 26 Komsomol and trade union officials, 67 directors of factories and construction projects, 18 directors of *sovkhozes* and MTS, 15 education and public health officials, 17 *sovnarkhozi* officials, 80 writers, artists, etc., 55 generals and other high-ranking officers, 116 collective farmers (including collective farm chairmen and former members of collective farms), and 78 workers (including former workers).[42] 78 workers and former workers (in British terms this would cover Sir William Carron) versus 67 directors of factories and construction projects!

The social composition of congresses of the CPSU is no different. At the 20th Congress, out of the 1,355 delegates, 506 were

Party officials, 177 Government officials, 116 army officers (not one private!), 12 trade union officials, 8 Komsomol officials, 98 writers, artists, actors, 251 were 'directly engaged in production' in industry, and 187 in agriculture. This does not mean that they were workers, but probably mainly directors of factories, *kolkhozes, sovkhozes,* etc. One may expect as little from the CPSU – in Deutscher's words the 'guardian of public ownership' – egalitarianism, as one would expect from the Catholic Church – the guardian of 'patrimonium pauperum' – the freeing of the serfs.

### Lacing the Story with 'Inside' Information and Accommodation to the Accomplished Fact

When dealing with current developments, Deutscher tries to cover his weakness in sociological analysis and general shallowness with a special stylistic device: presenting his speculations as facts, reporting conversations between Soviet leaders in inverted commas as though he had eavesdropped on them. One description reads as follows:

'Pointing at Molotov and Kaganovich, he (Kruschev) exclaimed: "Your hands are stained with the blood of our party leaders and of innumerable innocent Bolsheviks!" "So are yours", Molotov and Kaganovich shouted back at him. "Yes, so are mine", Kruschev replied. "I admit this. But during the Great Purges I only carried out your orders. I was not then a member of the Politbureau and I am not responsible for its decisions. You were." '[43]

Unfortunately this 'style', the lacing of his hypothesis with 'inside information', very often boomerangs on Deutscher himself, exposing the complete hollowness of much of this 'information'. Thus in April 1953, Deutscher reported that Beria was one of the chief liberalisers.[44] And side by side with him and Malenkov, stood their fellow spirits Voroshilov and Kaganovich![45] Kruschev is not mentioned even once in this connection, and is referred to only once in the whole book, in passing! With the fall of Beria, we are informed that the most diehard Stalinist leader, surpassing even Molotov, is Kruschev.[46]

However when it becomes incontrovertibly clear that Kruschev has won against the 'liberalisers' Beria, Kaganovich, Voroshilov, *et al*, Deutscher hurries along with new 'inside information'. We are informed in July 1957 that the 'Stalinist diehards' are very antagonistic towards Mao – of all people – and that 'they adopted toward him an attitude so hostile that if it had become official it would have led to a momentous breach between the USSR and China.'[47] Molotov and Co. are cast as enemies of Mao, Kruschev as his friend. How wrong can 'inside information' be?

Or again, on the eve of the greatest chauvinistic outburst of all (Russian responsibility for inventing everything from the locomotive to penicillin!) Deutscher could write: 'The most striking feature in Russian life during the first months of peace has been the ebb of the nationalist mood.'[48]

Then again, in June 1957 Deutscher announced that China had entered its NEP period, that Mao 'leaves us with no doubt that he envisages no such "second revolution" (as Stalin's of 1929–32) for China', and that he stands for the 'inevitability of gradualness';[49] and this a few months before the 1958 'Great Leap Forward' and the People's Communes.

Deutscher shows not only a great capacity for changing his tune, but also of 'speaking authoritatively' no matter what the zigzags of the Kremlin policies. In his first dispatch from Germany to the **Observer** he reported that some of the German soldiers on the Eastern front had been 'very favourably impressed by the collective farms in which, they said, they saw efficiency as well as social justice.'[50] In 1953 he endorsed Stalin's rejection of the proposed transfer of the Machine Tractor Stations to the *kolkhozes*, saying that this 'might indeed mark the beginning of a powerful development of modern capitalism in Russian farming', and that 'Stalin is undoubtedly right' in believing that 'the result would be an enormous strengthening of the anti-socialist elements in the Soviet economy.'[51] But a few years later, when the MTS were dissolved by Kruschev and all agricultural machinery transferred to the *kolkhozes*, he endorsed the move completely.[52]

Deutscher also shows a ready inclination to accept official Communist statistics uncritically. Thus we are informed in 1960 that while the Indians are growing hungrier the Chinese are facing abundance:

'Meantime the Chinese are greatly increasing their food output – they are said to grow more rice than is produced in the rest of the world, and to distribute it to their workers virtually free of charge. The contrast could not be more striking; and it would become most dramatic if indeed many millions of Indians were to be threatened with famine and China's rice surplus were to secure their survival. This would be a signal development in the struggle between communism and anti-communism in Asia.'[53]

A year later China had to admit hunger, and, cap in hand, beg grain from Australia and Canada!

Deutscher had to wait for Kruschev's revelation in order to be forthcoming about Stalin's labour camps. (**The Prophet Outcast**). In his biography of the creator of these camps he hardly mentions them at all.

## Is Stalinism an Offspring of the Revolution?

In **Stalin**, Deutscher explains that 'the broad scheme' which brought about the metamorphosis of triumphant Bolshevism into Stalinism, has 'been common to all great revolutions so far.' (And from his arguments would seem to be common to all popular revolutions in the future.)

In the first phase of these revolutions, 'The revolutionary party is still marching in step with the majority of the nation. It is acutely conscious of its unity with the people and of a profound harmony between its own objectives and the people's wishes and desires.[54] This phase lasts little longer than the Civil War. By then the revolutionary party faces an exhausted people and a reaction sets in.

'The anti-climax of the revolution is there. The leaders are unable to keep their early promises. They have destroyed the old order; but they are unable to satisfy the daily needs of the people. To be sure, the revolution has created the basis for a higher organisation of society and for progress in a not very remote future. This will justify it in the eyes of posterity. But the fruits of revolution ripen slowly; and of immediate moment are the miseries of the first post-revolutionary years. It is in their shadow that the new state takes on its shape, a shape that reveals the chasm between the revolutionary party and the people. That is the real tragedy which overtakes the party of the revolution.'[55]

In order to safeguard the achievements of the revolution, the Party now has to muzzle the people.

'The party of the revolution knows no retreat; it has been driven to its present pass largely through obeying the will of that same people by which it is now deserted. It will go on doing what it considers to be its duty, without paying much heed to the voice of the people. In the end it will muzzle and stifle that voice.'[56]

'The revolution had now reached that cross-roads, well known to Machiavelli, at which it found it difficult or impossible to fix the people in their revolutionary persuasion and was driven "to take such measures that, when they believed no longer, it might be possible to make them believe by force".'[57]

Now the Party is split.

'Some cry in alarm that the revolution has been betrayed, for in their eyes government by the people is the very essence of revolution – without it there can be no government for the people. The rulers find justification for themselves in the conviction that whatever they do will ultimately serve the interests of the broad mass of the nation; and indeed they do, on the whole, use their power to consolidate most of the economic and social conquests of the revolution.'[58]

Lenin and Trotsky led inevitably to Stalin. Deutscher claims to have

'traced the thread of unconscious historic continuity which led from Stalin's hesitant and shamefaced essays in revolution by conquest to the revolutions contrived by Stalin the conqueror. A similar subtle thread connects Trotsky's domestic policy of these years with the later practices of his antagonist. Both Trotsky and Lenin appear, each in a different field, as Stalin's unwitting inspirers and prompters. Both were driven by circumstances beyond their control and by their own illusions to assume certain attitudes in which circumstances and their own scruples did not allow them to persevere – attitudes which were ahead of their time, out of tune with the current Bolshevik mentality, and discordant with the main themes of their own lives.'[59]

One of the 'illusions' Lenin and Trotsky suffered from, according to Deutscher, was belief in the possibility of spreading the revolution westwards. If Lenin and Trotsky 'had taken a sober view of the international revolution' they might have 'foreseen that in the course of decades their example would be imitated (in any other country) . . . History produced the great illusion, and planted and cultivated it in the brains of the most soberly realistic leaders.'[60]

'. . . Stalin's scepticism regarding the revolutionary temper of the European working classes has so far seemed better justified than Trotsky's confidence.'[61]

It is implicit in Deutscher's scheme that the Trotskyists in the Russian revolution, as the Levellers in the English and the Hébertists in the French, are the 'utopians' who imperil the revolution, its conquests and its future.

Under Deutscher's pen, Stalinism is the legitimate child of the revolution. All revolutions have their utopian extremists who do not understand that the revolution could not satisfy the demands of the masses it inspired. The significance of the quotation from Machiavelli which stands at the head of **The Prophet Armed** is now clear. The prophet must be armed, precisely so that he can, when the people no longer believe in the revolution, 'make them believe by force'.

### Is Stalinism Revolutionary?

According to Deutscher Stalinism not only protects the achievements of the revolution, but also deepens and enlarges them.

'In 1920, five years after Lenin's death, Soviet Russia embarked upon her second revolution, which was directed solely and exclusively by Stalin. In its scope and immediate impact upon the life of some 160 million people the second revolution was even more sweeping and radical than the first.'[62]

'. . . Stalin . . . remained the guardian and the trustee of the revolution. He consolidated its national gains and extended them. He "built socialism"; and even his opponents, while denouncing his autocracy, admitted that most of his economic reforms were indeed essential for socialism.'[63]

As foreign policy is a continuation of domestic policy, Deutscher draws the conclusion that in the international arena also Stalinism plays a revolutionary role. He points out '. . . the theoretical and political difficulty which now beset Trotskyism, a difficulty that was to grow immensely' with time:

'How real indeed was the distinction Trotsky had drawn between the domestic (partly still progressive) and the international (wholly counter-revolutionary) functions of Stalinism? Could any government or ruling group have for any length of time one character at home and quite a different one abroad? If the Soviet body politic preserved the quality of a workers' state, how could this leave unaffected its relationship with the outside world? How could the government of a workers' state be consistently a factor of counter-revolution?'[64]

And in fact according to Deutscher at the end of the Second World War the revolution expanded into many countries, engulfing hundreds of millions of people:

'To Eastern Europe revolution was to be brought, in the main, "from above and not from outside" – by conquest and occupation; while in China it was to rise not as a proletarian democracy, spreading from the cities to the country, but as a gigantic *jacquerie* conquering the cities from the country and only subsequently passing from the "bourgeois democratic" to the socialist phase.'[65]

Accepting the international revolutionary role of the Russian state makes it an easy step to the conclusion that the struggle of the Powers in the Cold War is the main, or perhaps only, arena of struggle between socialism and capitalism. Deutscher informs us that from now on '. . . the class struggle, suppressed at the level on which it had been traditionally waged, would be fought at a different level and in different forms, as rivalry between power blocs and as cold war.'[66]

What role in **this** class-struggle can the workers play? How many H-bombs or sputniks have they? Compare Deutscher's conception of the socialist revolution with what Marx and Engels said of it. **The Communist Manifesto** states:

'All previous historical movements were movements of minorities or in the interests of minorities. The proletarian movement is the self-conscious independent movement of the immense majority, in the interest of the immense majority.'

Again in September 1879, Engels wrote, in Marx's name and his own, to the leaders of the German Socialist Party:

'For almost forty years we have stressed the class struggle as the immediate driving force of history, and in particular the class struggle between the bourgeoisie and the proletariat as the great lever of the modern social revolution; it is therefore impossible for us to cooperate with people who wish to expunge this class struggle from the movement. When the International was formed we expressly formulated the battle-cry: the emancipation of the working class must be achieved by the working class itself. We cannot therefore cooperate with people who say that the workers are too uneducated to emancipate themselves and must first be freed from above by philanthropic bourgeois and petty bourgeois.'

Today we should have to add to 'philanthropic bourgeois and petty bourgeois' also totalitarian despots.

### Posthumous Victory

Deutscher informs us that Mao's 'attitude in 1925-7 had often coincided with Trotsky's'[67] and Mao's rise to power was a final victory for Trotskyism: 'This, the "Chinese October" was, in a sense, yet another of Trotsky's posthumous triumphs.'[68]

If this were true it would mean that *jacqueries* could carry out the socialist revolution. Fantastic! Neither Marx nor Engels, Lenin nor Trotsky, nor for that matter any other Marxist, ever thought the peasantry socialist, collectivist. The peasants can be active in the struggle against feudalism, but this does not make them socialists. The October revolution was the fusion of two revolutions: that of the socialist working class, the product of mature capitalism, and that of the peasants, the product of the conflict between rising capitalism and the old feudal institutions. As at all times, the peasants were ready enough to expropriate the private property of the large estate owners, but they wanted their own small **private** properties. Whilst they were prepared to revolt against feudalism, they were not for that reason in favour of socialism.

To support his view, Deutscher distorts the historical record. Harold Isaacs in his book on the history of the Chinese revolution, to which Trotsky wrote an introduction, said the following about Mao's attitude in 1925-7:

'In Wuhan Mao had served as head of the Peasant Department of the Kuomintang, and there had carried out the policy of keeping the peasants in check while the counter-revolution advanced upon them.'[69]

Similar information is given by M. N. Roy who was the Comintern representative in China in 1937.[70] Again, the fact that Mao's **Selected Works** includes only one entry written prior to March 1927 says much about his role in the defeated revolution, for, as editor of a weekly paper for about four years before 1927, he must certainly have written more than one short article.

Trotsky too did not speak very favourably of Mao. Thus in November 1929 he criticised the peasant armies of Chu Teh and Mao for carrying out 'adventurous campaigns' in which 'the perspectives of a terrific debacle and of an adventuristic degeneration of the remnants of the Communist Party' were inherent.[71]

In November 1930 Trotsky wrote:

'The peasant war may support the dictatorship of the proletariat, if they coincide in point of time, but under no circumstances can it be substituted for the dictatorship of the proletariat.'[72]

Time did not improve matters according to Isaacs. In 1936,

'Mao Tse-tung far outstripped the opportunism of Chen Tu-hsiu (during 1925–27 – TC).'[73]

If Trotsky was never complimentary to Mao, neither was Mao to Trotsky or the Trotskyists. Thus in May 1937 he referred to the Trotskyists as 'jackals of Japanese imperialism.'[74]

And the **Fourth International,** organ of the American Trotskyist organisation, showed how Mao's thoughts were put into practice.[75] Speaking of the Trotskyists in Mao's Eighth Route Army, the Report states: 'But as soon as they were discovered, they were shamefully shot, one after another.' The Report continues by describing how Cheong Li Ming, Trotskyist commander of 2,000 guerillas in Eastern Chekiang was caught by the Stalinists and beheaded, how his wife was shot together with other Trotskyist captives, and how his six-year-old son was drowned in the sea.

The record does not tally with Deutscher's conclusions. To underline the point, practically the last political act of Natalia Sedova, Trotsky's widow, was to write a letter in **Azione Communista** in November 1961, refuting the idea that Mao Tse-tung was in any sense Trotsky's heir, and asserting that Russia and China were as far from socialism as Franco's Spain.

### From Illusions Regarding the Autocrat to Opposition to Popular Revolution

The belief that the death of an autocrat will bring **great,** fundamental changes in the whole system, are deeply rooted in slave or serf mentality. One need but remember the dreams born with the death of Tsar Nikolai I and the succession of his son Alexander II, in 1855. One of Alexander's first pronouncements was a declaration of his intention to abolish serfdom, which in 1861 he duly carried out.

However the emancipation of the serfs was carried out half-heartedly, and it did not turn them into really free wage workers, but in fact left the peasants with less land and a heavier economic burden to bear.

Following upon the emancipation of the serfs, Alexander implemented some other reforms:

(1) On 1 January 1864, he granted local government to the provinces and districts of European Russia.

(2) On 20 November 1864, he reformed the judicial institutions: trial by jury was introduced for all criminal cases and court proceedings were made public. (And there is no doubt that freedom of expression in the courtroom and the publicity given to trials helped greatly in the formation of democratic anti-tsarist public opinion.)

(3) 6 April 1865 saw the partial abolition of preventive censorship. (One of the results of this was the legal publication in Russian a few years later of Marx's **Capital**.)

That all these democratic reforms were very restricted was soon made quite clear. Thus, for instance, while the press was freed from preventive censorship, it was not allowed to publish accounts of any meetings of societies and clubs without special permission from the Provincial Governors; the Ministry of the Interior was empowered to inform editors of papers what subjects were 'unsuitable' and were of 'State significance'. The Tsarist police soon showed an iron hand. Many a radical was incarcerated.

In the first flush of Alexander II's promises of reform, many were eager to believe in his words. Thus Alexander Herzen, the founder and leader of Populism, prepared a banquet for all the Russians in London in honour of the Tsar's Manifesto of 19 February, 1861 abolishing serfdom. He drafted a speech, in which he recalled how in 1853, when the first page of the 'Free Russian Press' had been printed, if anyone had said that 'after eight years we should have come together, and the hero of the banquet would have been the Tsar of Russia, we should have thought that he was mad, or even worse.' And yet this was what had happened. True, 'the Manifesto of 19 February was only one milestone; the road was still long, and the coach was still in the hands of cruel Tartar and German drivers . . . In Russia it is impossible to denounce their intrigues, Speech has not yet been freed, and is still a slave of the censorship.' And so it was necessary to continue working abroad. But the fact remained that serfdom had been abolished in Russia. 'Let us raise our glasses to drink to our brothers who have been freed, and to honour Alexander Nikolaevich, their liberator.' But this toast was never drunk. The first bloody encounters in Warsaw, a few days after the emancipation, showed that the political oppression of the Russian Empire was still too serious for Herzen to be able to drink freely to Alexander II. 'Our banquet was sad. We lowered our hands. After the blood spilt at Warsaw it could no longer proceed.'[76]

Deutscher is a puny figure compared to Herzen. The blood of workers spilt in Budapest does not prevent him from proceeding with his toast to Kruschev. Deutscher opposed **all** the popular uprisings in Eastern Europe, from June 1953 in East Germany, to October 1956 in Poland and Hungary. He declared the latter to be counter-revolutions trying 'unwittingly to put the clock back.'[77] He cheered the Russian tanks which smashed the workers' uprisings:

'Eastern Europe (Hungary, Poland, and East Germany) . . . found itself almost on the brink of bourgeois restoration at the end of the Stalin era; and only Soviet armed power (or its threat) stopped it there.'[78]

## The Attraction of Deutscherism

The underlying theme of Deutscher's mode of presentation is that the Russian working class and the international working class were not ripe for anything but a passive role in the face of events, and that Stalin had to carry through the 'revolution from above' in

Russia itself (1929–32) and then 'export the revolution' from 1940 onwards. In the future too, it seems, only top people, who can play a decisive role in the cold war, thanks to the concentrated military power they hold, can be active participants in progress. This elitist approach – the assumption, if not spoken, implicit, that socialism can be imposed from above on an unwilling population or on an ignorant people – has a long tradition in the labour movement.[79]

It fits in perfectly with the values spread by all ruling classes, that only top people count. And as the ruling ideology in every society is the ideology of the ruling class, the concept of 'socialism from above' will have the upper hand in the labour movement . . . until the direct revolutionary activity of the masses destroys it along with the society it reflects. Deutscherism is attractive to tired socialists whose belief that the working class could emancipate itself was destroyed by the defeats of the movement in the 1930s and then by the general political apathy of the fifties and sixties. Stalinism, responsible to a large extent for both, becomes the beneficiary . . .

The undoubtedly important changes that have taken place in Russia also aid Deutscherism for a time. If the development from the industrial revolution to the 'welfare state', from the rough, shouting foreman, to the soft-spoken 'human-relations-orientated' personnel officer, from Malthus to Elton Mayo had been compressed into a space of forty years, the reformist illusions held here by Crosland and others – that capitalism has ceased to be capitalism – would be even stronger than they are. And this is basically what has happened in Russia. Kruschev's liberalisation is but a concentrated, less far-reaching reproduction of the process.

Deutscher's thesis that the bureaucracy can produce reforms and even its own self-liquidation, becomes more attractive in proportion to the extent to which it is believed that totalitarianism is and can only be a rigid, unchanging system of government – certainly an unrealistic picture. A comparison of Hitler's Germany with Franco's Spain or Salazar's Portugal shows this. Who could have imagined 120 intellectuals appending their signatures to a declaration against police brutality in breaking strikes in Nazi Germany? Who could have even imagined such strikes under Hitler? Who could have imagined a candidate in elections in Nazi Germany opposing the head of the Government, even if the elections were gerrymandered as they are in Portugal? If fascism has various species, so it seems reasonable to suppose has bureaucratic state capitalism, with its more dynamic political forms. Capitalism in its maturity and old age is different from capitalism in its youth, but it is still capitalism. The change from the rough, shouting foreman to the soft-spoken personnel officer does not abolish alienation nor exploitation, and the subordination of the workers to capital accumulation continues unabated. Kruschev's reforms give the bureaucracy a measure of security, 'normalise' its life, but in no way prevent the ossification of class privileges.

Deutscherism is acceptable to all who defend the *status quo*. The idea that socialism is nationalised property plus Kruschevite liberalisation should be welcome to Moscow apologists. In the West the idea that Stalinism and its natural successor, Kruschevism, are the necessary outcome of the Russian revolution, will also be very welcome, for it can be thrown back in the faces of all fighters for socialism in the West. Above all, the underlying theme in all Deutscher's writing is accommodation to state power. As the whole world lives today in the shadow of the omnipotent, omnipresent state, rising above society and blocking the free development of the members of society, the inclination to accommodation, to giving up the struggle for control over one's destiny, for freedom, is compelling.

### Deutscher and Trotsky

The association of state ownership of industry with the socialist revolution was natural for Trotsky. After all, the nationalisation of industry in Russia was the outcome of the revolution. Furthermore, for generations socialists fighting exploitation had had to combat the owners of private property, the bourgeoisie. And one always tends to see the future in the trappings of the past.

After the Second World War – with nationalised industry in Egypt and Ghana, in East Europe and China (and to a considerable extent in Britain and France), it becomes easier to see that there need not be a correlation between state ownership and proletarian revolution.[80]

Actually there is a dichotomy in Trotsky's views, between his concept of the role of the working class on the one hand, and the role of nationalised property on the other. The former is active, dynamic, revolutionary. Here Trotskyism is the principle of workers' democracy, of the struggle against all bureaucracy, of rank-and-file mass action against privilege. It is the reaffirmation (magnificently adapted to our time in the theory of the Permanent Revolution) of the essentials of Marxism. The central theme of Trotsky's life and struggle to the bitter end was that socialism can be achieved by the workers and not for them. The conception that Russia was a workers' state although the workers play no active role in it, but on the contrary, are objects of its suppression, is totally in contradiction to the first, main element in Trotsky's thought. The identification of the nationalisation of industry with socialism of any sort is formalism, a juridical abstraction, a subordinating of content to form. Unfortunately, many of Trotsky's so-called 'followers' see the main theme – if not the whole of Trotskyism – in the theory that Russia is still a workers' state, because of the nationalisation of industry. They try to stick to every jot and tittle of Trotsky's words, although they would of course be the first to deny that the whole of Leninism is contained in Lenin's criticism of the theory of the

Permanent Revolution. Deutscher follows this logic to the end.

For Deutscher the masses play a passive, secondary, if not a nuisance role, threatening the achievement of the revolution. Deutscher has thrown out the kernel of Trotskyism and kept the husk. His affinity to Trotskyism is fundamentally only extrinsic and verbal. The spirit of Trotsky the fighter is completely missing. Of him Trotsky could well have said: 'I have sown dragon's teeth, and harvested fleas.'

### In the 'Watchtower'

What role remains to our 'critic' of Stalinism?

'It seems that the only dignified attitude the intellectual ex-communist can take is to rise *au-dessus de la melée*. He cannot join the Stalinist camp or the anti-Stalinist Holy Alliance without doing violence to his better self. So let him stay outside any camp. Let him try to regain critical sense and intellectual detachment. Let him overcome the cheap ambition to have a finger in the political pie. Let him be at peace with his own self at least, if the price he has to pay for a phoney peace with the world is self-renunciation and self-denunciation.

'This is not to say that the ex-communist man of letters, or intellectual at large should retire into the ivory tower. (His contempt for the ivory tower lingers in him from his past.) But he may withdraw into a **watchtower** instead. To watch with detachment and alertness this heaving chaos of a world, to be on sharp lookout for what is going to emerge from it, and to interpret it *sine ira et studio* – this is now the only honourable service the ex-communist intellectual can render to a generation in which scrupulous observation and honest interpretation have become so sadly rare.'[81]

Deutscher does not tell us what is the difference **in practice** between inhabiting an ivory tower and a watchtower. In both cases no action is expected. And this is said in the name of Marxism, the science of revolutionary action![82]

How fitting to Deutscher are Trotsky's derogatory remarks regarding Otto Bauer and his friends, 'for whom theoretical analysis consists merely of the learnt commentaries of passivity':[83]

'The essence of their nature is adaptation, yielding to force. They will never make a revolution.'[84]

1. The works of Deutscher referred to are: *Stalin*, Oxford University Press, 1949; *The Prophet Armed*, OUP, 1954; *The Prophet Unarmed*, OUP, 1959; *The Prophet Outcast*, OUP, 1963; *Russia After Stalin*, Hamish Hamilton, 1953; *Heretics And Renegades*, Hamish Hamilton, 1955; *The Great Contest*, OUP, 1960. Only a few of Deutscher's articles have been consulted.

2. *Kapitalismus und Sozialismus nach dem Weltkrieg, Erster Band: Rationalisierung-Fehlrationalisierung*, Otto Bauer, Vienna, 1931, p225. Quoted in 'Prospects for the

Soviet Dictatorship: Otto Bauer', M Croan, in *Revisionism,* Ed. L Labedz, London, 1962, p289.

3. *Ibid,* p223, Labedz, p290.
4. *Zwischen Zwei Weltkriegen?,* Bratislava, pp160–1.
5. *Ibid,* p163.
6. *Ibid,* pp163–4.
7. *Ibid,* p166.
8. *Heretics and Renegades,* pp194–5.
9. *Ibid,* pp204–5.
10. 'Russia in Transition', I Deutscher, *Dissent,* New York, Winter, 1955.
11. *The Great Contest,* p21.
12. *The Prophet Outcast,* p419.
13. *Russia After Stalin,* p164.
14. *Ibid,* p173.
15. *Ibid,* p110.
16. *Marx-Engels Selected Correspondence,* London, 1941, p355.
17. Compare the above with the growth of heavy industry:

|  | First Plan Target | Actual Output 1961 |
|---|---|---|
| Electric Current (milliard kwh) | 22 | 327 |
| Coal (million tons) | 75 | 510 |
| Pig Iron (million tons) | 10 | 50.9 |
| Steel (million tons) | 10.4 | 70.7 |
| Oil (million tons) | 21.7 | 166 |

18. *Vedomosti verkhovnogo soveta SSSR,* Nos. 19, 21, 22 and 27, 1961.
19. 'Town Planning and Housing', T Sosnovy, *Survey,* London, October, 1961.
20. *The Development of Urban Centres in Soviet Russia,* T Sosnovy.
21. *Sovetskie profsoyuzy,* No. 8, 1961, p44.
22. *Pravda,* 14 July 1959.
23. *Pravda,* 15 February 1956.
24. *Pravda,* 25 December 1958.
25. *Pravda,* 13 August 1954.
26. *Pravda,* 6 August 1954.
27. *Pravda,* 13 August 1954.
28. *Industriya,* 18 July 1940.
29. *Voprosy Ekonomiki,* 1936, Nos. 11–12, p109.
30. *Task of Further Development of Industry, Technical Progress and Better Organisation of Production,* N A Bulganin, Moscow, 1955, p21.
31. *Foundations of Economic Accounting,* (Russian), Ya Kronrod, Moscow, 1956, p186.
32. *Trybuna Ludu,* Warsaw, 18 November 1956.
33. *Economic Competition Between the Two World Systems,* (Russian), ed. A M Alekseyev, Moscow, 1957, p118.
34. *Plenum of the Central Committee of the CPSU,* 15–19 December 1958, (Russian), Moscow, 1958, p80.
35. *Mao's China,* Y Gluckstein, London, 1957, pp421–2.
36. *Pravda,* 30 January 1959.
37. *Kommunist Vooruzhennykh Sil,* No. 2, 1962, p19.
38. *The Red Executive,* D Granick, London, 1960, p310.
39. *Sovetskaya Kirghiziya,* 26 February 1960.
40. *Sovetskaya Moldaviya,* 29–30 January 1960.
41. *Pravda Ukrainy,* 17 February 1960.
42. *Zarya Vostoka,* Tbilsi, 28 January 1958.
43. *The Prophet Unarmed,* pviii.
44. *Russia After Stalin,* pp129–30.
45. *Ibid.*
46. *Heretics and Renegades,* p178.
47. *The Times,* 10 July 1957.
48. *The Observer,* 11 November 1945, quoted in 'Deutscher as Historian and Prophet', L Labedz, *Survey,* April 1962, p126.

49. *New Statesman,* 29 June 1957.
50. 29 July 1945, Labedz p136.
51. *Heretics and Renegades,* pp164–5.
52. *The Great Contest,* pp15–16.
53. *The Great Contest,* pp76–77.
54. *Stalin,* p174.
55. *Ibid,* pp174–5.
56. *Ibid,* p175.
57. *The Prophet Armed,* p506.
58. *Stalin,* p176.
59. *The Prophet Armed,* p515.
60. *Ibid,* p293.
61. *Heretics and Renegades,* p89.
62. *Stalin,* p294.
63. *Ibid,* p360–1.
64. *The Prophet Outcast,* p461.
65. *Ibid,* pp257–8.
66. *Ibid,* p518.
67. *The Prophet Outcast,* p32.
68. *Ibid,* p520.
69. *The Tragedy of the Chinese Revolution,* H R Isaacs, London, 1938, p397.
70. *Revolution and Counter-Revolution in China,* M N Roy, Calcutta, 1946, p615.
71. *Problems of the Chinese Revolution,* L Trotsky, New York, 1933, pp233–5.
72. *Ibid,* p239.
73. Isaacs, *op cit,* p440.
74. *Selected Works,* Mao Tse-tung, London, 1954, Vol. I, p264.
75. See the article 'Trotskyism in China. A Report', *Fourth International,* July–August 1947.
76. *Roots of Revolution,* F Venturi, London, 1960, pp108–9.
77. *Universities and Left Review,* Vol I, No. 1, p10.
78. *The Prophet Unarmed,* p462. It is characteristic of Deutscher's attitude to the masses that in the thousands of pages of his writings the term 'workers' control' is mentioned in passing only once, or perhaps twice, and without any enthusiasm! In all the books by Deutscher referred to in this article, the term does not occur once in any index.
79. See 'The Two Souls of Socialism', Hal Draper, *International Socialism,* No. 11, Winter 1962.
80. It is interesting that in the last few days of his life Trotsky came very near to a separation of the two elements. In notes for an article found on his desk he wrote, 'The nationalisation of railways and oil fields in Mexico has of course nothing in common with socialism. It is a measure of state capitalism in a backward country which in this way seeks to defend itself on the one hand against foreign imperialism and on the other against its own proletariat. The management of railways, oil fields, etc., through labour organisations has nothing in common with workers' control over industry, for in the essence of the matter, the management is affected through the labour bureaucracy which is independent of the workers, but in return completely dependent on the bourgeois state. This measure on the part of the ruling class pursues the aim of disciplining the working class, making it more industrious in the service of the common interests of the state, which appear on the surface to merge with the interests of the working class itself.' (*Trade Union in the Epoch of Imperialist Decay,* London, n d, pp14–15.)
81. *Heretics and Renegades,* p20.
82. In the same watchtower spirit, Deutscher argues that it was futile for the Trotskyists in Russia to oppose Stalin. He puts it very neatly: 'It was true that the capitulators to Stalin committed political suicide; but so also did those who refused to capitulate.' (*The Prophet Unarmed,* p451.) Success, comrades, success, that is the main thing!
83. *History of the Russian Revolution,* L Trotsky, London, 1934, p815.
84. *Trotsky's Diary in Exile,* London, 1959, p41.

# Trotsky on substitutionism

TWENTY YEARS ago Trotsky was assassinated. The best tribute one can pay to this great revolutionary, who so despised all cant, would be a critical study of some of his ideas. We offer the following study of one problem he so brilliantly posed as a very young man, a problem that plagued him for the rest of his life, and that is still with us: the problem of the relation between party and class and the danger of the former substituting for the latter.

Quite early in his political activity, when only 24 years old, Trotsky prophesied that Lenin's conception of party organisation must lead to a situation in which the party would '*substitute* itself for the working classes', act as proxy in their name and on their behalf, regardless of what the workers thought or wanted.

Lenin's conception would lead to a state of affairs in which 'The organisation of the party substitutes itself for the party as a whole; then the Central Committee substitutes itself for the organisation; and finally the "dictator" substitutes himself for the Central Committee . . .'[1]

To Lenin's type of centralised party made up of professional revolutionaries, Trotsky counterposed a 'broadly based party' on the model of the Western European Social Democratic parties. He saw the only guarantee against 'substitutionism' – the term he coined – in the mass party, democratically run and under the control of the proletarian masses.

He wound up his argument with the following plea against uniformity: 'The tasks of the new regime will be so complex that they cannot be solved otherwise than by way of competition between various methods of economic and political construction, by way of long "disputes", by way of a systematic struggle not only between the socialist and capitalist worlds, but also many trends inside socialism, trends which will inevitably emerge as soon as the proletarian dictatorship poses tens and hundreds of new . . . problems. No strong "domineering" organisation . . . will be able to suppress these trends and controversies . . . A proletariat capable of exercising its dictatorship over society will not tolerate any dictatorship over itself . . . The working class . . . will undoubtedly have in its ranks quite a few political invalids . . . and much ballast of obsolescent ideas, which it will have to jettison. In the epoch of its dictatorship, as now, it will have to cleanse its mind of false theories and bourgeois experience and to purge its ranks from political phrasemongers and backward-looking revolutionaries . . . But this intricate task cannot be solved by placing above the proletariat a few well-picked people . . . or one person invested with the power to liquidate and degrade.'[2]

In Trotsky's words about the danger of 'substitutionism' inherent in Lenin's conception of party organisation, and his plea against uniformity, one can see his prophetic genius, his capacity to look ahead, to bring into a unified system every facet of life.

The history of Bolshevism since 1917 seems to have completely vindicated Trotsky's warning of 1904. But Trotsky never returned to it again. In the present article we shall try to find out why he did not, to reveal the roots of 'substitutionism' in particular and to look at the problem of the relation between the party and the class in general.

## The Problem of Substitutionism

'Substitutionism' is in the tradition of the Russian revolutionary movement. In the sixties and seventies of the nineteenth century, small groups, mere handfuls, of intellectuals, pitted themselves against the mighty autocracy, while the mass of peasants in whose name and interests these heroic Narodniks (Populists) acted remained indifferent, or even hostile to them.

In the morass of general apathy, before a mass movement of any kind appeared, these mere handfuls of rebellious intellectuals played an important, progressive role. Marx was not the least to accord them the greatest praise and admiration. Thus for instance, he wrote to his eldest daughter, in the very year in which the *People's Will* was crushed: 'These are admirable men, without any melodramatic pose, full of simplicity, real heroes. Making an outcry and taking action are two things completely opposite which cannot be reconciled.'

'Substitutionism', however, becomes a reactionary, dangerous element when a rising mass movement already exists and the party tries to substitute itself for this. Trotsky was too scientific a thinker to believe that in the conception, right or wrong, of the party about its role and its relations with the class, one can find sufficient guarantee against 'substitutionism' and for real democracy in the workers' political movement.

The objective conditions necessary to avoid it were clearly formulated by Trotsky a few months before he wrote the above-quoted work, when he said at the Second Congress of the Russian Social Democratic Workers' Party (London, 1903): 'The rule of the working class was inconceivable until the great mass of them were united in desiring it. Then they would be an overwhelming majority. This would not be the dictatorship of a little band of conspirators or a minority party, but of the immense majority in the interests of the immense majority, to prevent counter-revolution. In short, it would represent the victory of true democracy.'

This paraphrase of the **Communist Manifesto** is absolutely in harmony with Trotsky's struggle against 'substitutionism'. If the majority rules, there is no place for a minority to act as its proxy.

During the same period Lenin was not less emphatic in saying that any dictatorship of the proletariat when this was a small minority in society must lead to anti-democratic and, in his words, 'reactionary conclusions'.

When Trotsky, putting aside his own words, called for a workers' government as an immediate aim of the revolutionary movement in Russia, Lenin answered sharply: 'That cannot be! It cannot be because a revolutionary dictatorship can endure for a time only if it rests on the enormous majority of the people . . . The proletariat constitutes a minority . . . Anyone who attempts to achieve socialism by any other route without passing through the stage of political democracy, will inevitably arrive at the most absurd and reactionary conclusions, both economic and political.'[3]

Trotsky's warning against 'substitutionism' and his emphasis on the rule of 'the immense majority in the interests of the immense majority' as the only guarantee against it is indeed a crying contradiction to his call for a workers' government in 1905 and 1917, when the workers were a tiny minority. Trotsky is torn in the contradiction between his consistent, socialist, democratic conception of opposition to any form of 'substitutionism' and his theory of the Permanent Revolution, in which the proletarian minority acts as a proxy for all the toilers, and as the ruler of society. Alas, this contradiction is not the result of any failure in Trotsky's thinking, of any inconsistency, but is a reflection of actual contradictions in the objective conditions.

The nature of the revolution, including its actual timing, are not dependent on the size of the working class alone and not even on its level of class consciousness and organisation, but on many mixed and contradictory factors. The factors leading to revolution – economic stresses, wars or other political and social upheavals – are not synchronised with the enlightenment of the proletariat. A whole number of objective circumstances impel the workers to revolution, while the unevenness in consciousness of different sections and groups in the working class can be quite marked. In a backward country, as Tsarist Russia was, where the workers' general cultural level was low, and traditions of organisation and mass self-activity weak, this unevenness was particularly marked. And there the working class as a whole was such a small minority that its rule, the dictatorship of the proletariat, had to be the dictatorship not of the majority but of a tiny minority.

To overcome the actual dilemma facing the revolution in Russia – to avoid minority rule on the one hand, and to avoid the passive abstentionist attitude of the Mensheviks ('the proletariat should not take power so long as it is a minority in society') – Trotsky looked to two main factors: the revolutionary impulse and activity of the Russian workers, and the spread of the revolution to more advanced countries where the proletariat made up the majority of society.

However, what was the fate of 'substitutionism' with the decline of the revolutionary impulse in Russia itself, and, not less decisive, with the breaking of the revolutionary struggles in the West on the rocks of capitalism?

### Substitutionism in Russia

While the relation between the party and the class was affected by the level of culture and revolutionary consciousness of the working class it was also influenced by the specific weight of the working class in society: by the size of the class and its relations with other classes, above all – in Russia – with the peasantry.

Now, if the Russian revolution was a simon-pure bourgeois revolution – as the Mensheviks argued – or if it was a simon-pure socialist one – as the anarchists and Social Revolutionaries who did not distinguish between workers and peasants argued – the question would have been simple. A relative social homogeneity of the revolutionary classes would have constituted a large enough anvil on which to batter out of existence any trend toward the Marxist Party substituting for the proletariat.

However, the October revolution was the fusion of two revolutions: that of the socialist working class, the product of mature capitalism, and that of the peasants, the product of the conflict between rising capitalism and the old feudal institutions. As at all times, the peasants were ready enough to expropriate the private property of the large estate owners, but they wanted their own small *private* properties. Whilst they were prepared to revolt against feudalism, they were not for that reason in favour of socialism.

Hence it is not surprising that the victorious alliance of workers and peasants in the October revolution was immediately followed by very strained relations. Once the White armies, and with them the danger of the restoration of landlordism, had been overcome, very little remained of the peasants' loyalty toward the workers. It had been one thing for the peasant to support a government which distributed land, but it was quite another matter when the same government began to requisition his produce to feed the hungry populations in the cities.

The conflict between the working class and the peasantry was expressed from the beginning of the October revolution in the fact that already in 1918 Lenin was compelled to take refuge in the anti-democratic measure of counting one worker's vote as equal to five peasants' in the elections to the Soviets.

Now the revolution itself changed the relative weight of the proletariat vis-à-vis that of the peasantry, to the detriment of the former.

First, the civil war led to a terrible decline in the specific weight of the working class. The working class victory in the revolution led paradoxically to a decline in the size and quality of the working class.

As many of the urban workers had close connections with the villages, considerable numbers of them hurried back to the country-side as soon as the revolution was over, in order to share in the land distribution. This tendency was further encouraged by the food shortage from which, naturally, the towns suffered the most. Moreover, in sharp contrast to the old Tsarist Army, the new Red Army included relatively more industrial workers than peasants. For all these reasons the town population, and particularly the numbers of industrial workers, declined very sharply between 1917 and 1920. The population of Petrograd fell by 57.5 per cent, of Moscow by 44.5 per cent, of 40 provincial capitals by 33 per cent, and of another 50 large towns by 16 per cent. The larger the city the greater was the relative loss in population. How sharp was the decline is further illustrated by the fact that the number of workers in industry fell from 3,000,000 in 1917 to 1,240,000 in 1921–2, a decrease of 58.7 per cent. The number of industrial workers thus declined by three-fifths. And the productivity of these workers declined even more than their number. (In 1920, the industrial production of Russia was only some 13 per cent of that of 1913!)

Of those remaining the big majority were the most backward workers who were not needed for the different military fronts or for the administration of the State, trade unions and party. The State administration and army, naturally, drew most of their recruits from that section of the workers with the oldest social tradition, the greatest political experience and highest culture.

The fragmentation of the working class had an even worse effect. The remainder of the working class was forced by the scarcity of food to behave rather as small, individualist traders than as a collective, as a united class. It has been calculated that in 1919–20 the State supplied only 42 per cent of the grain consumed by the towns, and an even smaller percentage of other foodstuffs, all the rest being bought on the black market.[4] The sale by workers of furniture and clothing, and also belts and tools from factories where they worked, was quite common.[5] What an atomisation and demoralisation of the industrial working class!

In their mode of living – relying on individual illicit trade – the individual workers were hardly distinguishable from the peasants. As Rudzutak put it to the Second Congress of Trade Unions in Janauary 1919: 'We observe in a large number of industrial centres that the workers, thanks to the contraction of production in the factories, are being absorbed in the peasant mass, and instead of a population of workers we are getting a half-peasant or sometimes a purely peasant population.'[6]

Under such conditions the class base of the Bolshevik Party disintegrated – not because of some mistakes in the policies of Bolshevism, not because of one or another conception of Bolshevism regarding the role of the party and its relation to the class – but because of mightier historical factors. The working class had become declassed.

It is true that in despair, or in desperation, Lenin could say in May 1921: 'Even when the proletariat has to live through a period of being declassed, it can still carry out its task of conquering and retaining power.'[7] But what an extremely 'substitutionist' formulation this is! Declassed working class rule – the Cheshire cat's smile after the cat has disappeared!

In the case of the Narodniks, the 'substitutionist' conception was not a primary cause, but a result of the general apathy and stupor of the people which in turn was rooted in objective social conditions. Now again, in the case of Bolshevik 'substitutionism', it did not jump out of Lenin's head as Minerva out of Zeus's, but was born of the objective conditions of civil war in a peasant country, where a small working class declined in weight, became fragmented and dissolved into the peasant masses.

An analogy might help to clarify the rise of 'substitutionism' after the October revolution. One must only imagine a mass strike in which after a prolonged period the majority of the workers become tired and demoralised and only a minority continue to man the picket line, attacked by the boss and derided and resented by the majority of workers. This tragic situation is repeated again and again on the battleground of the class struggle. In the face of the White Guard, with the knowledge that a terrible bloodbath threatened the people if the Bolsheviks gave up the struggle and with the knowledge of their own isolation, the Bolsheviks did not find a way out. 'Substitutionism', like all fetishisms, was a reflection of social impasse.

## Substitutionism in the Party

From here it is a short step to the abolition of inner-party democracy, and the establishment of the rule of officialdom within it.

Contrary to Stalinist mythology – as well as that of the Mensheviks and other opponents of the Bolsheviks – the Bolshevik Party had never been a monolithic or totalitarian party. Far from it. Internal democracy had always been of the utmost importance in party life, but for one reason or another, this has been glossed over in most of the literature dealing with the subject. It is therefore worthwhile to digress somewhat and devote a little space to setting out a number of cases which illustrate the degree of inner-party democracy and the lack of monolithism in the history of Bolshevism.

In 1907, after the final defeat of the revolution, the party suffered a crisis over the question of what attitude to take to the elections to the Tsarist Duma. At the Third Conference of the Russian Social Democratic Workers' Party (held in July 1907), in which Bolsheviks as well as Mensheviks were represented, a curious situation arose: all the Bolshevik delegates, with the sole exception of Lenin, voted in favour of boycotting the elections to the Duma; Lenin voted with the Mensheviks.[8] Three years later, a plenum of the Central Committee of the Bolsheviks passed a resolution calling for unity with the Mensheviks; again the only dissentient voice was Lenin's.[9]

When the 1914–18 war broke out, not one of the party's branches adopted the revolutionary defeatist position which Lenin advocated,[10] and at a trial of some Bolshevik leaders in 1915, Kamenev and two Bolshevik Duma deputies publicly repudiated Lenin's revolutionary defeatist position in court.[11]

After the February revolution the large majority of the party leaders were not for a revolutionary Soviet government, but for support of the Coalition Provisional government. The Bolshevik faction had 40 members in the Petrograd Soviet on 2 March, 1917, but when the resolution to transfer power to the bourgeois coalition government was put to the vote, only 19 voted against.[12] At a meeting of the Petrograd Committee of the Party (5 March, 1917), a resolution for a revolutionary Soviet government received only one vote.[13] **Pravda**, edited by Stalin at that time, had a position which can in no way be called revolutionary. It decisively declared its support for the Provisional Government 'insofar as it struggles against reaction or counter-revolution'.[14]

Again, when Lenin came to Russia on 3 April, 1917, and issued his famous 'April Theses' – a light guiding the party to the October revolution – he was for a time in a small minority in his own party. **Pravda's** comment on the 'April Theses' was that it was 'Lenin's personal opinion', and quite 'unacceptable'.[15] At a meeting of the Petrograd Committee of the party, held on 8 April, 1917, the 'Theses' received only two votes, while thirteen voted against and one abstained.[16] However, at the Conference of the Party held 14–22 April, the 'Theses' gained a majority: 71 for, 39 against and eight abstentions.[17] The same conference defeated Lenin on another important question, viz., whether the party should participate in the proposed Stockholm Conference of the Socialist Parties. Against his views, it decided in favour of full participation.[18]

Again, on 14 September Kerensky convened a 'Democratic Conference' and Lenin spoke strongly in favour of boycotting it. The Central Committee supported him by nine votes to eight, but as the vote was so nearly equal, the final decision was left to the party conference, which was to be constituted out of the Bolshevik faction in the 'Democratic Conference'. This meeting decided by 77 votes to 50 not to boycott it.[19]

When the most important question of all, the question of the October insurrection was the order of the day, the leadership again was found to be sharply divided: a strong faction led by Zinoviev, Kamenev, Rykov, Piatakov, Miliutin and Nogin, opposed the uprising. Nevertheless, when the Political Bureau was elected by the Central Committee, neither Zinoviev nor Kamenev were excluded.

After taking power, the differences in the party leadership continued to be as sharp as before. A few days after the revolution, a number of party leaders came out with a demand for a coalition with other socialist parties. Those insisting on this included Rykov, the People's Commissar of the Interior, Miliutin, the People's Commissar of Industry and Trade, Lunacharsky, the Commissar of Labour, Kamenev, the President of the Republic, and Zinoviev. They went as far as resigning from the government, thus compelling Lenin and his supporters to open negotiations with the other parties. (The negotiations broke down because the Mensheviks insisted on the exclusion of Lenin and Trotsky from the coalition government.)

Again, on the question of holding or postponing the elections to the Constituent Assembly (in December 1917), Lenin found himself in a minority in the Central Committee, and the elections were held against his advice.[20] A little later he was again defeated on the question of the peace negotiations with Germany at Brest-Litovsk. He was for an immediate peace. But at a meeting of the Central Committee and active workers, held on 21 January, 1918, his motion received only fifteen votes against Bukharin's motion for 'revolutionary war', which received 32 votes, and Trotsky's, for 'neither peace nor war', which received sixteen.[21] At a session of the Central Committee next day, Lenin was again defeated. But at last he succeeded, under the pressure of events, in convincing the majority of members of the Central Committee of his point of view, and at its session on 24 February, his motion for peace gained seven votes, while four voted against and another four abstained.[22]

However, inner-party democracy dwindled under the pressure of the objective circumstances referred to above. Isolated, the party became frightened to think aloud, to voice disagreements. It was as if they were in a small rickety boat in the midst of rapids. The atmosphere of free discussion necessarily died.

The breaches of inner-party democracy became worse and worse. Thus, K. K. Yurenev, for example, spoke at the Ninth Congress (April 1920) of the methods used by the Central Committee to suppress criticism, including the virtual exile of the critics: 'One goes to Christiana, another sent to the Urals, a third – to Siberia.'[23] He said that in its attitude toward the party, the Central Committee had become 'not accountable Ministry, but unaccountable government'. At the same Congress, V. N. Maximovsky counterposed 'democratic centralism' to the 'bureaucratic centralism' for which the Centre was responsible. 'It is said,' he commented, 'that fish begin to rot from the head. The party begins to suffer at the top from the influence of bureaucratic centralism.'[24] And Sapronov declared: 'However much you talk about electoral rights, about the dictatorship of the proletariat, on the yearning of the Central Committee for the party dictatorship, in fact this leads to the dictatorship of the party bureaucracy.'[25]

At the Eleventh Congress, Riazanov said: 'Our Central Committee is altogether a special institution. It is said that the English parliament is omnipotent: it is only unable to change a man into a woman. Our Central Committee is more powerful: it has already changed more than one very revolutionary man into an old lady and the number of these old ladies has increased incredibly.'[26] He further accused it of intervening in all aspects of party life. V. Kosior gave many examples of local leaders both of the party and of the trade unions being removed by decisions of the Political Bureau or the Orgbureau: 'Many workers are leaving the party. How to explain this? This, dear comrades, is to be explained by the strong hand regime, which has nothing in common with real party discipline and which is cultivated among us. Our party carries wood, sweeps the streets and even votes, but decides no questions. But the not very healthy proletariat finds itself in these surroundings, and cannot stand it.'[27]

At the Twelfth Congress Preobrazhensky complained that 30 per cent of the secretaries of the gubernia party committees were 'recommended' for the positions by the Central Committee of the party, thus violating the principle of election of all party officials.[28] From here it was but a step to the supreme rule of the General Secretary.

One can say without hesitation that the substitution of a ruling working class for a capitalist class – where capitalism was in its infancy and where the majority of the people were small capitalists (peasants) – was the cause of the substitution of the Marxist party for the working class, and that this led to the substitution of the officialdom for the party, and finally to the individual dictatorship of the General Secretary.

Marx and Engels dealt more than once with the question of what would happen if the working class took power before the historical prerequisites for the substitution of capitalist relations of production by socialist ones were present. They concluded that in such an event the working class would blaze a path for developing capitalism. Engels wrote: 'The worst thing that can befall a leader of an extreme party is to be compelled to take over a government in an epoch when the movement is not yet ripe for the domination of the class which he represents and for the realisation of the measures which that domination would imply . . . he necessarily finds himself in a dilemma. What he *can* do is in contrast to all his actions as hitherto practised, to all his principles and to the present interests of his party; what he *ought* to do cannot be achieved. In a word he is compelled to represent not his party nor his class, but the class for whom conditions are ripe for domination. In the interests of the movement itself, he is compelled to defend the interests of an alien class, and to feed his own class with phrases and promises, with the assertion that the interests of that alien class are their own interests. Whoever puts himself in this awkward position is irrevocably lost.'[29]

Only the expansion of the revolution could have spared Bolshevism from this tragic fate. And on this probability Bolshevism hinged its fate. Only abstentionists and cowards could advise the Bolsheviks not to go to the limit of the revolutionary potentialities of the Russian proletariat for fear of finding themselves at the end of the cul-de-sac. Revolutionary dynamism and international perspectives beat in the heart of Bolshevism.

### The Inherent Danger of Substitutionism

However, if the State built by the Bolshevik Party reflected not only the will of the party but of the total social reality in which the Bolsheviks in power found themselves, one should not draw the conclusion that there was no causal connection at all between Bolshevik centralism based on hierarchy of professional revolutionaries and the Stalinism of the future. Let us look at this question somewhat more closely.

The fact that a revolutionary party is at all needed for the socialist revolution shows that there is an unevenness in the level of culture and consciousness of different sections and groups of workers. If the working class were ideologically a homogeneous class there would not have been any need for leadership. Alas, the revolution would not wait until all the masses had reached a certain intellectual level, or level of class consciousness. Oppressed by capitalism, materially as well as spiritually, different sections of the workers show different levels of class independence. If not for this difference in consciousness among different sections of the working class, the capitalist class in the advanced countries would hardly find any social basis for itself. Under such conditions the class struggle would be the smoothest act of gradual progress. There would indeed scarcely be any class struggle to speak of: instead of which workers face the antagonism of other workers – the threat of strike-breakers (workers) and policemen and soldiers (workers in uniform). If the working class were homogeneous there would not be the need for a workers' state either: after the revolution, the power of coercion would be unnecessary. Alas, the revolution has nothing in common with such anarchist-liberal day-dreaming. Working-class discipline presumes, under capitalism and immediately after the proletarian revolution, not only the existence of more advanced and less advanced workers, i.e. the existence of leadership, but also the combination of conviction and coercion – the working class cannot free itself by a stroke from the birthmarks of capitalist barbarism.

Under capitalism discipline confronts the worker as an external coercive power, as the power which capital has over him. Under socialism discipline will be the result of consciousness, it will become the habit of a free people. In the transition period it will be the outcome of the unity of the two elements – consciousness and coercion. Collective ownership of the means of production by the workers, i.e. the ownership by the workers' state of the means of production, will be the basis for the conscious element in labour discipline. At the same time the working class as a collective, through its institutions – soviets, trade unions, etc. – will appear as a coercive power as regards the disciplining of the individual workers in production.

This conflict between the individual and the collective, the necessity of uniting conviction with its ugly opposite, coercion, the compulsion on the working class to use barbaric methods remaining from capitalism to fight capitalist barbarism, is but another affirmation that the workers are not liberated spiritually under capitalism, and would take a whole historical period to grow to full human stature. Agreeing with the anarchists that the state, even the workers' state, is an ugly offspring of class society and that real human history will start only by having a really consistent workers' state, it is nonetheless only on this basis that the state will ultimately wither away.

The fact that the working class needs a party or parties is in itself a proof of the cleavages in the working class. The more backward culturally, the weaker the organisation and self-administration of the workers generally, the greater will be the intellectual cleavage between the class and its Marxist party. From this unevenness in the working class flows the great danger of an autonomous development of the party and its machine till it becomes, instead of the servant of the class, its master. This unevenness is a main source of the danger of 'substitutionism'.

The history of Bolshevism prior to the revolution is eloquent with Lenin's struggle against this danger. How often he appealed to the mass of the workers – especially in the stormy months of 1917 – against the vacillating, compromising party leadership and its machine. As Trotsky so correctly summed up the inter-relation between Lenin, the masses and the party machine: 'Lenin was strong not only because he understood the laws of the class struggle but also because his ear was faultlessly attuned to the stirrings of the masses in motion. He represented not so much the party machine as the vanguard of the proletariat. He was definitely convinced that thousands from amongst those workers who had borne the brunt of supporting the underground party would now support him. The masses at the moment were more revolutionary than the party, and the party more revolutionary than its machine. As early as March the actual attitude of the workers and soldiers had in many cases become stormily apparent, and it was widely at variance with the instructions issued by all the parties, including the Bolshevik . . . On the other hand, the authority of the party machine, like its conservatism, was only in the making at that time. Lenin exerted influence not so much as an individual but because he embodied the influence of the class on the party and of the party on its machine.'[30]

Men make history, and if these men organised in a party have a greater impact on history than their relative number warrants, nevertheless they alone do not make history, and for better or worse, they alone are not the cause of their greater specific weight, neither of the general history of the class nor even of themselves in this class. In the final analysis, the only weapons to fight the 'substitutionism' of the revolutionary party for the class, and hence the transformation of the former into a conservative force, is the activity of the class itself, and its pressure not only against its social enemy, but also against its own agent, its party.

This is not the place to point out how far Trotsky in practice went in turning a necessity into a virtue, to what extremes of generalisation he turned to justify anti-democratic, anti-working class, 'substitutionist' practices.

It is enough to mention his arguments in 1921 for the 'militarisation of labour' – compulsory labour imposed by the state. The trade unions, he said, should be statified. We need 'a new type of trade unionist, the energetic and imaginative economic organiser who will approach economic issues not from the angle of distribution and consumption but from that of expanding production, who will view them not with the eyes of somebody accustomed to confront the Soviet government with demands and to bargain, but with the eyes of the true economic organiser'.[31] What about the defence of workers from the state, even from the workers state? Can the trade unions neglect this? Trotsky did not answer the question, did not even pose it. 'Militarisation', he said at the Ninth Congress, 'is unthinkable without the militarisation of the trade unions as such, without the establishment of a regime in which every worker feels himself a soldier of labour, who cannot dispose of himself freely; if the order is given to transfer him, he must carry it out; if he does not carry it out, he will be a deserter who is punished. Who looks after this? The trade union. It creates the new regime. This is the militarisation of the working class.'[32]

To cap his 'substitutionist' attitude, Trotsky went as far as to say in 1924: 'None of us desires or is able to dispute the will of the party. The party in the last analysis is always right, because the party is the single historical instrument given to the proletariat for the solution of its basic problems. I have already said that in front of one's own party nothing could be easier than to acknowledge a mistake, nothing easier than to say: 'All my criticisms, my statements, my warnings, my protests – the whole thing was simply a mistake. I cannot say that, however, comrades, because I do not think it. I know that one must not be right *against* the party. One can be right only with the party, and through the party, for history has no other road for being in the right. The English have a saying: "my country – right or wrong". With far more historical justification we may say: my party – in certain concrete cases – right or wrong . . . And if the party adopts a decision which one or another of us thinks unjust, he will say: Just or unjust it is my party, and I shall support the consequences of the decision to the end.'[33]

### Substitutionism Today

As a point of departure for an evaluation of the role of the revolutionary party in its relation to the working class, we cannot but return to the **Communist Manifesto's** statement: 'All previous historical movements were movements of minorities or in the interests of minorities. The proletarian movement is the self-conscious independent movement of the immense majority, in the interests of the immense majority.' From the much higher cultural level of the workers in the industrial countries than in Russia, their greater self-reliance and organisational habits and the relatively greater social homogeneity of the mass of the toilers in these countries (not engulfed by hordes of peasants) one may deduce that prior to the revolution, during it and after its victory, the unevenness in consciousness of the masses will be much smaller than it was in Russia, although it will not have disappeared completely.

From this a number of conclusions may be drawn.

First, about the size of the revolutionary party as compared with that of the working class as a whole. In October 1906 the Russian Social Democratic Workers' Party (including both Bolshevik and Menshevik factions) numbered 70,000. At the same time the Jewish *Bund* numbered 33,000, the Polish Social Democrats 28,000 and the Lettish Social Democrats 13,000. Altogether then, the *illegal* Socialist parties numbered 144,000.[34] In August 1917 the Bolshevik Party had 200,000 members. On the average, in 25 towns 5.4 per cent of the industrial workers were members of the Bolshevik Party.[35] If the proportion of party members among the working class were the same in the advanced countries as it was in 1917, or

1905, in Russia, the party would have to have millions of members.

Because the unevenness in consciousness and culture is smaller in the advanced countries than it was in Russia, the relative size of the party should be even larger than it was in Russia. (The legality of the workers' parties, also contributes to this.) Anyone who draws the opposite conclusion from the *actual* size of the reformist parties does not understand the real role of the masses in the revolutionary struggle. The reformist party is in the main an apparatus for attracting votes in parliamentary and other elections. Hence it does not need a really active mass membership. On the whole the supporters of such a party do not find it necessary to join it actively, or to read its press. Active support of masses for a revolutionary party must lead to a comparatively much greater number of workers joining it.

From this it is clear that little groups cannot in any way substitute for the mass revolutionary party, not to say for the mass of the working class.[36]

Now what about the relation between the revolutionary party and the class?

Every party, whether reformist or revolutionary, whether conservative or liberal, aims to get support in order to lead towards one aim or another. The revolutionary workers' party also aims to lead. But here the similarity stops. The methods by which this leadership is established and the nature of the leadership are totally different.

One can visualise three kinds of leadership that, for lack of better names we shall call: those of the teacher, the foreman and the companion in struggle. The first kind of leadership shown by small sects is 'blackboard socialism' (in Britain an extreme example of this sort is the SPGB) in which didactic methods take the place of participation in struggle. The second kind, with foreman-worker or officer-soldier relations, characterises all bureaucratic reformist and Stalinist parties: the leadership sits in a caucus and decides what they will tell the workers to do, without the workers actively participating. What characterises both these kinds of leadership is the fact that directives go only one way: the leaders conduct a monologue with the masses.

The third kind of leadership is analogous to that between a strike committee and the workers on strike, or a shop steward and his mates. The revolutionary party must conduct a dialogue with the workers outside it.[37] The party, in consequence, should not invent tactics out of thin air, but put as its first duty to *learn* from the experience of the mass movement and then generalise from it. The great events of working-class history have shown the correctness of this emphasis beyond all measure of doubt. The workers of Paris in 1871 established a new form of state – a state without a standing army and bureaucracy, where all officials received the average worker's salary, with the right of recall of all officials, etc., *before* Marx began to generalise about the nature and structure of a workers' state. Again, the workers of Petrograd, in 1905, established a Soviet independently of the Bolshevik Party, actually in opposition to the local Bolshevik leadership and in face of at least suspicion, if not animosity, on the part of Lenin himself. Therefore one cannot but agree with Rosa Luxemburg when she wrote in 1904: 'The main characteristics of the tactics of struggle of Social Democracy are not "invented", but are the result of a continuous series of great creative acts of elementary class struggle. Here also the unconscious precedes the conscious, the logic of the objective historical process comes before the subjective logic of its bearer.'[38]

The role of Marxists is to generalise the living, evolving experience of the class struggle, to give a conscious expression to the instinctive drive of the working class to reorganise society on a socialist basis.

Because the working class is far from being monolithic, and because the path to socialism is uncharted, wide differences of strategy and tactics can and should exist in the revolutionary party. The alternative is the bureaucratised party or the sect with its 'leader'. Here one cannot but regret Trotsky's sweeping statement that 'any serious factional fight in a party is always in the final analysis a reflection of the class struggle'.[39] This verges on a vulgar materialist interpretation of human thought as growing directly out of material conditions! What class pressures separated Lenin from Luxemburg, or Trotsky from Lenin (1903–1917), or what change in class pressures can one see in Plekhanov's zigzags: with Lenin in 1903, against him in 1903, against him in 1905, with him again (and at last breaking, it is true, with Lenin and with the revolutionary movement and joining the class enemy)? Can the differences in the theory of imperialism between Lenin and Luxemburg be derived from an analysis of their position in class society? Scientific socialism must live and thrive on controversy. And scientists who start off with the same basic assumptions, and then use the same method of analysis, do differ in all fields of research.

In order that the party should be able to conduct a dialogue with the masses, it is necessary not only that the party have confidence in the tremendous abilities of the working class in action, but also that the party understand correctly the situation in the country and the conditions of the working class, materially and morally. Any self-deceit on its part must cut short the dialogue and turn it into a boring monologue.

The party has to be subordinated to the whole. And so the internal regime in the revolutionary party must be subordinated to the relation between the party and the class. The managers of factories can discuss their business in secret and then put before the workers a *fait accompli*. The revolutionary party that seeks to overthrow capitalism cannot accept the notion of a discussion on policies inside the party without the participation of the mass of the workers – policies which are then brought 'unanimously' ready-made to the class. Since the revolutionary party cannot have interests apart from the class, all the party's issues of policy are those of the class, and they should therefore be thrashed out in the open, in its presence. The freedom of discussion which exists in the factory meeting which aims at unity of action after decisions are taken, should apply to the revolutionary party. This means that all discussions on basic issues of policy should be discussed in the light of day: in the open press. Let the mass of the workers take part in the discussion, put pressure on the party, its apparatus and leadership.[40]

Above all, the revolutionary party should follow the guide of the **Communist Manifesto** when it says: 'In what relation do the Communists stand to the proletarians as a whole? The Communists do not form a separate party opposed to other working class parties. They have no interests separate and apart from the proletariat as a whole. They do not set up any sectarian principles of their own, by which to shape and mould the proletarian movement. The Communists are distinguished from other working-class parties by this only:

(1) In the national struggles of the proletarians of the different countries, they point out and bring to the front the common interests of the entire proletariat, independently of all nationality.

(2) In the various stages of development which the struggle of the working class against the bourgeoisie has to pass through, they always and everywhere represent the interests of the movement as a whole.

The Communists, therefore, are on the one hand, practically, the most advanced and resolute section of the working-class parties of every country, that section which pushes forward all others: on the other hand, theoretically, they have over the great mass of the proletariat the advantage of clearly understanding the line of march, the conditions, and the ultimate general results of the proletarian movement.'

The *whole* of the working class will have to mix its level of consciousness and organisation, through a prolonged struggle, including a struggle of ideas. As Marx said to revolutionaries who flattered the German workers in his time: 'While we say to the workers: you have 15 or 20 years of bourgeois and national wars to go through, not merely to alter conditions but to alter yourselves and make yourselves fit to take political power, you tell them on the contrary that they must take over political power at once or abandon all hope.'

1. N Trotsky, *Nashi Politicheskye Zadachi*, Geneva 1904, p54.
2. *Ibid*, p105, quoted in I Deutscher, *The Prophet Armed*, London 1954, pp92–3.
3. V I Lenin, *Sochenenya*, ix, p14.
4. L Kritsman, *Geroicheskii Period Velikoi Russkoi Revolutsii*, Moscow 1924(?), pp133–6.

5. *Chetvertye Vserossiikii Sezd Professionalnykh Soyuzov,* Vol 1, 1921, pp66, 119.
6. *Vtoroi Vserossiikii Sezd Professionalnykh Soyuzov,* 1921, p138.
7. V I Lenin, *Sochenenya,* xxvi, p394.
8. vKP *(b) v Rezoliutsiakh,* 4th ed, Vol 1, p126.
9. *Ibid,* 6th ed, Vol 1, pp154–60.
10. L Trotsky, *History of the Russian Revolution,* London 1932, Vol 1, p59.
11. *Ibid,* and Lenin, *Sochinenya,* xxi, p432.
12. A Shliapnikov, *The Year Seventeen,* in Russian, Moscow 1924, Vol 1, p197.
13. A S Bubnov and others, vPK *(b),* Moscow-Leningrad 1931, p113.
14. *Pravda,* 15 March 1917, quoted in Trotsky, *op cit,* p305.
15. *Pravda,* 8 April 1917.
16. Bubnov, *op cit,* p114.
17. vKP *(b) v Rezoliutsiakh,* 4th ed, Vol 1, p258.
18. V I Lenin, *Sochinenya,* 3rd ed, xx, p652.
19. *Ibid,* xxi, p526.
20. L Trotsky, *Stalin,* London 1947, pp341–2.
21. Bubnov, *op cit,* p511.
22. *Ibid,* p512.
23. *9 Sezd* RKP *(b),* p52.
24. *Ibid,* pp62–3.
25. *Ibid,* pp56–7.
26. *11 Sezd* RKP *(b),* p83.
27. *Ibid,* p134.
28. *12 Sezd* RKP *(b),* p133.
29. F Engels, *The Peasant War in Germany,* London 1927, pp135–6.
30. L Trotsky, *Stalin,* London 1947, p204. It is sad to point out that when Trotsky dealt with the question of the dangers of bureaucratic conservatism in the Trotskyist organisations he pooh-poohed the idea, taking flight in a simplicist materalist interpretation of bureaucratism. When J P Cannon, the American Trotskyist leader, was accused of bureaucratic conservatism, Trotsky said that the accusation was 'a bare psychological abstraction insofar as no specific social interests are shown underlying this "conservatism".' (L Trotsky, *In Defense of Marxism,* New York, 1942, p81.) What 'special social interests' were underlying the 'Committee-men' of pre-1917, of which Stalin was the archetype? This Trotsky did not try to show – quite rightly – in his last work, *Stalin,* whose central theme is the conservative, anti-democratic nature of the 'Committee-men'.
31. Trotsky quoted in L Deutscher, *Soviet Trade Unions,* London 1950, p42.
32. *9 Sezd* RKP *(b),* p101.
33. *13 Sezd* RKP *(b),* pp165–6. Trotsky's and Lenin's attitude to the Kronstadt rebellion is often quoted by Mensheviks, anarchists and also some other left critics of Trotsky and Lenin as an example of bureaucratic oppression. Actually the main aspect of Kronstadt was a peasant and semi-peasant rebellion against the towns. Hence all the inner-party oppositions – including the Workers' Opposition of Shliapnikov and Kollontai – took an active part in its suppression, and in its footsteps came the policy of concessions to petty capitalism, to the peasantry – the NEP. However the question of Kronstadt as well as the different opposition groups which existed prior to Trotsky's going into opposition and which in 1923 joined him under his leadership is a fascinating study which deserves a separate study.
34. V I Lenin, *Sochinenya,* x, p483.
35. *6 Sezd* RKP *(b),* Moscow 1958, p390.
36. Nobody in Russia doubted that Trotsky's group alone – the *Mezhrayonka* – which in August 1917 had some 4,000 members was much too small to be able seriously to affect the march of events. Similarly one can understand Trotsky when in 1921 he referred to the Communist Workers' Party of Germany (KAPD) as being slight: 'no more than 30,000–40,000' members (L Trotsky, *The First Five Years of the Communist International,* London 1953, Vol 2, p26).
37. Rosa Luxemburg put it thus: 'Of course through the theoretical analysis of the social conditions of struggle, Social Democracy has introduced the element of

consciousness into the proletarian class struggle to an unprecedented degree; it gave the class struggle its clarity of aim; it created, for the first time, a permanent mass workers' organisation, and thus built a firm backbone for the class struggle. However, it would be catastrophically wrong for us to assume that from now on all the historical initiative of the people has passed to the hands of the Social Democratic organisation alone, and that the unorganised mass of the proletariat has turned into a formless thing, into the deadweight of history. On the contrary, the popular masses continue to be the living matter of world history, even in the presence of Social Democracy; and only if there is blood circulation between the organised nucleus and the popular masses, only if one heartbeat vitalises the two, can Social Democracy prove that is it capable of great historical deeds.' (*Leipziger Volkszeitung,* June 1913, pp26–8.)

38. *Die Neue Zeit,* 1904, p491.
39. L Trotsky, *In Defense of Marxism,* New York 1942, p60.
40. Some cases of secrecy are justified and every worker will understand this. Just as factory meetings can be closed to the capitalists and their newspapermen and other agents, so there are moments in the life of a revolutionary party which have to be kept secret. But in all cases the party should be able to justify this to the workers and convince them that no basic decisions of policy are being hidden from them.

# Labour's addiction to the rubber stamp

RALPH MILLIBAND, in his book on the Labour Party, points out:
'Of political parties claiming socialism to be their aim, the Labour Party has always been one of the most dogmatic – not about socialism, but about the parliamentary system. Empirical and flexible about all else, its leaders have always made devotion to that system their fixed point of reference and the conditioning factor of their political behaviour . . .

'The leaders of the Labour Party have always rejected any kind of political action (such as industrial action for political purposes) which fell, or which appeared to them to fall, outside the framework and conventions of the parliamentary system. The Labour Party has not only been a parliamentary party; it has been a party deeply imbued by parliamentarism. And in this respect, there is no distinction to be made between Labour's political and industrial leaders. Both have been equally determined that the Labour Party should not stray from the narrow path of parliamentary politics.' (**Parliamentary Socialism**, p. 13.)

A number of historical factors have conditioned the mass of British workers to accept parliamentarism. Above all, parliament, for over a century, has been at the centre of reforms granted to the workers.

## Competition

All through the nineteenth and well into the twentieth centuries, the typical employer was a great deal smaller than he is today. And the market in which he sold his goods was extremely competitive. Not only were firms much smaller in size than today, but there were far more of them in any particular line of production. Being small, and being in fierce competition amongst themselves, these firms could not on the whole afford individually to pay their workers more or grant them greater concessions than their competitors. An employer who granted his workers very much more than his competitors ran the risk of putting himself out of business.

The economy was subject to a cycle of booms and deep slumps and the heavy unemployment characteristic of this earlier stage in the capitalist economy provided employers with a reserve army of unemployed workers. In this situation, the employers felt no especially strong need to compete with each other for labour by offering their workers a little more to stay with them. And, to a greater extent than today, workers' skills (or lack of skills) were more transferable between factories and industries. This was true of skilled and unskilled workers alike.

When the employers were forced to grant reforms to the workers, they tended to do this all together and all at once through such agencies as parliament. The nineteenth century and the early twentieth century were the great periods of reforms won for workers through parliament. It was through national agitation and propaganda, focused on the parliamentary centre, that workers made many of their gains through their representatives (or their misrepresentatives!). When, to avoid worse trouble, the employers paid out for these reforms, they applied to all workers equally, and the cost of them was borne by employers equally. In this way no employer was put at a competitive disadvantage with his rivals.

So long as sharp competition between workers for scarce jobs and cut-throat competition between capitalists were predominant features of the economy, reforms through parliament were central to workers' lives.

Over the last two decades the situation has changed. The typical employer of today is a great deal bigger and there are far fewer employers. As firms have grown in size their monopoly control over the market has increased and competition, in the national market at least, has become much less cut-throat. Because of their size, and because they are less afraid of their competitors than they were, they are more ready to grant reforms to their workers one at a time and on their own.

### Shortage

Also, with some exceptions in backward areas like Northern Ireland, the British economy since the beginning of the Second World War has had almost full employment and today there is a shortage of workers. With the virtual disappearance of the reserve army of the unemployed, labour has become a scarce commodity – and the employers are worried about recruiting and keeping their workers.

Machinery and technical processes in factories nowadays are a great deal more expensive than in the past and far more complicated. Because of technical changes, in many industries – and especially in the new, fast-growing and technologically advanced industries – it is becoming increasingly expensive to train workers and increasingly expensive to lose them. The employers hate labour turnover today almost as much as they hate strikes.

The workers therefore turn their attention and their militancy toward the shop floor, which is the most important area where wage gains and fringe benefits can be won, and away from parliament, which has ceased to be a central locus of reform.

### Indifference

The workers have become more and more indifferent towards parliament. A Gallup Poll showed that many people do not know who George Brown is: some think he is a band leader, others that he is an escaped train robber! Everyone, of course, knows the Beatles. The explanation is probably quite simple: one gets more pleasure from the Beatles than from Brown.

While parliament has ceased to be a locus of any serious reforms, and hence hardly in the centre of workers' attention, it gets a further knock by showing itself completely impotent in face of the real powers that be. The legend of the sovereignty of the British national parliament has shown itself to be a complete sham.

Today Britain is no longer the capitalist 'workshop of the world', but merely one among a number of advanced capitalist countries. It is by no means the largest, and its share in world trade drops year by year as other nations enter the market as industrial producers.

The British government is not the only, or even the most important, agency deciding what happens in Britain. This is particularly clear with regard to its 'social welfare' policies. Even if the Labour government had wanted, for instance, to give the old age pensioners their increased pensions immediately it came to power in October, 1964, the pressure of *international* banking opinion made this impossible. The same is true of its 'incomes policy', the present squeeze, the wage freeze, and so on. International business opinion sets the policies of a British capitalist government within quite narrow limits.

This is true of all capitalist countries, of course, but it is especially true of Britain, which is disproportionately 'open' to the pressures of the world market. The fact that the pound is maintained as an international reserve currency, that Britain is dependent on the world market for its importing and exporting activities, and so on, places severe limits on the freedom of movement of any British government that accepts the existing capitalist rules.

Governmental decisions are not made in parliament. They are made at the points of intersection of industry, finance and the civil service, in the Cabinet, the new 'planning' bodies and so on – anywhere, indeed, except in parliament. Parliament largely exists now to rubber-stamp decisions made elsewhere. Questions of central importance are made without reference to parliament at all: the decision to manufacture the atom bomb is a famous example, when even the Defence Minister, Shinwell, was not informed of the decision by Attlee and the Chief of Staff.

Even today, knowledge about how the government made its decisions about the Suez campaign is kept a closely guarded secret. At no stage was parliament given a chance to vote on the growth patterns for different industries proposed in the National Plan. George Brown's Plan was drafted on the basis of discussion with the management side of industry and on information supplied by business. Not even the Labour MPs, let alone the rank-and-file of the labour movement, were consulted about it. The first time the Plan was discussed by the parliamentary Labour Party was on the morning of 3 November – the eve of parliament's re-assembly after the summer holidays, and some six weeks after the Plan was published.

The rising role of Royal Commissions, State Boards and government inquiries is further evidence of the decline of parliament. Its complete impotence as a focal citadel of power becomes clear in every financial crisis. Lord Cromer, the Governor of the Bank of England, managed to negotiate a 3,000 million dollar loan in one night in November 1964.

The atrophy of parliament radically affects Labour MPs. If power corrupts, lack of power corrupts absolutely. If the 'gnomes of Zurich' – or international capitalism, of which British big business is a part – decide the central policies of Britain, why should we bother to send MPs to parliament, each costing us £3,250 a year. Wouldn't we do better to send a delegate to Zurich?

### Independent

With increasing capitalist planning, with the continued merging of big business and the state, and with the growing importance of the state, the executive becomes more and more independent of parliamentary decisions. There is an increasing consensus between the heads of government executives, Tory or Labour, and the needs of planned capitalism, above all with regard to the planning of wages.

It is true that remnants of old, traditional Labourism remain in the present, more modern, Party. Just as within and alongside the new planning, old capitalist anarchy can still be found, so inside the Wilsonian Labour Party there are still footholds of the old reformism, particularly in the defensive actions on behalf of workers in depressed areas or declining industries.

### Irrelevant

Suspended between state monopoly capitalism above and an indifferent mass of people below, Labour MPs are completely powerless and more and more irrelevant.

Until 1914, Marxists called the parties of the Second International – to which the British Labour Party belonged – socialist parties. It was the traumatic experience of August 1914, when the very same leaders who year in and year out inveighed against imperialism and war, jumped on the nationalist bandwagon and rushed to vote for the military budget, that caused Lenin and Luxemburg and their friends to change their characterisation of these parties.

They were no more called socialist parties but reformist parties, which did not intend to overthrow capitalism but to preserve it while, at the same time, carrying out some reforms within its framework – in other words, tinkering with it. They were called parliamentarian-reformist, as they were attached to the bourgeois parliament as the arena for carrying out reforms.

### Discipline

In the present stage of planned state-monopoly capitalism social democracy enters its third state: it is neither socialist, nor even authentic parliamentary reformist. It is much less than this. Its main task is to discipline the workers to the needs of state-monopoly capitalism.

The struggle of the left inside the Labour Party, and the attitude of socialists towards the party, will be the subject of our next article. This subject is of particular importance, for the overwhelming majority of organised workers still by tradition, see in the Labour Party *their* political organisation.

# Notes on democratic centralism

■ Our group has for a long time been a purely propaganda organisation – publishing books, theoretical journals, holding schools, etc. The structure fitting this situation was a loose federative one; all branches were like beads on a string.

■ Over the last year or two we have moved towards agitation. This demands a different kind of organisational structure. A revolutionary combat organisation – especially if it becomes a party – needs a democratic centralist structure.

■ In the first International the Proudhonist and the Bakuninists (both Anarchists) wanted a federal structure. Hence logically they argued that the International was a working-men's organisation, and only workers should be its members and representatives.

Marx argued that as the prevailing ideology under capitalism is the ideology of the ruling class, revolutionary politics *does not* reflect the current ideas of the class. As there cannot be a revolutionary movement without a revolutionary theory, the leadership of the International would not necessarily be workers, and could not be delegates on a federative principle (hence, Marx was the Russian 'representative' on the General Council of the International although he was not a Russian nor had he ever been in Russia; hence also the Central Committee of the Bolshevik Party had only one worker and all members were from one city; the same applied to the Mensheviks, to Luxemburg's Spartakusbund, etc.).

■ The Federal Principle – the idea that the Executive of a revolutionary organisation should be made up of one delegate per branch – is untenable:

IS Internal document June 1968

(a) It is undemocratic.

If a branch has 50 members who divide on a central issue 26 to 24, what is democratic about one person casting the votes of 50?

If a minority of the whole organisation – let us say 20 per cent – has one set of policies separating it from the majority – it will not be represented at all – or at most by a derisory number of people on the Executive.

(b) The inner-organisation struggle of ideas that is so vital, will be directed from issues to organisational frustrations and combinationalism.

(c) The Organisation cannot grow beyond a certain size: with 1,000 members and let's say 100 branches, no Executive could work.

(d) It is incompatible with the cell structure: the latter should be small and tight (it will probably replace the branch as the unit of work and education).

(e) It is incompatible with specialisation and division of labour. As Marx and Engels, Lenin and Trotsky, Luxemburg and Liebknecht were too busy to be able to be involved in local branch activities they could never have been eligible for election to the Executives of any revolutionary organisation.

(f) In conclusion: the federal structure is unstable and inefficient.

(In our own terms, with the expansion of the Group and the transition to a cell structure, half the Political Committee, including the editor of our agitational weekly, would not be able to be on the Executive, as they might be inactive locally in a branch. A revolutionary organisation whose two top Committees – the Executive and the Political Committee – are elected on opposite principles, could not work effectively.)

■ A democratic centralist organisation is based on the following:

A Delegates' Conference – meeting once or twice a year – decides the policies – the principles and strategy of the organisation.

An Executive, Political Committee, etc., are elected by the Conference as individuals, or on a list of candidates where there are factional groupings: each group of delegates is entitled to elect the number of people to the Committees in proportion to their share at the Conference.

All decisions of Conferences and between Conferences of the Executive are binding on all members of the organisation.

A revolutionary combat organisation faces the need for tactical decisions – daily and hourly – hence the need for great centralisation.

The most important decision for a revolutionary party – the decision to take State power – was taken by the Central Committee of the Bolshevik Party; in a revolutionary situation one cannot afford to waste a day (not to say a month – the time necessary to organise a Conference). The decision on War or Peace – the

Brest-Litovsk discussion – was again taken by the Central Committee of the Bolshevik Party. Or again the historical statements of the First International on the Paris Commune were written by Marx and agreed by a handful of people who turned up to the meetings of the General Council – without reference to the national sections of the International, not to speak of their mass rank and file.

If a minority of the branches – let us say 20 per cent – find it necessary to call an Emergency Conference – the Executive is bound to carry this out. New decisions and new elections can ensue.*

■ In practice because of the size and uneven nature of IS, we have to have a transitory structure: from federalism to democratic centralism.

At present all branches with ten members or more have a member on the Executive except for three branches: E. London, Croydon and Richmond. I suggest the addition of one from each of these branches.

The London Regional Committee – covering some half of the members of IS – should be strengthened. (It could organise demonstrations, schools, etc. The fact that it is based on a delegate per branch does not guarantee its functioning.)

Meetings of comrades in specific fields should be convened (as the teachers do regularly).

Two-way communication is vital: up to now there is much more information going from the EC and Administrative Committee to branches, than in the opposite direction. Criticism and self-criticism is absolutely vital. Above all, more politics, more theory, are necessary, hence the need for more centralism. (The worst 'economism' and organisational frustrations have come about in many local activities that were completely autonomous.) (Of course, any arrangement the September Conference decides should not run for more than a few months, as the IS – 800 or so at present – is bound, we hope, to grow considerably.)

---

*In arguing against Democratic Centralism anarchists and Social Democrats say: 'But see, the Bolshevik Party with such a structure led to Stalinism'. It was the lack of Bolshevism in Germany and elsewhere that led to the isolation of the Russian revolution and hence to the rise of Stalinism. (See especially Cliff, **Rosa Luxemburg**, pp63–64.)

# On perspectives: the class struggle in Britain

### Introduction

THE CENTRAL problem always facing Marxist revolutionaries is how the struggle of workers inside capitalism is related to the struggle against capitalism. For social democracy even in its heyday – the last decade of the nineteenth century and the first of the present – the problem was not even posed. There was no need to link reform with revolution. The organisation separated completely the minimum programme (i.e. the damands that can be achieved under capitalism) from the maximum programme (the demand for the end of capitalism). The maximum goals of socialism were relegated to the far future. The partial day-to-day struggle was for reforms. Socialism did for May Day speechifying.

In direct opposition to social democracy, Lenin repeated hundreds of times that reforms are the by-product of revolutionary struggle: 'partial improvements can be (and always have been in history) merely a by-product of revolutionary class struggle'.[1] 'The truth that reforms are possible only as a by-product of a movement that is completely free of all narrowness of reformism has been confirmed a hundred times in world history and is *particularly* true for Russia today.'[2]

This statement fitted perfectly the Russian experience. In Russia wages were practically stagnant up to the 1905 revolution. The average earnings of a factory worker were:

---

First printed: International Socialism (1) No 36

| 1901 | 201 rubles | | 1906 | 231 rubles |
|------|-----------|---|------|-----------|
| 1902 | 202 rubles | | 1907 | 214 rubles |
| 1903 | 208 rubles | | 1908 | 242 rubles |
| 1904 | 213 rubles | | 1909 | 236 rubles |
| 1905 | 205 rubles | | 1910 | 242 rubles |

Average for five
years: 206 rubles

Average for five
years: 238 rubles

This shows that the year 1905 was a turning-point: between the two averages was '32 rubles more per year . . . an increase of 15.5% . .

The year 1905 improved the workers' living standard to a degree that normally is attained during several decades.'[3]

Russian workers were beaten in the majority of their conflicts with the employers, except for the period of revolution itself. 'The statistics show that during ten years, 1895–1904, the employers won 51.6% of the strikes (according to the number of strikers involved); in 1905, 29.4%; in 1906, 33.5%; in 1907, 57.6%; in 1908, 68.8%.'[4]

The situation in Western Europe has been very different since the Second World War. Except for the first couple of years after the war, in all advanced countries the relation between reform and the revolutionary struggle has been very tenuous indeed. There has probably never been in the history of capitalism a period of twenty years in which real wages rose as quickly as in this period. In Britain real wages have doubled since the war. In the five years 1959–64 hourly earnings rose in Britain by 35%, in France by 50%, in West Germany by 54%, in Italy by 74%.[5]

The stabilisation of Western capitalism on the cone of the H-bomb made it possible for reforms to be achieved over a long period, independently of revolutionary politics.

However, things have begun to change over the last few years. The stability of Western capitalism is beginning to falter. This does not mean that Western capitalism is faced with the kind of collapse of the inter-war years. In the coming years we can expect an unevenness in the rate of economic growth, and intermittent expansions. The contradictions in the permanent arms economy, partly reflected in the international liquidity crisis, will inhibit systematic growth of the economies of Western Europe. The hurdles on the path of reform are becoming higher and higher. The period of decline in the working-class political movement is at an end.

## The Generalised Employers' Offensive

It is less than ten years since the first major productivity deal was negotiated at the Esso Oil Refinery at Fawley, Hampshire. How many workers who read of this strange new phenomenon would have guessed that in such a short time the same type of deal would come to dominate the lives of so many. The Fawley deal was signed in July 1960.[6] In December 1966 the Government Prices and Incomes Board (PIB) estimated the spread of productivity deals thus:

> 'Over the last six years, productivity agreements . . . have probably affected no more than half a million workers'.[7]

But immediately after the publication of this report there was a rapid increase in the adoption of productivity criteria throughout the national industrial negotiating machinery. In 1967 the number of productivity deals registered at the Department of Employment and Productivity (DEP) averaged about 60 per month. Once the rush had started, the pace grew more intense. For the first five months of 1968 the number of deals registered rose to 75 per month, and the number shot up in June of that year to a level of about 200 per month for the remaining seven months of the year. Since the beginning of 1969 the number of productivity deals registered at the DEP was at a lower level but still double that of the first half of 1968.

In February 1969 this register recorded some 2,500 cases covering around $4\frac{1}{2}$ million workers, or 20% of all employed workers . . . at the end of June 1969 the register recorded some 3,000 cases covering approximately 6 million workers, or 25% of all employed workers.[8]

It took about a hundred years for the piecework payments system to spread until it encompassed two-fifths of the British working class. Productivity deals engulfed some 25% in a few years.

With justified satisfaction the **Financial Times** declared:

> 'the country's present obsession with productivity probably exceeds the wildest dreams of those who were trying to spread the word five years ago.[9]

The implementation of productivity deals was facilitated by the government's incomes policy. On the face of it this policy had hardly any impact at all on the pattern of wage changes. All in all, in the four years of income policies – October 1964 to October 1968 – average hourly earnings (excluding the effects of overtime) rose by 27%, as against 23% in the four preceding years.[10]

Even Aubrey Jones, Chairman of the PIB, was very cautious regarding the effectiveness of the incomes policy. He believed that the net effect of the policy had been that the 'average annual increase in earnings in recent years may have been just under 1% less than otherwise it would have been'.[11]

This was a very tentative conclusion. Of course, there is no certain way to tell what would have been the increase in earnings had there been no incomes policy. Nevertheless, neither a Declaration of Intent nor a law could stop well-organised workers in their trade unions from pushing their wages upwards to try to keep pace with rising prices. But the indirect effect of the incomes policy was much greater than its direct effect. For the incomes policy prepared the ground for the spreading of productivity deals, a far more sophisticated weapon for the employing class.

Aubrey Jones dotted the 'i's and crossed the 't's:

'All that we have heard suggests that the effect of government policy, especially since July 1966, has been to direct the attention of both the employers and trade unionists away from conventional bargaining and towards productivity bargaining.'[12]

The Labour government blocked the path to a direct advance of wages, but left wide open the trapdoor of productivity bargaining.

One should not, however, draw the conclusion that the incomes policy has served only as a prelude to the introduction of productivity deals. The failure of incomes policy in itself contributed to the pressure for productivity bargaining. The failure of incomes policy to hold down wages dictated the move towards productivity deals – i.e. making workers pay, by working harder, under worse conditions, for their wage increases. This is where the employers' offensive springs from. The years of effort to impose the incomes policy located the main obstacle: shop-floor organisation. Hence the determination to eliminate this power not by direct confrontation but by fundamental alterations in the structure of industrial relations, which would be designed to isolate and undermine this power.

### Strengthening the Power of Management

One of the main aims of productivity deals, in the words of Allan Flanders, publicist of the famous Fawley Productivity Agreement, is to put an end to the abrogation of management authority by workers:

'This is the aspect of productivity bargaining that I particularly want to stress. I find it difficult to see how the accumulated disorder, which is the heritage of two decades of post-war growth in the unofficial system of collective bargaining, can be cleared up without the help of productivity agreements. The re-establishment of order and control is central to my case for productivity bargaining, because in the long run this may be far more important than the immediate gains that can be found in terms of increased labour productivity.'[13]

And wish considerable relish, the same author reports:

'More and more managements seem to me to be becoming aware that the labour situation has drifted dangerously far and that they are faced with the need to re-establish control over their workers. And since in the modern world they cannot re-establish control unilaterally, the plant productivity bargain seems to them a logical first step towards a modern viable system of managerial control over pay and effort.'[14]

Productivity deals are seen by employers as a means to curb the militant shop steward. They achieve this by the following means;

(1) Reorganising their payments systems in such a way as to remove from the bargaining table the issues over which stewards

have traditionally argued and in doing so gained their leverage. These issues concern mainly the wages levels associated with piece-work rates but also include such questions as waiting times, availability of materials, etc.

(2) Denying stewards the right to bargain on details of new work systems such as Measured Day Work (MDW).

(3) Increasing the number of supervisors substantially and trying to channel workers' grievances through these lower rungs of management – thereby bypassing the shop steward.

(4) Introducing highly formalised grievance procedures within the factory which enable the management to exclude shop stewards and replace them by local union officers.

(5) Under cover of flexibility clauses, establishing the right to move militants around the factory whenever they begin to build a base and win support among workers in a particular shop.

(6) Under cover of the Deal, stepping up the indoctrination of stewards by means of joint management/union sponsored courses.

The extent to which the employers are successful in these objectives depends very largely on the strength of the factory organisation. What the productivity deal does is to open the way for the acceptance of such changes which, under normal circumstances, would not even be countenanced by the best organised workers.

### For 'Partnership' of Employers and Unions

The real aim of the Donovan Report, of **In Place of Strife**, and numerous other similar documents was basically not to smash the unions, or even to weaken them as organisations, but to integrate them with management. This 'partnership' was to be embodied in productivity deals and formalised procedures in the plants.

The introduction of comprehensive formal agreements at factory level is the normal result of productivity bargaining and the central proposal of the Donovan Report. The reasoning behind this proposal is most clearly expressed by Allan Flanders, whose theoretical arguments strongly influenced Donovan, and who has been rewarded with a £6,500 job on the Commission for Industrial Relations.

Flanders diagnoses the central problem, for management and the government, as

'a progressive loss of managerial control over pay and work and therefore over labour costs, at plant level.'[15]

To say that management has lost control is to say that workers have *won* an area of control: over piece-rate bargaining, overtime, manning, allocation of work, pace of production. All these areas of control which workers have been able to wrest from management – and which productivity deals are intended to restore to management – have arisen, Flanders argues, because collective bargaining at factory level is

'largely informal, largely fragmented, and largely autonomous.'[16]

Bargaining takes place *at the point of production*, where workers'
power is most effectively organised and where management is
weakest. Lower-level supervisors – whose overriding concern is to get
production out, and whose own reputation in the eyes of their
superiors can be damaged by a strike – can be pressured into
making concessions, informally, which top management would
never sanction. And stewards can press hard, knowing precisely
what are the feelings of their members, and being largely free of the
restraining influences to which full-time officials are subject.

Informal plant bargaining, based on strong shop steward
organisation, is an open expression of a relationship of conflict.
Workers use their collective power to win concrete concessions in
pay and working conditions, and to *carve out an area of control*. Because
the inherent conflict is so obvious, the principal limit to workers'
demands is their own consciousness of their strength. And it is their
increasing awareness of this strength which is so frightening to the
ruling class. But formal plant bargaining necessarily means that the
relationship is *apparently* transformed. Management meets union
representatives as 'equal partners' in discussing the organisation of
work. Their negotiations aim at 'joint regulation' of managerial
questions. And the procedure under which these negotiations take
place is mutually agreed. In place of conflict, there is co-operation.
Of course such 'co-operation' is one-sided; as Flanders cynically puts
it, 'management regain control by sharing it'. Management can
allow union participation in 'joint regulation' only if the rules are
stacked in its favour, and if the basic economic aims of the company
are unquestioned; there must be, Flanders makes clear,

'a common system of joint control based on real objectives.'[17]

In return, many an employer expressed sympathy with the
plight of the union full-time official who faces rebellious shop
stewards. Lord Rootes had this to say:

'We would like to make it clear that in our view there is
considerable identity of interest between employers in industry
and responsible trade unionism, and we prefer to see an
improvement brought about by means of strengthening the
position of the trade unions and enabling them to control their
members more effectively than hitherto, so that agreements
which are freely entered into on both sides are honoured.'[18]

And John Davies, at the time Director-General of the Confeder-
ation of British Industry (CBI), added:

'We believe that trade unionists genuinely do not want this
unconstitutional, irresponsible behaviour by their members in
breaking agreements which the union has gone into. We all
know many prominent trade union figures, who in the past and
today, have expressed themselves in most forthright terms on
this subject – you would think perhaps their greatest enemies

were not employers but those of their rebel members who were bringing the unions into disrepute.'[19]

Because productivity bargaining is a 'soft' option in wage negotiations both Right-wing as well as Left-wing trade-union leaders are inclined to accept this willingly. The Right-wing leaders' commitment to an incomes policy does not exclude getting extra money for his workers by selling conditions. The Left-wing top brass is happy to oppose the incomes policy without defending workers' conditions. The only one that suffers is the worker. When it comes to productivity deals the limitations of the Left union leaders become very clear. Productivity deals pose in the most acute form the dilemma – either to go through the procedure and according to the rules laid down by the government (this must mean 'productivity' concessions) – or take direct action to win increases. Tied to procedure union officials are also thereby tied to productivity.

Trapped as they are in the logic of their own positions and reacting to mass pressure more than they initiate it, it is no wonder that the 'soft option' of wage rises through productivity deals appeals to the top union officials – even the most 'Left' of them. Scanlon of the Amalgamated Engineering Workers Union and Jones of the Transport and General support the principle of productivity deals. The Communist Party controlled Electrical Trades Union (ETU) was crucial in carrying through the Fawley agreement.[20] As a general rule, full-time officials are not averse to productivity deals precisely because these are bound to increase the power of the officials vis-à-vis the shop stewards.

### The Ideological Offensive: Production – for What?

A central theme in the whole productivity bargaining campaign is the need for 'efficiency' and 'modernisation' in the interests of the nation. By raising the issue of productivity the government and the employers are forcing politics on to the shop floor. Socialists must take up the challenge. Government incomes policy was the soil upon which productivity deals mushroomed. Government deflationary policy softening workers' resistance helped also the spread of productivity bargaining. When the government and the employers talk of efficiency, socialists have plenty to say on that score; about the anarchy and waste of capitalist production; the fact that more is spent on advertising than on basic research; that millions are wasted on armaments; that constant re-tooling of car plants takes place not because tools are worn out but because competition demands accelerated obsolescence and never-ending 'new models'.

The very purpose of production becomes an industrial issue. Should production be aimed at benefiting the workers, the old-age pensioners, or serve only to raise the profits of the rich?

The ideological offensive is in full swing. From government ministers, industrial tycoons and the political pundits of TV and the press we hear the same tune: 'Forget about inequalities of wealth – that's all old hat – if we all pull together and increase productivity then everyone will benefit.' It all sounds so plausible. If industry produces more then there will be more goods and services to go round. In a socialist society this would be true – by raising the productivity of labour we would give ourselves a choice; either a higher standard of living or shorter working hours. Today there is no such choice, because industrialists see higher productivity as a means to higher profit and in fact often have no wish to *increase output at all*. We see this contradiction most clearly in the motor industry. Although they are unable to sell all the cars they make at present, the manufacturers are desperate to push up productivity and make their workers work even faster. It is vital that we expose the employers' pious talk about 'efficiency' and 'production in the national interest'. If British Leyland (BLMH) lay off 20% of their workers and still maintain the same level of output then there is a very obvious gain for BLMH. For the 20% who get the sack, and for the community as a whole, there is nothing gained at all. In the economy as a whole 'productivity' can and is going up while production stays still – and structural unemployment grows.

The demands for increased productivity in the interest of greater profit should be countered by the socialist idea of production for use. By talking in terms of the 'national interest' the ruling class is attempting to divert attention from the really important question of the *distribution* of income and wealth between classes. Of course, the wealthy want to treat this question of distribution as being of minor importance – after all their portion of the cake is in fact growing from year to year. For us, however, these are the important questions and it is here that our challenge must be made.

## Shop Stewards' Organisations: Weaknesses and Strengths

The shop stewards are the representatives of shop-floor democracy and hence the pillars on which any real revolutionary socialist policy must rely. In evaluating the shop stewards' organisations at present, it is important that trade unionists and socialists be very clear about their weaknesses and their points of strength.

The most significant weakness of shop stewards' organisation today is its fragmentation. As the concentration and centralisation of capital have increased, through the processes of merger and takeover, the great combines running a number of plants across the country have become very prominent. The need to combine and co-ordinate the activities of shop stewards at least between the plants of a single combine is self-evident. But moves towards such co-ordination have been quite slow and faltering. Nor are the reasons difficult to understand. Negotiations have been carried on at a local basis, in a particular factory or even a particular shop. There is a great unevenness in strength of organisation, in traditions of militancy, and so on.

Even when there are shop stewards' combine committees, they are usually very weak indeed and their weakness is revealed clearly during industrial disputes.

Besides fragmentation, there is another associated weakness of the shop stewards' organisations of today: on the whole, the horizons of these organisations are quite narrow. They tend to react to events more than they shape them, and they pay more attention to wages than they do to the equally important question of redundancy.

Above all, the problems of people who cannot defend themselves very well – people like old-age pensioners, nurses – are not central in workers' activities and thinking. It is true, of course, that thousands of workers – lorry drivers, dockers, engineers – showed generosity of spirit in going on sympathy strike in support of the nurses' pay claim in May 1962. But still action like this is the exception, not the rule.

The shop stewards reflect their supporters, and while this is their strength, it is also their weakness. When the majority of workers are not really socialist or even militant, the shop stewards they elect cannot be either.

A most insidious trend appearing in recent years is the increase in the number of full-time convenors, shop representatives, deputy-convenors, works committee members, etc. – who spend an increasingly long period away from their increasingly nominal jobs. In many factories the ordinary worker who is elected shop steward very rapidly finds himself (if he is good at representing his men) taken away from the shop floor more and more often. Then he gets put on a 'soft' job, to allow management to take him away without disrupting production. It is no wonder that many get completely divorced from their base. With factory convenors this is particularly strongly felt. Often the only contact they have with the workers is when they appear to try to persuade the men not to walk out over a grievance. The only answer to this process of incorporation is to insist on regular shop floor meetings.

In many cases workers become alienated not only from the union officials but even from the shop stewards. They see them as a buffer between themselves and management. Hence the growing phenomenon, in the motor-car industry especially, of *unofficial* unofficial strikes in which the workers act on their own without even the endorsement of their shop steward. Sir Jack Scamp reports:

> 'At Morris Motors Limited, Cowley, for instance, the Council found that in 1965 256 out of 297 stoppages of work had occurred before the senior shop steward had even had a chance to put the grievance into procedure.'[21]

## The Widening of the Front

With a replacement of piece-work by Measured Day Work

(MDW), with the abolition of tens of hundreds of wage levels in a plant and their substitution by a few grades, with plant negotiation instead of piecemeal negotiations, the ground is being prepared for a wider unity of workers in struggle. Whatever the intentions of management, workers' solidarity could be strengthened by these changes.

This becomes obvious by comparing the pattern of strikes in Fords, based on MDW, grading, etc. and British Leylands, where Payments by Results (PBR) prevails. The strikes in the former have been on the whole on a much greater scale and continuing for a longer period.[22] Also the issues in the strikes, in the case of Fords, have been, on the whole, more fundamental, dealing with managerial prerogatives, production matters on the one hand and victimisation of workers on the other.[23]

As a matter of fact, productivity deals in themselves tend to provoke workers into greater militancy. At least, after the gilt on the gingerbread starts peeling off, it becomes clear that it means a much greater effort for the workers for relatively little or no extra money.

Take the case of the Post Office Engineers (POEU). In a fanfare of publicity they signed a productivity deal in January 1966. Three years later the first national strike in the 82-year history of the union took place. Similarly with the dustmen. In March 1967 the PIB suggested productivity bargaining for manual workers employed by local authorities, involving time and motion study, etc., for the magnificent wage rise of 5%, or some 14s.[24] During the whole of the summer of 1969 the unions were negotiating for the dustmen a wage increase of 18s and then at the beginning of October the dustmen went on strike. Their demands were not dampened at all by the past experience of productivity bargaining; on the contrary, they demanded an additional £4 11s, which would have brought their basic wage up to £20 a week. In the event, they were almost immediately offered a 50s a week rise in London (or 16%) and 30s (10%) in the provinces.

The miners followed suit and under the threat of a national strike (which actually broke out on a different issue and was the biggest miners' strike since 1926 and the biggest ever unofficial strike) won 27s 6d for the surface workers – the largest wage rise in the history of the mines!

The firemen followed the example. Under threat of a strike on the eve of Guy Fawkes, London firemen won £4 10s and the provincial firemen a £3 10s wage rise.

Electrical power workers were next in line. In September 1967 the PIB, in reply to a request for a 5% wage rise put forward by the unions, offered 3.7% with very heavy new productivity conditions attached.[25] Instead, the workers in electrical power supply followed the example of the firemen and threatened to strike (in a few stations it even came to actual strike) so getting a wage rise of 10%.

The teachers took up the baton. The employers offered them a

£50 interim rise on the annual basic wage (under 4%). The union leaders declared this 'derisory'. Quite rightly, **The Times** explained:

> 'An offer of £50 would have satisfied most teachers six weeks ago, but since then there have been awards of 16% to the dustmen, 9% to miners and 12% to firemen. Now even the Right wing of the NUT [National Union of Teachers] will not be prepared to accept an offer of less than £70.'[26]

It is very possible that productivity bargaining contributed indirectly to the size and height of the strike waves. Workers' expectations rose when they heard from State and employers' representatives about the benefits of productivity deals, while the reality was . . . so much poorer. After a time all productivity deals become tarnished. (Other elements that caused the recent burst of wage levels are the failure of low-paid workers and workers not paid on piece-rates to keep up with the rising cost of living, and the worsening of their earnings relatively to the earnings of other workers.)

The incomes policy propaganda and the big rumpus about productivity bargaining concentrated the attention of workers on comparing wages. Hence the current phenomenon of the, so to say, epidemic wage demands: the dustmen inspired the miners, the firemen, the teachers. Similarly a couple of years ago the figure of £17 a week became a magic formula in Merseyside: once the dockers at the end of 1967 got £17 basic, the Liverpool busmen fought for the same, then the lorry-drivers and then the tugmen.

The factor of comparability – and the struggle for parity – increases also as a result of mergers. It is not an accident that with the rise of British Leyland the struggle for parity has raised its head inside the corporation (hence the long strike of the five Preston factories). The same is true in the car industry in general. Similarly, and previous to the rise of British Leyland, it was the joining of Morris and Austin into BMC that pushed the Morris Oxford factories, that used to be very peaceful, on to a much stormier course.

### Sharpening of Class Conflicts

With the increasing advance of inflation, the capitalist class and its State are driven into a sharper and sharper, wider and wider confrontation with the working class.

At the time of writing, October 1970, public authorities have confronted a very wide section of the working class: local govern-ment manual workers, municipal busmen and miners, more than a million in all.

The employers in the private sector of the economy have also hardened their position. A couple of years ago the employers offered productivity deals in which the bitter pill was well covered with a thick coat of sugar. Now the sugar they offer is much thinner, especially if one takes into account the speed in the rise of the cost of living. Thus, for instance, in GKN Sankey, Wellington, the workers asked for £8 10s a week without strings to bring them up to the Birmingham standard of wages in the car industry. The employers offered the majority of the workers only a miserable £2 with many productivity strings. The top union officials of all the unions involved – from the Right of the General and Municipal Workers' Union to Bob Wright, 'Left' leader of the AEF – sided with management. After six weeks of unofficial strike the workers knuckled under. The general trend with regard to productivity bargaining is that the strings are becoming thicker and the positive inducements weaker.

An integral part of the tougher employers' offensive is the Tory trade-union legislation. Carr's Industrial Relations Bill, **Consultative Document** (October 1970), is incomparably more harsh than Barbara Castle's **In Place of Strife** (January 1969) or even the Tory **Fair Deal at Work** (April 1968). Carr's document puts the unofficial striker completely out of legal bounds. It aims to smash shop-floor democracy. It is symptomatic that in the thousands and thousands of words in the document two words are not mentioned even once, shop steward!

### The Offensive of the Employers

For a whole generation there has been great apathy among workers about the trade unions. It seemed good enough to know who the shop steward was – who cared about who controlled the union as a whole? Now, with plant negotiations the foundations of all productivity bargaining, this apathy emerges as the source of a very dangerous weakness – the workers are unarmed.

Apathy towards politics was natural when reforms could be achieved on the factory floor, and while the only politics visible were those of Tweedledum and Tweedledee, of Parliamentary Toryism and Parliamentary Labourism. However, with productivity deals now thrusting politics onto the factory floor, political backwardness can be clearly seen as the Achilles heel of the working class.

The fragmented industrial struggle has been accompanied *at many levels* by a narrow, fragmented contradictory consciousness. *Support for organised political opposition to the system dwindled* while the path of improving one's own conditions seemed to be open. (That this path was not a real solution to workers' problems was beside the point.) *Productivity bargaining by its direct attack on working conditions and the remaining workers' organisations changes all this: it generalises workers' experiences and resentments.* Parochialism and shortsightedness become impossible impediments.

The implementation of productivity deals is associated with a comprehensive attack on workers, using all weapons: the State (incomes policy and anti-trade-union legislation), the trade-union bureaucracy, 'science' (time-and-motion study), and ideology (the ideology of 'national interest', of 'partnership of labour and capital'). The aim of the employers' strategy is to split the workers, to subdue the shop stewards and integrate them into the union machine and incorporate the unions into the State. The workers need a total, a general, class strategy to confront the employers' offensive, to move from defence to attack.

For some two decades the picture of Western capitalism as expanding, with ups and downs but still in a fairly orderly way, and its concomitant, a fragmented working class, more or less fitted reality. Today the picture is much more complicated.

The fragments have not ceased to exist, but the boundaries between them are not unchanging. The vast subsoil of the old fragmentation is still there, but on top of it new kinds of unity are arising. The picture is a mosaic, patchy and inelegant. But this is the picture of a transitional stage which we find ourselves in today.

With the increasing fusion of State and business (incomes policy and labour legislation) the boundaries between fragments have become more and more conditional and dynamic. Something new grows out of the old – different 'stages' appear simultaneously. In such a situation sharp changes, sudden turns, unexpected combinations of different and conflicting elements of struggle, consciousness and organisation in the working class are bound to appear again and again. The whole movement can develop only as the result of very long and numerous struggles.

### The Contradictions in the Present Transitional Period

Over the last few years, it must be repeated, the economic-social-political scene in the working class has been very different from that of the two decades following 1948. However, from this one should not come to the conclusion that we are living in a revolutionary or at least in a pre-revolutionary period similar to those, let us say, of other proletarian revolutions in the past. To make this point clear it is useful to compare the present situation in Western capitalist countries with a previous revolutionary or pre-revolutionary situation – for example, 1905 in Russia.

To bring things into a clear focus we will compare the highest stage of the revolutionary crisis in Western Europe in recent years – May–June 1968 in France – with the Russian revolution of 1905, the dress rehearsal for the October revolution of 1917.

### May 1968 – a Turning-point

On 22 May, 1968 the French Prime Minister, Pompidou, told the National Assembly: 'Nothing will ever be exactly the same.' Today such a statement sounds platitudinous. Just as between 1789 and 1848 the imagery – the personnel, the dramatic events – of the first French Revolution were the terms of reference for all revolutionaries, so when one reads Lenin or Plekhanov prior to 1905, events of 1848 and 1871 are central in evaluating the current events in Russia decades later. So France 1968 will be central to the analysis of the tasks and perspectives of revolutionaries in advanced industrial societies in the years to come.

First of all the general strike in France far surpassed in magnitude anything that happened in Russia in 1905. In France at the height of the strike some ten million workers were involved. In Russia, in the month of October 1905, when the strike was at its peak, a little more than half a million workers participated.[27]

However, the duration of the revolutionary wave in France was incomparably shorter. The Russian revolution stretched over a period of some three years. It started in January 1905 and reached its apex in the December insurrection of the same year. This insurrection ended in defeat and the Tsarist autocracy went on to the offensive. In 1906 workers' strikes and peasants' and soldiers' outbreaks were much weaker than a year earlier, but were still very formidable. In 1907 the workers' struggle grew weaker still. However, only at the end of 1907, after three long years, can one speak of the end of the revolution. The wave declined completely, and the level of struggle returned to the pre-1905 standard. The picture becomes clear when one follows the strike statistics given later.

The form of the revolutionary organisation of the working class in Russia in 1905 was far ahead of France in 1968. The year 1905 witnessed the birth of Soviets – of workers' councils – the characteristic organisation of workers and the embryonic form of workers' power. The first Soviets arose out of the strike movement even prior to the October General Strike. In May 1905 a Soviet was formed in Ivanovo-Voznesensk, a month later in Kostroma, while in September, Soviets of printing, tobacco and other workers were formed in Moscow. In October a Soviet was formed in St Petersburg. Shortly before the December insurrection in Moscow, the Moscow Soviet of Workers' Deputies came into being, its example being followed in Kiev, Kharkov, Rostov-on-Don, Odessa, Nikolayev, Ekaterinoslav, Vladikavkaz, Revel, Novorossisk, Saratov, Chita, Irkutsky, Krasnoyarsk, Baku and elsewhere.

In France not one workers' council was formed. In fact in only a very few instances were strike committees even democractically elected. In practically every plant the trade union nominated the delegates to the strike committee. In Renault there were a few attempts to get elections by the rank and file, but with the exception of one department, they were quashed by the *Confédération Générale du Travail* (CGT, the Communist trade-union federation). In the chemical factory Rhône-Poulenc-Vitry the demand for a rank-and-file committee was so strong that the official one was overthrown and a new one was elected by union and non-union workers alike. It is interesting that even in Citroën, where for sixteen years there had not been a strike, and where only 7% of the workers were organised in trade unions, the union bureaucrats still managed to prevent the election of a democratic rank-and-file strike committee, and imposed a nominated one. They hastened to do this even before the strike began, as they were afraid that things might get out of hand with such a weak organisation. This is also the reason why the CGT full-time officials took the initiative in calling the strike. The most obvious lack in the strike was an independent network connecting the different strike committees. It did not exist even for factories belonging to the same firm.

|      |             | Number of strikers [28] |
|------|-------------|-------------|
| 1903 |             | 86,832      |
| 1904 |             | 24,904      |
| 1905 | 1st quarter | 810,000     |
|      | 2nd quarter | 481,000     |
|      | 3rd quarter | 294,000     |
|      | 4th quarter | 1,277,000   |
| 1906 | 1st quarter | 269,000     |
|      | 2nd quarter | 479,000     |
|      | 3rd quarter | 296,000     |
|      | 4th quarter | 63,000      |
| 1907 | 1st quarter | 146,000     |
|      | 2nd quarter | 323,000     |
|      | 3rd quarter | 77,000      |
|      | 4th quarter | 193,000     |
| 1908 |             | 64,166      |
| 1909 |             | 46,623      |

If the CGT could not stop the strike, it was able to sabotage it by fragmenting the movement – taking what had been a mass movement of the class as a whole and reducing it to a series of disconnected struggles in different industries. Thus on 27 May the Administrative Commission of the CGT declared: 'What the government and employers have not agreed on at a national inter-trades level, we must obtain from them on other levels by means of negotiations which we must demand immediately in each separate branch of industry and trade, such as are being carried on in the nationalised and public sectors.' Thus negotiations with different employers transformed the strike from being general into a collection of separate strikes.

Not only was there no network of strike committees, but in practice the trade-union bureaucracies did their best to isolate one strike committee from another. Thus, for instance, the Renault Billancourt CGT refused on 23 May to receive a delegation of Renault Flins.

In Russia the revolutionary political organisations were incomparably larger, more massive and more influential than the *groupuscules* in France. In November 1906 there were 150,000 members in the Russian Social Democratic Party: 33,000 Bolsheviks, 43,000 Mensheviks, 13,000 Letts, 28,000 Poles, and 33,000 members of the Bund.[29] Lenin was, of course, not satisfied with the size of the Party. He wrote: 'We must learn to recruit five times and ten times as many workers for the Party.' 'We suffer from routine, we must fight against it . . . Our slogan is: for a larger Social-Democratic Labour Party.'[30]

The membership of the French revolutionary organisations is still counted in hundreds, and this from a working class far larger than that of Russia in 1905-7. The revolutionary press in France is puny compared to that of Russia in the period under comparison. In Petrograd alone three social-democratic daily papers were published, with a circulation ranging from 50,000 to 100,000.[31] Trotsky and Parvus, with no organisation, took over a tiny paper, the **Russian Gazette**, and transformed it into a mass popular paper. 'Within a few days the circulation rose from thirty thousand to one hundred thousand. A month later it reached the half-million mark.'[32] In France there was not one revolutionary daily, and the circulation of the weeklies was only a few thousand.

In part the explanation of the difference between the pattern of events in France in 1968 and in Russia in 1905 lies at the organisational and ideological levels. In France there is a strong conservative workers' party, beside which there are small weak revolutionary groups. The resilience of the French Communist Party, and the difficulties facing the *groupuscules* in gaining credibility in the eyes of the masses, are important factors.[33]

But this is only part of the explanation of the failure of the French struggle to develop to a higher level. The strength of the reformist organisations and ideas and the 'crisis of leadership' are inherent in the objective situation. The two decades of capitalist expansion since 1948 have profoundly affected the labour movements of Western Europe, resulting in 'the fragmentation of the working class', 'privatisation', or in conventional terms 'apathy'. This false consciousness was defined by E. P. Thompson as the idea that individual and sectional problems, which are essentially social, can be solved by individual and sectional efforts.

The other side of the coin of apathy – both cause and effect – is the increasing bureaucratisation of the traditional workers' organisations, the parties and trade unions, and their increasing collaboration with employers and State.

The alienation of workers from their traditional organisations has developed over a whole generation. This expresses itself in a number of ways. Before the First World War the British Labour Movement had two daily papers -- the **Daily Citizen** and the **Daily Herald**. Today, with the Labour vote much larger than sixty years ago, the Labour Movement has not even managed to maintain its weekly **Reynolds News**, later renamed the **Sunday Citizen**.

The French Communist Party, with some four million voters, finds it difficult to maintain **L'Humanité** whose print order is less than 200,000 (of which a proportion goes to Russia and Eastern

Europe). It is true that the Labour Party has six million members, but it is doubtful if 10% of these know that they are members. The process of alienation is not a conscious act of rejection; the majority of workers are unconscious agnostics, not real atheists, towards their traditional organisations.

The Russian revolution of 1905 came after a decade of continuous development of the workers into a more and more united, politically conscious, class. The 1968 events in France followed a long period of fragmentation and privatisation. In Russia the revolution followed a decade of increasing politicisation of the working class; in France it followed years of depoliticisation.

The new phenomenon, the May-June mass struggle, has not wiped out the inheritance of twenty years. Actually it must be explained as an outgrowth of this same background. The new, the revolutionary, grew out of the general period of fragmentation, political lull and apathy. This is, basically, how the revolutionary struggle was channelled into a struggle for such puny, reformist aims.

For decades Marxists used to infer the state of mass consciousness from a few institutional barometers – membership of organisations, readership of papers, etc. The deep alienation of workers from traditional organisations eroded all such barometers. This is why there was no way of detecting the imminence of the upheaval in May 1968. And also, more important, it explains the extreme, explosive nature of the events. If the workers in France had been accustomed to participate in the branch life of the trade unions or the Communist Party, these institutions would have served both as an aid and as ballast, preventing the rapid uncontrolled spread of the strike movement. The concept of apathy or privatisation is not a static concept. At a certain stage of development – when the path of individual reforms is being narrowed, or closed – apathy can transform into its opposite, swift mass action. However, this new turn comes as an outgrowth of the previous stage; the epilogue and the prologue combine. Workers who have lost their loyalty to the traditional organisations, which have shown themselves to be paralysed over the years, are forced into extreme, explosive struggles on their own.

Traditional barometers are missing, the policies of the bosses and the State, as well as those of the trade union bureaucrats, are much less sure, much more vacillating, than before. Their reaction, even to marginal challenges, may be unexpected, brutal and seemingly irrational.

The forms by which the ruling class exercises its political and ideological control will become more contradictory. During the period of steady economic expansion, the bosses in Britain were ready to accept a practically autonomous shop stewards' organisation inside the factory and more or less 'liberal' policies outside. The economic faltering means that many of those tolerant attitudes will have to go. The political impact of the contradictions in capitalism under such conditions must far exceed their economic significance. By itself apathy, or a declining interest in the traditional reformist organisations (the Labour Party, Communist Party, etc.), does not mean the overcoming of reformist ideology. For this, a long struggle is necessary, in which all sections of society are involved, in which all parties and ideas are put to the test, and in which the victory of revolutionary ideas over reformist ideas takes place.

## Young Workers and Other Workers

To add to the complexity of the picture one must not only remember that all the boundaries between 'fragments' of the working class are dynamic but that cutting across the class is the division between young and not-so-young workers.

The student rebellion had some effect in radicalising at least one section of the French working class – the young workers. They, more than anyone else, are affected by the economic crisis of French society. It is very difficult for them to find jobs and if they do they are often dead-end jobs. From childhood many are roughed up by the police as 'delinquents' or rebels. They are affected by the ideological and moral crisis of society.

When the students proved on the 6th May that not only were they ready to fight the police but they were also able to stand their ground against them, thousands of young workers joined them. The number increased even more on the 10th May, the Night of the Barricades. After that thousands of workers started visiting the Sorbonne.

The young workers are very similar to the students in their attitudes to society. They rebel against the whole set-up. The old workers' thinking is basically concrete. It grows from bread-and-butter issues that are with the worker all his life, from trade-union consciousness. The young workers have usually been in a particular factory only a short time and they have no great interest in the specific work conditions. Socialist consciousness transcends trade-union consciousness. The young workers, like the students, are practically free of trade-union consciousness.

The young workers can provide much of the enthusiasm necessary for sustaining a revolutionary organisation. When massive working-class resistance to the system is lacking, youth protest can focus the aspirations of many working-class militants, and give confidence to old-timers who have been let down time and again by the traditional organisations and feel isolated among the more backward workers. In France the young workers showed much greater self-confidence than the old ones. Unfortunately the clea-vage between the age groups caused many of the young workers to leave the factories during the struggles and to move to a milieu more congenial to them – among the students in the Latin Quarter.

For Marx the concept of exploitation transcends that of alienation. The latter describes the situation of the individual in an inimical society; the former promises the cohesion of collective workers in opposition to the ruling class. The young workers cannot sustain a struggle unless they unite with workers of all ages in organisations based on the place of work to oppose the ruling class.

### Difficulties for Revolutionaries

The old forest of reformism is withering. The trees are without leaves, the trunks are dying. But, in society, old ideas are not wiped out unless they are replaced by new ones. The shoots of revolution are very small indeed in the British Labour Movement. Reformism can never be defeated by programmes. It can only be defeated by deeds. The education of the masses can never be separated from independent political revolutionary struggle. Only action discloses to the workers the magnitude of the struggle, widens their horizons, and clarifies their mind.

The point of departure of a revolutionary organisation is the experience – the action, thinking and organisation – of the workers, and the aim of its activity is to raise the initiative and drive of the working class.

The weakness of revolutionaries in Britain at present is quite obvious. Small in number, often isolated because of their social composition – white collar and student – from the main sections of the working class, split into a number of groups, and above all lacking experience in leading mass struggles. But these weaknesses can be overcome. Readiness to learn, readiness to experiment systematically, above all readiness to try and translate the general theories into practical activities – this is what is necessary. In a complex and rapidly changing situation, readiness to move from simple tasks to more difficult ones, above all readiness to overcome one's own mistakes is crucial. 'The fighting party of the advanced class need not fear mistakes. What it should fear is persistence in mistakes, refusal to admit and correct the mistakes . . .'[34]

The greatest defect of revolutionaries who have been isolated for years from the mass movement is their inclination to make a virtue out of necessity, and concentrate on theories to the exclusion of practice, forgetting that above all the duty of a revolutionary is to raise theory to the level of practice.

After the war, because of the general expansion of capitalism and the great improvement in workers' wages, a propaganda that tried to generalise from the fragments had no impact to speak of.

Now with the new stage – the increasing similarities between the experiences of workers in the different fragments and the trend towards uniting the fragments, a revolutionary agitation that is both general and specific can start having a greater impact than ever before.

International socialism, up to now at best a theoretical trend, now faces the challenge and opportunity to become linked with the mass working-class movement. To say that we are in a transitional period is not enough. We must be clear what is specific to the transition, and devise forms of propaganda and organisation that will take account of the specific characteristics of the situation. The main features of the immediate period are, to recapitulate: quick changes, fluctuations, economic, social and political, reflecting both the expansion of capitalism, and its intermittent, patchy nature; reactions on the part of bosses and State that are disproportionate to the economic challenge, and hence appear as irrationally nasty; the withering away of loyalties to traditional organisations – the 'vacuum on the Left' – and inertia of old reformist ideas, so long as they are not positively replaced by revolutionary ones.

Fatalism, that is inimical to Marxism in general, exposes its poisonous nature especially under such dynamic conditions. The initiative and perseverance of revolutionaries are at a special premium.

## References

1. Lenin, *Collected Works*, Vol. 26, p170.
2. *Ibid*, Vol. 19, p327.
3. *Ibid*, Vol. 28, pp258–9.
4. *Ibid*, Vol. 26, p385.
5. *Financial Times*, 10 March 1965.
6. The section dealing with productivity deals in the present article is largely based on the author's book *The Employers' Offensive: Productivity Deals and how to Fight them*, Pluto Press, 1970. The reader will find useful the articles by Tony Topham, 'Shop Stewards and Workers' Control' in *New Left Review*, No. 25, 1964; *Productivity Bargaining and Workers' Control*, Nottingham, 1968; and 'Productivity Bargaining' in the *Trade Union Register*, 1969.
7. Prices and Incomes Board (hereafter PIB) Report No. 23. *Productivity and Pay during the Period of Severe Restraint*, Cmnd 3167, p8.
8. PIB Report No. 123, *Productivity Agreements*, Cmnd 4136, p3. Among the number included in the DEP register are some which were regarded by the department as not authentic productivity agreements. In August 1968 the number of such agreements was considered to be some 130, covering about 48,000 workers.
9. *Financial Times*, 29 September 1969.
10. *Statistics on Incomes, Prices, Employment and Production*, March, 1969.
11. PIB Report No. 77, p12.
12. PIB Report No. 36, *Productivity Agreements*, Cmnd 3311, p1.
13. A Flanders in Engineering Employers Federation, *Productivity Bargaining Symposium*, 1969, p14.
14. *Steel Review*, July 1966, p6.
15. *Collective Bargaining – Prescription for change*, 1967, p25.
16. *Ibid*, p28.
17. *Ibid*, p32.
18. Donovan Commission: Report No. 23, *Evidence of the Motor Industry Employers*, p889.
19. Donovan Commission Report No. 69, *Evidence of the CBI*, p2988.
20. 'The ETU's attitude . . . was particularly interesting. Not only did this union have a Communist leadership nationally at the time [of the signing of the Fawley

Agreement – TC] but the [full-time official – TC] and the senior steward were also avowed and long-standing members of the Communist Party. Anyone naive enough to conclude that the union must therefore be hostile to such management co-operation as the Blue Book implied would be mistaken. Throughout the negotiations the ETU [full-time official – TC] who was chairman of the CUC [Croft Union Committee – TC] adopted a very constructive attitude and in this was strangely supported by his senior steward . . .' (Flanders, op, cit., p112.)

21. Ministry of Labour, Motor Industry Joint Labour Council, *Report by Sir Jack Scamp*, 1966, p10.
22. Turner, Clark and Roberts, *Labour Relations in the Motor Industry*, Chapter 9.
23. Ibid., p263.
24. PIB Report No. 29, *The Pay and Conditions of Manual Workers in Local Authorities, the National Health Service, Gas and Water Supply*, Cmnd 3230.
25. PIB Report No. 42, *Pay of Electricity Supply Workers*, Cmnd 3405, p22.
26. *The Times*, 7th November 1969.
27. Lenin, *Collected Works*, Vol. 23, p247.
28. Ibid., Vol. 19, pp534–6.
29. Ibid., Vol. 11, p265.
30. Ibid., p359.
31. Ibid., Vol. 23, p248.
32. L Trotsky, *My Life*, p177.
33. T Cliff and I Birchall, *France, The Struggle Continues*, International Socialism Publications, 1968, pp45–50.
34. Lenin, *Collected Works*, Vol. 26, p58.

# After Pentonville: The battle is won but the war goes on

THIS HAS been the greatest victory for the British working class for more than half a century. The battle has been won, but the war against capitalism is still going on.

After such a great victory it is important to take stock, view the battlefield as a whole and, while full of enthusiasm and the will to struggle, keep a cool head and think out the strategy, tactics and organisational measures necessary to lead the struggle forward.

The motive behind the Tories' attack on the working class is not the nastiness of the rulers, nasty though they be, but the deepening crisis of world capitalism.

The weapons the ruling class uses are determined largely by the immense strength of workers' organisation and workers' resistance. In fact, as Lenin put it, there is no crisis of capitalism the capitalists cannot find a way out of if the workers are ready to pay the price.

The workers' resistance makes it more and more difficult for the bosses to get their way. Let us look at the weapons they have been using for the last few years.

*Incomes Policy:* the aim of this is to shift the distribution of the national income from wages to profits.

In the 1920s and 30s, with massive unemployment and a weak shop organisation, the employers never dreamed of offering a wage rise of $3\frac{1}{2}$ per cent or 5 per cent. Instead they cut wages all round.

*Productivity Deals:* pay homage to working-class strength. Basically, a productivity deal is a bitter pill in terms of worse conditions, speed-up, etc., but it is covered with sugar.

In the 1920s and 30s management didn't dream of saying, 'We

will give you an extra £3 a week on condition you accept deterioration in working conditions.' They simply dictated: 'If you want a job, have it. If you don't, out you get.'

*Key Wage Settlements:* The idea of taking on the postmen and keeping down their wages, plus setting an example to other sections of the working class, is again homage to working-class strength.

In the 1920s and 30s the employers reduced all workers' wages. There wasn't one weak section to become an example to the strong sections – all sections of the working class were weak.

*Anti-trade Union Legislation:* Again homage to our strength. When shop organisation was weak and unemployment massive, the philosophy of capitalism was non-intervention of the state in labour relations.

Let there be a free for all and the best man win. And you can guess who won.

But, because of the present strength of workers' resistance, the capitalist machine does not work the way the bosses want. The driver steers and the machine doesn't turn. He presses the accelerator and it doesn't speed up. He puts on the brake and it doesn't stop.

What, in heaven's name, is affecting the engine? The answer is, the workers' will and ability to resist.

For example, the question of key wage settlements: It is true that the government managed to beat the postmen at the beginning of 1971. They got only a 9 per cent rise. This meant a cut in real wages of some 5 or 6 per cent.

When the cost of living is rising by 10 per cent the workers must get 15 per cent – as a third of any wage rise goes in deductions – just to stay in the same place. But the defeat of the postmen did not prevent Chrysler workers getting a rise of £6 a week in the same month.

Ted Heath and before him Harold Wilson believed that unemployment would introduce discipline on the wages front. (Remember Wilson's 'shake-out of the labour market'?)

For nearly two decades Paish's Law was accepted as a holy truth. Professor F. W. Paish of the London School of Economics had been economic adviser to the Tory government. His theory was that a certain level of unemployment – anything between 2 and $2\frac{1}{2}$ per cent – would break workers' resistance and put them in their place, so that wages would be contained. However, even with unemployment running at a million, Paish's Law did not work at all.

Workers' organisation is too strong for unemployment of the present magnitude to break their will to fight. Actually, unemployment in many cases spurs workers on to further wage claims. A Dundee building worker told me about a year ago: 'Because of the heavy unemployment among builders in my town we decided not to work for less than £1 an hour.'

The Paish logic on the other hand is that if under conditions of more or less full employment a building worker is ready to work for

75p, he will come cap in hand to the boss and be ready to accept a wage of 60p if there is unemployment.

But the workers argue exactly the opposite. 'If I am sure of 40 hours a week, then I can manage on 75p. But if there is unemployment I must demand at least £1.'

Finally, the *Industrial Relations Act* didn't work the way the Tories expected or hoped. Now we don't have to waste too much space to prove this, emerging as we are from five days that shook Tory rule.

It is true that if a ship loses its rudder the captain may use the left engine and stop the right, and then use the right and stop the left.

But this is a costly and ineffective way of moving a ship. If the five rank-and-file docks' militants had to be freed from prison perhaps pliable Jack Jones can serve now as the disciplinarian of the rank and file.

The threat of £55,000 over his head may serve to soften him up. We always knew that we have the best trade union leaders money can buy!

Workers' memories, however, aren't as short as all that. Perhaps two months ago a £55,000 fine would have terrified the rank and file, at least for a time, into submission. But why should workers stop picketing Midland Cold Storage even if Jack Jones has to pay the £55,000?

There is no compulsion on him to pay. He can fight back. If a strike can free the five, it can also prevent the imposition of a fine. If the TUC declared in advance that they would bring the country out on a one-day strike every time a fine was imposed, the ruling class would find the gain not worthwhile.

Every day workers in this country produce goods and services to the value of £150 million, so let's say to our rulers; 'You fine us £55,000 and we will take it back not in thousands but in millions.' That is only fair. It is not an equal exchange, but then we do not live in an equal society. So again this weapon of the ruling class somehow doesn't hit the target.

*Partial Struggles:* The other side of the coin of the ineffectiveness of Tory oppression is the fragmentation and volatility of the workers' struggle. If we juxtapose the great victory of the dockers and workers who came to their aid over the five days, against the fight of the Fine Tubes workers for more than two years, we see how fragmented the struggle is.

The management of Fine Tubes are far smaller in calibre, in weight, in resources than the executive committee of the capitalist class as represented by the state. On the other hand, the workers of Fine Tubes are members of two of the biggest trade unions in the country – the TGWU with 1,700,000 members and the AUEW with 1,400,000.

How is it that unions with more than three million members cannot crack a peanut the size of the Fine Tubes management? The answer is that the trade union bureaucracy was much more effective in paralysing aid to the Fine Tube workers than in paralysing the dockers and the workers who came to their aid.

But the struggle is fragmented also in another way. Take the miners. They won a magnificent victory. They smashed the Tory wage norm. They wiped the smile off Ted Heath's face.

But they could not prevent the rise in the cost of living, or the loss of Family Incomes Supplement, free milk, etc. What they held in their hand largely slipped through their fingers.

Again, the dockers five weeks ago saved three of their members from going to prison. But the very same weekend the giants of the City of London went on strike and they and other big businessmen transferred hundreds of millions of pounds out of this country.

The result? The floating pound and rising prices. The docker can prevent his mates being arrested but he cannot prevent his children losing school milk or the rise in prices now or after Britain joins the Common Market.

Every partial struggle under capitalism means that no victory is really complete.

*Volatility:* The working-class movement has been suffering the last few years not only from fragmentation, from the partial nature of the struggle, but also from extreme volatility.

If one looks back to the 1920s or 30s the struggle was largely systematic in its development. One event followed another in practically a straight line.

If one looks at the 1940s and 50s until the middle 1960s, again for a whole generation we face a systematic development in the class struggle. Year by year workers' real wages improved practically everywhere. Strikes were small in size, short in duration and practically always victorious.

Of course to all these steady developments there were important exceptions. After all, capitalism is an anarchic system and there cannot but be many exceptions to any rules governing the way it works.

As against this long period from the First World War to the middle 60s, the last few years has seen great volatility in the movement. To take only a couple of examples.

The defeat of the postmen led to the same or lower wage settlements involving millions of workers. 1971 was a year of declining wages all round, with important exceptions. Then came the miners' victory and following it the railwaymen's. A fantastic zigzag!

The volatility is even clearer in the case of the struggle against the Industrial Relations Bill. On 8 December 1970, half a million workers came out on strike against the Industrial Relations Bill. The struggle rose.

On 21 February 1971, 140,000 workers demonstrated against the Bill. There must have been many hundreds of thousands if not millions that identified themselves with these demonstrations in Liverpool, Manchester, Birmingham, Glasgow, and so on.

On 1 March 1½ million workers came out on official strike against the Bill. On 18 March a similar number came out again. On that day the TUC made it clear they were not ready to give a lead in the general struggle against the Bill. The result? There was an immediate 180 degrees turn.

The militants' slogan now was 'Stop the Retreat'. From an offensive posture they turned to a defensive one. This volatility affects largely the advanced sections of the working class. It is rooted in (1) the feeling of the militant that quite often he cannot carry the majority of his own workmates with him, and (2) his isolation from militants in other places of work and even more, in other industries.

*Three Cog Wheels:* The trade union movement with 11 million members and 250,000 shop stewards is a powerful cog, with far the strongest shop organisation of the working class anywhere in the world.

Let's assume that we had in this country a revolutionary socialist party, a combat organisation, steeled in struggle and schooled in the art of strategy and tactics for the overthrow of capitalism. Let's assume that we, the International Socialists, who are building such an organisation, had 50,000 members.

There is no question that this would indeed be a powerful cog wheel. However, one cog wheel of this size could not have moved the cog wheel of 11 million. If it tried it would only break its cogs. A connecting cog wheel is necessary between the two.

This is the organisation of militants in different unions and industries who work together round specific issues, issues wider than those affecting a small group of workers in one place of work and not going as far as to aim at a complete emancipation of the working class by the overthrow of the capitalist system.

IS members participate in building such a cog wheel in the form of rank and file organisations round papers like **The Carworker, The Collier** and **Rank and File Teacher.** The aim of these is to influence the policies of the trade unions.

The rising conflict will disclose to workers the magnitude of the struggle, will widen their horizons and will help to clarify their ideas. It is very important for members of IS to do their best to recruit militants into our political organisation as well as to strengthen all existing rank and file industrial and trade union organisations.

*Generalise the Struggle:* One of the main strengths of the dockers' five days' struggle was the clear unity between the particular life and death interest of the docker protecting his livelihood and the general interest of the working class to break the yoke of the Industrial Relations Act.

In the coming stage of the dockers' struggle, this unity has to be preserved. There is no doubt that the media, television and the press, that serves big business, will do their best to show the dockers' struggle as a struggle of one group of workers in their own selfish interests against other workers.

It is extremely important that the dockers make it absolutely clear that their struggle is a struggle for the right to work. Now more than ever it is important to have leaflets and posters by the thousands putting this case.

It is important that dockers themselves should go around factories, power stations, mines and so on and put this case clearly forward. One live docker can make more effective propaganda for the truth than a thousand copies of the **Daily Express**.

In the new stage the question of generalisation rises in another way. During the five days' struggle the rank and file showed itself in all its glory while the trade union bureaucracy, including Jack Jones, showed their complete bankruptcy. Now that the dockers' strike is official, the danger is that those bankrupt full-time officials will take over the running of the strike.

It is even more important now that the joint Port Shop Stewards' Committee is central in actively running the strike, in publicising the issues and in developing the strategy and tactics of the struggle.

The question of generalisation arises also in yet another way. The Tory press is arguing that a docks strike can go on for a long time without damaging the economy, that is, big business. To some extent it is whistling in the dark.

However, the experience of 1970 with a $2\frac{1}{2}$ weeks docks strike makes it clear that to spread the struggle is important. A docks strike affects exports but it also affects imports.

When the miners' strike started, the Tory press was confident that the government would win because it assumed that the miners would simply picket the mines. But the rank-and-file miners were 100 per cent right when they showed their initiative in picketing the power stations. This is a lesson that the dockers should not overlook.

The question of generalisation of the struggle also raises a question of new institutions created in struggle. In the short five days struggle very close relations were created between the dockers and the printers in Fleet Street. It is important that those close relations continue.

It won't be amiss if the printers refuse to print particularly obnoxious attacks on the dockers. After all, we are told we live in a free, democratic country and if six owners of the press have a right to dictate what is being published in their papers, why shouldn't the printers also have some say?

In the five days of struggle the embryo of a Council of Action connecting dockers and printers and other workers was in the making. In new, more prolonged, wider struggles the question of a Council of Action will really come to the fore.

The last point in terms of generalisation: Episodic struggles are very prone to accidents. Their outcome depends on the relation of forces in every specific situation.

Because the ruling class is highly centralised, its ability to manoeuvre is much greater than any individual section of the working class.

Therefore the need for a revolutionary party, to repeat, as a school of strategy and tactics, and at the same time an active combat organisation, will become more vital than ever.

# 1972: A tremendous year for the workers

1972 WAS A tremendous year for Britain's working class. The struggle rose to new heights, both in terms of the number of workers involved, the size of strikes and their length, and above all in the quality of the struggle.

There have been far more large-scale and prolonged strikes this year than in the previous ten years, as the table below shows.

November and December figures have not yet been published, but there is no doubt that the total number of strike days has reached or exceeded 30 million this year. If one excludes miners' strikes, only once in British history has the number of strike days been greater – that was in 1919.

The 1972 figure is more than four times 1969, and some nine times the yearly average for the previous twenty years.

1972 saw the first national miners' strike since 1926 – and this time the miners won – and the biggest building strike ever – 300,000 out over twelve weeks. The last similar confrontation was in 1923, when the employers locked the builders out.

The quality of the struggle has also been very advanced. There has been a purely political strike, to free the Pentonville Five. There has been a solidarity strike of 50,000 Birmingham engineers in support of the miners, 10,000 of them marching to Saltley Coke Depot. For the first time we have had strikes in support of old age pensioners, 6,000 construction workers in Anchor, near Scunthorpe, coming out.

The workers have shown great initiative.

But the trade union bureaucracy has been treacherous. Look at the miners' strike. The government offered the miners only £2. The official claim of the miners' union was £9, £6 and £5. Joe Gormley declared on the eve of the strike that if the government had raised the offer just a little the strike would not have taken place – he would probably have signed for £3.

The Tory press was absolutely convinced the government would win this round as they won against the postmen. They were looking for a confrontation. It was the initiative of the miners' rank and file, in picketing power stations instead of wasting effort on picketing the pits, that led the way. Helped by railwaymen, lorry drivers and workers in the power industry, they won a magnificent victory.

While 60 per cent of the miners of Barnsley went on picket duty outside Yorkshire, the Labour MP for Barnsley contributed to victory by standing for a whole ten minutes on the picket line at Battersea power station. By sheer accident the television cameras were there at the same time.

We shouldn't criticise. It was cold, and he had to rush back to the House of Commons for some important vote, probably on dog licensing.

The Shadow Minister for Fuel and Power, Harold Lever, attacked the Tories for mismanaging the dispute, declaring that if Labour had been in power they would have settled the miners' wage claim for less than the Tories.

While the leaders did not manage to prevent the miners' victory, they did manage to sign an agreement sabotaging future battles, by allowing the date of the agreement to be shifted from November to February. Until now the annual agreement has run from November to November. The present one runs until February 1973.

If at the end of February the coal board rejects the NUM claim, the executive will have to organise a ballot and prepare miners for action, which will take a month or two. For miners to go on strike in summer is not the best of tactics. The 1926 general strike, remember, started in May.

Ice-cream workers should have agreements from May to May, miners from November to November. Although the rank and file miners won the battle in spite of the bureaucrats, the latter managed to sabotage the next round.

Again, look at the dockers' struggle. It was a magnificent victory over the government when the five dockers were freed.

The strike was unofficial. Jack Jones kept his mouth shut, and did nothing at all the help the dockers. Reg Prentice, the Shadow Minister of Labour, attacked the five dockers for breaking the law, and seeking self-advertisement.

Barbara Castle was more hypocritical. The Pentonville Five were arrested on the anniversary of the Tolpuddle Martyrs. 'In Place of Strife' Babs put a wreath on the grave of one of them. If he were not dead, and if she were in power, she would surely have put *him* in Pentonville instead.

After the Five were freed Jack Jones threw his weight and that of the union on the side of the dockers and job security, declaring an official strike, which lasted three weeks. If 41,000 dockers could win an unofficial strike, the support of a union of 1,700,000 should surely have won them the official one.

But the result was the Aldington-Jones sell-out. Lord Aldington, former Tory MP, former vice-chairman of the Tory Party who gave £30,000 to buy Morning Cloud for Ted Heath, the vice-chairman of GEC that sacked more than 50,000 workers over four years, was sold to the dockers by Jack Jones with promises of job security.

After the Pentonville Five affair the Tory government was reeling. In July and August, the Tory press spoke of Ted Heath's government being bankrupt.

But in September, the TUC snatched victory out of defeat for this government. It was Vic Feather and the TUC who suggested the idea of an incomes policy at the September conference in Brighton. Ted Heath spelt it out by suggesting an all-round price of £2, and thus the ground was prepared for the 90-day freeze.

The fantastic potential power of the rank and file and the treason of the trade union bureaucracy make it necessary now, more than ever, to build rank and file organisations in the unions to fight for democratic control, and to create combat organisations connecting workers from different places of work, so that they can discuss questions of strategy and tactics.

The struggle over the past year has also shown that it is important to bridge the gulf that exists in many factories and other places of work between the militants and the rest of the workers. For a long time battles were won in individual shops by mobilising a small number of workers, or by threatening to do so. With today's mass confrontations, the key problem is how to involve a massive number of workers in the struggle.

Often militants in one factory are without any contact with workers in the factory next door, or with the workers in another factory of the same empire. No less serious, however, is that militant shop stewards do not always involve their own workers in discussing the strategy and tactics needed to raise their fighting strength and understanding of the issues facing them.

During 1972 members of the International Socialists participated in launching a number of rank and file papers – **The Collier, The Steelworker, The Dockworker**, among others. We decided also to build **Socialist Worker** groups in factories.

The aim is to discuss with workers the general question of socialist politics facing the working class. Such groups should be active and intervening at all stages of the struggle. They should dig deeper roots for **Socialist Worker** inside the factory, by increasing its sale, getting reports for it, criticising it, and collecting donations.

The paper is more and more a workers' paper – not a paper just for workers. It is written to a large extent by workers in struggle. But however good the paper, improvements and criticism are always necessary.

When Lenin said the paper is an organiser, he meant not only, say, the carworkers' paper, but also separate factory bulletins in different car factories, written by militants in the factory itself, read by the whole workforce in the factory, not only the minority of militant socialists.

If decisive proof were needed that cabbage-patch militancy is not enough, the case of James Goad and the Lucas Birmingham factories has given it.

The Sudbury Lucas workers, where Goad used to work, went on strike against the Industrial Relations Court's £50,000 fine on the Engineering Union and called on their Birmingham colleagues to come to their aid. But under the influence of the right-wing officials, the Birmingham Lucas shop stewards decided not to take any action.

If they had decided differently and the 20,000 Lucas workers had come out in solidarity with Sudbury, the impact would have been tremendous. The snowball effect could have been as big as the Pentonville Five.

Things could have turned out very differently if the left in Lucas Birmingham were better organised. Many of the militant stewards did not know about the stewards' meeting. Not one of the stewards knew that a request from the Sudbury strikers to send a delegation to the Birmingham meeting had been turned down by the district secretary.

For lack of space I cannot deal adequately with the bankruptcy of the AUEW leadership in the Goad affair – a subject I will return to in the next few weeks.

Members of the International Socialists and other militant workers in Lucas Birmingham factories started a monthly bulletin called **Lucas Worker** about a month ago. Had they started, say, a year earlier . . . if . . . if . . . A different initiative from the local Lucas leadership could have brought a totally different outcome.

The struggle in one field – in Birmingham Lucas – can become decisive for the whole labour movement. In the great chain of events, even an individual link can be decisive at a particular point in time. Socialists, organising in their place of work, should see their work as relevant not only to the workers directly involved, but also, potentially, to the whole of the working class.

In the second issue of the **Dockworker**, published a few days ago, a docker's wife wrote a marvellous letter. I shall quote just the final paragraph: 'After trying for 10 years "officially" to get these [thalidomide] kids some money, without success, it's about time that something was done "unofficially". I am surprised that dockers have not done something about blacking Distillers' products, which I am sure are exported through some docks in the country.'

She is absolutely right. The dockers who could free the Five have the industrial power to force Distillers to cough up money for those unfortunate children.

The workers have the power to force the Tory government to give a £16 pension to the old age pensioners. They have the power to smash the Tory government. They have the power to blow capitalism to kingdom come.

1972 has gone. Welcome to 1973.

| | Number of workers involved (000s) | Number of working days lost (000s) | Average number of days per worker on strike |
|---|---|---|---|
| 1953–64 (average) | 1,081 | 3,712 | 3.3 |
| 1965 | 876 | 2,925 | 3.3 |
| 1966 | 544 | 2,398 | 4.4 |
| 1967 | 734 | 2,787 | 4.0 |
| 1968 | 2,258 | 4,680 | 2.1 |
| 1969 | 1,665 | 6,876 | 4.1 |
| 1970 | 1,801 | 10,980 | 6.1 |
| 1971 | 1,171 | 13,551 | 12.1 |
| Jan–Oct 1972 | 1,353 | 22,202 | 17.1 |

# The use of Socialist Worker as an organiser

LENIN SPOKE about a socialist paper as an organiser of workers. He saw it in three fields: (1) the workers as writers for the paper, (2) as sellers of the paper, (3) as donors of money. Now, let's look at Socialist Worker's role in those three fields. There is no question that Socialist Worker has improved radically over the last few years in terms of involvement of workers in writing for it. There is no question that it is by far the best socialist paper on the left for decades in this country. However, we shouldn't be complacent. Still to a large extent workers' writing is limited to a small area of the paper. From time to time excellent pieces written by workers appear in 'Under the Influence' and some other articles written by workers. A new very important contribution by workers is, of course, the Letters Page which has improved radically over the last few months. Still the criticism that Trotsky levelled at the American Socialist Appeal on 27 May 1939 is not completely irrelevant to Socialist

Worker although let's make it clear – Socialist Worker is much better than Socialist Appeal. Let's quote Trotsky:

'As it is, the paper is divided among various writers, each of whom is very good, but collectively they do not permit workers to penetrate to the pages of the Appeal. Each of them speaks for the workers (and speaks very well) but nobody will hear the workers. In spite of its literary brilliance, to a certain degree the paper becomes a victim of journalistic routine. You do not hear at all how the workers live, fight, clash with the police or drink whiskey. It is very dangerous for the paper as a revolutionary instrument of the party. The task is not to make a paper through the joint forces of a skilled editorial board but to encourage the workers to speak for themselves. A radical and courageous change is necessary as a condition of success . . .'

The fact that nearly half the IS membership are manual workers is not reflecting itself well enough in the paper. It is important that workers should write, not only about strikes in their place of work but about their children and their education, about everything that is relevant to their life. To a large extent the paper must become a workers' diary. Now of course workers find it diffficult to write. When they speak quite often they are incomparably better than when they write because their concreteness, their colourfulness, their individuality comes through – and after all, for Marxism it is always central that the truth is always concrete. When workers write quite often they adapt their style to what they think the style *should* be and therefore it becomes dull and jargonised. Therefore the use of a tape recorder and then editing the story while keeping the flavour intact is very, very important and should be used. This will mean of course a fantastic burden on our journalists. It is much easier for Paul Foot, for instance, to write a whole page on his own than to edit five or six stories written by workers that will also fill a page. Therefore, the use of more workers' material will probably mean the need for more journalists. Our organisers in the field will have to do their part. Every factory branch will have to be supplying stories, articles, letters for the paper. Lenin's **Pravda** in 1912, when the party was illegal and with a working class much smaller than ours, managed to print in one year 11,000 items written by workers. It is true that the Bolsheviks had much better roots than we have but still it will not be beyond our reach if we aim to, say, have 50 items a week written by workers in the paper. For them we need not only perhaps more effort put in by the editorial board of the paper and the organisers, but above all a clear decision that items written by or told by workers *have* to find a place in the paper in one way or another. (Of course even to this we must have exceptions.) There is not a capitalist paper in the country that can afford more than 3,000 reporters – we can.

The question of workers' writing for the paper raises the question of the identification of workers with the paper. In bourgeois journalism the hierarchical concept in which a small bunch of the people from the centre supply the consumption needs of the millions is the prevailing one. For a workers' paper the question of the **involvement** of the 'consumer' is central. The abolition of the abyss between producer and consumer is central. Therefore a story written by a worker that perhaps will interest directly only a few tens of workers directly next to him at his place of work is of fantastic importance. This is the way the paper becomes rooted deeper in the class.

Now to the question of workers as *sellers* of the paper. The fact that nearly half of the membership of IS – to repeat – are manual workers does not reflect itself at all in the sale of the paper. Less than 20 per cent of the sales of the paper is from inside places of work and this is a very, very serious defect. To some extent it is a result of the question of the relation between readers and workers as writers. But to some extent it is a question that stands on its own. We were so busy in the last few years in turning an organisation with hardly any workers into an organisation that involves workers in it that we didn't use effectively enough our periphery around the organisation. In reality we posed to every worker two possibilities – join IS, and then of course you pay subs, come to meetings, etc., or otherwise buy a copy of the paper. Now we have to approach our periphery and ask every one of them to take a few copies of the paper. If we reach let's say in three months' time a thousand non-IS members, who will take say two or three copies of the paper each, it will be an important change in our position.

A worker that buys one copy of the paper has a very different attitude to it than the one who sells a couple of copies. If he buys he doesn't have to read the paper, he doesn't have to take a position on the different ideas in the paper. If he sells the paper he can't avoid doing both because always he faces the possibility of one of the buyers arguing with him about the paper. In reality people never grasp ideas clearly unless they have to fight for those ideas and therefore if one paper is sold it doesn't create a conflict of ideas – if five are sold in the same place, it does. It is not therefore only a quantative change but a radical, qualitative change in the relation of the individual to the ideas and to the organisation that propagates those ideas.

Thirdly, about the workers donating money to the paper. Lenin put it clearly that it is very important that the collection of money is done regularly and systematically. The weekly payment of one kopek that in relative terms to our wages in Britain is something like one new penny a week, was expected from every buyer of **Pravda**. And these by the way were the party subs. In Britain, for obvious reasons, it is much more difficult to organise such a net of money donators – and we will have to start probably with a much more modest target of let's say 10p per month, to be collected on the first pay day in the month. This is not only a question of money – it is much more a question of politics. By giving money workers declare that they are really identifying themselves to some extent with the paper. When they give money they look more critically at the paper, at the same time more appreciative of the paper because they know that their money helps make the appearance of the paper possible. Therefore from such small beginnings quite long term results can come. If we got, let's say, a thousand donors over the coming six months it will be quite an important bridgehead.

All the above changes will bring quite a serious transformation in the whole working of our organisation. Above all it will make it possible for workers to come to the front in the running of our organisation because in every aspect the organisation will appear less and less often the by-lines of the Paul Foots, Laurie Flynns and more as a workers' organisation. Workers will have to be encouraged to be the main speakers of the organisation on platforms, their names will have to appear in the paper more and more often and less and less often the bye-lines of the Paul Foots, Laurie Flynns and Tony Cliffs. At the same time, their influence in determining the educational role of the paper will increase over time.

All the above changes cannot be done by a campaign. It is not a question of a campaign. When we turned our organisation towards industrial activity it took us years of struggle. This time making Socialist Worker into a workers' paper in order to make IS into a workers' party will also take a long time. This doesn't mean that a few *technical* and immediate measures are not necessary. The fact that we published a book on productivity deals did not transform our organisation into a workers' organisation but helped in the process of doing it. The technical decisions we have to take immediately are; that every factory branch should send at least one article, report or story once a month, that every organiser should see to it that from his area we get at least one article or story a week – if need be, we will have to increase the number of journalists on the paper with the emphasis on them being in the field. We will have to organise the transformation of the buyers of the paper into sellers, without putting an individual target that is meaningless for branches or districts, we will have to monitor our successes and failures. Thirdly we will have to organise the collection of let's say 10p a month from the buyers of the paper.

These are the technical things that have to be organised immediately.

# Lenin:
# His ideas are the future

Lenin. Turned into a peepshow and a god by Stalin and the gravediggers of the Russian Revolution. Painted as a tyrant and dictator in the west by the capitalist opponents of socialism.

He was neither of these parodies. He dedicated his life to the emancipation of working people, not only in Russia but throughout the world. He fought to build a tough party of revolutionaries to organise the struggle for power.

Above all, Lenin placed his belief in the ability of working people to throw off the chains of their oppressors. To mark the 50th anniversary of Lenin's death, Tony Cliff rescues the revolutionary leader from his enemies on both sides of the 'Iron Curtain'.

FIFTY YEARS ago the great revolutionary socialist leader Vladimir Ilyich Lenin died.

At the anniversary of his death, Moscow and its friends on the one hand and Western opponents of Communism on the other, did their best to distort the real historical role of this great man.

The legend was cultivated over a long period that Lenin was the father of Stalinism, a man that believed in totalitarian dictatorship. Nothing can be further from the truth.

What happened to Lenin was prophetically foretold by him in his brilliant work, **State and Revolution**, when he described the fate of revolutionary leaders in the past:

'During the lifetime of great revolutionaries, the oppressing classes constantly hounded them, received their theories with the most savage malice, the most furious hatred and the most unscrupulous campaigns of lies and slander. After their death, attempts are made to convert them into harmless icons, to canonise them, so to say . . . while at the same time robbing the revolutionary theory of its *substance*, blunting its revolutionary edge and vulgarising it.'

Above all, Lenin had supreme confidence in the creative abilities of the masses. Thus, for instance, he wrote in June-July 1905:

'Revolutions are festivals of the oppressed and the exploited. At no other time are the mass of the people in a position to come forward so actively as creators of a new social order, as at a time of revolution. At such times the people are capable of performing miracles, if judged by the limited, philistine yardsticks of gradualist progress.'

Workers learn in the struggle. They learn from their own experience in battle. The role of a really consistent revolutionary socialist workers' party is not to lecture to the workers but to learn from the workers in struggle and teach them in struggle.

'When bourgeois gentry and their uncritical echoers, the social reformists, talk about the 'education of the masses', they usually mean something schoolmasterly, pedantic, something that demoralises the masses and instils in them bourgeois prejudices.

'The real education of the masses can never be separated from their independent political, and especially revolutionary, struggle. Only struggle educates the exploited class. Only struggle discloses to it the magnitude of its own power, widens its horizon, enhances its abilities, clarifies its mind, forges its will.'

The aim of the revolutionary socialist party is to tap the natural potential resources of energy and ingenuity hidden in the masses. The party has to learn from the workers in struggle:

'There is an enormous amount of organising talent among the 'people', i.e. among the workers and the peasants who do not exploit the labour of others. Capital crushed these talented people in thousands; it killed their talent and threw them on to the scrapheap.

'We are not yet able to find them, encourage them, put them on their feet, promote them. But we shall learn to do so if we set about it with an all-out revolutionary enthusiasm, without which there can be no victorious revolutions.'

To learn from the masses the party must also be able and ready to learn from its own mistakes, to be very self-critical. As Lenin put it:

'A political party's attitude towards its own mistakes is one of the most important and surest ways of judging how earnest the party is and how it fulfills *in practice* its obligations towards its *class*, and the *working people*. Frankly acknowledging a mistake, ascertaining the reasons for it, analysing the conditions that have led up to it, and thrashing out the means of its rectification – that is the hallmark of a serious party; that is how it should perform its duties, and how it should educate and train its class, and then the masses.'

The open debate is ever more vital and essential at the period of direct revolutionary struggle. So Lenin wrote in a leaflet, 25–26

April 1906:

'In a revolutionary epoch like the present, all theoretical errors and tactical deviations of the party are most ruthlessly criticised by experience itself, which enlightens and educates the working class with unprecedented rapidity.

'At such a time, the duty of every socialist is to strive to ensure that the ideological struggle within the party on questions of theory and tactics is conducted as openly, widely and freely as possible, but that on no account does it disturb or hamper the unity of revolutionary action of the Social-Democratic proletariat.

'The party of the revolutionary proletariat is strong enough to openly criticise itself, and unequivocally call mistakes and weaknesses by their proper names. The fighting party of the advanced class need not fear mistakes. What it should fear is persistence in a mistake, refusal to admit and correct a mistake out of a false sense of shame.'

Of course, inner-party discussions must not lead to lack of discipline and unity of action. But on the contrary, inner-party democracy has to serve as a base for unity in action. As Lenin so well put it:

'We have more than once already enunciated our theoretical views on the importance of discipline and on how this concept is to be understood in the party of the working class. We defined it as: *unity of action, freedom of discussion and criticism*. Only such discipline is worthy of the democratic party of the advanced class.

'. . . The proletariat does not recognise unity of action without freedom to discuss and criticise . . . there can be no mass party, no party of a class, without full clarity of essential shadings, without an open struggle between various tendencies, without informing the *masses* as to which leaders and which organisations of the party are pursuing this or that line. Without this, a party worthy of the name cannot be built.'

Contrary to Stalinist mythology – as well as that of liberal opponents of Bolshevism – the Bolshevik Party has never been a monolithic or totalitarian party. Far from it.

Internal democracy had always been of the utmost importance to party life. Thus for instance, when the most important question of all, the question of the October insurrection in 1917 was the order of the day, the leadership was sharply divided: a strong faction led by Zinoviev, Kamenev, Rykov, Piatakov, Miliutin and Nogin, opposed the uprising.

Nevertheless, when the political bureau was elected by the central committee, neither Zinoviev nor Kamenev were excluded.

After taking power, the differences in the party leadership continued to be as sharp as before. A few days after the revolution, a number of party leaders came out with a demand for a coalition with other socialist parties.

Those insisting on this included Rykov, the People's Commissar of the Interior, Miliutin, the People's Commissar of Industry and Trade, Lunacharsky, the Commissar of Education, Kamenev, the President of the Republic and Zinoviev.

They went as far as resigning from the government, thus compelling Lenin and his supporters to open negotiations with the other parties. The negotiations broke down because the right-wing socialists insisted on the exclusion of Lenin and Trotsky from the coalition government.

Again, on the question of holding or postponing the elections to the Constituent Assembly in December 1917, Lenin found himself in a minority in the central committee, and the elections were held against his advice.

A little later he was again defeated on the question of the peace negotiations with Germany at Brest-Litovsk. He was for an immediate peace. But at a meeting of the central committee and active workers, held on 21 January 1918, his motion received only 15 votes against Bukharin's motion for 'revolutionary war', which received 32 votes, and Trotsky's for 'neither peace nor war', which received 16.

At a session of the central committee next day, Lenin was again defeated. But at last he succeeded, under the pressure of events, in convincing the majority of members of the central committee of his point of view, and at its session on 24 February his motion for peace gained seven votes, while four voted against and another four abstained.

As a result of the weakness of the Russian working class, after nearly seven years of war and civil war, the isolation of the Russian revolution following the betrayal of the German revolution by right-wing labour leaders – including the murder of the great socialist leaders Rosa Luxemburg and Karl Liebknecht – the Stalinist bureaucracy rose in Russia.

It consolidated itself after the mass murder of Lenin's old comrades in arms during the 1930s. One-man management in the factories where managers earn 100 times more than workers, where workers have no right to strike and are deprived of all freedoms, became the hallmark of the Stalinist regime.

But the future belongs to the ideas of Marx and Lenin. The basic tenets of Marxism-Leninism:

*That the working class is the agent of socialism.*

*That the working class needs a vanguard party to lead it, to raise its combative ability, consciousness and organisation.*

*The need to smash the bureaucratic militarist police state machine of capitalism and replace it with democratic workers' councils, where all officials get the same wages as the workers they represent, with regular elections of all officials and the right to recall them.*

These ideas are of vital importance to workers everywhere, whether in Britain or Russia, the United States, China or India.

The future belongs to the ideas of Marx and Lenin.

# The great incomes policy con-trick

WHAT DO politicians mean by incomes policy? Is it anything more than a policy to restrain wages?

When Labour introduced its first incomes policy in 1965, it stressed that it would be perfectly fair because it would apply equally to all incomes. Is there any truth in this claim?

## Can Profits Be Controlled?

There is a qualitative difference between wages and profits: wages are a necessary part of the costs of production while profits are not; profits are what is left over after production and sale, while wages are not; wages are negotiated between two sides, while profits are not. It is nonsense to talk of putting the same restraints on profits and wages since profits cannot be planned.

Profits, moreover, are the motor of capitalism and its only reliable guide to how well an enterprise is doing.

Profit is the life-blood of capitalism. If you are allergic to profit then you just can't run a capitalist economy. Therefore, as long as the Labour leaders are committed to such an economy they cannot and dare not harm, or gag, profits.

Profits are what is left from the sale price of a commodity after its costs of production have been deducted. So, to control profits, there must also be control of prices. But price control is also an impossible task.

The number of price changes is fantastically large. The Department of Economic Affairs estimated that something like three million prices are altered each year, that is 12,000 for each of the 250 members of the Price Commission staff.

These poor people have to evaluate all the price increases requested, check the quarterly returns, make spot checks on a myriad of small firms, and make sure that all the figures they are given are valid, even though they have nothing better than unaudited accounts to deal with, or alternatively year-old audited ones.

And if they do get anywhere, the maximum fine that can be imposed for illegal price increases is £400 – what a deterrent!

In the first five months of Phase Three, only one company had to defy a Commission order to reduce prices – there were no others, which is not surprising since price increases of up to 80 per cent were being allowed through.

The 1964–1970 Labour incomes policy was launched against a background of economic growth and expansion. Now we're in the middle of a crisis.

So incomes policy Mark II will be different from Mark I. It will be accompanied by a massive propaganda effort around the theme that incomes policy is necessary to avoid catastrophe – to prevent massive unemployment and spiralling inflation.

Labour will try to convince workers that they should not press for an improvement in living standards, but aim at best to defend existing ones. The TUC's 'Social Contract' fits the bill perfectly.

### Does the Social Contract help the low-paid?

Many workers believe that incomes policy is a good thing in principle, even if they don't agree that it should apply to themselves at present. Many believe that it makes sense for better-off workers to practice restraint in order to improve lower-paid workers' wages.

But in fact the whole thing is based on a misunderstanding: if ICI workers were to hold back on a claim for another £1 a week, would the management of ICI transfer the money they have saved to, say, the nurses, or would they transfer it to ICI's bank account? To ask the question is to see the answer.

The way wages are won under capitalism is simple: workers in the strongest sections, in the technologically advanced industries, where they are best organised, win increases, and the rest of the working class keep up by comparing their own wages with those received by the strongest and best-paid, and following.

If a worker in a strong position gets a small wage rise, the one in a weaker position will get even less. This is why wage differences within the working class have declined considerably over the years as the workers' strength grew. Skilled workers, who were getting twice as much as the unskilled in the years before 1914, were only 15 or 10 per cent ahead by the fifties.

If anything was needed to explode the myth that incomes policy would act as the angel of social justice for the lower-paid workers, it was the Prices and Incomes Board's refusal of the railwaymen in January 1966.

In their report, wages per standard week (excluding overtime) were given as follows: porters £10.18s; leading luggage room attendant £12.5s; second-year guard £12.19s; qualified fireman £14.8s; qualified train driver £16.19s (National Board for Prices and Incomes, Pay and Conditions of Service of British Railways Staff, Cmndt 2873, January 1966, pp. 32–33).

There they are, low-paid grades in plenty – but still no suggestion that more pay should be given to the wretchedly underpaid sections.

The strongest and best-organised workers must not hold back, for if they do the whole working class will be held back with them.

### Is the Social Contract fair?

Harold Wilson tried a voluntary incomes policy when he first came to office. It fell to pieces in the rebellion of the lower-paid in 1969. This time, with inflation four or five times higher than last, his incomes policy will be doomed even faster.

Talk of its fairness cannot stick when workers read about nine-carat gold neckchains for cats – price £85 (**Observer Magazine**, 20 May 1974), or velvet 'Marie Antoinette' kennels for £148, and small doggy winter coats – in mink – for £400 at Harrods (**London Evening News**, 10 December 1973), or penthouse suites at £35,900 each on the QE2's 91-day round-the-world cruise (**Daily Mail**, 25 January 1974), or Michael Noble, Tory MP for Argyllshire's bottle of Chateau Mouton Rothschild, which went for a record £3,538 (£100 a glass) (**Daily Express**, 24 May 1972).

Long queues of pensioners form each morning outside Greggs' bakery shop in Westgate Road, Newcastle, The reason? Stale cakes and bread returned from the firms' other shops are sold to the pensioners for half price.

A spokesman for the firm said that previously 'the bread used to be destroyed and it was normal for it to be sent to pig farms' (**Morning Star**, 17 July 1974).

Workers are more suspicious of government propaganda than before. The fact that, on the eve of the October general election, there was a fantastic strike wave shows how little leeway they will allow for government, including a Labour government.

In 1969 it was the workers with no traditional militancy or strength of organisation that broke through the wage restraint. This time the breakthrough will come much more quickly, and through the activity of workers on a much wider front, from relatively well-paid carworkers to ancillary workers in hospitals.

# Portugal: The lessons of the 25th November

The Portuguese revolution suffered its first major setback on 25 November 1975. After paratroopers had seized a number of airbases and the national radio and television station, the right wing staged a counter-coup. The outcome was the disarming and disbandment of those left-wing military units in the Lisbon area that had supported the struggles of workers.

The main organisation of the workers movement in Portugal remain intact, but it can no longer look to support from the best armed sections of the army. Indeed, the monopoly of organised military power now lies with generals most of whom are well to the right of the present coalition government and who would relish the idea of turning Portugal into another Chile.

THE PORTUGUESE revolutionary movement suffered its first major defeat on 25 November since the overthrow of fascism.

Its base among the military units in the Lisbon area has been destroyed and scores of left-wing soldiers and officers are in jail. The ruling class has regained a more or less complete monopoly of armed force.

Prime responsibility for the defeat lies with the Communist Party leadership, which initiated the rebellion and then abandoned it to its fate.

---

*COPCON:* Continental Operations Command. Highly radicalised crack troops.
*RAL I:* Lisbon barracks light artillery regiment. Very radical.
*CRTSM:* Councils of Revolutionary Workers, Soldiers and Sailors. They were not Soviets since they organised only a minority of the most class conscious workers.
*PRP:* Revolutionary Party of the Proletariat.
*MES:* Left grouping which tended to act as a pressure group on the Communist Party.
*SUV:* Soldiers United Will Win.
*RADIO RENASCENCA:* Radio station owned by Catholic hierarchy, occupied by the workers. Reported sympathetically on workers struggles in Portugal and abroad. An important symbol of the revolution.

---

**Pamphlet first published in Portuguese December 1975**

Communist Party aligned officers agitated for the paratroops to seize airbases.

The revolutionary organisations seem to have been quite taken by surprise.

But once the paratroopers had taken action, they saw no choice but to support them. It was then that the PRP and MES issued a joint statement that 'the hour had come to give a lesson to the bourgeoisie'.

But within hours, the Communist Party leadership had copped out of the struggle. It called no strikes to back up the paratroopers – although it had been able to initiate a successful two-hour general strike the day before – but did issue a leaflet calling on the workers to stay calm. It left the revolutionaries, and even some of its own officers, isolated in the face of attacks from the right.

The Communist Party campaigned against strike action by the workers at the very moment when such action was the only way to prevent the advance of reaction.

In October, we wrote in the Portuguese edition of the pamphlet **Portugal at the Crossroads** – that the bourgeoisie would attempt to strangle the revolutionary left, 'to provoke it to engage in battle before there existed either soviets or a mass revolutionary party. The right will do everything in its power to dupe the working-class vanguard.'

It succeeded on 25 November through the Portuguese Communist Party.

Now this treachery looks like being rewarded, as right-wing military figures such as Melo Antunes and Charais call for the Party to be kept in the government, while the left-wing officers are in jail.

But the treachery of the Communist Party was to be expected. To explain the defeat, it is necessary to know why the revolutionary left could not counteract that treachery.

Sections of the middle class, even those most favourable to the working class, will always vacillate when it comes to decisive confrontations. The job of a revolutionary organisation is to inculcate this lesson into the ranks of the workers and soldiers before the crunch comes.

### Lack of Organisation

Above all what characterises the events of 25 November is the lack of any serious organisation of the revolutionary soldiers when it came to the crunch.

Too much trust was put in revolutionary officers and no real structure of organisation of the rank and file existed able to lead at the testing time. As was stated in an interview in Lisbon on 27 November by a couple of revolutionary comrades:

'There was no co-ordination, no real co-ordination. The CP expected Copcon to do it. Copcon didn't. It hesitated, wavered, and so on. The same thing happened with the so-called revolutionary units because they were caught in a totally defensive position, discussing and so forth. Inside the barracks they did not take a single initiative. Yet they were exposed to the extent that they never pledged themselves to the military commanders and did not follow this or that order.

'No-one offered resistance (to the commandos). There were only a few shots in the case of the military police. And even there the top commander of the military police opened the door to them. He surrendered himself after a little shooting – and not from the other side.

'What happened at RALIS? (at the time of the interview RALIS had not yet surrendered). Last night the soldiers were still there and wanted to do something but they lacked military direction (their commander, Denis da Almeida, had surrendered).'

One of the military police, a soldier, told me how annoying it was for these soldiers who were prepared and organised for an insurrection for the socialist revolution. 'As soon as the two commanders – Tome and Andrade disappeared – one surrendered, the other was captured – they didn't know what to do. There wasn't anyone to give orders. Although the soldiers were refusing military discipline, they didn't know how to operate in any other way.'

'The so-called revolutionary officers are finished.'

■■■■■■■■■■■■■■■■■■■■

### Weakness of the Revolutionary Left

The decisive factor in the defeat of the 25 November was the weakness of the revolutionary left. When it came to the decisive test, the reformists were shown to have incomparably more weight within the working class than the revolutionaries. And even within the left-wing army units, the reformists were able to prevent a full mobilisation.

A few weeks ago, the revolutionary left was able to mobilise for demonstrations through SUV many thousands of soldiers. Over the last year on a number of occasions the revolutionary left also mobilised tens of thousands of workers, despite the complete or partial opposition of the CP (on 7 February, on the CRTSM demonstration in the early summer, on 20 August, on the SUV demonstrations of 25 September, on the demonstration to liberate Radio Renascenca). But the failure of the working class to respond en masse to the calls from the paratroopers on 25 November show that over the class as a whole, even in the Lisbon area, the paralysing grip of the reformists is much stronger than the directing influence of the revolutionaries.

It is a quite different thing for workers to demonstrate in defiance of reformist leaders than to enter upon the insurrectionary path. No worker will risk his livelihood, and even his life, in an insurrection without a feeling of the probability of success. If he feels that only a minority in the class back insurrection, he will foresee the defeat and abstain from the movement.

On 25 November the weakness of the revolutionary left meant it was not even able to mobilise the workers for a defensive general strike. The reformists were still strong enough to sabotage mass resistance to the extreme right.

On 25 November, even those soldiers who first moved – the paratroops – hesitated as soon as they saw that the mass of the class was not moving with them.

It is this which explains why the soldiers' committees and SUV, which seemed so powerful (even to the ruling class!) on 24 November, collapsed like a house of cards on the 25th.

As we wrote in our paper **Socialist Worker** of 25 October:

'The greatest weakness of the revolutionary movement is the unevenness between the soldiers and the workers. The workers' movement lags far behind the soldiers movement . . .

'The unevenness cannot go on forever. If the workers do not rise to the level of the revolutionary soldiers, there is great danger that the soldiers' level of consciousness and action will go down to the level of the workers . . .

'If the workers do not catch up with the soldiers, the danger is that the soldiers' spirit will be dampened . . . The soldiers will be wary of marching forward on their own to seize state power . . .

'In fact, armed forces substituting for the proletariat will not even do for Lisbon in 1975 what the Blanquists did for Paris in 1839. Then a small minority of a few thousand could take power because the rest of the population was unorganised. This cannot be repeated in Lisbon. The Communist Party is too well implanted in the class to allow it.'

Shortly before 25 November some revolutionaries were saying that the 'objective conditions for a successful insurrection' existed. Now certainly many of the conditions were present: the deep divisions within the armed forces, the splits within the ruling class on how to deal with these, the growing wave of struggle of the workers. But one crucial thing was missing – a mass party of revolutionaries, with members in every workshop, fighting for its policies in every workers' committee, counterposing its policies to those of the reformist bureaucrats in the unions, everywhere able to put across to the broad mass of workers direct and immediate arguments to counter the treacherous twists and turns of the reformists.

The revolutionary left did have influence in a few of the leading workers' committees. But when it came to the class as a whole, its influence was much weaker than that of the Communist Party.

Under such conditions it was easy for the CP first to disorientate the revolutionary left with the coup and then to isolate the revolutionary left by betraying the movement it had helped initiate.

It was able to play on certain mistakes of the revolutionary left – above all on the confusion between propaganda and agitation. In the weeks before 25 November the best elements of the revolutionary left had quite rightly made propaganda among advanced layers of workers, stressing that only through an armed insurrection could the class prevent counter-revolution. But often the propaganda was presented in such a way as to give the impression to many workers that it was an agitational call for immediate insurrection. So although the leaders of the revolutionary organisation seem to have been clear that the coup of 25 November could not be the insurrection, those who followed them in the class were not always so clear.

In a revolutionary period, the timing of slogans is crucial. The revolutionary organisation has to make absolutely clear the distinction between its propaganda for insurrection, its call to prepare the political conditions for insurrection, and its immediate agitational demands. Otherwise thousands, tens of thousands of workers who are new to political activity can be confused and demoralised unnecessarily.

### Reaction Wins a Battle – Not the War

The capitalist class has regained a practical monopoly over armed power. One must not underestimate the defeat for the revolution. On the other hand one should not exaggerate it. Neither complacency nor panic are good guides to revolutionary action. Above anything else workers need the *truth*. The defeat for the revolution is not yet total. Army units have been dissolved, but not workers' committees and the trade unions remain more or less intact. The right wing does not yet feel strong enough to take them on directly.

The disaster is not as in Chile. Reaction has won a notable battle, but full-blooded counter-revolution is not triumphant.

Reaction to counter-revolution is as reform to revolution. We may call victories of reaction those changes in the regime which bring it in the direction desired by the counter-revolution without altering radically the balance of forces, without smashing the organisation and confidence of the proletariat.

After July Days when the Bolshevik Party was slandered as being German agents, when hundreds of Party members were thrown into prison, when Lenin and other Party leaders were in hiding. Lenin posed the question: was this a victory of counter-revolution or only a victory of reaction? The key question was whether the working class had lost its confidence and ability to fight. Some time after July Days Lenin explained how one incident clarified to him completely that counter-revolution had not been victorious, that although a battle was lost the war was far from being ended.

'After the July Days . . . I was obliged to go underground . . . In a small working-class house in a remote working-class suburb of Petrograd, dinner is being served. The hostess puts the bread on the table. The host says: "Look what fine bread. They dare not give us bad bread now. And we had almost given up thinking that we'd ever get good bread in Petrograd again."

'I was amazed at this class appraisal of the July Days. My thoughts had been revolving around the political significance of these events, analysing the situation that caused this zigzag in history and the situation it would create, and how we ought to change our slogans and later our Party apparatus to adapt it to the changed situation. As for bread, I who had not known want, did not give it a thought. I took bread for granted . . .

'This member of the oppressed class, however . . . takes the bull by the horns with that astonishing simplicity and straightforwardness, with that firm determination and amazing clarity of outlook from which we intellectuals are so remote as the stars in the sky. The whole world is divided into two camps: "us", the working people, and "them", the exploiters. Not a shadow of embarrassment over what had taken place; it was just one of the battles in the long struggle between labour and capital. When you fell trees, chips fly.

' " 'We' squeezed 'them' a bit; 'they' don't dare to lord it over us as they did before. We'll squeeze them again – and chuck them out altogether," that's how the worker thinks and feels.' (Lenin, **Collected Works**, Vol. 26, p. 120).

Historical experience shows that in revolutionary times a victory of reaction can be followed swiftly be revolutionary victories.

To chart only the chronology of events in Germany in 1919–1920: in January 1919 Rosa Luxemburg, Karl Liebknecht and hundreds of other revolutionaries were massacred – then January 1919 defeat of the German proletariat was incomparably more costly than the defeat of the Portuguese on 25 November. On 3 March a general strike broke out in Berlin; on 21 a general strike broke out in the Ruhr; a year later, on 13 March 1920 the Right organised a coup and took power; on 14 the Social Democratic leaders afraid for their own skins called a general strike that toppled the right-wing Kapp four days later; in October that same year 300,000 members of the USPD (Independent Social Democratic Party) joined en bloc the Communist Party and thus transformed it from a small organisation of a few tens of thousands into a mass party.

These points all lead to one conclusion: the 25 November was not the final battle. It was not like the coup in Chile. If historical analogies are needed, it is better to look at the defeat suffered by the German revolution in January 1919 (at a much greater cost than the defeat of 25 November) which still left the German working class with the strength to fight in March 1919 and against the Kapp putsch in 1920.

If the SUV demonstration of the 25 September or the building workers' mass demonstration besieging the government officers for thirty-six hours on 13 November for example, were semi-insurrections or quarter insurrections then the victory of reaction on 25–26 November was a semi-victory of the counter-revolution.

There is no doubt at all that the 300,000 workers who went on a demonstration in Lisbon on 16 November and 90 per cent of the workers in the Lisbon area who went on strike on 24 November could not have lost their soul, their confidence, their ability to fight, notwithstanding the cruel coup by the right on the 25th.

Symptomatic of the weakness of the Government is its inability to impose a curfew in Lisbon. As a Lisbon comrade wrote on 27 November: 'Lots of people have been ignoring the curfew. The military do not have the means of implementing it.'

### Win the workers to Revolution

If up to 25 November revolutionaries put the emphasis on winning power, on the immediate winning of power by the proletariat, now the centre of all party agitation must be the *winning of the majority of the proletariat*. The march towards the dictatorship of the proletariat of necessity has become *longer and will take a more roundabout path*.

Unable to take power – for lack of a mass revolutionary party – the proletariat will have to lay down the gauntlet in the economic and social field.

The pressure of the international economic crisis continues to be felt by Portuguese capitalism. It cannot expect real relief from these until an upturn in the world economy. This will not come for 6–8 months *at the minimum* – and in any case will be shortlived, leading to renewed world inflation, and to a renewed world crisis within two years.

The government and the council of the revolution will be compelled to proceed at top speed with their 'austerity' plans – price increases, enforced sackings, factory closures, a clamp down on wage increases.

Under these circumstances the economic struggle of workers will most likely very rapidly regather momentum. The great struggles of recent weeks (the metal workers, the builders) involving whole layers of previously passive workers will be followed by further struggles. *The most important thing for the recuperation of the forces of the revolutionary left will be to be able to relate to these struggles.*

Because of the partial defeat for its forces, as well as those of the revolutionary left, the CP will be in a much weaker position for bargaining over the price it has to pay for remaining in the government.

Those who were victorious on 25 November will only let the CP retain its positions if it does its utmost to dampen down the economic struggles of workers.

Revolutionaries could well find themselves as in the first months after 25 April, being the only people to support the most elementary economic struggles of workers.

That is why it is essential to understand the key role which the economic struggles of workers play in any revolution.

As the great Polish-German revolutionary Rosa Luxemburg noted sixty years ago, 'Every new rising and new victory of the political struggle simultaneously changes itself into a powerful impetus for the economic struggle by expanding the external possibilities of the latter . . . After each foaming wave of political struggle, a fructifying deposit remains behind from which a thousand strikes of economic struggle shoot forth . . . The ceaseless state of economic war of the workers with capital keeps the fighting energy alive at each political pause. It forms, so to speak, the ever-fresh reservoir of strength of the proletarian class, out of which the political struggle continually renews its strength.' (**Mass strike**.)

It was because she saw this that after the first defeat of the German revolution at the hands of reformism, in December 1918, she stressed that the fight by revolutionaries for leadership of the class meant moving, for a brief period, from direct political confrontation to economic confrontation: 'In the first period of the revolution, the revolution remained exclusively political. Only in the last two or three weeks have strikes broken out quite spontaneously. Let us be clear: it is the very essence of this revolution that strikes will become more and more extensive, that they must become more and more the central focus . . . No-one will dispute that we alone are on the side of the striking and fighting workers.' In this way, she argued, the hold of reformism would be shaken over even the most backward strata of workers and the base of the revolution would expand hugely.

No-one in Portugal today can afford to ignore that lesson. After the political change of 25 April followed a period of intense economic struggle. Now, after a period in which political questions have dominated everything, the class will recupe its powers through economic struggle.

In the past phase of continual political crisis, there has been a tendency for revolutionaries to dismiss the economic struggle as 'out-dated'. But that is to make a dangerous confusion.

It is true that Portuguese capitalism can no longer afford reforms to the benefit of the workers. It is true also that some of the most advanced workers find themselves in a situation where wage demands threaten the economic viability of enterprises controlled by their own workers' committees, and therefore draw revolutionary political conclusions. But the vast mass of workers are not yet at this level of consciousness. The fact that they have followed the wage demands of the reformist unions shows it. Instead of the revolutionaries telling these workers that the economic struggle is surpassed, it is necessary to fight alongside them for the economic demands, to suggest forms of organisation appropriate to winning them, to fight within the workers' committees and the unions against the inevitable tendency of the reformist leaders to bow to the needs of Portuguese capitalism and renege on the fight even for reforms. Revolutionaries must not merely comment on the fight for wage improvement: they must do their utmost to propel it forward, to unite the strength of the workers round partial economic demands, in order to raise the level of unity and combativity of the class, so that the political question of state power is posed to wider ranks of workers than ever before.

The embryonic organs of Popular Power by and large showed themselves to be inadequate on 25 November. This is because many of their activities remained remote from the everyday activities of workers – from the daily struggle for better wages and conditions, for better housing, against unemployment and rising prices. Workers vaguely supported them, but did not feel intimately and organically involved in their actions. The building of real organs of Popular Power will depend upon overcoming this fault, upon making them central to the partial, economic struggles of workers, as well as seeing them as an embryo of working-class power.

In the period immediately ahead, groups of revolutionaries in each factory will only be able to recuperate their strength and to overcome the weaknesses of 25 November if they do more than pose, abstractly, the question of state power, and make themselves the centre of the struggle against the austerity programme of the government. That means formulating demands for a fight back on the economic front, using regular factory bulletins and newspapers to counter the betrayals of the reformists on this front as well as on the political front.

Revolutionaries will have to seize every opportunity to link themselves to workers' struggle through legal 'front' organisations.

To repeat, the revolution has not yet suffered a *decisive* defeat. The revolutionary left can still rally support and turn the tide. The struggle now is a struggle to convince workers that all the gains of the revolution to date are at risk. The economic offensive which the rulers must launch, the offensive to break the industrial power of the working class, is now the centre of the battlefield. On this battlefield, working class unity around a militant programme can still be achieved.

On that basis the revolutionaries can begin to build the party that was so clearly missing on 25 November. If they learn the lessons of that defeat, it will not be long before they rise again.

### Building the Mass Party

Even with the best elements of the revolutionary left there is a failure to understand the need to organise politically those workers who are breaking with reformism. The notion is widespread that the job of the party is to deal with technical questions, like the organisation of the insurrection, while the functioning of organs of workers' power can be left to the 'non-party' bodies themselves. In practice this means that the Party is seen as being made up of small, highly trained (in military terms) cadres, which does not need to permeate every single section of the class.

This aversion to a stress on building up the organisation of the Party and its periphery is perhaps a natural reaction to the crude, Stalinist notion of the Party peddled both by the Communist Party and the Maoist sects (which leads the Maoists to counterpose building the Party to the tasks of the mass movement). But it is extremely dangerous at present.

In Russia in 1905 Lenin stressed again and again the need of the Party to draw to it tens of thousands of workers, to grab at every single worker who in any way was drawing close to revolutionary politics.

He recognised that if the revolutionary party did not seize on them and win them to its full position by joint activity in a common organisation, they could all too easily be pulled back into the orbit of reformism or even reaction.

'We need young forces. I am for shooting on the spot any one who presumes that there are no people to be had. The people in Russia are legion; all we have to do is recruit young people more widely and boldly, more boldly and widely and again more widely and boldly, without fearing them (Lenin stress) . . . Get rid of all the old habits of immobility, of respect for rank, and so on. Form *hundreds* of circles of Vperyod-ists from among the youth and encourage them to work full blast . . . We must with desperate speed, unite people with revolutionary initiative and set them to work. Do not fear their lack of training, do not tremble at their inexperience and lack of development. In the first place, if you fail to organise them and spur them to action, they will follow the Mensheviks and the Gapons and this inexperience of them will cause five times more harm. In the second place, events themselves will teach them in *our spirit* . . . This is a time of battle. Either you create *new*, young, fresh energetic battle organisations everywhere for revolutionary . . . work of all varieties among all strata, or you will go under wearing the aureole of "committee bureaucrats".'

His words apply absolutely in Portugal today. Everyone moving to the left who is not won to an organisation will be pulled into the orbit of reformism, centrism of sectarian Maoism, and will present insuperable problems for the revolutionaries in the future.

The danger can be avoided but only if the revolutionary left sharply alters the priority which it gives to Party building.

Above all, regular and popular press is needed. Without it there is no pressure on members of the revolutionary party to bring contacts to the organisation. They have no automatic organisational link with those who waver between them and the reformists, Maoists or centrists, not yet being willing to join the Party. They have no ready way of explaining the Party's view of day to day events to the large number of workers attracted to revolutionary ideas. They have no easy way to open up a dialogue with the dissident Communist Party members or even those Maoists and centrists bemused by the behaviour of their organisations.

Of course, the Party cannot be built merely by proclaiming it, or by counterposing it to the development of the mass struggle (as most of the Maoist groups believe). But it can be built by an organisation that shows in practice that it knows what needs to be done by the class and insists openly and clearly again and again to the rest of the class that it has only been able to do so because it exists as a party around a certain programme.

To enter upon the road of insurrection and civil war without a mass Party is the most dangerous thing conceivable for revolutionaries.

In Portugal, there is no possibility of evading for more than a few months (*at most*) sharp, armed clashes between the classes. That is why the most urgent task for the revolutionary left is to build the political organisational structure within the class. A failure to do so will not only condemn the Portuguese working class to defeat: it will also throw away the best opportunity for a revolutionary breakthrough in Europe since 1917.

### The road to power

To aim to win power without first winning over the mass of the proletariat is ultra-left adventurism. To win the proletariat to the party as an aim is simply opportunism. To win the proletariat to the revolutionary party in order to win power is the only realistic revolutionary path open now in Portugal.

A long time ago Lenin, who was destined to lead the only successful mass proletarian insurrection up till now, explained how the organisation of the revolutionary party dovetails with the preparation for an armed insurrection. He wrote in 1902: 'Picture to yourselves a popular uprising. Probably everyone will now agree that we must think of this and prepare for it. But *how?* Surely the Central Committee cannot appoint agents to all localities for the purpose of preparing the uprising! Even if we had a Central Committee it could achieve absolutely nothing by such appointments under present day Russian conditions. But a network of agents that would form in the course of establishing and distributing the common newspaper would not have to 'sit about and wait' for the call for an uprising, but could carry on the regular activity that would strengthen our contacts with the broadest strata of the working masses and with all social strata that are discontented with the autocracy, which is of such importance for an uprising. Precisely such activity would serve to cultivate the ability to estimate correctly the general political situation, and consequently, the ability to select the proper moment for an uprising. Precisely such activity would train *all* local organisations to respond simultaneously to the same political question, incidents and events that agitate the whole of Russia and to react to such 'incidents' in the most vigorous, uniform and expedient manner possible; for an uprising is in essence the most vigorous, most uniform and most expedient answer of the entire people to the government. Lastly, it is precisely such activity that would train all revolutionary organisations throughout Russia to maintain the most continuous, and at the same time most secret, contacts with one another, thus creating *real* party unity; for without such contacts it will be impossible collectively to discuss the plan for the uprising and to take the necessary preparatory measure on its eve, measures that must be kept in the strictest secrecy.' (Lenin, **Collected Works**, Vol. 5 pp. 525–6.)

Only when the mass revolutionary party is implanted deeply in the proletariat can it lead to a successful insurrection. A necessary condition for the victory of the proletarian insurrection is that the decisive sections of the proletariat will it. Lenin wrote in 1917: 'To be successful, insurrection must rely not upon a party, but upon the advanced class. That is the first point. Insurrection must rely upon a *revolutionary upsurge of the people*. That is the second point. Insurrection must rely upon that *turning point* in the history of the growing revolution when the activity of the advanced ranks of the people is at its height, and when the *vacillations* in the ranks of the enemy and *in the ranks of the weak, half-hearted and irresolute friends of the revolution* are strongest. That is the third point.' (Lenin, **Collected Works**, Vol. 26 pp. 22–3.)

'Military conspiracy is Blanquism, *if* it is organised not by a party of a definite class, *if* its organisers have not analysed the political moment in general and the international situation in particular, *if* the party has not on its side the sympathy of the majority of the people, as proved by objective facts, *if* the development of revolutionary events has not brought about a practical refutation of the conciliatory illusions of the petty bourgeoisie, *if* the majority of the Soviet-type organs of revolutionary struggle that have been recognised as authoritative or have shown themselves to be such in practice have not been won over, *if* there has not matured a sentiment in the army . . . against the government . . . *if* the slogans of the uprising have not become widely known and popular, *if* the advanced workers are not sure of the desperate situation of the masses and the support of the countryside, a support proved by a serious peasant movement or by an uprising against the landowners and the government that defends the land-owners, *if* the country's economic situation inspires earnest hopes for a favourable solution of the crisis by peaceable and parliamentary means'. (Lenin, **Collected Works**, Vol. 26, pp. 212–3.)

Some people have claimed that the example of the Cuban revolution shows that such conditions need not be fulfilled in Portugal. But the conditions under which the Cuban revolution occurred are quite different from those of Portugal today.

The guerilla movement in Cuba was able to win because when it came to the decisive test, none of the major classes was prepared to support Batista against the rebel army. The local bourgoisie in Cuba was weak and divided, to such an extent that some of its representatives joined Castro's first government. Even sections of the US state department were prepared to show a benign neutrality to Castro at this stage. Remember, at the time of taking power and smashing the established army of Batista, Castro was still claiming that the revolution would not be an anti-capitalist revolution. He only proclaimed its socialist intentions on 16 April 1961.

Conditions in Portugal today are quite different. The bourgeoisie are much stronger than they were in Cuba. They have a wide measure of support among the petty bourgeoisie and the northern peasants. The bourgeoisie are aware that their whole social position is threatened by any intensification of the revolution and are determined to fight to the end against it. The US government does not show 'benign neutrality' but bitter hostility to the revolution.

All this makes the hold of reformism much harder to deal with than was the case in Cuba. The reformists can impede an all-out struggle against the forces of the right: this was shown conclusively on 25 November. No insurrection can be successful until their hold in the factories is already challenged in a decisive fashion by the revolutionaries. It cannot be the case that, as in Cuba, the insurrection takes place and then the CP is forced to accept it. And it is worth remembering that even in Cuba the hold of the reformists continued to be crucial after the insurrection, forcing the leaders of the rebel army to make an alliance with them that explains many of the deformations in Cuba today.

As a guide to revolutionaries in Portugal, as elsewhere in the world, not Castro but the Communist Manifesto should serve when it states: 'All previous historical movements were movements of minorities or in the interests of minorities. The proletarian movement is the self-conscious independent movement of the immense majority.'-

The working class is ready for the armed seizure of power only when both objective and subjective conditions are ripe. Thus Lenin never raised the slogan for the insurrection prior to September 1917 – when the Bolsheviks won a majority in the soviets of Petrograd and Moscow. In April 1917, a leading Bolshevik in Petrograd, Bogdatev, secretary of the Putilov Bolshevik Committee issued a leaflet calling 'Down with the provisional government'. Lenin attacked him as ultra-left and his action was condemned by the party, because of the danger that the workers would see this as a call to immediate action before the party had the support of the class.

In a revolutionary situation tenses are more important than grammar.

For revolutionaries, there cannot be a gap between words and deeds. Therefore when a party makes propaganda about the need for insurrection it must allow no confusion at all to exist in the eyes of the workers that this is an immediate call for action. Every statement, every leaflet must make this distinction clear. No call can be put to the workers in a way that will be seen as a call to action unless the party is fully prepared for the essential consequences that will follow.

If revolutionaries work correctly in Portugal today, they can create the conditions for the organisation of a successful struggle for power. But that means recognising that in the forefront of those conditions is winning the working class for the revolution.

The hold of reformism, so decisive on 25 November, can be shaken. But only if revolutionaries recognise that it is necessary to go backwards a little in order to go forward, to relate to the many economic struggles we can expect in the months ahead in order to prepare the ground for renewed political struggle.

The attempt of the government to solve the economic problems of Portuguese capitalism will lead to many sharp clashes between it and sections of workers. If revolutionaries know how to relate to these economic struggles, it will be easy to push them to the point at which political issues are raised – the role of the police, the role of the purged army, the role of the government and all its components (including the CP) the need for class action against it and for corresponding organisations of struggle and power.

The contradictions within the forces who were victorious on 25 November mean that the next major political conflict may not be far away. Already sections of the military want to go much further in their repression than do Antunes and sections of the Socialist Party leadership.

Revolutionaries have very little to build the organisational strength in the class that did not exist on 25 November. But if the opportunities available are seized the revolution can still be saved.

The defeat of 25 November should be used to teach every worker in Portugal and elsewhere the key lessons needed for the achievement of proletarian victory in the future. An army that has been licked is the better for it if it draws the lessons from its beating.

# Why we need a socialist workers party

FOR A NUMBER of years, the International Socialists was a propaganda group.

But, increasingly over the last year, IS acted more and more as an organisation which initiates action.

That is the meaning of the Right to Work Campaign, the Campaign against Racialism and so on.

In the course of the last year, our organisation has become a party. But we should not have illusions of grandeur. To use sporting terms, we are still in the fourth division.

For a time, the Communist Party tried to deny the fact that we were more or less the same size from the point of view of active membership. But, if nothing else, the recent parliamentary by-elections proved that we are in the same league.

In Walsall North in October 1974, the Communist Party got 465 votes. In November, our candidate got 574 votes on a lower poll.

Last November's Right to Work Conference made the point once again. In terms of delegations represented, it was bigger than the last three Liaison Committee conferences, whose main initiator was the CP.

But it is important to be clear that while our capacity for initiating activity is greater than that of the Communist Party, the ideas of the CP and of the Labour Left – which are indistinguishable from one another – are far more widespread than ours.

*The ability of these organisations to prevent action is still greater than our ability to get real action going.*

For two years after Labour came to power, until last spring, our membership slowly and gradually went down from 3,300 members to around 2,650 members. In recent months things have changed.

In June we recruited 64 members, in July 77, in August 100, in September 174, in October 192, in November 243, and in the first three weeks of December 155, making a total of over 1,000 in just over seven months.

For the first time in the history of our organisation, there are more manual workers than white-collar workers. And all of this is indicative that the deepening general crisis of the system, plus the crisis within the Labour movement, gives us great opportunities to build the organisation.

At the same time, the purpose of recruitment must be clearer now than ever before. The events in Portugal, where a revolutionary party has been, and is being, frittered away, underline the key role of a revolutionary party in transforming a revolutionary situation into a victory for the working class.

The greatest victory so far of the international working class, that of the October revolution in Russia, also showed the key role of the mass revolutionary party.

There is no doubt that in a few years' time, perhaps six, perhaps eight, perhaps ten, Britain will face a level of unemployment of three or four millions.

Under such conditions, two alternative policies will appear as a solution to this unemployment.

One is the revolutionary socialist alternative – the overthrow of capitalism and the establishment of socialist planning. The other is the fascist solution: 'If there are three million unemployed get rid of black workers, the Irish and the Jews'.

If, at the beginning of the revolutionary crisis, there is a mass revolutionary party of sorts, it can grow quickly in the months of the crisis so it is able to lead the working class to power.

*In February 1917, the Bolshevik Party had 23,600 members. By July, it had nearly 250,000.*

When, at the beginning of July, the capitalist press started a massive slander campaign against Lenin, accusing him of being a German agent, the flood of denigration was stopped by the mass party with one in ten of the workers.

Imagine if the party had only one per cent of the workers. Perhaps every member would have convinced ten or fifteen workers that the capitalist press was lying. But the majority of the class would have fallen into the trap.

The conclusions for us are clear. If, when the revolutionary crisis comes to Britain, we have 40,000 members, there is no question that we can grow to 400,000 or perhaps half a million.

If, on the other hand, the revolutionary organisation has only a few thousand members, it is even possible that the party appears as irrelevant and does not grow at all. A certain size *is* necessary for take off.

Recruitment is the first task we have to carry through. But an army which is simply collected together is no good at all unless it is at the same time involved in struggle.

That is the importance of building our fractions, building the factory and workplace branches, building the rank and file movement.

In building the party, **Socialist Worker** is one of the most important weapons we have, involving both party members and the periphery in activity in the working class struggle and in building the party.

In the years 1912 to 1914, the Bolshevik Party had 3,000 members in Petrograd. The party paper had a circulation in the city of 30,000.

In 1917, party membership in Petrograd reached 32,000. And there is no doubt that those who bought the paper in 1912 became, a few years later, party members.

So when we sell **Socialist Worker** the aim is not by any means only to raise 10p or even make propaganda. Above all it is to organise round our policies.

*Our organisation must become an accepted part of workers' lives where they work and where they live.*

Finance is also increasingly important. Raising it is a political act. Without it, we could not have printed the hundreds of thousands of leaflets to combat the racists. Without it we cannot do the many more things we need to do.

It is extremely important to raise this money not only from the members, but from workers sympathetic to our ideas. The 5p a week paid by unemployed IS members is every bit as important as the £5 paid by a well-to-do comrade.

If we believed that the way to socialism was through parliament, the structure of the party should basically be that of branches based on constituencies.

But because we believe that the class struggle is the way to achieve socialism, the revolutionary party has to build itself by and large in workplaces, though we are still far too weak to have the majority of our members in factory and workplace branches.

We have to build there more and more, especially now, when there is a growth of the class struggle and of recruitment.

But we must be careful how we build. The reformists always have a difference between their words and their deeds. After all, Harold Wilson did not appear on TV to say Vote Labour and Double Unemployment.

*Revolutionaries should never have a difference between their words and their deeds.*

One can be very **'Revolutionary'** by promising things you can't deliver.

Suppose I was in the business of making promises I couldn't deliver. I'd promise my child a gold-plated Rolls Royce in 1999. It is a safe promise.

First I'll probably be dead by 1999. If not he'll probably forget my promise by then. And if those two things don't work, I'll have 22 years to think of excuses.

So if we have comrades who are teachers they can't at the moment deliver a general strike against teacher unemployment. But they can carry a no-cover policy and they can build from there.

We have to orient ourselves more and more to the specific, to the factory bulletins. With these you can't start with general statements about unemployment or racism. You have to talk about specifics, about an overtime ban here, a specific instance of discrimination against black workers there.

In February and March this year we will be holding some 200 meetings with the central theme of building the Socialist Workers Party. The aim of them will be to recruit – and recruit quickly.

To prepare the ground, we have a marvellous new booklet written with compassion and passion, titled **Why you should be a socialist – the case for the Socialist Workers Party.**

We intend the comrades to have a month or so of selling this pamphlet, seeing as many of the buyers as possible and getting them to the meeting with a clear knowledge of what the meeting is for.

*It is possible, and vital, to build the organisation quickly. But it is also a fact that many of us suffer from conservatism in doing that.*

As a result of two tough years many of us are putting the sights far too low. We are afraid of being hurt and therefore look for safety. And, of course, if you try to recruit no-one, you are 100 per cent successful.

The present members of our party are not the salt of the earth, the select few. If any elitism exists in our organisation it is necessary to uproot it completely.

Some revolutionaries do suffer from elitist notions. They think of the barricades as follows: In the front row there is an Imperial Father of the Chapel representing craft workers in all their glory. He is wearing his gold chain of office to pay homage. Or is it perhaps to say 'you have nothing to lose but your chains'.

And then there are some representatives of section one of the Engineering Union.

Only then if there is enough room in the street they would in their generosity allow some blacks, a few women and some youth – if they know their place, that is.

Revolution has nothing at all to do with this hierarchical concept.

Anyone who is in any doubt about it has no need to look further than the boys and girls of Soweto.

# Why socialists must support gays

In CLASS-INFESTED society there is oppressor and oppressed in all walks of life. Employer oppresses employee; man oppresses woman; white oppresses black; old oppresses young; heterosexual oppresses homosexual.

The true socialist is able to overcome all these divisions. An engineering worker who can only identify with other engineering workers may be a good trade unionist but he has not proved himself to be a socialist. A socialist has to be able to identify with the struggles of all oppressed groups.

We are all the children of capitalism, so we tend to conceive of the future – even the socialist future – in an ordered and hierarchical way.

It is as though the socialist revolution will be led by the Father of the Chapel in the print union, the NGA working on Fleet Street. Second in command will be an AUEW Convenor Section 1 from the toolroom in a big car factory. The lieutenants of the revolution will all be forty-year-old white male shop stewards.

If there is enough space then we'll allow blacks and women and gays to take part – providing they stand quietly at the back!

A lot of socialists still have difficulty believing that gays will be taking part in the revolution at all.

*On the contrary we should look forward now to the first leader of the London workers' council being a 19-year-old black gay woman!*

The system rules by dividing us. This means there is no natural way by which one oppressed group identifies with another. The most racist extremists in the Southern States of America are the *poor* whites – not the rich whites.

In the same way blacks do not *automatically* support women and women do not automatically support blacks. Gays will not *automatically* support other oppressed groups.

The Nazis sent thousands of gays to concentration camps. In Chile gays were castrated and left bleeding on the street.

But it is not true that, even given these facts, gays automatically become anti-fascist.

Tens of thousands of gays supported Hitler. Many were in the

Brownshirts. After Hitler took power he turned on the gay support and slaughtered them in the Night of the Long Knives.

How can we explain gays joining the Nazis?

If you are an *oppressed* gay putting on a Nazi leather jacket and leather boots gives you for the first time a sense of power. It makes it easy to put down Jews, women and anyone else.

For any oppressed group to fight back there is need for *hope.*

If you are on the way *down* you feel despair. You look for a victim to kick.

If you are on the way *up* you look for a back to pat.

That's why only by building a socialist movement can you unite workers with oppressed blacks, women and gays.

And that's why it is so important for gays to organise for demonstrations like at Brick Lane and to feel able to identify themselves proudly as gays and – where possible – as revolutionary socialist gays.

Karl Marx wrote that capitalism unites the forces of opposition. But it also divides us. We have to struggle *consciously* for that unity.

We are one – all of us together – but only when we *fight* together.

# Ten years on: 1969 to 1979

THE FIRST FIVE years was a period when the class struggle achieved a level unprecedented in British working class history for generations.

We had two national miners' strikes. One of them smashed to pieces the incomes policy of the Tory Government. The other forced the government to introduce a three-day week and then to lose power.

The last general strike of miners before this was in 1926, and this was a very different experience. The miners were beaten, driven to their knees.

In 1970 we had the first national dustmen's strike in British working-class history and this one ended in victory.

We had a national unofficial docks strike challenging the government's Industrial Relations Act. It led to the imprisonment of five dockers. The government capitulated to the strike and the Pentonville prisoners were set free.

The same period saw the first ever national building workers' strike, the first national teachers' strike and the first national hospital workers' strike.

**Socialist Worker 631, 26 May 1979**

We had a national strike by the engineers against the Industrial Relations Act which forced the government to lift the court fine on the AUEW.

Workers facing sackings and factory closure in over 200 factories occupied them, a tactic completely new to the British working class.

If one compares the years 1969–74 with even the best period of militancy in Britain of 1900–14 there is no question that this time the struggle was on a much higher level, much more generalised, and the hatred of the government was all prevailing, all encompassing.

This chapter ended abruptly with the electoral victory of Labour in February 1974. The next five years since were radically different.

We did not have one national strike in any key section of the class, although we had the national strikes of bakers, of lorry drivers and of provincial journalists.

The struggle was incomparably more fragmented, the level was far lower. One has only to remember that the number of days on strike in 1976 was the lowest for ten years.

One reason given for this change is that it was simple loyalty to Labour that cut the level of struggle.

This wouldn't wash in 1969. The strikes of the dustmen and the teachers *did* smash through Wilson's incomes policy. Loyalty to Labour by itself would not have held the dam.

A second reason put forward is the fact that there was an incomes policy. Perhaps this dampened down the struggle. However, all the historical experience, from Selwyn Lloyd's incomes policy to Harold Wilson's, showed that incomes policy by itself only stemmed the battle for a year, or at best, two years.

The third reason given is that militancy was dampened by unemployment and the threat of the sack.

Again, historical experience shows that well-organised workers can be whipped into *greater* militancy by the threat of the sack. This is exactly what happened under Ted Heath's government when unemployment rose by half.

To understand the downturn in the class struggle in 1974–79 one must look to the cause in the weaknesses of the labour movement – general causes that were very much in evidence in the first five years.

I gave a list of workers struggles that ended victoriously in the years 1969–74. Alas a whole number of important battles in the same period ended in defeat.

In 1970 the national strike of the gas workers was defeated.

In 1971 the seven week long and bitter strike of the postmen ended in a complete victory for the employers.

In 1972 the wage claim of two million engineering workers ended in the dust.

In 1973 the building workers' strike, with all its militancy and flying pickets, was accompanied with the arrest and imprisonment of the Shrewsbury pickets. They were *not* freed.

In other words sectionalism was still rampant in the labour movement.

There were only a few miners, the best organised and the most militant and powerful section of the working class, who came to the aid of the hospital workers in 1973.

The generalising and unifying element in all those strikes was a deep anti-Tory feeling. The alternative to the Tories meant the Labour Party. Once Labour was in power that general opposition collapsed.

In all the struggles of 1969–74 the union officials kept complete control over the national strikes.

The spearhead of union bureaucracy at that time were the left leaders, Scanlon and Jones.

With Labour in power all the union leaders moved towards the social contract – this time spearheaded by the same 'terrible twins'.

In the strikes of 1900–14 (which were on the whole on a lower level in terms of size than in 1969–74) independent rank and file socialists played a far greater role and were far more cohesive, far more influential than in the 1970–74 strikes.

In 1969 there were probably something like 500 full time convenors.

Ten years later the number rose to about 6,000. This gave a much wider base to union bureaucracy than existed before (the total number of full time union officials is 3,000).

Because of the massive productivity deals of the late 1960s, and because of incomes policy and unemployment, the power of the individual shop steward, which was largely based on his ability to set piece rates and bonus rates, declined quite seriously.

Wage drift, the difference between national wage rates and the 'going rate' on the shop-floor, ten years ago was one of the most important expressions of the power of individual shop stewards. That has now practically disappeared from industry.

Therefore we are in a period in which the struggle must become much wider than the individual shop.

But the organisation inside the factory relating the individual shop stewards to each other *still* goes through the convenor. And many of them are collaborating with management through partici- pation schemes. Faced with participation and the new wave of productivity deals the shop stewards feel less and less able to act collectively.

In describing a period in our history there is always a danger of a one-sidedness. It was clear that 1969–74 was not only a period of successes for the working class but also a time in which important sections of workers were badly beaten.

Similarly, the period 1974–79 should not be seen simply as a time of decline in the struggle. The picture was far more mosaic.

Hundreds upon hundreds of factories entered the struggle, involving workers that never knew strike action. Women and black workers entered the battle.

While the traditional key sections of the working class – miners, engineers and dockers – were by and large acquiescent, other sections came to the fore, especially at the end of the Callaghan government, during last winter. These were hospital workers, local government workers and white collar workers.

Alas, this section, in terms of even the statistics of strike records, didn't fill the gap left by the others.

In the years 1966–76 hospital workers struck for only eight per cent of the number of days that workers in manufacturing industry did.

Similarly, amongst white collar workers, the number of strikes was only ten per cent compared with a similar number of workers in manufacturing industry.

The worst inheritance of the trade union bureaucracy during the social contract was that scabbing became respectable.

Ten years ago hardly any union official would have dreamt of instructing members to cross picket lines of workers in other unions.

But this happened in Port Talbot when the electricians went on strike. The AUEW and the ISTC and other unions instructed their members to cross the lines.

In Leyland when the toolroom workers went on strike other workers were instructed to cross the picket line. When maintenance engineers in Heathrow went on strike other workers were told to cross.

Blacklegging not only remained the domain of the top union officials now. We must remember how Jimmy Airlie, the convenor of Govan shipyard, scabbed on the yard workers of Swan Hunter in Newcastle, accepting the blacked Polish ships.

This is remarkable when one remembers that Govan shipyard in 1971 was the centre of national mobilisation of workers in defence of their jobs – Upper Clyde Shipbuilders.

To cap the respectability of scabbing came the Concordat between the Labour Government and the TUC.

It aimed at castrating the picket line, at weakening solidarity between workers.

Labour laid the foundations and the Tories will now build the structure by using the law.

### The role of the SWP

In the first five-year period the International Socialists (at present the Socialist Workers Party) expanded from a group of a few hundred – mainly students and white collar – to an organisation of three to four thousand members.

Something like a third of these were manual workers. We

managed to implant ourselves in a number of factories, in a whole number of trade unions, both manual and white collar.

We were involved in the establishment of a whole number of rank and file groups, with rank and file papers in different unions.

In the second five years the SWP found the going much tougher.

With the Social Contract, not only the trade union leaders, but also the Communist Party – the main organisation of the left in industry – veered strongly to the right.

The SWP decided quite rightly to steer left. The organisation was kept intact, but quite a heavy price was paid. Its members found themselves very often isolated and they had to hold on by their fingertips to their positions in the movement.

The organisation has been steeled. The period was not only a period of marking time. We managed to carry out quite important initiatives like the Right To Work Campaign, and the ANL, which established our credibility widely in the movement.

To some extent the two periods we are dealing with are similar to two periods in the history of the Bolshevik Party.

At the time of the 1905 revolution the Bolshevik Party expanded massively, reaching a membership of 30,000 in 1907.

However, in the period of reaction following, demoralisation in the class and police persecution smashed the Party.

Of course the years of 1969 to 74 in Britain didn't see a revolution but saw a massive rise in the class struggle.

The years 1974–79 did not see the victory of reaction and counter-revolution, but did see a serious shift to the right.

The Socialist Workers Party is much better poised at present to take a part in the new advance of the class struggle than it has ever been before.

No individual, and certainly not the movement, can be completely free from the past.

Our experience of 1969 to 1974 as well as 1974–79 will affect our movement in the coming days, months and years.

Now, when the Tories are back in power, even if their policies are not harsher than those of Callaghan, they will raise incomparably more anger than he has done.

The government, as the enemy, will help generalise the struggle. With the increasing and deepening crisis of world capitalism the attack on workers is bound to come.

The possibility of once more building a rank and file movement, far more independent of the union bureaucracy than in 1969–74, is with us.

The prize of victory will be much greater, but also the penalty of defeat will be much more severe.

Loyalty to the Labour Party, reliance on the trade union leaders, and sectionalism, are the main impediments that workers have to overcome.

# Books by Tony Cliff

**Imperialism in the Middle East**, Palestine 1944, unpublished
**Stalin's Satellites in Europe**, as *Y Gluckstein*, London 1952
**The nature of Stalinist Russia**, London 1955
   retitled and expanded:
**Russia, a Marxist analysis**, London 1963
   retitled:
**State Capitalism in Russia**, Pluto Press, 1975
**Rosa Luxemburg**, London 1959, republished Bookmarks 1980
**Incomes Policy, Legislation and Shop Stewards**, (with Colin
   Barker), London 1966
**Mao's China**, as *Y Gluckstein*, London 1957
**The employers offensive: Productivity deals and how to fight them**,
   Pluto Press, 1970
**Lenin**
   *1. Building the Party,* Pluto Press 1975
   *2. All power to the Soviets*, Pluto Press 1976
   *3. Revolution Besieged*, Pluto Press 1978
   *4. The Bolsheviks and World Revolution*, Pluto Press 1979
**The Crisis: Social Contract or Socialism**, Pluto Press 1975

To be published: **Women and the struggle for socialism.**

Of these titles, State Capitalism, Lenin, Rosa Luxemburg and The
Crisis are still in print.

# Bookmarks

**Never Again! The hows and whys of stopping fascism**
*by Colin Sparks*
Fascism, born out of the economic crisis of the 1930s, brought the barbarism and
death camps of World War II. Now, as another crisis deepens, it raises its head
again. This book looks at how and why fascism grows, how and why its opponents
failed in the 30s and how and why it can be stopped today.

*£1.35 plus 30p postage*                                    *ISBN 0 906224 02 0*

**Rosa Luxemburg**
*by Tony Cliff*
Before she was murdered in Berlin during the German Revolution of 1919, Rosa
Luxemburg made important contributions to socialist and Marxist thinking – on the
role of the party, on imperialism, on the importance of strikes, on reform and
revolution. This is a short account of her life and thought.

*£1.35 plus 30p postage*                                    *ISBN 0 906224 03 7*

**Anger on the Road**
*by Jimmy Reilly*
How the TUC learned to hate the Right to Work march – one man's account of the
fight against unemployment by the Right to Work Campaign and the march to the
TUC in Brighton in 1978. With cartoons by *Phil Evans* and pictures by *John Sturrock*.

*75p plus 25p postage*                                      *ISBN 0 906224 01 2*

**We Shall Be All**
edited by *Laurie Flynn*
Chapters in the working class history of Scotland – the sort they leave out of the
official history books.

*90p plus 25p postage*                                      *ISBN 0 906224 00 4*

*Other books by members of the*

# Socialist Workers Party.

**Trotsky's Marxism**
*by Duncan Hallas*
Trotsky, one of the architects of the Russian Revolution of 1917, also chronicled and
analysed the degeneration of the new regime. This is a handbook and guide to his
unique contribution to Marxist thought.

*£2 plus 40p postage*

**Bureaucracy and revolution in Eastern Europe**
*by Chris Harman*
East Germany 1953, Poland 1956, Hungary 1956, Czechoslovakia 1968, Poland 1970
. . . this book looks at how Eastern Europe turned 'Communist' and at the turbulent
relationship between workers and regimes ever since. Written before the present
upheaval in Poland, but indispensible for understanding the background to those
events.

*£2.50 plus 50p postage*

### The mandate of Heaven: Marx and Mao in modern China
*by Nigel Harris*
China has been transformed from a poor country devastated by war into a major world power, and by a regime that claims to be socialist. How was it done? How do the peasants and workers of China live? Is this socialism? Nigel Harris explains.

*£4.25 plus postage*

### Workers Against the monolith
*by Ian Birchall*
Once the Communist Parties led the workers towards power. Now they are parties of order in The West, of counter-revolution in the East, and of betrayal in Latin America and Asia. Berlin 1953, Hungary 1956, Indonesia 1965, Czechoslovakia and France 1968, Italy 1969, Chile 1973 . . .

*£2.95 plus 40p postage*

### Solidarność: From Gdansk to military repression
*Colin Barker and Kara Weber*
On 13 December 1981 Jaruzelski's army moved in to crush Solidarność. The most powerful workers movement since the war was halted in its tracks.
*How could it happen?*
Drawing on a variety of original Polish material Colin Barker and Kara Weber trace the unfolding crisis and debates it provoked within Solidarność. They argue that Solidarność was too rooted in the factories to be co-opted, that real revolutionary possibilities existed, but tragically, this was only realised by the radical wing of Solidarność too late.

*£1.95 plus 50p postage*

**All available by post from:**
**Bookmarks, 265 Seven Sisters Road, London N4 2DE**

**Bookmarks** is a socialist bookshop in North London, where you'll find two floors of books on socialism, trade unionism, working class history, women's issues, economics, internationalism, socialist novels . . . and much more. You'll find us at 265 Seven Sisters Road, just around the corner from Finsbury Park tube station. If you live too far away to call in, we run a socialist mail order service too . . . so why not drop us a line.